Merry Christmas Charles
love Elaine

Editor: Victoria Pybus

Assisted by Clare Last

Distributed in the USA by
Peterson's;
202 Carnegie Center, Princeton, N.J. 08543-2123

Published by Vacation-Work
9 Park End Street, Oxford

First published by Vacation-Work in 1978 and annually thereafter.

Twenty-first edition 1998

ADVENTURE HOLIDAYS 1998

ISBN 1 85458 197-X (softback)
ISBN 1 85458 198-8 (hardback)
ISSN 0143-389 X

Cover photography by kind permission of Guerba

Imageset and Printed by
Unwin Brothers Ltd.
Old Woking, Surrey

Contents

Multi Activity Holidays **7**

Young People's Holidays **36**

Airsports **47**
- General 49
- Ballooning 49
- Gliding 50
- Hang Gliding and Paragliding 51
- Parachuting and Parascending 53
- Power Flying and Microlighting 55

Cycling **57**

Hiking and Rambling **68**

Mountain Pursuits **92**
- General 94
- Climbing and Mountaineering 97
- Skiing 104
- Snow Boarding 110

Overland **111**

Riding and Trekking **120**

Specialist Activities and Courses **131**
Agriculture — Angling — Archaeology & History — Arts and Crafts — Cattle Ranching — Caving and Cave Studying — Conservation — Historical Re-creation — Just Women — Management Courses — Motor Sports — Murder and Mystery Weekends — Orienteering — Painting — Photography — Powerboating — Shooting — Survival Courses — Winetasting — Other

Special Tours and Expeditions **148**
Aid Expeditions — Anthropological — Archaeological & Historical — Arctic & Antarctic Exploration — Camel Caravanning — Horse Drawn Holidays — Husky Sledging — Inland Cruising — Motorcycling — Photographic — Rail Tours — Research Expeditions — Wine Tours — Other

Watersports **166**
General 171
Canoeing and Rafting 174
Sailing 181
Scuba Diving and Snorkelling 190
Windsurfing and Surfing 196

Wildlife **200**
General 200
Birdwatching 208
Botanical 211
Safari 212

Maps and Charts
National Parks and National Trails of England and Wales 74
Windchill Chart 98
East African Game Parks 218

Index of Companies and Organisations 220

Making Bookings and Enquiries

Bookings. For most holidays you should book direct with the operator. For organisations noted as members of the Association of British Travel Agents (ABTA), however, you may book through any other ABTA member. Before making a firm booking, check exactly what the price includes and the organisation's policy on applying surcharges between booking and the commencement of the holiday.

Telephone. Numbers outside the UK are shown in the internationally accepted form (+123) 45-67890; the + represents the international access code (00 from Britain), 123 is the country code, 45 the area code and 67890 the subscriber's number. Note that if you are calling from within the same country, you should omit the country code and usually add a zero before the area code.

Linkline numbers (prefix 01345) can be dialled for the price of a local call from anywhere in the UK. Toll-free numbers (prefix 0800) can be dialled free of charge from within the UK, and American numbers beginning 1-800 are free when made in the USA.

The author and publishers have every reason to believe in the accuracy of the information given in this book and the authenticity and correct practices of all organisations, companies, agencies etc. mentioned; however, situations may change and telephone numbers, visa requirements, exchange rates etc. can alter, and readers are strongly advised to check facts and credentials for themselves. Readers are invited to write to the author c/o Vacation Work, 9 Park End Street, Oxford OX1 1HJ if there is any organisation or company they would like to see included in the next edition.

Preface

For more than two decades the tourist industry has been catering to the demand for a more enlivening alternative to the traditional week or two on a Mediterranean beach with its accompaniment of badly-behaved fellow holidaymakers, polluted seas and a fair chance of skin cancer. There is no sign in the adventure travel trend abating, despite our growing obsession with risk when travelling. Perhaps it is the restrictive nature of daily life that drives us to seek freedom, with or without thrills, in near or far flung corners of the globe. Certainly there is no doubt that adventure holiday business is expanding through its own inventiveness. .The range of alternatives to the 'traditional' package holiday has never been greater so that it seems no corner of the globe or activity is not reachable or doable on one or other specialist holiday: exploring Antartica, skiing in Greenland, horse riding in China, studying humpback whales in Hawaii or making your own Guitar, are not just pipedreams but available holidays (provided you have £1500 to £3000 to spare). Money, rather than feasibility is the only limit on your ambitions. However, even the financially challenged can experience a holiday-with-a-difference be it on an organic farm in France working for keep, or with an international crowd on a conservation holiday in Britain, Ireland or elsewhere in Europe. These will cost you little more than the cost of getting there. In between, there are hundreds of possibilities priced from a couple of hundred pounds a week.

As the number of small, independent holiday operators with expertise in precise destinations and activities grows, so also does the number of travellers and tourists visiting unusual and remote regions. The impact of tourism on the popular resorts or destinations is all too familiar and most of us share a concern to avoid rampant commercialisation and defacement happening to the world's remaining beautiful places. A Campaign for Environmentally Responsible Tourism (P O Box 4246, London SE21 7ZE; 0181 299 6111) has been one response from concerned tourist companies, but in the end it is up to each one of us to ensure that we pass through beautiful places leaving them as we found them lest we trample on our dreams (or someone else's).

This fully-revised 1998 edition of Adventure holidays contains more exciting, interesting and unusual holidays than ever before. It is for anyone, however experienced or otherwise who wants an exciting, interesting or unusual holiday or who wants to learn something new or improve existing skills. You may wish to go on a watersports or multi activity sampler holiday to find out which sport or activity you like best. Or you may already have enjoyed cycling in Cornwall and wish to ride a bike in China or Mexico, or wish to go winetasting in Australia. Would-be or accomplished naturalists, climbers, divers, conservationists, riders, sailors or dog-sled drivers and others, are bound to find a holiday that appeals. This book tells you what is available, where, when and for how much. The choice is yours.

Victoria Pybus

Abbreviations for national and international Authorities, Associations, Clubs and Societies.

AALA	Adventure Activities Licensing Authority
ABRS	Association of British Riding Schools
ABTA	Association of British Travel Agents
AITO	Association of Independent Tour Operators
AMI	Association of Mountaineering Instructors
AOPA	Aircraft Owners and Pilots Association
ASTA	American Society of Travel Agents
ATOL	Air Tour Operator's Licence
BAHA	British Activity Holidays Association
BAMG	British Association of Mountain Guides
BAPC	British Association of Parachute Clubs
BBAC	British Balloon and Airship Club
BCU	British Canoe Union
BGA	British Gliding Association
BHGA	British Hang Gliding Association
BHPA	British Hang Gliding & Paragliding Association
BHS	British Horse Society
BMC	British Mountaineering Council
BMIF	British Marine Industries Federation
BOF	British Orienteering Federation
BPA	British Parachute Association
BGSF	British Grass Ski Federation
BSA	British Surfing Association
BS-AC	British Sub-Aqua Club
BSF	British Ski Federation
BTA	British Tourist Authority
BWA	British Waterski Association
BWSF	British Waterskiing Federation
ETB	English Tourist Board
FIYTO	Federation of International Youth Travel Organisations
IATA	International Air Traffic Association
IYHF	International Youth Hostels Federation
IWS	International Windsurfer Schools
MIC	Mountaineering Instructors Certificate
MLTB	Mountain Leaders Training Board
NAUI	National Association of Underwater Instructors
NFSPS	National Federation of Sailing and Powerboat Schools
NFSS	National Federation of Sea Schools
NSFGB	National Ski Federation of Great Britain
PADI	Professional Association of Diving Instructors
PSCA	Professional Sailboard Centres Association
RYA	Royal Yachting Association
SCGB	Ski Club of Great Britain
SSC	Scottish Sports Council
TIA	Travel Industry Association (USA)
UIAGM	Union International Associations Guides Montagnes
YCA	Yacht Charter Association
WARP	Welsh Association of Residential Providers

Multi Activity Holidays

The best way to begin a directory of adventure holiday opportunities is by dealing with organisations which offer holidays involving a variety of activities. These multi activity centres provide the chance to sample a very wide range of pursuits, and enable you to choose which to follow up at a later date.

Multi activity centres are a growth industry in Britain and abroad. Many are specifically arranged for young people of school age. The custom of going off to summer camp spread to the UK from North America where it has been practised for decades. It seems likely that an annual visit to an activity centre will soon become the rule rather than the exception. See *Young People's Holidays* (beginning on page 36 for the opportunities available and for an update on the on safety provisions at UK outdoor centres.

Whether young or old, you can choose a multi activity centre which offers canoeing and climbing, windsurfing and walking, and much more. Prudent participants will probably want to take out insurance designed to cover those on activity holidays. Two organisations worth contacting are specialist insurance companies Worldwide Travel Insurance (0541-508080) and Crispin Speers & Partners Ltd. (0171-480 5083). Another company, Columbus Travel Insurance offers policies for action adventure holidays with over a dozen named sports; however, these do not include mountaineering and caving. Another specialist broker is Leisurecare Insurance (01793-514199) of Swindon who can arrange cover for most activities and sports. Insurers usually have different rates for Europe and worldwide. You should always check with the insurer which if any sports or activities are covered by the policy and whether you are insured for third party liability (particularly for jet-skiing).

Prices at multi activity centres normally include all meals and accommodation, so the only extra expenses are for transport, pocket money and postcards. But most visitors are far too busy, or exhausted to write home.

Worldwide

CLUB MED
106-110 Brompton Road, London SW3 1JJ (tel 0171-581 1161; brochure line 01635-565065).
Member of ABTA, CAA ATOL and IATA.
Club Med, now 45 years old, organises all-inclusive holidays (sun and wintersports in over 100 *villages* worldwide for singles, families and mature travellers. Activities include tennis, golf, archery, sailing, windsurfing, waterskiing, snorkelling and scuba diving. Prices include flights and transfers, full board and wine/beer with meals, use of sports facilities, tuition if required, entertainment, children's clubs and full travel insurance.

GANE & MARSHALL INTERNATIONAL LTD
266 East Barnet Road, East Barnet, Herts. EN4 8TD (tel 0181-441 9592; fax 0181-441 7376).
Proprietor: Jeremy Gane.
In business since 1993.
ATOL and CAA bonded.
Climb Kilimanjaro or trek the Cuban Sierras. Combine a week's safari with walking and camping in the uninhabited and vast Selous reserve in Tanzania or a week on

Zanzibar with unspoilt beaches and Moorish architecture. Try scuba diving off desert islands or a special interest tour of Cuba. Activities include mountain walks, climbing, diving and cycling in a range of diverse destinations worldwide. Prices of around £1400, including accommodation and flights.
Some holidays are suitable for the physically challenged.

KUMUKA EXPEDITIONS
40 Earls Court Road, London W8 6EJ (tel 0171-937 8855; fax 0171-937 6664; BROCHURE 01233-211666).
In business since 1987.
Member of East African Wildlife Society.
Holidays for over 2000 arranged annually.
Adventure holidays worldwide covering Lake Malawi, Serengeti, Ngorongoro Crater, the Victoria Falls, Masai Mara and the Okavango Delta. Wide range of activities available including horse riding, walking safaris, white water rafting, hot springs, deep sea fishing, scuba diving, dune boarding, game drives and bungy jumping. Prices from £450 to £1500. Camping accommodation. A small amount of participation in the day-to-day running of camps is expected.
Age range: 18 to 40 years.

ORIGINS
Woodcock Travel Ltd, 25-31 Wicker, Sheffield, S3 8HW (tel 0114-2729619; fax 0114-2722709).
Directors: B Waller, I Taylor, P Major, P Broadhead, B Cummings.
In business since 1980.
Member of ABTA, ATOL, IATA, GBTA.
Holidays for 150 arranged annually.
Nature, Travel and Adventure holidays located worldwide and in the U.K. all year round. Destinations and activities include dog-sledging in Lapland; canoeing, hiking and riding in British Columbia; rafting in the Grand Canyon; hiking in Poland; archeological tours to Jordan, Peru and Japan; wildlife photographic tours to Yellowstone, Borneo, Baja, Botswana and the Hebrides of Scotland. Tours last seven to 31 days for individuals and groups of six to 12 people. Prices from £900-£5000 including half or full board accommodation in hotels, guesthouses, mountain huts or camping, airport taxes and entrance fees.
'We travel carefully, respecting wildlife and cultures through small group sizes and minimal disturbance'.
Minimum age: 12 years (accompanied).

SPORTIF INTERNATIONAL
Fleets, Spatham Lane, Ditchling, East Sussex BN6 8XL (tel 01273-844919; fax 01273-844914).
Directors: Mr D J Thomas and Mrs A C Thomas.
In business since 1989.
Member of ATOL, RYA and Caribbean Windsurfing Association.
Holidays for 2500 annually.
Sporting activities in worldwide destinations, all year round. Try windsurfing, diving, multi-sports, tennis, golf, riding and mountain biking in the Canary Islands, Spain, the Caribbean, Venezuela, the USA, Turkey and Egypt. Prices £270-£1500, depending on resort.

TRAVELBAG ADVENTURES
15 Turk Street, Alton, Hampshire GU34 1AG (tel 01420-541007; fax 01420-541022).
Directors: M Wright, D Williams, B Wood, D Betsworth & L Webber.
In business since 1996.
Member of ABTA, ATOL, IATA, AFTA & PATA.
Holidays for 2000 arranged annually.
Wide range of adventure activity holidays in over 30 countries worldwide, from Argentina to Yemen, including white water rafting, wildlife and nature tours, jeep safaris, sea kayaking, diving and snorkelling. Group sizes number no more than 6 people. Transport varies depending on the tour; from minibuses to Land Rovers, local buses and rickshaws, ferries to dugout canoes; even elephants. Accommodation ranges from tribal huts, homestays and camping to guesthouses and hotels. Holiday prices from £495-£2595. Sleeping bags and walking boots are not included in the price.
Ages: 14 years (17 years unaccompanied, 5 years on Special Family Adventures) to 60 years.

TREK & DIVE
The Travel Trading Company, Trowfarth, Clwyd LL22 8BW (tel 01492-650225; fax 01492-650093). E-mail: sales@travel-trading.demon.co.uk
Proprietor: Robert Jones.
In business since 1989.
Member of England's North Country Tourist Board.
Tailor-made multi activity holidays in the U.K., India, South-East Asia and South America. Activities include trekking, diving, white water rafting, 4x4 jungle safari's, camel safari's and wildlife treks. Individuals, and groups of any size catered for. Some

experience may be necessary to achieve the most from the holiday, although tuition is possible. Receive as much or as little assistance as required. Prices
from £1000, to £1800 inclusive of flights.
Physically challenged people catered for in the U.K. No age limits.

England

ACORN ACTIVITIES
P O Box 120, Hereford HR4 8YB (tel 01432-830083; fax 01432-830110).
Partners: C H Cordle, K A R Cordle.
In business since 1989.
Holidays arranged for 10,000 annually.
Activity and special interest holidays in Herefordshire, Shropshire and Wales throughout the year for families, couples, singles and groups. No experience necessary. Over 100 activities to choose from including: abseiling, canoeing, motorsports, airsports, watersports, fishing, golf and arts & crafts. Choice of hotels, farmhouses, group accommodation, and self-catering. All equipment provided and instructors fully accredited. Accommodation from £22 per night, activities from £40 per day.

ALLNATT CENTRES
Joseph Allnatt Centres Ltd, 35 Ulwell Road, Swanage, Dorset BH19 1LG.
Directors: D V Martin, D M Wright, M Piper.
In business since 1924.
Member BAHA, FIYTO, BITOA, NAOE, SCOE. Activity Centre Operating Licence.
Holidays for 13,000 arranged annually. Low cost accommodation and facilities in Lyme Regis and Swanage, Dorset and the Isle of Wight all year round for groups of ten to 200 people. Wide spectrum of activities from abseiling and archery through to watersports and trampolining. Led by experienced and qualified instructors. Also popular environmental educational courses and facilities Price £70-£140 + VAT per person includes specially converted hotels and hostel-type accommodation with full board.
Minimum age: eight years; maximum age: 21 years.

ALSTON TRAINING AND ADVENTURE CENTRE
High Plains Lodge, Alston, Cumbria CA9 3DD (tel 01434-381886).
Director: D Simpson.
Multi activity holidays in the North Pennines. Activities include canoeing, climbing, abseiling, mountain biking, underground exploration, fell walking, dry skiing and snow skiing when available. Prices from around £30 per day, including accommodation and meals.

ANGLIAN ACTIVITY BREAKS
29 Yarmouth Road, Norwich NR7 OEE (tel 01603 700770; fax 01603 701166).
Directors: Paul W King, Sarah J Harris.
In business since 1993.
Holidays for 5000 arranged annually.
Over 100 activities and adventures available in East Anglia all year round. Choose from sailing, riding, painting, abseiling, raft building, paintballing, watersports, hang gliding, archery, ballooning, parachuting, tank driving, quad biking and more. For singles, families and groups up to 40. No experience needed for any activity. Prices from £52 for a half day of motorsports, £17 for dry slope skiing. Accommodation in a range of luxury hotels, guest houses and budget group categories. All equipment provided.

AVON SKI CENTRE/MENDIP RIDING CENTRE
Lyncombe Lodge, Churchill, Somerset BS19 5PQ (tel 01934-852335).
Proprietor: S Lee.
In business since 1973.
British Ski Schools Operators' Association, West Country Tourist Board, BHS approved.
Riding and skiing in the Mendip Hills, all year round. Individuals and groups of between ten and 40 catered for. No experience is required. Prices from £140 (weekend). Low season skiing and riding combination £265 + VAT; riding only £245 + VAT. Prices include dormitory accommodation, half board and all equipment.
Unaccompanied young people accepted from seven years.
Physically and mentally challenged people welcome if accompanied by an able-bodied person.

BLENHEIM LODGE GUEST HOUSE
Brantfell Road, Bowness-on-Windermere, Cumbria LA23 3AE (tel 01539-443440; fax 01539-445440).
Proprietors: Jackie and Frank Sanderson.
Dalesway Association Members. Home Cooking and Accommodation Awards.
Well planned wildlife walks and tours where the air is so pure that many rare plants abound, and where birds and red squirrels

come to look at you. Oil painting for beginners. B&B from £23-£40 per day; dinner from £18.

BOWLES OUTDOOR CENTRE
Eridge Green, Tunbridge Wells TN3 9LW (tel 01892-665665).
Educational Charitable Trust.
Owned by Bowles Rocks Trust Ltd.
Patron: HRH The Duke of Edinburgh.
In business since 1961.
Holidays for 2600 arranged annually.
Activity holidays including skiing, rock climbing, camping, orienteering and canoeing. Prices for a weekend from £74, five days from £153); full board and accommodation included. All equipment is provided. Specialist courses are also offered in each of the activities (see individual activity entries). No experience needed.
Physically challenged students catered for.
Minimum age: eight years (accompanied); nine years (unaccompanied).

CALVERT TRUST KIELDER
Kielder Water, Hexham, Northumberland NE48 1BS (tel 01434-250232).
Northumbria Calvert Trust; registered charity no. 511851.
Director: P Cockerill.
In operation since 1984.
Multi activity holidays for the physically challenged and their families and friends. Open all year. Price includes activity, instruction equipment, fully accessible accommodation and meals. Also available, short term Respite Care, and courses for school groups.

CINNAMON ADVENTURE
Haland House, 66 York Road, Weybridge, Surrey KT13 9DY (tel 01932-842221; fax 01932-840005).
Sole Trader: Paul Maung-Maung.
In operation since 1995.
Holidays for 250-300 arranged annually.
Multi activity breaks located in the Peak Distict, Solent and Cornwall, starting at half-day to week long courses, available all year round. Activities vary between centres, including canoeing, mountain biking, caving, pot holing, climbing, abseiling, hill-walking, paragliding, sailing and surfing. Discover splendid moorland views, pony trekking in the New Forest or the mountain biking trails of Bodmin Moor. Individuals and groups of up to 30 catered for. Prices range from £25 half-day to £450 for a weeks activities and half board in a hotel. Accommodation ranges from hotels to residential centres depending on holiday location.
Ages: 16-60 years. Unaccompanied young people not accepted.

COMPASS WEST ISR
9 Mayon Green Cresent, Sennen, Penzance, Cornwall TR19 3BS (tel/fax 01736-871447).
Proprietors: R Edwards and E Edwards.
In business since 1982.
Holidays for 250 arranged annually.
Climbing, walking and mountain biking holidays in Cornwall from July-September. Small groups of up to eight catered for. Prices from £290 per week. Self-catering accommodation. No experience necessary. All equipment included except climbing boots.
Minimum age: 18 years. Unaccompanied young people not accepted.

DORSET ADVENTURE HOLIDAYS
Sea Barn Farm, West Sleet, Weymouth, Dorset DT3 4ED (tel 01305 785852; fax 01305-775396).
Directors: M Hodgson and J Coombe.
In business since 1989.
Adventure Activities Licence.
Member of Tourist Development Action Programme — Weymouth/Portland.
Holidays for around 1000 arranged annually.
Multi activity and multi adventure holidays for adults, families and groups in Fleet and Weymouth all year round. Wide range of activites possible including climbing, abseiling, canoeing, swimming, windsurfing, sailing, raft building, water and jet skiing, riding, archery, orienteering, caving and initiative games. Multi-choice breaks, corporate days, women-only breaks and family choice weekends. Prices from £39/£270 for short weekends/seven days including all meals and any specialist equipment. Tented accommodation in the Canvas Village near Weymouth, with swimming pool, club house and bar. Alternative accommodation can be arranged. All instructors are experienced and qualified in their specialist activities, (a detailed staff qualification list is available on request).
Minimum age: eight years (accompanied); twelve years (unaccompanied) (see *Young People's Holidays*).

EASTBOURNE MARINE
11 Wrestwood Avenue, Willingdon, Eastbourne, East Sussex BN22 OHA (tel 01323-502674).
Proprietor: P Towner.
In business since 1982.
RYA Affiliated.
Multi activity holidays including sailing, windsurfing, canoeing and mountain biking. Two-day and five-day holidays from April to September. Individuals and groups of up to 12. Prices from £150. A variety of accommodation can be arranged locally.

HIGH ADVENTURE
Yarborough House, Nettlecombe Lane, Whitwell, Isle of Wight PO38 2QA (tel 01983 730075; fax 01983-731441).
Proprietor: Philip Keen.
In business since 1981.
Member of BHPA and Southern Tourist Board.
Courses for 500-1000 arranged annually.
Five-day multi activity courses on the Isle of Wight based at the guest house. Activities include hang-gliding, para-gliding, sailing, canoeing, surfing and mountain biking. Summer and winter. Prices from £175 per week for courses inclusive of instruction and equipment except hire of mountain bikes at £12 per day or £60 per week. Accommodation extra from £17 per night.
Minimum age: 14 years (accompanied); 16 years (unaccompanied).

JOHN BULL SCHOOL OF ADVENTURE
12 Littlethorpe Park, Ripon, Yorks HG4 1UQ (tel + fax 01765-604071).
Proprietor John Bull.
In business since 1984.
BCU, RYA, Yorkshire Tourist Board.
Holidays for 2000-3000 arranged annually.
Day and residential adventure holidays involving outdoor activities on rivers, lakes, mountains and rocks. Day, weekend and week-long courses. Individuals, families and groups of up to 20. All levels from beginner upwards. Prices: day rate £35, weekend course £90 and week's course £210, including full board and accommodation in a converted watermill. Non-residential rates also available. Bespoke courses can be arranged for junior management and graduate trainees.
Age ranges: eight to 80 years.
Physically challenged people welcome.

LYNCOMBE LODGE
Churchill, Somerset BS19 5PQ (tel 01934-852335; fax 01934-853314).
Proprietor: Mrs S A Lee.
In business for over 20 years.
British Ski Slope Operators Association and BHS approved.
Holidays arranged for around 500 annually.
Activity holidays in the Mendip hills, in the heart of the West Country. Specialising in riding holidays the lodge also offers dry slope skiing — with tuition or purely recreational, pistol shooting, caving, orienteering, swimming, canoeing, cycling and hiking as well as fishing and golf. For individuals, families and groups of up to 30. Prices from £250 for children and £300 for adults. Farmhouse and half board accommodation. Vegetarians catered for.
Minimum age: seven years (unaccompanied).
Some facilities for physically challenged people.

MEDINA VALLEY CENTRE
Dodnor Lane, Newport, Isle of Wight PO30 5TE (tel 01983-522195; fax 01983-825962).
Non-profit making company.
Executive Director: Peter Savory.
In business since 1963 (formerly The Christian Sailing Centre until 1977).
Recognised by RYA and NFSS.
Activity holiday weeks suitable for individuals and families at the attractive riverside locationon the Isle of Wight. Activities include dinghy sailing, walking, painting & drawing and natural history.Qualified instructors and all safety gear provided. Courses on residential and non-residential basis. Also holiday base accommodation.
All ages, all abilities.
Free colour brochure and tariff on request.

MENDIP OUTDOOR PURSUITS
Laurel Farmhouse, Summer Lane, Banwell, Weston-super-Mare BS24 6LP (tel 01934-820518/823666).
Owner: J Hayward.
Operating since 1988.
BCU approved, BOF accredited and RYA recognised centre. Adventure Activity Licence.
Activity holidays and weekends for individuals or groups of six or more. Activities

include caving, climbing, canoeing, abseiling, orienteering, archery, sailing, windsurfing, raft builing and assault course. Beginner to intermediate level. Courses can be tailored to suit the needs of clients. Corporate team building a speciality. Some activities involve use of local accommodation including caravan sites, holiday cottages, bunk house, hostels and hotels. Courses are suitable for children and adults and are also available half-day, day etc. non-residential basis.
Minimum age: eight years unaccompanied.
Physically challenged people welcome depending on activity and disability.

MILLFIELD HOLIDAY VILLAGE
Millfield School, Street, Somerset BA16 0YD (tel 01458-445823).
Course Director: Douglas Humphrey.
In operation since 1971.
Recognised by ETB.
Holidays for 2500 arranged annually.
Almost 300 holiday courses in July and August covering a very wide spectrum of interests from aerobics through to clay pigeon shooting and bridge to yoga. The cost of two courses with residence (in school houses) with all meals is around £290 per week.
Minimum age (accompanied) three years; cr'eche facilities available. Minimum age for unaccompanied children: eight years.
Physically challenged people catered for.
See also *Young People's Holidays*, England for details of special multi activity holidays for those aged five to 12 years.

MILL ON THE BRUE
Trendle Farm, Tower Hill, Bruton, Somerset BA10 0BA (tel 01749-812307; fax 01749-812706).
Partners: T & T Rawlingson Plant.
In business since 1982.
Gained Investor in People & National Training Awards.
Holidays for 3500 arranged annually.
Residential and day multi activity adventures in Somerset and specialist 12 days on the Isle of Mull, Scotland, during the summer holidays. Groups (including adults and special needs) taken from the end of January to December. Activities include climbing, canoeing, high ropes course, problem solving and group tasks. Prices: £25 for a day visit; unaccompanied children/teenagers £289 per week includes full board, shared bedrooms, all instruction and specialist equipment.Special rates for groups .
Minimum age: eight years (unaccompanied); maximum: none.

NORTH YORK MOORS ADVENTURE CENTRE
Ingleby Cross, Northallerton, North Yorks DL6 3PE (tel 01609-882571).
Director: Ewen Bennett.
Recognised by BCU, BMC, ETB, NCOETR and AHOEC.
In business since 1978.
Activity or field studies courses centred on a traditional, stone-built farmhouse in the North York Moors National Park. Courses can be tailored to suit groups or individuals. Activities available include: canoeing, rock climbing, caving, hill walking, camping, orienteering, pony trekking and mountain biking. Full board catering for a maximum of 24 guests. Multi activity weekends or weeks with specialist, qualified instructors. Prices from £50-£200, fully inclusive.
No equipment necessary.
Minimum age: 12 years (unaccompanied).

OUTDOOR ADVENTURE
Atlantic Court, Widemouth Bay, Nr Bude, Cornwall EX23 ODF (tel 01288-361312).
Partners: Jeff Gill, Richard Gill.
In business since 1981.
Member: RYA, BCU, BSA, BAHA.
Multi activity adventure sports weeks, three-day breaks and weekends for adults, from March-Nov. Activities include windsurfing, canoeing, sailing, surfing, climbing and mountain biking. Individuals and groups catered for. All equipment (including wet suits), experienced and qualified instruction and local transport included. Week prices from £288, weekends £123, includes full board in twin rooms at the seafront centre, with lively bar. Vegetarian and special diets catered for. Beginners and all abilities welcome.
Minimum age: 16 years.

THE OUTDOOR TRUST
Belford, Northumberland NE70 7QE (tel & fax 01668-213289).
Head of Centre: Peter Clark.
Established as a Charitable Trust 1995 (previously Windy-Gyle Outdoor Trust founded 1974).
Recognised by the RYA, BCU.
Adventurous holidays including rock climbing, orienteering, sea, river and white water kayaking and other watersports. Weekends, five days or seven days.
'We offer the opportunity of overcoming your fears and learning new skills, all

conducted within a framework of impeccable safety'.
Minimum age: nine years.

OUTWARD BOUND TRUST
Watermillock, Cumbria CA11 OJL (tel 0990 134227).
Established 1941.
Courses for 12 000 arranged annually.
Outward Bound programmes are available to all over the age of 11. Age bands: 11-13, 14-15, 16-17, 18-24, 25 plus and 50 plus. A choice of centre-based or expedition courses at three UK venues are illustrated in a free brochure and video.

PEAK NATIONAL PARK CENTRE
Losehill Hall, Castleton, Derbyshire S30 2WB (tel 01433-620373).
Director: Peter Townsend.
1992 winner of English Tourist Board's England for Excellence Awards.
Natural History, walking, navigation skills, painting, photography and heritage holidays for individuals and groups. Holidays for two, three or four nights all year. Prices from £125 including luxury en suite accommodation, full board, tuition, evening talks and activities. No single room supplement.
Minimum age: eight years old if accompanied by legal guardian. Holidays can be tailor-made for groups of 12+ people.

PLEASURE IN LEISURE
Tirobeck, Keldwyth Park, Windermere, Cumbria LA23 1HG (tel 015394-42324; fax 015394-88288).
Proprietor: Babs Matthews.
In business since 1982.
Member of Cumbria Tourist Board, Adventure Activity Licence.
Holidays for around 1000 arranged annually.
Adventure programme includes abseiling, rock climbing, windsurfing, raft building, canoeing, gorge scrambling and caving. Other activities include orienteering, Go-Karting, quad-bikes, archery, clay pigeon shooting and horse riding. Holidays located in the Lake Distict, Cumbria and West Yorkshire. Individuals and groups catered for, including team events and challenges, Stag and Hen parties and corporate groups. Prices vary depending on activity and duration, ranging from two-hour sessions to weekly programmes. Choice of half or full-day option programmes for groups. Prices vary depending on group size and option choice. Example: Groups of six to ten enlisting for full-day Option 1 (Go-Karting, quad bikes, archery, horse riding, JCB digger races) costs £54 per person. Accommodation can be arranged locally in guest-houses, hotels or youth hostels. All equipment is provided.
'Friendly, caring and professional instruction in the most beautiful corner of England.'
Minimum age: 8 years (accompanied); 12 years (unaccompanied).
Physically and mentally challenged people welcome in groups of four minimum.

ROCK LEA ACTIVITY CENTRE
Station Road, Hathersage, Hope Valley, S32 1DD (tel 01433-650345).
Proprietors: Caroline and Iain Jennings.
In operation since 1977.
Founder member of BAHA. Recognised by Heart of England Tourist Board and DARE. Adventure Activities Licence.
Adult holidays arranged for 100's each year.
Weekend, four-day and six-night multi activity holidays all year round (except Christmas). Rock climbing, caving, sailing, water-skiing, windsurfing, orienteering, treasure hunts, mountain biking, walking, abseiling and canoeing. Suitable for beginners. Prices from around £349 for six nights, £99 for a weekend. Individuals and groups of up to 20 in single, double/twin shared rooms and dormitories. Accommodation also in adjacent hotels, B&B's, hostels and bunkhouses. Group discounts available.
'Friendly, house-party atmosphere, very safe professional staff, and intensive action in beautiful surroundings'.

SHORELINE OUTDOOR PURSUITS
11a Crooklets Beach, Bude, Cornwall, EX23 8NE (tel 01288-352451).
Partners: N Hammond and S Hammond.
Established 1979.
BCU approved, Adventure Activities Licence.
Holidays provided for 1000 each year.
Multi activity holidays in Cornwall from May to October. Activities include canoeing, surfing, climbing/abseiling and archery. Also guided studies of the history, wildlife and ecology of the area. Walks of varying lengths also arranged. Holidays last five, six or seven days. Short sessions also available. Two star accommodation and fine cuisine. Junior schools, groups, families and individuals catered for. All equipment provided.

SKERN LODGE OUTDOOR CENTRE

Appledore, Bideford, North Devon EX39 1NG (tel 01237-475992).

Partners: Martin Robinson and Andrew Milne.
In operation since 1975.
Member of BAHA; recognised by BCU, ETB etc.
Holidays for 2000 arranged annually.
Canoeing, riding, orienteering, climbing, abseiling, archery, water skiing, sailing, surfing and snorkelling for individuals and groups of up to 120, throughout the year. Dormitory accommodation and all meals provided. Flexible programmes of activities supervised by highly qualified instructors. Opportunities for overnight bivouacking, coastal exploration, abseiling on local crags, capsize drills and rafting on improvised rafts. Specialist courses available (see appropriate chapters for details). Prices from £80 for a weekend, and from £154 for a week excluding VAT. All specialist equipment is included. No experience needed.
Minimum age: nine years (unaccompanied).
Physically challenged people welcome.

SPICE: SPECIAL PROGRAMME OF INITIATIVE, CHALLENGE AND EXCITEMENT

Head Office: 18 Henrietta Street, Old Trafford, Manchester M16 9GA (tel 0161-872 2213).

Birmingham branch: 7 Wentworth Court, Kingbury Road, Erdington, Birmingham B24 8QN (tel 0121-382 5501).
East Midlands branch: 19 Quayside Close, Turneys Quay, Nottingham NG2 3BP (tel+fax 0115 986 6188
North Lancs. branch: 847 Chorley Old Road, Bolton BL1 5SL (tel 01204 849848).
South London branch: 66 Robin Hood Lane, Sutton, Surrey SM1 2SA (tel 0181 661-7794; fax 0181 661-7796).
South Yorkshire branch: 47 Middleox Gardens, Halfway, Sheffield, S19 5SR (tel 01142-488161).
Thames Valley branch: 14 The Dell, Kingsclere, Newbury, Berks RG20 5NL (tel 01635-298733; fax 01635-299998).
West Yorkshire branch: 112 West St. Lindley, Huddersfield, W Yorks HD3 3JX (tel 01484-461113).Scotland East branch: 72 Ratcliffe Terrace, Edinburgh EH9 1ST (tel 0131 662-9600; fax 0131 662-9601).
National Co-ordinator: David Smith.
In operation since 1980.
An 'adventure social club', 9000 members strong, offering a wide range of activities lasting from a few hours to several weeks throughout Britain and abroad. Membership is limited and costs £45 for the first year, £50 thereafter.
'The adventure group for ordinary people who want to do extraordinary things'.

ST GEORGES HOUSE CHRISTIAN OUTDOOR CENTRE

Georgeham, Braunton, North Devon EX33 1JN (tel 01271-890755; fax 01271-890060).

Charitable Trust.
In business since 1978.
Holidays for about 2,000 arranged annually.
Members of BSA, CCI/UK.
Week-long multi activity holidays in North Devon, operating mainly March-October. Activities include sailing, canoeing, surfing, mountain biking, water skiing and climbing. Individuals and groups catered for. Basic, fully catered accommodation provided. Price: £150. Individual participation is expected in the day-to-day running of the holiday.
'Highly flexible; challenges set to ability of the individual. Spectacular surf beaches.'
Minimum age: 8 years (accompanied); 16 years (unaccompanied).
Maximum age: 45 years.

SUMMITREKS ADVENTURE SERVICES

14 Yewdale Road, Coniston, Cumbria LA21 8DU (tel 01539-441212; fax 01539-441055).

Directors: Ron Rutland and Hilary Hills.
In business since 1986.
Member of Cumbria Tourist Board and AMI, BMC, health and safety inspected.
Holidays for 5000 arranged annually.
Wide range of multi activities in the Lake District. Choose from mountain biking, windsurfing, canoeing, climbing, abseiling, aquaseiling, gorge scrambling and leaders' certificate courses. Prices from £12 per half day to £199 per week.
Minimum age: 11 years (accompanied); 16 years (unaccompanied).
Physically, visually and mentally challenged people welcome.

TRIG POINT 49

Staithes, Nr Whitby, N. Yorkshire TS13 5AD (tel/fax 01947-840757).

In business since 1988.

Member of Yorkshire & Humberside Tourist Board and Marine Conservation Society.

All year residential and educational outdoor activity centre in the North York Moors National Park. Activities include: canoeing, kayaking, climbing, abseiling, orienteering, rope/assault courses, expeditions, bivouacing, archery, team work challenges, raft building & racing, mountain biking and pony trekking. The centre caters for groups of ten and over, schools, colleges, youth clubs, corporate bookings.The centre has a recreation room, playing fields etc. and accommodates large groups of people, full board, in bunk house accommodation; also self catering units. Telephone or write for a full brochure.

WHITE HALL CENTRE FOR OPEN COUNTRY PURSUITS
Long Hill, Buxton, Derbyshire SK17 6SX (tel 01298-23260).
Administered by Derbyshire Outdoors.
Outdoor Education courses for all ages, from pre-school to the retired. Specialises in outdoor and adventurous activities. Linked with Lea Green Centre (Lea, Matlock DE4 5GJ, 01629-534561) which offers field studies and sports courses. Accommodation in self-catering facilities is available.

WIGHT WATER ADVENTURE SPORTS
19 Orchardleigh Road, Shanklin, Isle of Wight P037 7NP (tel/fax 01983-866269.
Member of RYA, BCU and BSA. Adventure Activities Licence.
Watersports and landsports holidays in Sandown Bay on the Isle of Wight from April to September. Activities include: windsurfing, sailing, canoeing, wave-skiing, surfing and bodyboarding.
No experience necessary. Courses are non-residential but plenty of accommodation is available locally.

YHA ACTIVITY CENTRE
Rowland Cote, Nether Booth, Edale, Derbyshire S30 2ZH (tel 01433-670302; fax 01433-670243).
Member of BAHA & BCU.
Multi and individual activity breaks featuring mountain, water and airsports activites, adventure courses, archery and more in the Peak District and North Wales. Individuals, groups and families. Fully qualified and experienced instructors cater for all levels, from novice to advanced participants. Prices from £71 for a weekend to £259 for seven nights include full-board accommodation in dormitories sleeping from two to ten people and all activities. Vegetarians and special diets catered for.

YMCA NATIONAL CENTRE
Fairthorne Manor, Curdridge, Southampton SO3 2GH (tel 01489-785228; fax 01489-798936).
Owned by the National Council of YMCAs.
In business since 1947.
Member of Southern Tourist Board, RYA, BCU, MLTB & GNAS.
Open residentially from March to October, daily all year. Activities available include canoeing, climbing, archery, obstacle course, raft building, orienteering and sailing on the Hamble River. All equipment included. Also day camps for five to 12-year-olds during Easter and summer holidays.
Groups with special needs welcome.

YMCA NATIONAL CENTRE
Lakeside, Ulverston, Cumbria LA12 8BD (tel 015395-31758; fax 015395-30015).
In operation since 1940.
Member of BCU, RYA, BOF and MLTB.
Outdoor Education, training courses and multi activity holidays based on the centres estate in the Lake District all year round. Activities are mountain and water based. Prices from £120 include accommodation, all meals and activity programme. Boots and waterproofs are available for hire. Open to individuals and groups including families.
Minimum age: ten years (unaccompanied).

Scotland

ABERNETHY TRUST
Nethy Bridge, Inverness-shire PH25 3ED (tel/fax 01479-821279).
Administrator: Jan Brush.
In operation since 1972.
Holidays for thousands arranged annually.
Canoeing, windsurfing, rock climbing, hill walking, skiing and sailing for all standards at a Christian Centre, December to Octobert. Accommodation, meals and specialist equipment provided. Prices from £215 per week.
No experience needed.
All ages.
Unaccompanied children from ten years +.

ABERNETHY TRUST — ARDEONAIG
by Killin, Perthshire FK21 8SY (tel 01567-820523; fax 01567-820955).
Centre Director: Philip Simpson.
In business since 1984.
Recognised by BCU. Adventure Activity Licence.
A residential outdoor adventure centre offering a full range of instructed activities around Loch Tay. Sports hall and games room on site. Weekends £52 including one day of instruction, board and lodging. One-week holidays from January-October. 'Breakthrough' teambuilding and leadership courses for all ages. Price for one week £225 includes instruction, equipment, accommodation and meals.
Minimum age: 14 years unaccompanied; ten years in a group.

ARRAN OUTDOOR CENTRE
Shiskine, Isle of Arran KA27 8EW (tel 01770-860333; fax 01770-860301).
Centre Director: Peter W Jones.
In business since 1982.
Recognised by Scottish Tourist Board (Isle of Arran).
Holidays provided for up to 1200 annually.
Multi activity weekends and weeks at a Christian centre on the Isle of Arran from February to November. Activities include canoeing, hillwalking, fishing, cycling and environmental studies, Groups of up to 40 can be catered for. No experience required. Price for seven days full board and four days instructed activities: adults £170 + VAT, children £150 + VAT. Activity weekends £41 + VAT.

CAIRNWELL MOUNTAIN SPORTS
Gulabin Lodge, Glenshee, by Blairgowrie, Perthshire PH10 7QE (tel & fax 01250-885255).
Director: G Fischnaller.
In business since 1973.
Member of Perthshire Tourist Board, BHPA, Association of Ski Schools, Adventure Activity Licence pending.
Mountain pursuits based at Glenshee operating all year round. Activities include skiing, nordic skiing, mountaineering, hill walking, mountain skills and hang-gliding. Typical price for multi activity holiday: £100 + VAT. Accommodation can be arranged in local hostels, with B&B or full board available. Individuals and groups of up to 20 catered for.
No experience necessary.

CALEDONIAN DISCOVERY
The Slipway, Corpach, Fort William PH33 7NN; tel 01397 772167; fax 01397-772765).
Week-long activity holidays aboard a large (126ft) Belgian barge that sleeps twelve, cruising the Great Glen with its canal sections linking the spectacular highland lochs including Loch Ness and Loch Lochy. Multi activity weeks include canoeing, sailing, windsurfing, walking and mountain biking using the barge as a base. Guests can also just relax on the barge and enjoy the scenery of the Caledonian canal. Some weeks specifically designed for ramblers, cyclists or families, some with a music or art theme. In winter the barge offers comfortable accommodation for walkers and skiers and well as for winter mountaineering courses. £335-£390 for six days. Price includes all activities, full board and accommodation in comfortable double cabins. Central heating, hot showers, spacious saloon. Individuals and groups catered for and all levels from beginnner to expert. No age limits.

COMPASS CHRISTIAN CENTRE LTD.
Glenshee Lodge, by Blairgowrie, Perthshire PH10 7QD (tel 01250-85209; fax 01250-885309).
Directors: C Mackel, J Craib, A Grassick, M Leiper, E Thomson, D Frew, D Mair.
In business since 1967.
Adventure Activities Licence.
Multi activity and environmental studies holidays based in the Eastern Highlands for individuals, families and groups of up to 42. Dormitory accommodation, meals and specialist equipment provided. Inter-denominational Christian centre with all activities run to national guidelines by experienced and qualified staff. Activity Weekends £49 (2 days instruction). Open all year. All ages. No experience necessary. Self-catering accommodation also available.

CRAIGOWER LODGE
Outdoor Centre, Golf Course Road, Newtonmore, Inverness-shire PH20 1AT (tel 01540-673319).
Proprietors: Bob and Suzanne Telfer.
In business since 1982.
Holidays for 1200 arranged each year.
Activity holidays in the Highlands. Orienteering, hillwalking, climbing, mountain biking, canoeing and kayaking, skiing and visits to places of interest. Prices from £210-£235 for six days, including full board,

activities, use of equipment and instruction. Weekend packages also available.
Minimum age: eight years.

GLENCOE OUTDOOR CENTRE
Glencoe, Argyll PA39 4HS (tel 01855-811350).
Multi-activity holidays in and around Glencoe for individuals and groups of up to 35. Activities include canoeing, sailing, hill walking, windsurfing, orienteering, rock climbing and abseiling. Prices from around £70 per person for a weekend including full board, accommodation, qualified instruction and use of equipment. Non-residential packages available. The Centre can also be hired by groups who wish to arrange their own activities.
Minimum age: six years (accompanied); 12 years if (unaccompanied).

GLENMORE LODGE NATIONAL OUTDOOR TRAINING CENTRE
Glenmore Lodge, Aviemore, Inverness-shire PH22 1QU (tel 01479-861276; fax 01479-861212).
Operated by the Scottish Sports Council Trust Company, Caledonia House, South Gyle, Edinburgh EH12 9DQ (tel 0131-317 7200).
Principal: Tim Walker.
Canoeing, kayaking, climbing, hill walking, skiing and adventure courses in the Cairngorms. Weekly courses at all standards throughout the year. Sampling and young people's courses available in the summer. Prices from £185 includes equipment, instruction, accommodation and all meals. Courses are subsidised by the SSC. All courses supported by a comprehensive evening programme of lectures, talks and seminars.
Minimum age: 17 years.

GREAT GLEN SCHOOL OF ADVENTURE
South Laggan, Nr Spean Bridge, Inverness-shire (tel 01809 501381; fax 01809 501218).
Leisure Manager: Donnie McCartney.
In business since 1989.
Member: Scottish Rafting Association; RYA approved.
Adventure Activity Licence.
Multi activity holidays with waterskiing, sailing, windsurfing, rock climbing, mountain biking, jetbiking, walks, archery, air rifles, down-the-line clay pigeon shooting, wake boarding (single ski water-skiing), knee boarding, skiing and white water rafting on a dam-released river (i.e. guaranteed water level) in north west Scotland all year round. Accommodation not included in the price but full facilities available locally and there is a restaurant on site. Nearby chalets can be booked with Hoseasons through travel agents.

LOCH RANNOCH OUTDOOR CENTRE/LOCH RANNOCH HIGHLAND CLUB
Kinloch Rannoch, Perthshire PH16 5PS (tel 01882 632 201; fax 01882 632 203).
Multi activities offered include white water rafting, dry/snow skiing, sailing, windsurfing, canoeing, kayaking, climbing and mountain biking. Hotel/lodge accommodation with facilities including indoor heated pool, sauna and solarium. Strict safety standards adhered to.

PERTHSHIRE ACTIVITY LINE
Perthshire Tourist Board, Lower City Mills, West Mill Street, Perth, Scotland PH1 5QP (tel 01738-444144; fax 01738-630416).
In business since 1993.
30 different activity and special interest holidays throughout Perthshire all year. Choice of multi activity, multi sports, or single activity holidays. Adventures include river rafting, off-road driving, quad biking, skiing and watersports. Activities include alternative therapy, golf and fishing. Individuals and groups accepted. Also available — one day 'tasters', tailor-made, 'a la carte' and twin centre holidays. Prices from £22. Various accommodation: activity centre, B&B, hotel and self catering depending on holiday and area. All activities are inclusive of instruction and equipment. No experience necessary.
All ages and abilities.
Physically challenged people welcome by arrangement.

RAASAY OUTDOOR CENTRE LTD
Raasay House, Isle of Raasay, by Kyle of Lochalsh, Ross-shire IV40 8PB (tel 01478-660266).
Director: L Rowe
Established 1984.
Recognised by Isle of Skye and SW Ross Tourist Board and RYA approved.
Holidays provided for 500-700 annually.
Multi activity holidays throughout the year on the Inner Hebridean Isle of Raasay. Activities include canoeing, sailing, windsurfing, cycle hire, climbing and abseiling, expeditions, orienteering, gorge walking

and archery. Groups of up to 50 catered for. No experience required. Prices from £330 per week for adults, £279 per week for children. Accommodation in twin, double, family and alpine-style bunk rooms in a Georgian mansion. Full board, tuition and all equipment provided.
'Many beautiful walks and varied wildlife'.
Unaccompanied young people accepted from nine years.

UIST OUTDOOR CENTRE
Cearn Dusgaidh, Lochmaddy, Isle of Uist HS6 5AE (tel/fax 01876-500480).
Proprietor: Niall Johnson.
In business since 1992.
Member of the Western Isles Tourist Board.
Multi activity holidays based in Lochmaddy, North Uist, Outer Hebrides all year round. Activities including: abseiling, sea kayaking and other watersports, walking, wildlife watching and climbing. Individuals and groups of up to 20. Prices: from £85 a week with self catering hostel accommodation up to £305 a week for full board accommodation. All equipment is included.
Minium age: eight years (unaccompanied).
'The ultimate location for outdoor adventure on hill, beach, loch and sea'.

Wales

BLACK DRAGON OUTDOOR EXPERIENCES
7 Ethelbert Drive, Charlton, Andover Hampshire SP10 4EP (tel 01264-357313).
Partners: Paul Cammack and Kevin Hatherill.
In business since 1993.
Member of BMC, MLTB, BAEML and NAOE.
Mountain walking, navigation, mountain saftey, scrambling, rock climbing, and more, in the Brecon Beacons and Snowdonia national parks, all year round. Also in the Austrian Alps (summer) and Scottish Highlands (winter). Individuals and groups catered for. Experienced and qualified leaders. Prices from £140. Wide range of accommodation and catering options. No experience required. Courses can also be organised in other areas.

BLACK MOUNTAIN ACTIVITIES
P O Box 5, Hay on Wye HR3 5YB (tel 01497-847897).
Exciting, action packed courses for families, individuals and groups in the Brecon Beacons National Park. Black Mountain Activities offer courses for all abilities. Activities include white water rafting, abseiling, climbing, canoeing, kayaking, mountain biking, walking, caving, archery, clay pigeon shooting and raft building. Clients are given the opportunity to mix and match programmes. A wide range of accommodation is available locally to suit all budgets.

BUTTERFIELDS
Pen-y-Nant Cottage, Minera, Wrexham LL11 3DA (tel/fax 01978-750547).
Partners: Ken and Janet Butterfield.
In business since 1985.
Holidays for around 60 arranged annually.
Multi activity holidays for deaf and hearing impaired children, young people and adults offered all year round. Activities include climbing, abseiling, canoeing, watersports, mountain walking, swimming, pony trekking and biking. Weekend or weeklong courses (five days/six nights) based at the centre overlooking Minera Mountain. Groups of up to ten catered for. Prices from £248 for a week long course, including accommodation in a self-contained residential block, all meals, transport, equipment and activities. Emphasis is placed upon safety, flexibility and hospitality.
Minimum age: five years (accompanied); 11 years (unaccompanied). No maximum age limit.
'Deaf children, young people and adults have full access to their first language (British Sign Language) throughout their holiday'.

CMC — PENSARN HARBOUR
Pensarn Harbour, Llanbeds, Gwynedd LL45 2HU (tel/fax 01341-241718).
Registered Charity.
Chairman: Mr Denis Jones.
In operation since 1966.
MLTB approved training and assessment centre. Member of Christian Camping International. Affiliated to Welsh Canoeing Association. BCU approved centre and Welsh Tourist Board Certified Centre.
Holidays for 900-1000 people arranged annually.
A variety of activities including climbing, abseiling, canoeing, sea-level traversing, gorge walking, kayaking, mountain biking and mountain craft, for two to seven days all year round. For individuals and groups of up to 50. The centre is situated in Snowdonia National Park, beside a tidal estuary.

Field studies, environmental studies and technical training courses also available in mountain walking, canoeing and rock climbing. Prices from £130 for seven days, including full board and accommodation, all equipment including rucksacks, waterproofs, instruction and all transport during the course.
For watersports, clients must be comfortable in water wearing a buoyancy aid.
Minimum age (unaccompanied): nine years.

CLWYCH FARM

Clwych Farm Cottages, Bwlch, Powys LD3 7JJ (tel 01874-730460; fax 01874-730948).
Canoeing, abseiling, birdwatching, walking, riding, climbing and shooting all available within the 300 acre Cilwych Farm estate or the surrounding Brecon Beacons National Park. Accommodation in four self-contained cottages, catering for a maximum capacity of 30 people. Specialising in family group holidays, outdoor weekends and training groups. Prices (for groups over 12 people) short breaks: £50 per person, one week: £150 per person. Fully equiped, self-catering accommodation. Meals available on request.
Minimum age: 8 years.

CINNAMON ADVENTURE

Haland House, 66 York Road, Weybridge, Surrey KT13 9DY (tel 01932-842221; fax 01932-840005).
Multi activity breaks located in Snowdonia, Llangollen and the Black Mountains. Week-long trekking holidays in the Snowdonia National Park with a choice of two moderate to strenuous treks, both covering up to ten miles a day. Prices of around £395 per week including accommodation in hotels, inns or B&B's (based on two people sharing).
Activities at Llangollen and the Black Mountains include climbing, abseiling, canoeing, white water rafting, gorge walking, mountain biking, pony trekking and kayaking. Prices from £40 per day to £195-£250 for a five-day multi activity break. Choice of accommodation in local hotels and guesthouses providing half or full board.
Individuals and groups of up to 30 catered for.
Ages: 16-60 years. Unaccompanied young people not accepted.

CLYNE FARM CENTRE

Westport Avenue, Mayals, Swansea SA3 5AR (tel 01792-403333; fax 01792-403339).
Owner: Geoff Haden.
In business since 1988.
Member of Wales Trekking and Riding Assoc., BAHA, WTB accredited centre. Complies with activity criteria where applicable, under licence from the Adventure Activities Licensing Authority.
Winner of Prince of Wales Award, Civic Trust Commendation, and the Wales Tourist Board Special Green Award.
Holidays provided for up to 2000 annually. Multi activity holidays including pony trekking, canoeing, climbing, caving, wildlife, assault course, and field study on the Gower Peninsula throughout the year. Individuals and groups of between four and 100 catered for. Activities may also be pursued separately. Other courses include: Pink Pyjamas, women only; Stag & Hen Parties, residential activity weekends; Art & Painting and Conservation & Environmental Issues. Prices between £160 and £230 (typical price £180 for seven days). This includes all equipment and accommodation in rooms sleeping one to six in a converted stone barn. No experience is necessary.
Unaccompanied young people accepted from 8 years. Provision for people with special needs.
Trekking in Nepal to Everest base camp and adventure trips to South America are part of a new Clyne Farm overseas venture.

CWM PENNANT OUTDOOR EDUCATION CENTRE

Cwm Pennant, Garndolbenmaen, Gwynedd, Wales LL51 9AQ (tel 01766-530682).
Run by the London Borough of Hillingdon — Youth & Community Service (Local).
In operation since 1966.
Member of Welsh Tourist Board, BCU and BMC.
Accommodation for up to 60.
Tailor-made activity courses to suit a range of budgets, on the North West boundary of Snowdonia National Park well-situated for a full range of challenging and adventurous land, water and mountain based activities, available all year round. Choose from mountain scrambles, abseiling, climbing, gorge walking, raft building, kayaking, canoeing, surf skiing, mountain biking and overnight bivouacking camps. Prices: £6-£13 per night for young people, £8-£15 per night for adult groups. Special out of season rates.

Accommodation in dormitories on self-catering, half or full-board basis. All specialist equipment is provided. All activities are supervised by qualified and experienced instructional staff.
Unaccompanied young people from 18 years.
Physically, visually and mentally challenged people welcome.

LLANGOLLEN YHA ACTIVITY CENTRE
Tyndwr Hall, Tywdwr Road, Llangollen, Denbighshire LL20 8AR (tel 01978-860330; fax 01978-861709).
Welsh Tourist Board accredited.
Group, individual and childrens multi activity breaks (summer camps for 9-16 year olds) featuring mountain, water and airsports activities, adventure course, archery, gorge walking, caving, mine exploration and more, based in North Wales. Fully qualified and experienced instructors cater for all levels, from novice to advanced participants. Prices from £76 for two nights to £259 for seven nights, include full-board, dormitory accommodation and all activities. Vegetarians and special diets catered for.
Physically challenged people welcome.

MOUNTAIN VENTURES
120 Allerton Road, Liverpool L18 2DG (tel 0151-734 2477).
Directors: J S Lyon, J Kewley.
In business since 1968.
Member of BMC, BCU, MLTB, WTB Accreditation scheme for activities.
Courses arranged for 4000 annually.
Multi activity courses throughout the year at Llanberis at the foot of Snowdonia, north Wales. Groups of five to 200+. Prices from £50, for three-day activity breaks in dormitory accommodation (hotels can be arranged). Price includes hotel or dormitory accommodation and all meals. Equipment is not included but can be hired. Participation with day to day running sometimes expected.

OUTER LIMITS
Pwll-y-Garth, Prenmarhmo, Gwynedd LL25 0HJ (tel & fax 01690-760248).
Proprietor: Chris Butler.
In business since 1996.
Member of BCU, Association of Mountaineering Instructors.
Holidays for 20+ arranged annually.
Multi activity day, weekend and week long holidays offered all year round in North Wales. Activities include horse riding, white water rafting, mountain biking and caving. Prices dependant on numbers and requirements. Groups and individuals catered for. Accommodation available in local guesthouses, or the bunkhouse (£8.50 per night including breakfast). No experience necessary.
Minimum age: 14 years (accompanied); 16 years (unaccompanied).
Physically, visually and mentally challenged people welcome.

PLAS CAERDEON OUTDOOR CENTRE
Bontddu, Barmouth, Gwynedd LL42 1TH (tel 01341-430276).
Chief Instructor: Barry Skinner.
Member of the Mountain Leader Training Board, BCU, MIA, BOF and WTB accredited.
Outdoor multi activity courses situated over looking the Mawddach Estuary in Mid Wales. Also training given leading to a Mountain Leadership Certificate and a Single Pitch Supervisor's Award. Accommodation in a Victorian mansion or a self contained cottage in the grounds. Suitable for school groups or adults. All instructors are experienced and qualified in their particular field.

SEALYHAM ACTIVITY CENTRE LTD
Wolfscastle, Haverfordwest, Pembrokeshire SA62 5NF (tel 01348-840763).
Directors: D Richards, V Richards, M Hone.
In business since 1986.
WTB accredited, BCU, WCA approved.
Holidays for 3000 arranged each year.
Canoeing, climbing, archery, surfing, sailing, orienteering, rifle shooting, pony trekking, abseiling and rope courses in Wales from March-November. Numerous evening activities. Prices from £94 to £260 for six days, all inclusive. Individuals, adults and groups of up to 100 catered for.
Minimum age: eight years.

SNOWDONIA MOUNTAIN CENTRE
3 Bryniau Terrace, Mynydd Llandegai, Gwynedd LL57 4BJ (tel 01248 600589).
Sole proprietor: Gerard Lynch.
In business since 1977.
Member of WTB, MLTB, AMI and BCU.
Multi activities including hillwalking/scrambling, climbing, abseiling, canoeing, mine exploration, pony trekking and mountain biking in Snowdonia (also Scotland and the

Alps). Weekends, week and two-week holidays throughout the year. Cost from £114 weekends, £272-£351 a week includes Youth Hostel accommodation and full board.
Unaccompanied young people accepted from 14 years.

TWR-Y-FELIN OUTDOOR CENTRE
Twr-y-Felin, St. Davids, Pembrokeshire, South Wales SA62 6QS (tel 07000 Big Fun or 01437-721611; fax 01437-721838). E-mail: 100104.2022@compuserve.com
Proprietor: Andrew Middleton.
In business since 1986.
Member of Welsh Tourist Board, BCU, BMC, BSA, Pembrokeshire Coast National Park.
Multi activity weekend breaks, Stag and Hen weekends, half and full-day activity sessions, specialised courses in kayaking, surfing, rock climbing and coasteering. Multi activity programmes include canoeing, orienteering, walking and abseiling. Holidays available all year round based at the hotel centre in St. Davids. Individuals and groups catered for. Prices range from £15 for half-day to £200 for a weekends full board. Accommodation provided at the hotel on site. Facilities include: kitchen and bar, single, double and family rooms, bed and breakfast of full board.
Minimum age: 6 years (accompanied); 12 years (unaccompanied).

WILTON HOUSE HOTEL
6 Quay Street, Haverfordwest, Pembrokeshire SA61 1BG (tel 01437-760033; fax 01437-760297).
Partners: P H Bowie and K R Bowie.
In business since 1996.
Member of the Welsh Tourist Board.
Scuba diving, windsurfing, hiking and rambling based in Pembrokeshire National Park. Individuals and groups of up to 18 catered for. Five-day scuba diving course: £450. Prices range from £100-£500 for other activities, including B&B accommodation at the hotel. Additional expenses for hikers and ramblers requiring transportation to and from locations.
Ages: 18-80 years. Unaccompanied young people not accepted.

Ireland & Northern Ireland

ASSOCIATION FOR ADVENTURE SPORTS
Tiglin, The National Adventure Centre, Ashford, Co. Wicklow, Ireland (tel +353 404-40169; fax +353 0404-40701). E-mail: mail@tiglin.le
Voluntary organisation.
In operation since 1969.
Holidays for 3000 arranged annually.
Adventure Sport weeks and weekends based south of Dublin, eight miles from the sea. Water sports — canoeing and snorkelling, with rock climbing and orienteering also available. AFAS is the Irish National Adventure Sports body which runs courses to encourage activity and foster higher standards in the range of adventure sports for which it has a national responsibility. All courses are designed to present participants with controlled challenge and adventure. Four-bedded dormitory accommodation in Tiglin Centre; B&B also available. Prices for five days from IR£175; weekends from IR£70.
Minimum age: ten years.
Some facilities for physically challenged participants.

BURRENDALE HOTEL & COUNTRY CLUB
51 Castlewellan Road, Newcastle, Co Down, N Ireland BT33 OJY(tel 013967-22599; fax 013967-22328).
Proprietor: Sean Small.
In business since 1978.
Investor in People Award 1997.
Multi activity holidays including riding, golf and many other outdoor pursuits all year round. Prices: special breaks from £89 per person: £6 per hour riding, £20 per hour golf.
Minimum age: unaccompanied from seven years.
Won British Airways Tourism award for facilitating holidays for the disabled.

CARLINGFORD ADVENTURE CENTRE & HOLIDAY HOSTEL
Tholsel Street, Carlingford, Co Louth, Ireland (tel +353 42 73100/73816; fax +353 42 73651).
Directors: Mary McArdle, Tom McArdle.
In business since 1990.
Member of the Irish Sailing Association, Association For Adventure Sports.
Holidays for approximately 6000 each year.
Multi activities in the setting of a medieval village and all activities within walking

distance. Activities include kayaking, windsurfing, orienteering, sailing, raft building, canadian canoeing, rock climbing, archery, hill walking and indoor climbing wall. Individuals and groups of up to 60.One and two-day breaks, weeks. From mid-February to the end of November. Prices: from £89 (adults) and £64.50 (children) for two days including full board and all activities. Group rates available on request.

GANE & MARSHALL INTERNATIONAL LTD
266 East Barnet Road, East Barnet, Herts. EN4 8TD (tel 0181-441 9592; fax 0181-441 7376).
Gourmet and walking holidays, with accommodation in country houses, hotels and places of special interest. Individual and group itineraries. Flights and car ferry arrangements possible.
Minimum age: 18 years.
Some holidays are suitable for the physically challenged.

LAKELAND CANOE CENTRE
Castle Island, Enniskillen, Co. Fermanagh, Northern Ireland BT74 5BA (tel 01365-324250; fax 01365-323319).
Proprietor: Gary Mitten.
In business since 1992.
Member of RYA and BCU.
Holidays for 2000 annually.
Canoeing, windsurfing, sailing, mountain biking, caving, orienteering, archery and horse riding around the waterways of Lough Erne and the purpose built island centre, all year round. Prices from £7 for a half day, £50 for two days and £120 for five days, including hostel and camping accommodation, all meals and equipment. For individuals and groups up to 45, with management courses also possible. No experience necessary.
Minimum age: nine years (accompanied); 11 years (unaccompanied).
Physically, visually and mentally challenged people welcome.

LITTLE KILLARY ADVENTURE CENTRE
Salruck, Renvyle, Co. Galway, Ireland (tel +353 95-43411; fax +353 95-43591). E-mail: Killary@iol.ie
Directors: M & J Young.
In business since 1990.
Approved by the Irish Tourist Board and Association for Adventure Sports.
Holidays for approximately 2000+ arranged annually.
Holidays offered start at £89 for a weekend. Activities include kayaking, hobie-cat sailing, high and low ropes course waterskiing, mountain biking, hill walking, orienteering, rock climbing, abseiling, archery, scuba diving and horse riding.
Accommodation in centre in Connemara or local, depending on budgets. Primarily for adults but younger groups of people can be catered for.

SHARE CENTRE
Smith's Strand, Lisnaskea, Co. Fermanagh BT92 0EQ, Northern Ireland (tel 013657-22122/21892; fax 013657-21893).
Director: Dawn Latimer.
Registered Charity.
In operation since 1981.
Recognised by BCU, RYA.
Mixed ability holidays including sailing, canoeing, fishing, hill walking, banana skiing, archery and windsurfing. Monday-Friday and Friday-Sunday courses in March-June and September-October Prices from £35 all inclusive; one week courses in July and August from £146 all inclusive.
'The aim is for the integration of able-bodied and physically challenged people; all facilities are adapted for the disabled.
Minimum age (unaccompanied): 14 years.

UNIVERSITY OF LIMERICK ACTIVITY CENTRE
Two Mile Gate,Killaloe, Co. Clare, Ireland (tel (+353) 61-376622; fax (+353) 61-376765). E-mail: UL.Activity@ iol. ie
Directors: Karen Weekes.
In business since 1974.
Member of ISA, AFAS, ICU.
Multi activity holidays provided on Lough Derg and surrounding hill country and forests. Activities offered: sailing, windsurfing, kayaking, canoeing, orienteering, archery, hillwalking, lakeboating, mountain biking, initiative exercises, raft building and horse riding. Available March to December for single and up to five-day courses. Individuals and groups catered for. No accommodation is provided but is available locally.
Minimum age: nine years (accompanied); 16 years (unaccompanied).
Physically challenged people can be catered for.

Europe

ADVENTURE WORLD
P O Box 645, 3800 Interlaken, Switzerland (tel +41 33 8267711; fax +41 33 8267715).
Directors: Stephan Friedli.
In business since 1992.
Member of the Tourism Organisation Interlaken, Bungy Jumping Association.
Adventures arranged for 16,000 to 20,000 annually.
River rafting, canyoning, bungy jumping, mountain biking, rock climbing, hiking, flying fox, fun yak and incentive programmes in the Jungfrau region of Switzerland (area around Interlaken). Open all year round but activities mainly carried out from May to October. Activities are paid for on an individual basis so you can do as many or as few as you want. The price range for different activities is from 40-380 Swiss francs (about £17-£185). Guide, equipment, snacks and drink are included in the prices, but not meals or accommodation both of which are available locally. Photo and video services of clients in action cost extra. No experience needed for activities, but a basic fitness level (i.e. able to walk for one hour) is required.
Minimum age: 16 for bungy jumping, otherwise 12 years.

ALP ACTIVE
Unit 9, Cheterton Mill, French's Road, Cambridge CB4 3NP (tel 01223-568220).
Alpine based activity holidays in Les Gets, France, for families, groups and individuals. Activities include mountain biking, white water rafting, paragliding, horse riding, tennis and golf. Accommodation in catered or self-catered chalets and apartments. Daytime childminding service available for 2 days per week. One week adult prices: £185 (children £145) including return Dover/Calais ferry crossing, self-catering apartment for four, two days childminding and a one day 'leisure lake' pass. Holidays run June to September.

CHALLENGE ACTIV LTD
49 Eastwick Road, Walton on Thames, Surrey KT12 5AR (tel 01932-254501).
Directors: Mr S C Allen and Mrs A L Allen.
In business since 1993.
A flexible range of activities including skiing, mountain biking, rafting, mountain walking, canoeing, wind surfing, horse riding, tennis, ice skating, fishing, archery and others, in Morzine in the French Alps. Skiing Dec-April; other activities April-Oct. Prices from £120-£240 per week. A mixture of half-board and B&B accommodation in a luxury chalet, sleeping 23. Plenty of restaurants and supermarkets locally.
Minimum age: 18 unaccompanied.
Maximum age: 68 years.

COMPASS WEST ISR
9 Mayon Green Cresent, Sennen, Penzance, Cornwall TR19 3BS (tel/fax 01736-871447). Bookings also taken at: Calle Sin Salida 16, Finestrat, Alicante, Spain 03509.
Climbing, walking and mountain biking holidays in Spain from October-June. Small groups of up to 8 catered for. Prices from £290 per week. Self-catering accommodation. All equipment included except climbing boots.
Minimum age: 18 years.

CRYSTAL HOLIDAYS
The Courtyard, Arlington Road, Surbiton, Surrey KT6 6BW; (tel 0181-241-5128).
Offers multi activity holidays. Activities include, summer skiing, mountain biking, white water rafting, windsurfing, sailing and water-skiing. Operated in Austria, Italy, France, Switzerland and Slovenia from May to September. Groups, families, couples and singles catered for. Accommodation also available in bed and breakfast, half board or all inclusive properties.

ERNA LOW CONSULTANTS LTD
9 Reece Mews, London, SW7 3HE (tel 0171-584 7820; fax 0171-589 9531).
Managing Director: Joanna Yellowlees-Bound.
In business since 1981.
Member of ABTOF, ATOL, AITO
Holidays arranged for 10,000 annually.
SKi self drive family holidays organised in hotels and self catering apartments in La Plagne, Les Arcs and Flaine in the French Alps, with summer skiing and a range of other mountain activities available. Also spa holidays around Europe.

EXODUS EXPEDITIONS
9 Weir Road, Balham, London SW12 0LT (tel 0181-675 5550 or 0181-673 0859 24 hrs).
Directors: D Burlinson, J Gillies, D Gillespie.In business since 1974.

Fully bonded member of AITO and ATOL.
Holidays arranged for 8000 annually.
Trekking and discovery holidays in Bulgaria, the Czech Republic, Crete, Greece, France, Madeira, Mallorca, Romania, Spain, Switzerland, Turkey, Cyprus, Portugal, Italy and the CIS which include walking, wildlife-spotting, exploring historical sites, river rafting and boat cruises. Organised all year round, prices range from about £385 to £1095 for eight to 18 days. All trips graded according to difficulty.

EXPLORE WORLDWIDE LTD
1 Frederick Street, Aldershot, Hampshire, GU11 1LQ (tel 01252-344161; fax 01252-343170).
Directors: Travers Cox, Derek Cook and Peter Newsom.
In business since 1981.
Fully bonded member of AITO, IATA and ATOL licensed.
Holidays arranged for 25,000 annually.
Walking, hiking, cycling, rafting and wildlife adventure holidays across Europe — Spain, Portugal, The Azores, Italy, France, The Alps, Greece, Canary Islands, the Czech Republic, Bulgaria, Romania, Scandinavia, Iceland/Greenland and Russia. Organised all year round. Prices range from about £299-£1890 for eight to 22 days.

FINLANDIA TRAVEL AGENCY (NORVISTA)
3rd Floor, 227 Regent Street, London W1R 8PD (tel 0171-409 7334; fax 0171-409 7733).
Managing Director: Jussi Lahtinen.
In business since 1963.
Member of ABTA, IATA licensed, ATOL holder.
Holidays for 2500 arranged annually.
Operates in Finland, Sweden, Baltics and Russia. Offers Christmas/New Year breaks above the Arctic Circle in Finnish Lapland featuring several activities including reindeer driving, snowmobile safari, husky driving, Lapp baptism, tandem skiing and a rendezvous with Santa Claus. Suitable outdoor clothing supplied along with a local guide. Holidays last three days (two nights) or four days (three nights). Prices from £520 (adult), £385 (child) including flights, accommodation, full board and activities. Departures throughout December. Similar activities available throughout the winter.

HEADWATER HOLIDAYS
146 London Road, Northwich, Cheshire, CW9 5HH (tel 01606-48699).
Directors: Richard and Christine Bass, Catherine Crone.
In business since 1986.
Member of ATOL, AITO, CAA.
Multi activity holidays for independent travellers in France from April to October. Prices from £249, includes ferry travel, hotel accommodation, private bathroom, dinner, bed and breakfast. No experience required.
Physically challenged people catered for.

LENA & FRIENDS
Prospekt 50-Let Okiybrya 17-216, Petropavlovsk-Kamchatsky, Russia; tel +7 415 2231431; fax +7 415 2231431; e-mail: root@friend.kamchatkasu
UK agent: Russian Experience tel 0181-566 8846.
Director: Elena N Bugrova.
In business since 1995.
Holidays for 243 people organised in 1997.
Adventure tours in Kamchatsky, Russia including wilderness, hiking, eco tours, fishing and geological tours, heli-skiing and cross-country skiing. Individuals and groups of up to fifteen. Individual participation in day-to-day running of the holiday (e.g. help with cooking etc) expected. Accommodation can be a mix of hotels, flats, tents or huts depending on the tour. Sleeping bags and mats can be hired. Cost ranges from £600-£1,230. Book direct or through UK agent.

LSG THEME HOLIDAYS
201 Main Street, Thornton, Leicester LE67 1AH (tel 01509-231713).
Director: M Cornette.
In business since 1985.
Holidays for about 350 annually.
Holidays incorporating several different activities including painting, photography, conversational French, regional cookery, rambling, cultural discovery in various regions of France from the Dordogne to Provence. One or two weeks from May to mid-October. All levels catered for. Singles and 'no-theme' participants welcome. Also theme mini-breaks offered, including cookery, discovery and painting. Approximately 25-30 individuals on each holiday. Prices from £159 (mini-break) or £429 (eight days South of France) including single or twin rooms with en suite facilities and full-board.

Participants taking a painting option must provide their own materials. 'LSG offers several different activities running in parallel which means that couples, friends etc, with totally different interests can share the same holiday in superb surroundings whilst pursuing their own interest'.
24hour brochure request line (01509-239857).
Ages: 18 to 70+.

MOSWIN TOURS
Moswin House, 21 Church Street, Oadby, Leicester LE2 5DB (tel 0116-2719922; fax 0116-2716016).
Director: Marita Seth, H K Seth.
In business since 1981.
Member of ABTA, AITO, ATOL.
Holidays arranged for 4000-5000 annually.
Multi activity holidays in Germany throughout the year. Activities include: cycling, skiing, archaeology, wine harvesting, painting, music, steam railways, river cruises, rambling, health/spa holidays, sailing, motor racing, canoeing, golf, riding, ballooning and German Language tours. Individuals and groups of all sizes catered for. For cycling holidays bicycle hire is included. Various types of accommodation are available. All excursions on escorted holidays are included in the price, unless otherswise specified.
Unaccompanied young people accepted from 16 years.

NATURAL HEIGHTS
Holidays and Leisure, 10 Blandfield Road, London SW12 8BG (tel 0181-682 8990; fax 0181-673 7466).
In operation since 1995.
Holidays for all ages arranged annually.
Natural Heights is a holiday/leisure agent based in the western Algarve of Portugal. Operating from Burgau, in the middle of an unspoilt coastline. Tailor-made holidays include a choice of accommodation and activities including kite-flying, horse riding, mountain biking, walks, excursions, fishing, golf and watersports including snorkelling and scuba diving. More specialised courses include aromatherapy, massage and reflexology. There are weekly courses in most of the above. The main season is April to October. A typical holiday costs £300-£400 per person per week inluding, flights, a car and self-catering accommodation.

NEUCHATEL TOURISM
Hôtel des Postes, 2001 Neuchâtel, Switzerland (tel +41 32-889 68 90; fax +41 32 889 62 96).
Discover the Neuchâtel region in northwest Switzerland, the three lakes region. Choose from five hotel categories. Wide selection of cultural, sporting and discovery activities (one per day included in package). Special offers for families with children. Half board and breakfast included. Extend your stay as you please, sixth night with half board is free. Price from 199 Swiss francs (about £85) per person for three nights/four days with breakfast, half board and one activity per day.

NJHC DUTCH YOUTH HOSTEL ASSOCIATION
Prof. Tulpstraat 2, 1018 HA Amsterdam (tel +31 20 55 13155).
Director Mrs C P M Schilte.
In business since 1929.
Member International Youth Hostel Association, IYHF.
Holidays for 3000 arranged annually.
Operates 35 hostels geared towards young travellers. Most people travel from hostel to hostel on an individual basis. The NJHC also organises cycling and sailing holidays in Holland. Between seven and 14 days May-August plus autumn holidays. Professional instructors. Individuals and groups catered for in groups of 15-100. No experience needed. Prices from $112 (£70) to $450 (£295) for half-board youth hostel accommodation. Sheets and linen not included but can be hired.
Minimum age: 14 (unaccompanied).
Physically and mentally challenged people catered for in a limited number of hostels.
'Informal atmosphere, easy to make new friends, excellent opportunity to get to know Holland'.

PARALLEL PURSUITS
Chalet Le Rêve, Les Mouilles, 74430 St Jean D'Aulps, France (tel in the UK 01462-438574; in France: tel/fax +33 4-50795027).
Proprietors: P Player, M Evans.
In business since 1996.
Registered with Chambre De Commerce in France.
Holidays for 350 arranged annually.
Multi activity holidays in the Portes Du Soleil region of the French Alps. Summer

activities include mountain biking, white water rafting, canyoning, hiking, horse riding, hydospeeding, paraponting, tennis and golf. Winter activities concentrate on skiing. Winter holidays operate between Christmas and Easter, summer holidays between mid-June and mid-September. Individuals and groups of up to 14 catered for. Features include magnificent mountain scenery, excellent cuisine and private minibus transfers to activities. Prices from £199-£425, plus travel. Half board accommodation provided. No experience required.
Minimum age: 12 years (accompanied); 16 years (unaccompanied).

POLNET TRAVEL

10 The Mead, Beckenham, Kent BR3 5PE (tel 0181-650 0286; fax 0181-402 6678).
Directors: A Townsend & A Grazesik.
In business since 1996.
Holidays for 400 arranged annually.
Canoeing, kayaking, biking and trekking holidays in North-East and South-East Poland. Holidays last 9-13 days from May-September. Kayaking tours on the Czarna Hancza and Drawa Rivers, spending six hours daily in a kayak, with camping or hotel accommodation (meals included). Bike tours of the Pieniny and Bieszczady Mountains, and through Mazury. Accommodation in hotels and boarding houses. Twelve-day trekking tour through the West Carpathian Mountains. Accommodation in hotels and camping. Prices from £230-580, excluding travel to Poland.
Minimum age: 8 years (16 years unaccompanied).

ROUGH TRACKS

6 Castle Street, Calne, Wilts. SN11 ODU or FREEPOST (SN2051), Calne, Wilts SN11 OSZ (tel 07000 560749).
Multi activity adventures in northern Portugal May-June and September-October. Other dates available for groups by arrangement. Professional, high quality tours with a genuine personal touch. Example of price for an eight-day holiday, including two days of watersports (skiing, canoeing and inflatable tow), two days trekking and two days mountain
biking is £458. All meals, wine and comfortable accommodation, tuition, equipment and transfers are included.
Minimum age (accompanied): 12 years.
Unaccompanied young people from 14 years.

TALL STORIES

67a High Street, Walton on Thames, Surrey KT12 1DJ (tel 01932-252002; fax 01932-225145).
Partners: B M Makin and P J Rayfield.
In business since 1991.
Members of Travel Trust Association.
Holidays for 700 arranged annually.
Multi sports holidays for adults, single people, groups and 'family weeks' in Austria, Spain, Alpine France and Corsica. Weekends also available in the UK. Activities include paragliding, climbing, mountain biking, hiking, summer skiing, snowboarding, alpine trekking, rafting, sailing, scuba diving, snorkelling, water skiing, windsurfing, coastal exploration and canyoning. Prices between £399-£550 include half-board accommodation in hotels or chalets.
Minimum age: 13 years accompanied; 18 years unaccompanied.
Maximum age: 70 years.

TRAVELBOUND

Olivier House, 18 Marine Road, Brighton, East Sussex BN2 1TL (tel 01273-677777; fax 01273-600999; brochures and reservations 01273-696960).
J Bowden, M Bole, P Lower, A Lay, A Marriner and P Couchman.
In business since 1986.
Member of ABTA, FTO and CAA.
Holidays for 40,000 annually.
Specialist activity and watersports holidays. Specialist sports include netball, soccer, hockey, basketball, volleyball, tennis, badminton, golf, windsurfing and sailing.

Locations include Holland, Belgium, France, Germany, Austria, Spain, Greece and Malta.

Choose your sport, learn new skills, enjoy the excitment of playing an international and taking some excellent excursion and visit possibilities.

The programme also includes, sailsports and alpine adventure courses in the French and Austrian Alps. Tours can be tailored to groups of all ages, from schools to adults. Quotations available for groups (not individuals).

Other sporting holidays can be tailored world wide. Prices available on request. Physically, visually and mentally challenged people welcome.

TRAVEL CHOICE

27 High Street, Benson, Wallingford, Oxon OX10 6RP (tel 01491-837607; fax 01491 833838).

Directors: G F Roberts and G Roberts.
In business since 1980.
Member of ABTA and ATOL.
Holidays for 500 arranged annually.
Skiing, walking, painting and photographic multi activity holidays in France, Switzerland and Austria throughout the year. Prices from around £200 for B&B accommodation, self catering also available.
No minimum age.

TREKKING HELLAS

7 Filellinon Street, Syntagma Square, 10557 Athens, Greece (tel +30 1 3310323; fax +30 1 3234548).

Director: Michael Tsoukias.
In business since 1986.
Member of Hellenic Association of Tourist and Travel Agencies, and Greek Association of Mountain Guides.
Holidays for 5000 arranged annually.
Trekking, rafting, kayaking, canyoning, cycling, diving, micro-light and horse riding activities in Greece all year round. Locations include Mount Olympus, Meteora, Crete, Cyclades, Peloponnisos and the Ionian sea. Price for 6-nights half board at the Meteroa Activity centre: about £309 (camping) or about £390 (hotel). Evritania Activity Centre prices: about £335 (village guesthouse) or about £460 (hotel). Groups and individuals catered for. Specialist equipment included in the price.
Minimum age: 8 years (accompanied); 16 years (unaccompanied).

VALKENBURG & MERGELLAND (TOURIST OFFICE)

Th. Dorrenplein 5, Postbus 820, 6300 Av Valkenburg a/d Geul, Holland (tel +31 43-6098600; fax +31 43-6098500).

Director: Mrs A Huysse-Niewierra.
Oldest tourist office in Holland operating since 1885. Activities available in the marlstone country of Holland include, mountain biking, walking, climbing, karting, golf, canoeing, horse riding, micro-light flying, hot air ballooning, tobogganing and ice riding. Tailor-made itineraries for groups over ten people. Accommodation in hotels, B&B's and campsites. Cycle hire available. Contact the tourist office for detailed information.

VFB HOLIDAYS

Normandy House, High Street, Cheltenham, Glos. GL50 3FB (tel 01242-240310 brochure enquiries; 01242-240332 reservations; fax 01242-570340).

Directors: M Bruce-Mitford, F Julien (French Director), J Kirk (Operations) and J Beckett (Finance).
In business since 1971.
Member of AITO, ABTOF and AITOT.
Multi activity holidays for individuals but mainly families in July and August in the traditional alpine resorts of la Clusaz, Samoëns and Morzine in the Savoy Alps, plus les Deux Alpes in Isère VFB Representatives in the resorts help clients plan their activities and organise children's clubs, etc. Activities include: mountain walking, canyoning, windsurfing, scuba diving, canoeing/rafting, fishing, mountain biking, climbing, summer tobogganing, horse riding, hang gliding, summer skiing, archery and fencing. Prices from £416 for a family of four for seven nights, with self-catering accommodation or half-board hotels, insurance and ferry.
All ages.

VIGVATTEN NATUR KLUBB

Apartado Numero 3253, Vitoria — Gasteiz 01002, Spain (tel +34 45-28194; fax +34 45-281794).

Director: Laureano Varela.
In business since 1994.
Multi activity walking, hiking, mountain pursuits, night walking, trekking, mountain biking and mountain walking adventure holidays in rural settings in the Pyrenees, Urbion's Mountains and Basque country throughout the year. For five days, a week or a fortnight camp in some of the most beautiful places in Spain, closely in touch with the natural environment. Prices from £110-£200 per week including accommodation in tents, mountain huts and youth hostels, all meals and insurance. No experience necessary.
Minimum age: eight years (unaccompanied).
(See *Young People's Holidays* for further information).

Americas

AMERICAN ADVENTURES
64 Mount Pleasant Avenue, Tunbridge Wells, Kent TN1 1QY (tel 01892-512700; fax 01892-511896).
President: D Stitt.
In business since 1982.
Member of FIYTO, TIA and ABTA.
Specialists in action-packed adventure tours to the USA, Canada, Alaska and Mexico. Travel is in small groups from 1 to 6 weeks with a Tour Leader and a maximum of 13 passengers. Prices start from £265 per person for a seven-day tour from Los Angeles to San Francisco. The tour includes camping equipment and transport. Food is on a kitty basis $6 per day. Sleeping bags are not included, but may be hired. Participation in day-to-day running of the camp tours is expected. No age limit, but most passengers are in the 18-35 age group. Passengers can participate in a wide range of activities on the tours including whitewater rafting, mountain biking, bungy jumping, hiking, para-sailing, horseback riding, jet-skiing, roller-blading and much more.

CAMP ALASKA TOURS
P O Box 872247, Wasilla, Alaska 99687, United States of America (tel +1 907 3769438; fax +1 907 3762353).
Proprietor: Tim Adams.
Operating since 1984.
Member of the Travel Industry Assn. of America and the Alaska Visitor Association.
Overland camping tours in Alaska from June to September. A wide variety of trips are offered from one week trips departing from Anchorage, to three week tours including the Inside Passage, the Yukon and the Canadian Rockies. Each itinerary has a flexible schedule and choice of optional activities as you travel including, hiking, canoeing, kayaking and whitewater rafting. Tour groups are kept to no more than twelve adults, although families with children aged ten+ can go on the Alaska Family Safari (eight days) featuring Denali National Park, Prince William Sound and the Kenai Peninsula.
Price for a week is about $800 (about £500) including food and tent camping.

DRAGOMAN ADVENTURES
28 Camp Green, Debenham, Suffolk IP14 6LA (tel 01728-861133; fax 01728-861127).
Directors: M H Sykes-Balls, G J Durie, C H K Hopkinson.
In business since 1981
Three to 26-week journeys in North, South and Central America. Trips in Alaska, Canada, USA, Mexico, Belize, Guatemala, Honduras, Nicaragua, Costa Rica, Panama, Colombia, Ecuador, Peru, Bolivia, Chile, Argentina, Brazil, Paraguay and Venezuela. Accommodation in hotels and camping. Transport by expedition vehicle. Groups prepare three meals a day on equipment supplied, when camping. Optional treks, flights, whitewater rafting and boat trips. Price from £180 a week including fuel, tolls, equipment, vehicle, crew, plus kitty for food, campsites, etc.
Minimum age: 18 years.

EXODUS EXPEDITIONS
9 Weir Road, Balham, London SW12 0LT (tel 0181-675 5550 or 0181-673 0859 24 hrs).
Small group walking and adventure holidays with opportunities for wildlife spotting, snorkelling, cruising by boat, canoe expeditions, jungle safaris, fishing, riding, whitewater rafting and exploring the sights by light aircraft. Organised all year round with prices ranging from £940-£2695. Holidays are run in: Argentina, Bolivia, Chile, Costa Rica, Guatemala, Belize, Mexico, Patagonia, Venezuela, Ecuador and Galapagos, Peru, Brazil, Canada and Alaska. All trips are graded according to difficulty.

EXPLORE WORLDWIDE LTD
1 Frederick Street, Aldershot, Hants, GU11 1LQ (tel 01252-344161).
Walking, trekking the heights of Machu Picchu in Peru, white-water rafting, camping, hiking at the Grand Canyon and exploring the jungles of Guatemala and the Yucatan are some of the adventures in a range of holidays from Argentina, Chile, Paraguay, Bolivia, Brazil, Ecuador, Venezuela, Belize, Mexico, USA to Canada. Prices from £945 to about £3000 for 15 to 29 days.

GEODYSSEY
29 Harberton Road, London N19 3JS (tel 0171-281 7788; fax 0171-281 7878).
Directors: Gillian Howe and John Thirtle.
In business since 1993.
Range of activities and tours in Venezuela covering the country's 1500 miles of Caribbean coast, the magnificent rainforests, the high mountains of the Andes, the entire length of the Orinoco river, the surreal

landscape of the Grand Sabana and the Angel Falls, the tallest waterfall in the world. Choose from Rainforest River Journeys, Andes by Foot & Mule, Trek to the Lost World, The Birds of Venezuela and the Venezuelan Odyssey. Prices from £795-£1790 including most meals and accommodation in hotels, lodges, simple guest houses, hammocks and tents. Insurance and international flights are not included in the cost. Own sleeping bag needed on trekking tours, can be hired locally. No experience needed.
Minimum age: 14 years (younger people catered for on tailor-made family tours).
Maximum age: 65 years (without a doctor's certificate).

INCREDIBLE ADVENTURES
PO Box 77585, San Francisco, CA 94107, USA (tel +1 415 759 7071; fax +1 415 759 8464). E-mail: info@incadventures.com http://www.incadventure.com
Hiking and camping expeditions in California. Adventurous four-day and three-night camping trip to Yosemite National Park. Packed full of hiking, swimming, campfires, good food and good laughs. Off the beaten path to the wilder side of Yosemite. Price: $169 includes food, camping equipment, transportation, park entrance fee and tax. Departs downtown San Francisco. Also available for those with less time on their hands, one day trip for $75 (about £46).

LAST FRONTIERS
Swan House, High Street, Long Crendon, Bucks. HP18 9AF (tel 01844-208405; fax 01844-201400). E-mail: travelinfo@lastfrontiers.co.uk. Internet: http://www.lastfrontiers.Co.uk
Director: Edward Paine.
In business since 1991.
Member of ATOL.
Holidays for 300 annually.
South American and Caribbean multi activity holidays ranging from painting, photography, cycling, natural history, white water rafting, waterfall expeditions, fishing, riding, birdwatching, botanical tours, paragliding, walking and trekking, in Venezuela, Brazil, Chile, Ecuador, the Galapagos Islands, Grenada, Dominica and Argentina all year round. Tailor-made for individuals and groups. Best local guides and maximum cultural interchange. Prices from £1400-£2300 including half-board accommodation in small family hotels and lodges. Mountain bikes can also be hired.

MAPACHE LODGE WILDERNESS CAMP
Boca Taboga, Sierpe de Osa, Puntarenas, Costa Rica (tel +506 786 65 65; fax +506 786 63 58). UK agent: Mike Boston tel/fax 01631 770 214). Internet: http://www.greenarrow.com/travel/mapache.htm
Established 1995.
Corporation owned by Giuseppina Montarana.
Member: BTO, American Orchid Society, American Birding Association.
Holidays for about 120 people arranged annually.
Multi activity holidays including birdwatching, hiking, horse riding, kayaking, diving and snorkelling, fly fishing, big game fishing in the south of Costa Rica, on the Pacific Slope in and around the Osa Peninsula, the Corcovado National Park and the biological marine reserve of Cano Island. Holidays last for a minimum of four days up to usually 11 days from November to April. Can arrange holidays for a single individual up to a maximum of twelve people. Prices from $195 to $1990 (about £120-£1,228) including accommodation in tents cabins, ranger stations, full board (Italian, local, vegetarian and international cooking). Help is expected with tent rigging.
EXPEDITIONS: Corcovado Ring Adventure involving crossing virgin forest to dive into the Pacific Ocean and playing with whales. Ten days. Starting every 15 days from 8th December to 13th April (last departure date). The trip includes multi activities. Price $1350.
Minimum age unaccompanied: 16 years.

MONTANA RAFT COMPANY
Glacier Wilderness Guides, Box 535, W. Glacier, MT 59936, USA (tel +1 406-387-5555; fax + 1 406-387-5656).
Directors: Randy Gayner, John Gray, Cris Gayner and Doug Niemann.
In business since 1983.
Member of Glacier Country, Flathead Conventions and Visitors Association.
Holidays for 4000 arranged annually.
Backpacking, rafting and fishing adventures in Glacier National Park, Montana. Whether shooting rapids or relaxing on a scenic float, professional guides escort you down the wild and scenic Middle and North Forks of the Flathead River. Also overnight river adventures, hiking & horseback, ranch & raft combinations, from May-October. No experience necessary. Ecotourism of ultimate importance. Prices from US$100

(about £60) per day to US$1400 (about £864) per week, including all food and accommodation. Camping equipment needed, but can be hired.
Minimum age: from four years depending on trip.
Unaccompanied young people from 15 years.

THE PROJECT PARTNERSHIP
PO Box 9, Burgess Hill, West Sussex RH15 8JY (tel 0990-143610; fax 0990-168309).
Partners: J P & L M Richardson.
Established 1991.
Holidays for about 2,000 arranged annually.
Multi activity ranch holidays in the US all year round. Choose from riding, fishing, cattle drives, hot air balloons, white water rafting, mountain biking, wagon trains, winter ranching, golf and cross-country skiing. No experience needed. Typical cost of US$1,200 (about £740) includes all meals and activities, but not air fares. Ski hire and some overnight camping equipment extra.

RANCH AMERICA
19A Village Way East, Rayners Lane, Harrow, Middlesex HA2 7LX (tel 0181-868 2910).
Director: R Harris
In business since 1988.
Member ABTA, Association of Travel Agents Consortium.
Holidays for 700 people arranged annually.
Multi activity ranch holidays throughout the year in the USA. Activities available include riding, white water rafting, swimming, square dancing, tennis and hiking. Excursions from ranch sites sometimes available. Individuals and groups catered for. Prices £950-£1500 per week including room, all meals, flights and activities.

RAVEN TOURS
PO Box 2435, Yellowknife, Northwest Territories, Canada X1A 2P8 (tel +1403 8734776; fax +1403 8734856). E-mail: raventours@yellowknife.com
President: Mr Bill Tait.
In business since 1981.
Member of NWT Arctic Tourism, Northern Frontier Visitors Association.
Holidays for 5000 arranged annually.
Individual or group tours and packages to Yellowknife and the Northwest Territories in Canada. Summer tours include Caribou viewing, Yellowknife city tour and boat cruises on the Great Slave Lake. The Winter Aurora Season includes Caribou viewing ($395), Dog Sledding ($67) and Snowmobile tours ($67). The Aurora Tour consists of a 20-minute drive outside the city to view the Aurora Borealis, spending four hours at a lodge accompanied with a northern snack of Caribou stew ($85). All accommodation and services available in Yellowknife. Winter clothing available for hire. Bookings taken direct or from Pioneer Tours in the U.K.

REEF AND RAINFOREST TOURS LTD
Prospect House, Jubilee Road, Totnes, Devon TQ9 5BP; tel 01803-866965; fax 01803-865916.
Directors: A A P Godwin and A P Godwin.
In business since 1989.
Member of ATOL.
Holidays arranged for 250 annually.
Multi activity holidays in Central & southern America, S.E. Asia and also Madagascar. Destinations include Belize, Costa Rica, Honduras, Indonesia, Papua New Guinea, Venezuela, Ecuador, Peru and the Galapagos Islands. A wide range of adventures can be undertaken from horse riding along jungle trails to trekking in Chirripo National Park, canoeing on Laguna Verde, snorkelling/diving around the inner cays on Belize's Barrier Reef and the Bay Islands of Honduras, sailing the coast in a catamaran, white water rafting, lemur watching in Madagasca,, guided trekking to Mayan ruins, visiting Tortuguero National Park to see turtles nesting and Braulio Carrillo National Park to explore the cloud forest with spectacular butterflies. Prices from £1000-£2500 based on two people travelling on a tailor-made basis. Accommodation in lodges and ranches, most with their own nature reserve, with private facilities and full-board. Group tours to Costa Rica, Peru, Madagascar and Irian Jaya with various departures.
Minimum age: three years (no upper limit).

SOURDOUGH OUTFITTERS INC
P O Box 90, Bettles, Alaska 99726, USA (tel +1 907 692 5252; fax +1 907 692 5612). E-mail: sour@sourdough.com
In business since 1972.
Dog sledding, snowmobiling, canoeing, rafting, backpacking, trekking and sport fishing holidays in Alaska's Brooks Range, the last great wilderness.

Winter season 1 February to 1 May; summer season 1 June to 15 September. Individuals and groups of two/six people catered for. Prices for guided holidays range from $1,200 to $4000 and self-guided $350 to $2,000. Guided assisted trips are also available. Add $250 per day to the self-guided price plus guided related expenses. Typical price $1,500 for a guided holiday and $900 for self-guided. On guided trips all commuter flights, bush flights, meals and tent camping in the wilderness are included. On self-guided trips, clients supply their own food and equipment can be rented. Highlights of Alaska's Brooke Range include experiencing one of the last great wildernesses and understanding a self-contained eco-system. There are opportunities to view grizzly bear, musk ox moose, wolf packs on the run and the caribou during their spring and fall migrations. Starting in late August and through mid April the Northern Lights can be seen.

TRIPS WORLDWIDE
9 Byron Place, Clifton, Bristol BS8 1JT (tel 0117 987 2626; fax 0117 987 2627).
Sole Proprietor: Jo Campbell
Operating since 1991.
Member of Latin American Travel Association.
Holidays for about 800 arranged annually.
Wildlife, birdwatching, botanical, trekking, safari and rainforest trips worldwide but with emphasis on Central America. Runs a special interest & adventure travel agency. Does tailormade and also takes individuals.

Tailor made tours to Central America and the Alternative Caribbean including, Mexico, Belize, Guatemala, Honduras, Costa Rica, Cuba, Trinidad, Tobago, Dominica, Surinam and Guyana.

All itineraries for individuals and groups can be based around particular interests: diving, wildlife, Mayan culture, archaeology, conservation, birds, fishing and trekking.

Tailormade itineraries start at £1200 based on two people sharing for a two-week itinerary including flights and accommodation.

TUCAN SOUTH AMERICA
c/o Adventure Travel Centre, 131-135 Earls Court Road, London SW5 9RH (tel 0171-370 4555).
Multi activity holidays as part of, or separate from overland tours of Latin America. Activities include: hiking and trekking, white water rafting, horse riding and skiing.
Groups of up to 21.
All ages: from 18 years.

Africa

ADRENALIN PUMP
Safari Drive Ltd, Wessex House, 127 High Street, Hungerford, Berkshire RG17 ODL (tel 01488-681611; fax 01488-685055).
E-mail: safaridrive@compuserve.com
Directors: Charles Norwood and Meregan Turner.
In business since 1994.
Action holidays in Zimbabwe from ten days to three weeks all year round. The ultimate adventure and classic safari in one. Activities include big game tracking on foot, canoeing among herds of elephant, rafting the mighty Zambezi, microlighting, bungy jumping (300ft from a bridge) and helicopter rides. All inclusive prices from £1595. Accommodation in top quality hotels and bush camps. No previous experience necessary. Experienced professional guides accompany each trip.

DRAGOMAN ADVENTURES
28 Camp Green, Debenham, Suffolk, IP14 6LA (tel 01728-861133; fax 01728-861127).
Three to ten-week journeys in southern, central and East Africa. Multi activity trips in Kenya, Tanzania, Uganda, Zaire, Malawi, Zambia, Zimbabwe, Botswana, Namibia, Ethiopia, South Africa and Mozambique. Accommodation in hotels or camping. Transport by expedition vehicle. Groups prepare three meals a day on equipment provided. Optional treks, flights, whitewater rafting and boat trips. Prices from £180 a week including fuel, tolls, equipment, vehicle, crew, plus kitty for food, campsites, etc.
Minmum age: 18 years.

EXODUS EXPEDITIONS
9 Weir Road, Balham, London SW12 0LT (tel 0181-675 5550 or 0181-673 0859 24 hrs).
Expeditions and safaris including opportunities for sailing, hiking, game viewing and cruising in Kenya, South Africa, Tanzania, Uganda, Malawi, Botswana, Namibia, Swaziland, Zambia, Madagascar, Morocco, Egypt and Zimbabwe. Supported and self-help camping, hotels, mountain huts and tourist bungalows are used, depending on

area. Prices range from £1195 to £2095 for 15 to 25 days.

EXPLORE WORLDWIDE LTD
1 Frederick Street, Aldershot, Hants GU11 1LQ (tel 01252-344161).
African expeditions include game viewing, trekking, desert safaris and sailing in Morocco, Egypt, Ethiopia, Eritrea, Madagascar, South Africa, Malawi, Namibia, Kenya, Zimbabwe, Botswana, Tanzania and Uganda. Camping and hotel accommodation. Small groups of average 16 people.
No experience needed, but participants should be reasonably fit.
Minimum age: 17 years.

LET'S GO TRAVEL
P O Box 60342 Nairobi, Kenya (tel +254 2 213033/340331; fax +254 2 214713 & +254 2 336890). E-mail: letsgotravel@commsol.sprint.com Internet: http://www.kenyadirect.com/letsgo.
Established 1979.
IATA, Kenya Association of Tour Operators.
Mountain climbing including Mts. Kiliminjaro and Kenya. Camel safaris, horse back safaris, walking safaris, camping, gorilla tracking, deep sea diving, deep sea fishing and ballooning in Kenya, Tanzania, Uganda and Zaire.
Minimum age (accompanied) generally 13 years but depends on activity.

TUSK TOURS
Hawksfield, Uplands Road, Totland, Isle of Wight PO39 0D2 (tel 01983-756748; fax 01983-756758).
Directors: Mrs J A De La Rosa, Mrs T L Heaton.
In business since 1994.
Holidays for 200+ arranged annually.
Adventure holidays in Southern Africa all year round. Activities on offer include whitewater rafting, canoeing, kayaking, mountain climbing, walking safaris, bungee jumping, parachuting, cycling, horse riding, river boarding, micro-lighting and ultralighting. Individuals and groups of any size catered for. Prices for ground only, £400, or all iclusive from £1400 (two-weeks) including all accommodation, activities, transfers, all meals or just B&B. Accommodation varies depending on itinerary.
Physically, mentally and visually challenged people catered for.
Minimun age: 18 years (unaccompanied).

WILDLIFE TOURS (PTY) LTD
PO Box 24374, Windhoek, Namibia, Africa (tel +264 61 240817; fax +264 61 240818).
Directors: H H A Schroeter.
In business since 1993.
Expeditions in the deserts of Namibia, Botswana and Zimbabwe, including mountain biking through game areas, trekking, coastal and fresh water fishing, rafting, birdwatching and safari tours, all year round. Special interest tours also arranged in painting, geology and history. For individuals and groups.
To book contact the Wildlife Tours Office in Windhoek or through a local agent.

Arctic

ARCTIC EXPERIENCE LTD
29 Nork Way, Banstead, Surrey SM7 1PB (tel 01737-218800; fax 01737-362341).
Directors: C Stacey and M Leaney.
In business since 1985.
Member of ABTA, AITO, IATA, CAA.
Holidays arranged for 3000 annually.
Independent holidays, hotels and farmhouse based tours and action holidays to the Arctic and sub-arctic regions covering Iceland, Greenland, Lapland, Canada and the Faroe Islands. Holidays include luxury weekend breaks, farmhouse adventures, camping safaris, fly-drive holidays and husky sledge expeditions. From under £1000 spend a week touring in Iceland (inclusive of accommodation), weekend breaks from around £271.

Asia

DRAGOMAN ADVENTURES
28 Camp Green, Debenham, Suffolk, IP14 6LA (tel 01728-861133; fax 01728 861127).
Two to ten-week journeys in India exploring all aspects of the Subcontinent including the remote Orissa region. Accommodation in hotels and camping. Transport by expedition vehicle. Groups prepare three meals a

day on equipment provided. Prices from £180 a week including fuel, tolls, equipment,vehicle, crew, plus kitty for food, campsites, etc.
Minimum age: 18 years.

EXODUS EXPEDITIONS
9 Weir Road, Balham, London SW12 0LT (tel 0181-675 5550 or 0181-673 0859 24 hrs).
Small group trekking and adventure holidays in Nepal, India, Thailand, Borneo, Vietnam, Malaysia, Indonesia, Sri Lanka, Pakistan, Mongolia (China), Tibet, Siberia (CIS), and Bhutan. Activities include river rafting, game viewing, rail travel, trekking and botany. Self-help camping, hotels and mountain huts and tourist bungalows are used, depending upon the area. Prices range from £995 to £2325 for 15 to 28 days.

HIMALAYAN KINGDOMS
20 The Mall, Clifton, Bristol BS8 4DR (tel 0117-923 7163; fax 0117-974 4993).
Director: Steven Berry.
In business since 1987.
Multi activity Christmas adventure in Nepal, including rafting down the Trisuli River, game watching in the Chitwan National Park, trekking in the famous Annapurna region and celebrating the New Year like never before.
'Fifteen days of fabulous fun'. Further details available on request.

THE IMAGINATIVE TRAVELLER
14 Barley Mow Passage, First Floor, Chiswick, London W4 4PH (tel 0181-742 3113).
Active sightseeing and exploratory tours lasting one to three weeks with opportunities, in The Middle East, Turkey, India, Nepal, Central and South East Asia, Alaska, North, South & Central America, Africa, Europe, Australia and Great Britain. Innovative use of transport eg. Camel safaris through Rajasthan, white water rafting in Nepal, elephant back, jeep safaris; also cycling, sailing and walking. In Turkey: canoeing through the Taurus mountains, cruising the coast in traditional gulets. Trans Siberian Railway tour also available. No experience needed. Individuals, couples and small international groups. Group sizes vary depending on the holiday from 12 to 20 people. All styles of traveller catered for from budget to 1st class. Prices range from £160-£1500 excluding flights. Good flight details available. Accommodation includes camping, hotels, mountain lodges, palaces and castles.
Minimum age for groups: 18.
Tailor-made: open ages.

THE MALAYSIA EXPERIENCE
42/44 Station Road, North Harrow, Middlesex HA2 7SE (tel 0181-424 9548).
Operated by Bob Mortimore Travel Ltd.
In business since 1992.
Member of ABTA, ATOL, IATA and PATA.
Trekking, mountain climbing, canoeing, white water rafting, sailing, bird watching, jungle safaris, golf, special historical interest tours and Malaysia Ex-Service reunions over the whole of Malaysia, all year round. Prices from £639 including all accommodation and most meals.
Minimum age: 18 years (unaccompanied).

MYSTERIES OF INDIA
Pleasureseekers Ltd, 92 The Green, Southall, Middlesex UB2 4BG (tel 0181-5742727; fax 0181-5710707).
Directors: Mr S P Jain, Mr H Jain.
In business since in 1982.
Member of ABTA, ATOL, IATA.
Wildlife, trekking and white water rafting holidays in India and Nepal from October to April. Programmes and itineraries are tailor-made to suit individual needs. Rhinos of Kaziranga (4 days ex Delhi) £615 per person. Royal Trek Nepal (4 days ex Kathmandu) £375 per person. Accommodation in lodges and camping.
Unaccompanied young people not accepted.

TIGER TOPS NEPAL
P O Box 242, Kathmandu, Nepal (tel +977 1 411225; fax +977 1 414075/419126). E-mail tiger@mtn.mos.com.np
A wide range of adventures and activities are offered at Tiger Mountain Tharu Village, built on high ground overlooking the Chitwan National park. It is constructed in the traditional style of the Tharu tribe and consists of longhouses made of timber, grass reeds and clay. Guests' bedrooms are large and comfortable and are equipped with fans for summer. Showers are solar-heated. The resort offers Nepalese and western cuisine, swimming pool, village walks, boat rides, jungle safaris on elephants, horse and pony riding (and instruction), bullock cart and

horse drawn buggy rides, adventurous jungle treks and tennis. Pioneers of environmentally sensitive adventure holidays in Nepal.

TRANS INDUS
Northumberland House, Popes Lane, London W5 4NG (tel 0181-566-2729; fax 0181-840 5327).
Director: Mrs. A Singh.
Established: 1990.
ABTA, ATOL.
Trekking, wildlife safaris, fishing, golfing, cycling and white water rafting all over India and Nepal. Individuals and groups of six to 12 catered for. Prices from £1,500 including all equipment and full board on outdoor locations.

Australasia

PEAK INTERNATIONAL
15 Moor Park, Wendover, Aylesbury, Bucks HP22 6AX (tel/fax 01296-624225).
New Zealand, North Island bespoke programmes to include any or all of the following — mountain trekking, Canadian canoeing, bush walking, white water rafting, 'tube riding' through caves, sea kayaking and coastal mountain biking. One to four weeks. From £395 per week.

SUN BLESSED HOLIDAYS
19-21 Southbourne Grove, Bournemouth, Dorset BH6 3QS (tel 01202-434320; fax 01202-434313).
Managing Director: Gary David.
In business for over 30 years.
Member of AITO and ABTA.
Tailor-made adventure holidays for the independent traveller to Australia and New Zealand all year round. Offers experiences of out-of-the-way places and areas not on the regular itineraries. Budget, youth travel and YHA arranged. Activities include white water rafting, sea kayaking, cycling, ballooning, scuba diving off the Great Barrier Reef and more. Try the Triple Challenge or the Awesome Foursome in New Zealand with jet boating, rafting, helicopter rides and bungy jumping. Holiday prices start at £157 for ten days plus Australia or New Zealand flights from about £500.

Middle East

IMAGINATIVE TRAVELLER
14 Barley Mow Passage, Chiswick, London W4 4PH (tel 0181-742 3113).
Tours to Egypt and elsewhere in the Middle East including Syria. Activities include: sailing the Nile in traditional feluccas, camel safaris in the Sinai, jeep safaris in the Negev. Holidays provided all year round in small, international groups of 12 to 20 as well as tailor-made arrangements. No experience needed. Prices £160-£985 excluding flights but including meals, transfers, sights, transport etc. All styles of traveller catered for from budget to first class. Good contact also for flight deals.
Minimum age for groups: 18.
Tailor-made: open ages.

Young People's Holidays

Multi activity centres with special programmes for young people have considerable appeal to both parents and children. Ideally, these centres should provide a safe environment in which young people can enjoy a wide range of closely-supervised activities with well-qualified instructors. However, in the wake of the Lyme Bay canoe disaster in 1993 in which four out of eight teenagers drowned while under the supervision of two instructors and a teacher, came growing concern about insufficient supervision and the inadequacy or lack of instructors' qualifications. Surprisingly perhaps, the actual number of adventure holiday centres in the UK is unknown but estimate range from 2000 to 3000. In July 1994 an independent report claimed that at least 300 such centres were unsafe, if not very dangerous. In May 1994 the English Tourist Board introduced a voluntary accreditation scheme. The Activity Centres (Young Persons' Safety) Bill which went through Parliament two years ago led to new regulations governing safety standards being brought in on August 1st 1996. The Health and Safety Executive is responsible for implementing the new regulations. Safety inspection of the first 900 centres was completed in 1997, but of course, it is an ongoing process. The regulations apply only to centres offering four groupings of sports: caving, climbing (on natural outdoor features), trekking (includes mountain biking, horseback trekking and off-piste skiing), and a range of watersports, to the under 18's. Such centres will have to register for the safety inspection and licensing scheme. Other 'dangerous' sports such as hang gliding, bungy jumping, archery and quad-biking, carry no legal obligation to register but may be voluntarily registered for inspection. Inspections will concentrate on the qualifications and experience of the staff in the sports they are directing, staff first aid qualifications, emergency and contingency provision and frequency of equipment inspection and maintenance.

Any centre catering for children under eight years old, will, as before have to register with the local authority. Parents can check whether the centre has applied for an Adventure Activity Licence for the above mentioned activities with the Activity Licensing Authority, Tourism Quality Services (01222 755715).

The British Activity Holiday Association (BAHA) was the pioneer organisation set up with the aim of establishing a code of conduct for operators but membership of the association is voluntary and membership represents only a minority of centres. BAHA has about 32 members who between them run 70 of the operational sites in Britain. For further details, or a copy of the BAHA consumer guide contact BAHA (22 Green Lane, Hersham, Walton-on-Thames, Surrey KT12 5HD; tel: 01932 252994). The Wales Tourist Board and Association of Residential Providers (Davis Street, Cardiff CF1 2FU; tel 01222-475278) was the first British tourist board to set up and run its own accreditation and safety scheme for centres that cater for children and will only allow centres it has approved to be featured in its promotional literature. A brochure listing over 100 of them can be obtained from the above address.

The canoeing disaster off Lyme Regis five years ago (see above) highlighted the issue of safety at sea in particular. The correct precautions for a sea trip are, that the coastguard should always be informed in advance, a safety raft should be taken and if possible the leader should have an EPIRB (portable radio beacon with homing device).

The Department of Education issues a handbook *Safety in Outdoor Education* specifically for schools whose students take part in trips organised by outside bodies, in which the need for competent, qualified leaders and instructors is emphasised. It should be stressed that most adventure holiday organisations work within self-imposed, high safety standards. However, in a BBC documentary broadcast in 1993 it was found that some instructors in some of the best known companies were employing instructors without formal sports qualifications. In 1994, a BBC researcher with bogus qualifications applied to 20 commercial adventure holiday centres, none of which attempted to verify the qualifications; he was offered a job by six of the centres. It is hoped that the new regulations will make adventure companies much more stringent in checking qualifications of potential employees. The Sports Council (16 Upper Woburn Place, London WC1H OQP; tel 0171-273 1500) can supply an address list of the governing bodies of of the various sports. Most of the major ones can be found in the chapter introductions of this book, but for others like fencing, archery etc. send an s.a.e. to the Sports Council at the above address.

In any case, parents and others responsible for sending children and teenagers on adventure holidays should make their own sensible enquiries, including the ratio of staff to children on particular activities and the qualifications (including a knowledge of first aid) of the instructors.

Extra prudent parents will probably consider taking out insurance to designed to cover those on activity holidays. Extrasure Travel Insurance (0171-480 6871) offers a package called Activitysure with three levels of cover depending on the type of activity involved. Category A is for so-called low risk sports like hockey and orienteering; category B includes most watersports and outdoor endurance exercises while category C is for the higher risk sports including mountaineering, jetskiing and paragliding. There are different rates for Area One Worldwide (excluding the USA, Canada, Mexico and the Caribbean) and Area Two Worldwide (including the US, Canada, Mexico and the Caribbean). The insurance is not applicable to children under ten years.

The worldwide category at the beginning of this section lists organisations which offer young people who in their final school years or between school and university a challenging project in far off country. After worldwide the general section contains organisations offering holidays for young people throughout Britain. Many are multi activity organisations while others are specialists in certain activities such as music or sailing. Information about the RYA Young Skippers Scheme for ages 14 to 23 can be found in the introduction to the *Watersports* chapter. Those companies which offer holidays abroad are listed under their general geographical area of operation.

Worldwide

PROJECT TRUST
The Hebridean Centre, Isle of Coll, Argyll (tel 01879 230444; fax 01879 230357.
In operation since 1967.
Projects for about 200 young people arranged annually.
A one year voluntary service abroad for those between school and university/career. Applicants must be in full time education with a view to obtaining qualifications to UCAS standard. Projects include English language assistants, care work, health and community projects, educational projects and outward bound schools challenges. Countries in which projects are currently offered include Uganda, Zimbabwe, Namibia, Botswana, South Africa, Honduras, Guatemala, Brazil, Cuba, Chile, Thailand, China, Hong Kong, Pakistan, Sri Lanka, Indonesia, Japan, Egypt, Jordan, Vietnam, Malaysia and Guyana.
The average cost of a project is approximately £3450. Project raises £500 per head and assists volunteers in finding the remaining £2950 from charities and donors, sponsored events industry and local business.

Selection takes place October to December. Training courses are held on Coll in July and August.
Ages: 17-19 years.

WORLD CHALLENGE EXPEDITIONS
Black Arrow House, 2 Chandos Road, London NW10 6NF (tel 0181-961 1122; fax 0181-961 1551).
World Challenge is an eighteen-month scheme to enable teams of students aged 16-20 to create, fund, plan and lead a challenging expedition incorporating project-based and adventurous activities in remote parts of the developing world including Pakistan, India, Borneo, Nepal, Costa Rica, Ecuador, Venezuela, Bolivia, Vietnam, Uganda, Zimbabwe, Morocco, Namibia and Thailand.
Mainly organised through schools but some individuals accepted.

England

ACTION HOLIDAYS
Robinwood, Jumps Road, Todmorden, Lancashire (tel 01706-814554).
Directors: M Vasey, J Vasey, M Bailey, T Lovett.In operation since 1985.
Holidays for 2000 arranged annually.
Multi activity holidays in Surrey, Staffordshire and Lancashire during July and August. Options include watersports, horse riding, climbing, archery, gymnastics and tennis. Prices in range £136-£269 including full board with dormitory accommodation. Staff/children ratio of 1:4.Age range: five to 15 years.

ADVENTURE AND COMPUTER HOLIDAYS LTD
PO Box 183, Dorking, Surrey RH5 6FA (tel 01306-730716).
Member of BAHA and West Country and Cornish Tourist Boards.
Day camps in Surrey and residential holidays in Cornwall for individual children and school groups. Activities include: sailing, bicycle safari's, canoeing, rock climbing, fishing, horse riding and stable management, cycling, computing, art, craft, cookery, drama, sports, animal lovers and photography. For ages four to 14 in a safe and friendly environment.

ANGLIA SUMMER SCHOOLS
15 Inglis Road, Colchester, Essex C03 3HU (tel 01206-540111; fax 01206-766944.
Directors: J R Lucas, H C Baker.
In business since 1982.
Holidays for 150+ annually.
Residential theatre performance holidays in Essex. Six, nine and 13 days during April, July and August. Individuals and groups of up to 50. Students are tutored in small groups of up to ten, arranged according to age and experience. No previous acting experience needed. Prices from £310 for six days. Includes boarding school accommodation and full board. Travel not included but participants can be collected from nearby points of arrival.
Holidays are divided into age bands: 13 days in July for 13 to 19 year olds; six days in August (separately) for each of eight to 12-year olds; 12-16-year olds; 16 to 19-year olds.

Holidays include visits to live professional theatre performances and rehearsals for a performance (usually a revue) before family and friends on the last day.
A longer, nine-day holiday is offered for ten to 19-year olds at Easter in which the entire time is spent solely on the creation, rehearsal and performance of a new piece of musical theatre generated by the staff and participants. Hard work and intensive, but immensely rewarding.

AQUA SPORTS COMPANY
Mercers Park, Nutfield Marsh Road, Merstham, Nr Redhill, Surrey RH1 4EU (tel 01737-644288; fax 01737-645869).
Partners: E J Morgan and M J Noyle.
In operation since 1993.
Members of RYA and BCU.
Holidays for 100-150 arranged annually.
Weekend and week-long watersports holidays based at a country park in Redhill from March-October. Junior Summer Camps offered in school holidays. Activities include windsurfing, dinghy sailing and canoeing. Individuals and groups of all sizes catered for. Courses run from beginners to advanced. A completed Junior course is a prerequisite for Summer Camp entry. Prices from £50-£150 non-residential. Summer Camp: £150 including tents, food and equipment. Juniors are responsible for keeping their camp areas tidy. All equipment is provided on junior and beginner courses, but may need to be hired for advanced programmes — available from Aqua Sports.

Minimum age: eight years (unaccompanied) to 16 years.
Physically, visually and mentally challenged people catered for.

ARDMORE ADVENTURE
11-15 High Street, Marlow, Buckinghamshire SL7 1AU (tel 01628-890060).
In business since 1983.
Day and residential multi-activity holidays at centres in Oxfordshire, Buckinghamshire and Berkshire. Activities include swimming, archery, tennis, video film making, parachute games and earth-ball. Residential prices from £199 per week; day prices from £129.
Age range: six to 15 years.

AVRIL DANKWORTH NATIONAL CHILDREN'S MUSIC CAMPS
c/o David Edwards, 61 Crown Road, Sutton, Surrey, SM1 1RT (tel 0181-715 4048). E-mail: ncmc@edcrown.demon.co.uk
In operation since 1970.
Holidays provided for 256 children each year.
Non profit-making music camps run by Avril Dankworth, in the grounds of the home of her brother John and his wife, Cleo Laine, at Wavendon in Milton Keynes. There are four week-long camps held in August, each catering for 64 children. Two camps are for those between eight and 12 years, and the other two are for 13 to 17-year-olds. Children with all levels of musical ability are accepted, though they should have their own instruments. Accommodation is under canvas. Sports and arts and craft activities are also included in the programme. At the end of the week, the campers put on an operetta for their parents.

BATTISBOROUGH HOUSE
Holbeton, South Devon PL8 1JX (01752 873062; fax 01752 873062.
Sole Trader: Mr J Farrington.
In business since 1988.
BAHA member.
Holidays for 600-800 approx. arranged annually.
Multi activity courses including canoeing, caving, abseiling, climbing, gorge walking, archery, shooting, raft building, tennis, assault course and badminton. Children's activities courses start mid-July to the end of August. One, two or three-week stays possible. Prices from £250 per week; disount for two or more siblings. Transport from Bagshot, Surrey to Battisborough £30 return.
Also provides language/activity courses for overseas children. Price £295 a week.
Age range: nine to 16 years.

BRATHAY EXPLORATION GROUP
Brathay Hall, Ambleside, Cumbria LA22 0HP (tel & fax 015394-33942). E-mail: brathay.exploration@virgin.net Internet: http://freespace.virgin.net/brathay.exploration.
Administrator: Ron Barrow.
51st year of operation.
Member of Royal Geographical Society, Young Explorers' Trust.
The trust organises 12 youth scientific/adventure expeditions, plus leader training and mountain first aid courses annually. Expeditions take place in the UK and worldwide. Trips last from one to five weeks and take place mainly during the summer. Prices range between £250 and £2500, inclusive of all travel, food, accommodation (huts or camping) and insurance.
Age range: 16 to 25 years.

CALSHOT ACTIVITIES CENTRE
Calshot Spit, Fawley, Southampton SO45 1BR (tel 01703-892077).
Administered by Hampshire County Council.
In operation since 1964.
Recognised by the RYA, BCU, ESC, STB and Sports Council.
Holidays for 5000 children arranged annually.
Dinghy sailing, canoeing, windsurfing, dry slope skiing, track cycling, mountain biking, rock climbing, archery, rifle shooting, orienteering and problem solving. Expert tuition from experienced and nationally qualified staff. High saftey standards. All specialist equipment is provided. Six-day holiday courses are available for £225 fully residential.
Minimum age: nine years.

CASTLE HEAD FIELD CENTRE
Grange-over-Sands, Cumbria LA11 6QT (tel 015395-34300).
Directors: F C and J M Dawson, J Baker.
In business since 1979.
A mix of adventure sports (climbing, canoeing, rafting etc.) and wildlife watching (eagles, peregrines, badgers, deer) holidays arranged every summer. Accommodation and meals in Field Centre. Saturday-to-Saturday courses mainly in July and August.

No experience required; binoculars useful. Ages: eight to 16 grouped in age bands. Unaccompanied adults accepted.
Young Leader Training courses for 17 and 18 year-olds.

DORSET ADVENTURE HOLIDAYS
Sea Barn Farm, West Sleet, Weymouth DT3 4ED (tel 01305 785852; fax 01305-775396).
Adventure Activities Licence.
Multi activity and multi adventure holidays for young people between eight and 15 or 15 to 18 in Fleet and Weymouth all year round. Wide range of activities possible including climbing, abseiling, canoeing, swimming, windsurfing, sailing, raft building, water and jet skiing, riding, archery, orienteering, caving and initiative games. Prices from £39 to £270 for short weekends to seven days including all meals and any specialist equipment. Tented accommodation in the Canvas Village near Weymouth, with swimming pool and club house. Alternative accommodation can be arranged. All instructors are experienced and qualified in their specialist activities (a detailed staff qualification list is available on request). Non-residential day camps also available.
Minimum age: 8 years accompanied; 12 years unaccompanied.

EUROYOUTH
301 Westborough Road, Westcliff, Southend-on-Sea, Essex SS0 9PT (tel 01702-341434; fax 01702-330104).
Directors: E, and R Hancock.
In operation since 1961.
Holidays for 2000 arranged annually.
Tennis, riding, sailing, windsurfing and canoeing holidays for individuals and groups of 15-45, during the summer months. Accommodation arranged with families. Courses in individual sports available. Other activities include golf, football, educational and cultural visits. Paying guest visits abroad organised all year round.
No experience needed.
Minimum age: 14 years.
Unaccompanied teenagers: 16 years + .

FIELD STUDIES COUNCIL
Head Office, Montford Bridge, Shrewsbury SY4 1HW (tel 01743-850674; fax 01743-850178).
Opportunities at several FSC centres: Young People's Nature Week and Countryside Adventure Course, for unaccompanied young people at Preston Montford near Shrewsbury; Family Adventure Week including pony trekking, environmental activities, pond dipping and caving at Malham Tarn in the Yorkshire Dales; Family Wildlife Weekends and weeks at several centres. Prices include accommodation, all meals and tuition.

HYDE HOUSE ACTIVITY CENTRE
Hyde Near Wareham, Dorset BH20 7NX (tel 01929 471205; fax 01929-471911).
Member of RYA, BCU, BOF.
Residential multi activity centre situated in 150 acres of private woodland, lakes and rivers. Activities include windsurfing, climbing, waterskiing, abseiling, archery, kayaking, shooting, raft building and many more. Qualified instruction. Groups from schools, colleges, youth clubs and Price's Trust welcome throughout the year. Unaccompanied childrens holidays for groups or individuals run in August. Prices from £59 per person including full board and two full day sessions. Phone for brochure, availability and details.

ISCA CHILDREN'S HOLIDAYS
Bonnaford, Brentor, Tavistock, Devon PL19 0LX (tel 01822-810514).
Partners: Mr N P Shephard, Mrs M A Shephard.
Day and residential activity holidays in tennis, horse riding, and soccer at Bloxham School, Banbury during August. Additional activities include: canoeing, swimming, archery, ten-pin bowling, trampolining, ice skating, roller skating, squash, badminton, pottery, discos and many more. ISCA Soccer School and the Tennis Coaching Course offer intensive coaching. Family run centre ensures caring supervision, excellent food and homely atmosphere.
Ages: five to 15 years.

ISLAND CRUISING CLUB
10 Island Street, Salcombe, South Devon TQ8 8DR (tel 01548-843481; fax 01548-843929).
RYA recognised, Adventure Activities Licence.
Sailing courses available from the age of 5 years, cadet weeks (10-15 years) and student membership weeks (16-18 years). One or two weeks, weekend and mid-week courses available. Individuals, families and groups catered for. Dinghy and keelboat sailing, cruising, on modern traditional yachts, power boating and kayaking. Main sailing activities conducted from base ship moored in the Salcombe Estuary. Prices from £80 for

an early summer weekend course. Residential and non-residential option available. Specialises in working in partnership with educational groups from schools and colleges to create custom built courses from two days upwards.
People with sight or hearing difficulties can also be taught.

KIDS KLUB ACTIVITY HOLIDAYS
The Lodge, Finsborough Hall, Great Finsborough, Stowmarket, Suffolk IP14 3EF (tel 01449-675907; fax 01449-771396).
Directors: Mr Magnus Willatts, Mr Michael Willatts.
In operation since 1986.
Member of BAHA, East Anglian Tourist Authority.
Holidays for 3,000 arranged annually.
Multi activity and educational holidays based at four centres in East Anglia. Operating all year round for groups, and during Easter and Summer vacations for individuals. Choose from over 50 activities, everything from abseiling to volleyball. Daily prices for non-residents: £15. Price for one-week residency: £200 (including full board and accommodation). All equipment is included in the price; pocket money for excursions optional. Brochure available on request for bookings.
'An extremely wide range of activities on offer, exemplary saftey standards, good food and quality accommodation'.
Minimum age: 6 years (unaccompanied). Maxiumum age: 16 years.

MARLBOROUGH COLLEGE SUMMER SCHOOL
Marlborough, Wilts SN8 1PA (tel 01672-892388; fax 01672-892476).
Directors: T Rogers, D West, E Gould, B Williams, D Williamson, M Kwiatkewski, R Pick.
In operation since 1975.
Activity holiday courses at Marlborough College in July and August for young people aged three to 17. Those aged three to 12 have to be accompanied by adults (who are doing adult courses); those aged 13+ can come unaccompanied. The range of activities for those 12 and under includes art, crafts, gymnastics, games and tennis; weekly prices for residents are about £250 for dormitory accommodation including all meals; non-residents pay £150 per week. Over-13s select one or two options from a range of categories e.g. racquet sports, art courses, outdoor adventures etc.

MILLFIELD HOLIDAY VILLAGE
Millfield School, Street, Somerset BA16 0YD (tel 01458-445823).
A wide range of holiday courses in July and August, including special multi activity programmes for those aged five to 12 years. The cost with residence (in school houses) with all meals, approx. £290 per week.
Minimum age (unaccompanied): eight years.
Physically challenged people welcome.

MOUNTAIN WALKING IN LAKELAND
Old Strands Cottage, Wasdale, Seascale, Cumbria CA20 1ET (tel 019467-26258).
Proprietor: David Killick.
In business since 1984.
Fell-walking holidays for ten to 14-year-olds, July-August, in the Lake District. Guided walks to the tops of England's highest mountains. Price: £118. Full board accommodation in an 18th century farmhouse near Wastwater lake. Only four children accepted at a time. Walking boots are needed and should be worn in. Barn with table-tennis and pool and swimming nearby, 'as well as a beck to dam up'.

THE OUTDOOR TRUST
Belford, Northumberland NE70 7QE (tel/fax 01668-213289).
Two- five- and seven-day action holidays organised throughout the school holidays. Activities include: windsurfing, rock climbing, abseiling, canoeing, cliff jumping, bivouacking, body boarding and barbecues. Full day and evening programme arranged. 24-hour supervision.
Minimum age: nine years.

OUTWARD BOUND TRUST
Watermillock, Cumbria, CA11 OJL (tel 0990 134227).
Outward Bound programmes for teenagers. Call for a free brochure and video.

PENSHURST OFF ROAD CLUB
Grove Cottage, Grove Road, Penshurst, Kent TN11 8DU (tel 01892-870136; fax 01892-871187).
Director: Mike Westphal.
Estalished: 1993.
Childrens courses covering all aspects of off-road biking including bike set up, posture, mechanics, cornering, braking, uphill and downhill technique, fitness, nutrition and route planning. Individuals and group tuition available. Prices from £15 per day. Bike hire available.

PLEASURE IN LEISURE
Tirobeck, Keldwyth Park, Windermere, Cumbria LA23 1HG (tel 015394-42324; fax 015394-88288).
Proprietor: Babs Matthews.
In business since 1982.
Member of Cumbria Tourist Board, Adventure Activity Licence.
Choice of 14 activities including abseiling, canoeing, rockclimbing, raft building, orienteering and windsurfing. Activity durations from two hour sessions to intergrated two to five-day programmes offered all year round. Accommodation arranged in local guesthouses, hotels or hostels. Available to school, scout, guide and other organised youth groups only. Prices depend on group size and activity. All equipment provided. No experience needed.
Ages: 8 to 18 years.

PGL ADVENTURE LTD
Alton Court, Penyard Lane, Ross-on-Wye, Herefordshire HR9 5NR (tel Freecall 0500 749147; fax 01989-766306).
Floyd K Ballantyne: Managing Director.
In business since 1957.
Member of British Activity Holiday Association and ABTA.
Choice of over 75 different activities in any of the 25 centres in the UK and France. Individuals, groups and schools . No experience needed, full instruction by expert and qualified staff. Accommodation varies from camping to single rooms and other indoor accommodation. Prices: Weekend £79, Mini Breaks three/four nights £100-£150, Full Week £209-£300, Overseas holidays £250-£500. Can accommodate special needs groups by arrangement.
Minimum age: six years (unaccompanied).
Maximum age: 18 years.

SCRIPTURE UNION HOLIDAYS
207-209 Queensway, Bletchley, Milton Keynes MK2 2EB (tel 01908-856000; fax 01908-856111). E-mail: holidays@scriptureunion.org.uk
Holidays Coordinator: Mr J Hammett.
In operation since 1930s.
Registered charity. Member of Christian Camping International.
Holidays for 2500 arranged annually.
A wide range of holiday courses at Easter and during the summer, ranging from specialist activities to multi activity outdoor courses and community ventures. Help with simple domestic chores is expected on some holidays. Prices £40 to £135 including all food, accommodation (which varies from outdoor centres to canvas camping) and equipment. Groups of up to ten from any one school are catered for.
'Caring staff, a Christian atmosphere and action-packed holidays'.
Ages: nine to 20 years.
Special courses for physically challenged people.

SUNSAIL UK
The Port House, Port Solent, Portsmouth PO6 4TH (tel 01705-222224).
Sunsail's UK sailing school offers a comprehensive range of sailing holidays in southern England and Scotland. With a variety of RYA courses, you can learn to sail on a modern fleet of dinghies, keelboats and yachts in the sheltered waters of the Solent and The Clyde. The 5-day RYA young sailor and teenage cruiser courses, for eight to 17-year olds are taught by qualified instructors and run from April to October; no previous sailing experience is necessary. During July and August, residential junior activity weeks combine sailing and evening entertainment for fun from dawn to dusk. Prices start from £150 which includes 'cabin' style accommodation, meals, buoyancy aids and a certificate.

SUPERCHOICE LTD
191 Freshfield Road, Brighton, East Sussex BN2 27E (tel 01273-676467; fax 01273-676290). E-mail: reservations@superchoice.co.uk
Directors: Lloyd Smith, Stephen Haupt, Chris Storr.
In business since 1992.
Member of BAHA, BCU, BMC, BSAC, RYA, ABTA.
Holidays for 30,000 arranged annually.
Multi activity and adventure holidays for young people 7-16 years all year round at the holiday centres in Dorset and the Isle of Wight. Over 40 activities available for school children, youth groups and unaccompanied children including quad biking, karting, abseiling, climbing, sailing, film making and rafting. Specialist holidays available in motorsports, computer based or for horse lovers. Prices from £29 (youth group weekend) to £299 (full week summer camp) including all meals, accommodation in log cabin villages and equipment. Field study and educational courses available.

SUTHERLAND LODGE ACTIVITY CENTRE LTD
Cropton, Nr. Pickering, North Yorkshire Y018 8ET (tel 01751-417228; fax 01751 477024).
Director: Stuart Morley.
In business since 1981.
Holidays for 3000-4000 arranged annually.
Multi activity holidays in Yorkshire from February to December. £90 to £120 per week includes dormitory accommodation and full board.
Children from eight years accepted.

YHA ACTIVITY CENTRE
Rowland Cote, Netherbooth, Edale, Derbyshire S30 2ZH (tel 01433-670302; fax 01433-670243).
Young people's multi activity holidays in the Peak District and North Wales all year round. Experienced instruction in an atmosphere of fun and learning, with safety uppermost at all times. Activities include: climbing, abseiling, canoeing, archery, adventure course etc. All equipment provided. Prices from £81 (weekend) to £259 (days).
Ages: 12-15 years.

YOUNG ARCHAEOLOGISTS CLUB
Bowes Morrell House, 111 Walmgate, York YO1 2UA (tel 01904-671417; fax 01904-671384).
Co-ordinator: Juliet Mather BA(Hons).
Fieldwork projects in which young people can take part in are advertised in the Club's magazine, *Young Archaeologist*, published quarterly. Annual membership of the Club, which is open to nine to 16-year-olds, is £7.50. The Club has a number of local branches throughout the UK which organise their own events and activities.

Scotland

ABERNETHY TRUST
Nethy Bridge, Inverness-shire PH25 3ED (tel 0147982-1279).
Adventure Unlimited courses for ten to 11 (£220) and 12-13 year olds (£225) and *Adventure Plus* courses for 14-16-year-olds (£235), each covering a wide range of activities. 'The staff are qualified instructors and committed Christians and enjoy sharing their expertise and faith with visitors to the Centre'.

CRAIGOWER LODGE
Outdoor Centre, Golf Course Road, Newtonmore, Inverness-shire PH20 1AT (tel 01540-673319).
Multi activity holidays for young people in the Highlands. Orienteering, mountain activities, rock climbing, canoeing and kayaking, mountain biking and skiing. Holidays for individuals and groups of up to 50 throughout the year. Prices from £210 for six days including full board, activities, instruction and evening entertainment. Discounts for groups of ten or more.
Minimum age: eight years.

GLENMORE LODGE NATIONAL OUTDOOR TRAINING CENTRE
Glenmore Lodge, Aviemore, Invernessshire PH22 1QU (tel 01479-861276; fax 01479-861212).
Weekly courses in the Highlands include: hill walking, canoeing, kayaking and rock climbing. Sampling courses in summer, taking in several activities. Prices around £185 including instruction, comprehensive evening programme, accommodation and meals.
No experience needed.
Ages: 12-21 years.

JOHN BULL SCHOOL OF ADVENTURE
12 Littlethorpe Park, Ripon, Yorks HG4 1UQ (tel 01765-604071).
Children's (under sixteens) multi activity weeks in the Yorkshire Dales or the Lake District. Activities include abseiling, gorge running, cave rescue, mountain biking, white water canoeing and tube rafting as well as camping out and cooking own camp food. Price £125. Also, daily instruction and non-residential weekend courses for four to sixteen-year-olds, £28 (day), £70 (weekend) per child for a minimum group of four children. All leading instructors have NGB qualifications and first-aid.

Wales

CLYNE FARM CENTRE
Westport Avenue, Mayals, Swansea SA3 5AR (tel 01792-40333; fax 01792-403339).
Winner of Prince of Wales Award, Civic Trust Commendation, and Wales Tourist Board Green Award.
Multi activity holidays including pony trekking, canoeing, climbing, caving, wildlife,

and field study on the Gower Peninsula throughout the year. Individuals and groups of between four and 100 catered for. Activities may also be pursued separately. Prices range between £160 and £230. A typical price is £180 for seven days. This includes all equipment and accommodation in rooms sleeping one to six in a converted stone barn. No experience is necessary.
Provision is made for special needs clients.

CMC — PENSARN HARBOUR

Pensarn Harbour, Llanbedr LL45 2HU (tel 01341-241718).
Multi activity adventure courses including rock climbing, abseiling, canoeing, mountain walking, camping, sea-level traversing, mountain biking, gorge walking and kayaking. Price of £170 includes full board and accommodation, all equipment and travel concerned with the course. Swimming ability required for canoeing, windsurfing and rafting.
Ages: 10+.

FIELD STUDIES COUNCIL

Head Office, Montford Bridge, Shrewsbury SY4 1HW (tel 01743-850674; fax 01743-850178).
Opportunities at the FSC's centres in Wales in August: Nature for Children at Dale Fort in Pembrokeshire and Venture Snowdonia for unaccompanied young people at Rhyd-y-creuau in North Wales. Prices include accommodation, all meals and tuition.

HEART OF WALES RIDING HOLIDAYS

Tyddu, Dolau, Llandrindod Wells, Powys LD1 5TB (tel/fax 01597-851884).
Proprietors: B Brown.
In business since 1990.
Holidays for 300 arranged annually.
Instructional, children's riding holidays in mid-Wales. Easter half-terms and during July and August. Prices from £185-220 a week include riding, full board and dormitory accommodation. Participants are expected to look after the pony that they ride for the week.
Age range: eight to 18 years.
Mentally and physically challenged children are catered for on special Riding for the Disabled Association weeks.

MARLE HALL OUTDOOR EDUCATION CENTRE

Marle Lane, Llandudno Junction, North Wales LL31 9JA (tel 01412-581218).
Run by Warwickshire County Council.
Head of Centre: Dave Horley.
In business since 1971.
AALA, WTB accredited and Head of Outdoor Education Centre Association.
Multi activity holidays in North Wales from Monday-Friday during August. Price: £200 includes accommodation in the centre and full board. All equipment is included.
Ages: ten to 14 years.

MOUNT SEVERN CENTRE

Llanidloes, Powys, SY18 6PP (tel/fax 01686-412344).
Partners: G & J Novak.
In business since 1982.
Wales Tourist Board, Welsh Canoeing Association.
Open all year round. Multi activity holidays for families in July and August. Price of £240 per person per week includes full board and accommodation and all activities. Typical programme includes archery, canoeing, pony trekking, orienteering, white water rafting, abseiling, climbing, walking and ropes course.

Courses for schools, trainees and managers organised outside July and August.

PLAS MENAI NATIONAL WATERSPORTS CENTRE

Caernarfon, Gwynedd LL55 1UE (tel 01248-670964).
Multi activity youth weeks during half-terms and during the summer holidays. Activities include sailing, windsurfing, canoeing and mountain activities. Also RYA sailing courses for young people at all levels. Prices from £270 per week including full board and accommodation, 24 hour supervision, tuition and equipment.
Ages: 8 to 16 years.

TWR-Y-FELIN OUTDOOR CENTRE

Twr-y-Felin, St. Davids, Pembrokeshire, South Wales SA62 6QS (tel 07000 Big Fun or 01437-721611; fax 01437-721838).
E-mail: 100104.2022@compuserve.com
Five-day multi activity courses in May and July based at the hotel centre in St. Davids. Activities include coasteering, surfing, kayaking, canoeing, orienteering, walking,

climbing and abseiling. Evening activities also provided. Price: £260 includes accommodation in the hotel and full board.
Ages: 12 to 16 years.

Ireland

CARLINGFORD ADVENTURE CENTRE & HOLIDAY HOSTEL
Tholsel Street, Carlingford, Co Louth, Ireland (tel +353 42 73100/73816; fax +353 42 73651).
Multi activity holidays in the setting of the medieval village with all activities within walking distance. Activities include windsurfing, raftmaking, indoor climbing wall, canoeing, hill walking, bivouacking and archery. Youth programmes do not overlap with adult courses. Prices start from £49 for a two-day course including bunk bed accommodation and all meals and activities.
Age range: 9-17 years.

WEST OF IRELAND ACTIVITY CENTRE
Loughanelteen, Sligo, Ireland (tel/fax (+353 71-43528 24-hours). E-mail: wiac@iol.ie
Registered charity. Member of Irish Tourist Board and Christian Camping International.
Residential camping and activity centre for young people. Activities include sailing, abseiling, canoeing, archery, windsurfing, horse-riding and hill-walking. Differential price structure depending on activities undertaken, duration of stay and time of year.
Enquiries/bookings to the Programmes Manager at the above address.

Europe

ACTION VACANCES
30 Brackley Road, Stockport, Cheshire SK4 2RE (tel & fax 0161-442 6130 or 01904-489248).
Action Vacances is the British agent for the French activity organisation UCPA (Union des Centres sportifs de Plein Air) which promotes a summer programme for juniors in centres around France, including the outskirts of Paris, Brittany and the Aquitaine coast. Activities on offer include watersports, horse riding, tennis, golf canoeing and many others.
Ages: 12 to 17.

BLUE RIDGE TRAVEL
Consort House, Consort Way, Horley, Surrey RH6 7AF (tel 01293-825827; 01293-825828).
Directors: P Hopkins, D Lyne, R Fatah, E Mullaney, P Jackson.
In business since 1995.
Member of ABTA, ATOL.
Multi activity and watersports holidays for schools in France, Spain and Austria. Activities include windsurfing, sailing, mountain biking, pony trekking, climbing, canoeing and kayaking. Tours last up to 9 days catering for groups of any size. Prices range from £200-£2000 depending on destination and departure dates. Full board accommodation available.
Minimum age: 7 years.

DISCOVER LTD
Timbers, Oxted Road, Godstone, Surrey RH9 8AD (tel 01883-744392; fax 01883-744913). E-mail: info@discover.ltd.uk
Internet: http://www.discover.ltd.uk/net/
Directors: M McHugo, T Rowell, C McHugo, R Crofts, M Davis.
Adventure training and personal development courses for school children based at The Eagle's Nest Activity and Field Study Centre in the Cevennes, France. The area offers opportunities for caving, canoeing, and watersports on local reservoirs, also pony trekking and walking. The centre accommodates up to 80 people. Price around £350 for ten days including self-drive minibus hire and fuel from London and back, full board and accommodation and up to 200 miles of excursions from the Centre.
The Eagle's Nest Centre also specialises in fieldwork courses in biology, environmental studies, geography and history, based on the environs of the Centre.

PGL ADVENTURE LTD
Alton Court, Penyard Lane, Ross-on-Wye, Herefordshire HR9 5NR (tel Freecall 0500 749147; fax 01989-766306).
Choice of over 75 different activities in any of the 25 centres in the UK and France. Individuals, groups and schools. No experience needed, full instruction by expert and qualified staff. Accommodation varies from

camping to single rooms and other indoor accommodation. Prices: Weekend £79, Mini Breaks three/four nights £100-£150, Full Week £209-£300, Overseas holidays £250-£1500. Can accommodate special needs groups by arrangement.
Minimum age: six years (unaccompanied).
Maximum age: 18 years.

UCPA
c/o Action Vacances, 30 Brackley Road, Stockport, Cheshire SK4 2RE (tel/fax 0161 442 6130).
UCPA, established by the French Government to encourage young French people to experience the outdoors, has been the the French leader in outdoor activities for 30 years. increasingly their centres offer multi-activity holidays to young Europeans from many countries and many staff are bilingual in English/French. Packages can be arranged through a UK agent, mainly for school groups but individuals are also accepted. Typical programmes involve a combination of French language tuition and multi sports including water-based activities, sand yachting and mountain biking. Multi activity packages are available at a range of centres around France. A week's package costs about £300 and does not include transport. Parents can drop children at the centre or arrange an escort which costs extra.

VIGVATTEN NATUR KLUBB
Apartado Numero 3253, Vitoria-Gasteiz 01002, Spain (tel (+34) 45-281794; fax (+34) 45-281794).
Children's summer camps and young people's multi activity holidays in rural settings in the Pyreneess, Urbion's Mountains and Basque Country. Choose from walking, hiking, mountain pursuits, night walking, trekking, mountain biking and mountain walking. For individuals and groups. 5 days, a week or fortnight from £110-£125 per week, including accommodation in tents, mountain huts and youth hostels, all meals and insurance. No experience necessary. Some participation required in day-to-day running on the young people's camp holidays.
Minimum age: eight years.

Americas

AMERICAN WILDERNESS EXPERIENCE INC
P O Box 1486, Boulder, Co 80306, USA (tel +1 303 444 2622; fax +1 303 444 3999).
Dolphin discovery camp with dolphin swims, snorkelling, scavenger hunts, riding and nature hikes in Roatan, Honduras. Six days from June to the end of August. Camp size is limited to groups of six to fifteen children. Adults can participate in many of the activities or participate in the linked world class dive centre of Anthony's Key Resort. Child price is $500 based on shared room accommodation with adults booked on the standard adult dive package. Includes accommodation, all meals, camp activities and equipment.

BLUE RIDGE TRAVEL
Consort House, Consort Way, Horley, Surrey RH6 7AF (tel 01293-825827; fax 01293-825828).
Mountain and River Adventure holiday for schools in Quebec, Canada from April to October. Nine-day holiday with itinerary including two days horseback riding, river canoeing, guided mountain hike, white water rafting and city tours. Accommodation in hotels and apartments. Prices from £799-£859 including full board, flights and activity programme.
Minimum age: 10 years.

Africa

FIRST CHALLENGE
World Challenge Expeditions, Black Arrow House, 2 Chandos Road, London NW10 6NF (tel 0181-961 1122; fax 0181-961 1551).
First Challenge is an 8 day expedition to Morocco for groups of school pupils aged 14-16, designed as an introduction to expeditions. Team members complete a self-sufficient trek and spend time living with the indigenous people. Price is £645. Schools can take part during holidays or half-terms.

Airsports

Most people's experience of flying is confined to the inside of a jet airliner. Several more intimate forms of flying, however, have developed into increasingly popular leisure pastimes. Airborne activities are extremely varied in terms of length of time in the air, duration of necessary training, expense, technical equipment and knowledge required, degree of participation involved, risks entailed and excitement experienced. Among all those who fly there is a great sense of comradeship and a strong addiction to altitude.

Unfortunately, there was a big price hike for pleasure flights in 1995 when the government first levied 17.5% VAT to transport generally. Power flying and even ballooning have were also included in the price rises.

BALLOONING was man's first experience of flight over 200 years ago. However, it was not until the late 1960s that hot-air ballooning really developed in Britain. Probably the ultimate balloon flight was executed in October 1991 by pilot and photographer Chris Dewhurst and Leo Dickinson, when they flew over Mount Everest and other Himalayan peaks, reaching altitudes of 34,000 feet. Ballooning is a very tranquil experience and virtually passive as you are expected only to stand and look at the receding countryside, the mechanics of the flight being handled by experts. If you wish to learn to fly a balloon yourself and can afford it (they cost several thousand pounds), it is possible to buy your own, usually as part of a syndicate. Some manufacturers provide instruction or you can learn on an hourly basis at a club. The minimum age is 17 and you must provide a medical certificate. A booklet containing details of balloon companies offering flights can be obtained by phoning by calling the British Balloon and Airship Club (01604-870025) and asking for a BBAC directory.

GLIDING is a very graceful sport. Gliders are usually made of wood and covered with fabric. They fly as a bird does when soaring, that is when the speed of the air flowing over the wings is enough to cause it to lift. While training you will fly in a two seater with a qualified pilot and the first flight will last about 15-20 minutes. During a week's course with average weather conditions you can expect to do about 20 launches and it will take an average of 50 to be at the standard to enable you to fly solo. Occasionally novices can learn to fly solo by the end of a one-week holiday course. The minimum age for solo flying is 16. Introductory courses include subjects such as aerodynamics, navigation and meteorology. All equipment is usually provided by the club or can be hired. Suitable warm and waterproof clothing is very important as airfields are very exposed places and the air at 2,000 feet can be quite cool even in summer. Sunglasses are essential on a sunny day. Further information can be obtained from the British Gliding Association, Kimberley House, 47 Vaughan Way, Leicester LE1 4SE; tel 0116-253 1051.

HANG GLIDING is the fulfilment of man's dream of stepping off a hill or mountain and flying like a bird. It has made flying a possibility for almost everyone since it is relatively inexpensive and involves very little equipment. Training includes ground instruction in aerodynamics, wind conditions and possible hazards as well as learning how to manoeuvre with the glider. This is done from a hill facing into the wind and by the end of the course you should be able to make flights from the hilltop, turn left and right, land accurately at the bottom of the hill. By doing so, you should qualify for an

Elementary Pilot Certificatewhich will enable you to hire or buy a hang glider and use it without supervision. A five-day course is normally needed to reach this standard. The minimum age for flying solo is 16 (with parental consent). You should wear warm and waterproof clothing and a helmet. Once you have completed a course you can join one of the clubs which are governed by the British Hang Gliding and Paragliding Association, The Old School Room, Loughborough Road, Leics. LE4 5PU (tel 0116-261 1322).

PARAGLIDING or foot-launched parascending is one of the newer airborne pursuits. The pilot begins with the canopy open above him or herself and then launches from a ridge or hillside. Most paragliding in the UK is therefore done in the northern hilly areas or from clifftops such as the South Downs. By using air currents and skill it is possible to remain aloft for several hours. In the Alps you can paraglide (or *parapente*) as it is known in France) from the mountains, and a winter variation is to do it with your skis on.

Paragliding in the UK comes under the auspice of the BHGPA (see *Hang Gliding* above) and further details can be obtained from them.

PARAMOTORING comes somewhere between para gliding and microlighting but also comes under the BHGPA (see above). It is the newest and simplest form of aircraft flying and consists of a paraglider (or hang glider) and a back pack power unit which resembles a fan in cage. The unit weighs about 25kg and can be stowed in a car boot. New paramotors cost from £2,600. This form of flying has been legalised in the UK since 1996 and takes about eight days to learn. Para motoring can be done over long distances across country and take off can be achieved in approximately ten metres. Many hang gliding and para gliding centres now offer this form of flying. For further details contact the BHGPA or individual para gliding centres.

PARACHUTING, although terrifying at first, is probably one of the most thrilling and exhilarating of the airsports. It is not as dangerous as it may seem as very thorough training is given and high standards of safety have to be met. The training — which usually takes place over two days-includes study of the equipment used, exit drill from the aircraft, theory and practice in a suspended harness, canopy handling, landing falls and emergency procedure. The first jump is made from about 800 metres with an automatically opening parachute attached to the aircraft by a static line, and a reserve in case of malfunction. After six static line jumps you may progress to free fall descents from about 3,000 feet. Another way of parachuting is the tandem jump where the instructor and student are linked together by a harness and the instructor has control of the canopy.

It is very important that you should take a course only at a member club of the British Parachute Association (BPA) which will have qualified instructors. the BPA (0116-2785271) will provide a list of clubs and a membership application form.

POWER FLYING is the most expensive way to take to the air and it takes three to four weeks of intensive training to complete the course for a Private Pilot's Licence (although those with gliding experience can qualify in less). Many clubs offer instruction on an hourly basis but holiday courses are sometimes arranged. The PPL training consists of both flying practice including take offs, landings and cross-country navigation, and ground instruction in related subjects. The minimum age is 17 and before embarking on a course you must have a medical examination by a Civil Aviation Authority doctor. Further information and details of clubs and schools offering instruction, can be obtained from the Aircraft Owners and Pilots Association, British Light Aviation Centre, 50a Cambridge Street, London SW1V 4QQ; tel 0171-834 5631.

MICROLIGHTING is less expensive and glamorous than power flying and a microlight is a much smaller machine. It is in fact a very small powered aircraft for one or two persons and some are open pods and others have enclosed cockpits. Maximum speed varies depending on the machine but about 75mph is average. There are about 2000 microlight pilots in Britain and the overseeing body is the British Microlight Aircraft Association (BMAA) at the Bull Ring, Deddington, Oxfordshire (01869 338888).

General

ACORN ACTIVITIES
PO Box 120, Hereford HR4 8YB (tel 01432-830083; fax 01432-830110).
Airsports holidays with wide range of activities including: ballooning, flying, gliding, helicopter flights, hang-gliding, microlighting, parachuting, paragliding. Half hour tasters and one to five-day courses. Choice of hotels, farmhouses, group accommodation and self-catering. All equipment provided. Fully qualified instructors. Prices for accommodation from £22 per night and for activities from £40 per day.

SKYDRAGONS PARAGLIDING
Ruthin, North Wales LL15 1LB (tel 01824-707171).
Proprietor: Audrey Humphreys.
In business since 1989.
Member BHPA.
Foot-launched paragliding, parachuting, paramotor flying, gliding, flights, micro light flying and hot air ballooning flights and courses in North Wales. Operates all year round. One day 'taster' courses or four-day courses. Course fees include all equipment but not accommodation which is available locally in B&B, camping, farmhouses and hotels.

Ballooning

England

ADVENTURE BALLOONS
Winchfield Park, London Road, Hartley Wintney, Hants RG27 8HY (tel 01252-844222).
Director: K S Hull.
Member of BBAC and CAA Air Operator's Certificate.
Flights for 3000 arranged annually.
One hour hot air balloon flights (price £115) from launch sites in Berkshire, Hampshire, Hertfordshire, Surrey and over the city of Oxford, March to October, throughout the week, subject to weather conditions. Flights are made in the early morning or evening when winds are lightest and the whole experience takes three to four hours. Individuals and groups can be accommodated, and the company has seven balloons with sizes ranging from four to 16 passengers. Also special flights over London from launch sites close to Tower Bridge on weekday mornings, April to September.

BATH BALLOON FLIGHTS
24 Gay Street, Bath, Avon BA1 2PD (tel 01225-466888; fax 01225-336167).
Directors: J E Mansell and M Mansell.
In business since 1986.
Member of the Balloon and Airship Club.
Licensed by Civil Aviation Authority.
Hot air balloon flights from Royal Victoria Park in Bath, Ashton Court in Bristol, South Wales and the Vale of the Usk, and from Staverton Flying School at Gloucestershire airport. Flights all year round. Individuals and groups of up to 38 may be catered for. You should be able to stand for an hour, and children must be over four feet high so that they can see over the basket. Champagne is served upon landing. Guests are invited to help inflate the balloon. Prices start at £110 from Bristol and Bath for flight and insurance. Group discounts for ten or more people (each balloon takes twelve passengers). The company has arrangements with local hotels and guest houses for accommodation.
Minimum age: 18 years, unless accompanied.

VIRGIN BALLOON FLIGHTS LTD
54, Linhope Street, London NW1 6HL (tel 0171-706 1021).
Member of CAA.
Hot air ballooning all year round throughout the UK, with over 200 take-off sites to choose from. Flights last around one hour and you are returned to the starting point by the recovery team for the traditional

toast with champagne and commemorative flight certificates. Balloons of varying capacity carry 8 to 16 passengers. Price: £135 per person.
Minimum Height: 4ft 6ins.

Gliding

England

BRISTOL AND GLOUCESTERSHIRE GLIDING CLUB
Nympsfield, Nr Stonehouse, Gloucestershire GL10 3TX (tel 01453-860342; fax 01453-860060).
In business since 1955.
Member of BGA.
Gliding courses from April to October for complete beginners (and the more experienced pilot) in a friendly club atmosphere. All tuition is given by fully qualified BGA instructors, and is tailored to individuals needs. Price including tuition, flying, accommodation and main meals from £390 for 5 days.
Minimum age: 14 years if accompanied, otherwise 16 years.

DERBYSHIRE & LANCASHIRE GLIDING CLUB
Great Hucklow, Tideswell, Derbyshire SK17 8RQ (tel 01298-871270).
In business since 1935.
BGA, East Midlands Tourist Board.
Holidays for 200+ arranged annually.
Gliding courses in the Peak District National Park, Derbyshire from April-Sept. The club is based around a converted eighteenth century farmhouse which provides sleeping accommodation, convivial bar and dining facilities. Prices from £314-£349 for a week's course include six nights, full board, single or double room. All levels from beginner are catered for. For experts there is the possibility of ridge hopping and lee wave conditions are commonplace. There is a refund system if bad weather limits flying.
Minimum age: 16 years (unaccompanied); 14 years if accompanied.

MIDLAND GLIDING CLUB
The Long Mynd, Church Stretton, Shropshire SY6 6TA (tel 01588- 650206; fax 01588 650532).
Ltd. Company registered under the Friendly Societies Act.
Established 1934.
Member of the BGA.
Holiday courses arranged for 200-250 annually.
Gliding instruction at all levels. Courses are held weekly from mid-March until mid-October. Individuals and groups of up to ten. Price for a five-day course is £350-£490 depending on the season. Prices include bunkhouse accommodation and full board and tuition and equipment as well as a guarantee of minimum flying hours. Gliders are winch launched but aerotow available at extra cost. Gliders can also be bungy-launched (catapulted from the side of a hill) in suitable weather conditions.
Minimum age: 14 years (accompanied) by adult Club member, otherwise 16 years.

THE SOARING CENTRE
Husbands Bosworth Airfield, Lutterworth, Leics. LE17 6JJ (tel 01858-880521).
Directors: B Toulson, M Hughes, C Spiers.
In business since 1952.
Member of BGA.
Holidays for around 250 annually.
One to five-day gliding courses from April to September. Prices from about £105 per day and from about £205 for five days including flying, instruction, winch and aerotow launches. Individuals or groups. Typically, the cost of training to solo standard is about £800. Accommodation is not included but bunk-bed caravan may be available on site for an extra charge.
Minimum age: 15 years (unaccompanied).

Scotland

SCOTTISH GLIDING CENTRE
Portmoak Airfield, Scotlandwell, by Kinross KY13 7JJ (tel 01592-840543).
Chairman: A Bauld; Secretary: J Provan; Course Secretary: Brian Phillips.
Established over 50 years.
Affiliated to the BGA.
Holidays arranged for around 200 each year.
Gliding courses offered from May to October, although gliding takes place all year round. Residential 5 day gliding courses are

intended for beginners although more experienced pilots can be catered for. Flying skills are taught by a fully qualified instructor in a dual control glider. Prices from £195 excluding flying fees, but including full board and accommodation. Flying fees are £15 per hour and £5 per winch launch. Budget flying fees of £150 for an average weeks activity.
Unaccompanied young people accepted from 16 years. From 14-16 years must be accompanied by family member or responsile friend.

Hang Gliding and Paragliding

England

ACTIVE EDGE PARAGLIDING
Albert Terrace, Glasshouses, Harrowgate, North Yorkshire HG3 5QN (tel 01423-711900).
Holidays provided for 400 annually.
Paragliding and hang gliding holidays from one to seven days all year round. Groups of up to 15 people. Prices: Funday £65; four days £210; seven days £275, unlimited days £399. Accommodation not included but available locally. Insurance of £29 for three months necessary. Individual participation expected.
Minimum age: 16 years.
Pysically challenged people catered for.
'There is nothing to beat the sheer excitement and exhilaration of this activity'.

AIRBORNE HANG GLIDING & PARAGLIDING CENTRE
Hey End Farm, Luddendenfoot, West Yorkshire HX2 6JN (tel 01422-834989 or 01973-845616; fax 01422-836442).
Directors: Tony Delaney and Sue Whitehouse.
In operation since 1973.
Member of AFFP.
Holidays for 1000 arranged annually.
Hang gliding holidays based in the Whitworth Valley, half an hour from Leeds and Manchester, all year round. Prices from £75. Student Pilot Courses from £295 (four days). Also now offering paramotoring (hang gliding with an engine strapped to your back).Accommodation is not included but is available locally from about £15 per night for bed and breakfast. Also paragliding holidays in Tenerife from £275.
Ages: 12-65 years.

HIGH ADVENTURE
Yarborough House, Nettlecombe Lane, Whitwell, Iow PO38 2QA (tel 01983-730075; fax 01983-731441).
Hang gliding and paragliding training throughout the year for beginners, through intermediate to advanced levels. Instruction in groups of ten to 20. One-day, weekend or week long courses to BHPA syllabuses. Prices from £59 for a one-day introductory course. Five-day midweek Elementary Pilot Certificate hang gliding courses £260. Six to seven-day combined student pilot and club pilot paragliding courses £350. Also multi activity courses (see *Multi Activity* section). Accommodation in the guest house, Monday to Friday bed and breakfast four nights mid-week £60;. otherwise bed and breakfast per night £17. Courses also available at various sites in the UK and abroad in winter. Surf sports, sailing and mountain biking also available.
Minimum age: 14 years (accompanied); 16 years (unaccompanied).

PEAK DISTRICT HANG GLIDING CENTRE
York House, Ladder Edge, Leek, Staffordshire ST13 7AQ (tel day 07000-426445).
Proprietor: Mike Orr.
In business since 1974.
BHPA registered.
Courses organised for around 400 each year.
Hang gliding in the Peak District throughout the year. Individuals and groups of up to 20 may be catered for. No experience is required. Prices from £43 for a day to £175 for five days, including all equipment. Various types of accommodation are available locally. You will need to be a member of the BHGA, which costs between £8 and £29.
Minimum age: 16 years. Unaccompanied young people accepted.

PEAK SCHOOL OF HANG GLIDING
The Elms, Wetton, Nr. Ashbourne, Derbyshire DE6 2AF (tel 01335-310257).
Proprietor: J H Clarke.
In business since 1978.
Member BHPA.
Courses for 500 arranged annually.
Hang gliding courses offered year round in the Peak District. Groups of up to 30 or

individuals. Two-day introductory course £98. Five-day Elementary Pilot Certificate £229, first step in hang gliding training. Club Pilot Certificate, designed to produce pilots of high standard before they join clubs. Dual soaring course also available. No experience necessary. Courses taught by qualified instructors. All equipment provided. Accommodation available locally in youth hostels, bed and breakfasts, hotels, camping etc.
Featured in the BBC2 *Alternative Holiday Show* and *Great Outdoors* magazine.
Minimum age: 16 years, for unaccompanied young people.
Maximum age: 60+.

SKY SYSTEMS
Truleigh Sands, Edburton, Near Henfield, West Sussex (tel 01273-857700; fax 01273-857722).
Directors: M Carnet and K Carnet.
In business since 1989.
Holidays for approximately 550 arranged annually.
Paragliding, hang gliding and paramotor courses on the South Downs, near Brighton all year round. Individuals and groups of up to 16 (paragliding) or 10 (hang gliding). Price for a beginner course £299, or one-day £79, plus mandatory insurance. Accommodation and board are not included, but a variety of accommodation is available locally. Sky Systems also offers introductory Dual Paragliding Flights at £39 including insurance. Phone for an information pack.
Minimum age: 16 (unaccompanied).

SUSSEX HANG GLIDING AND PARAGLIDING
Dairy Farm, Wick Street, Firle, Nr Lewes, East Sussex BN8 6NB (tel 01273-858170; fax 01273-858177).
Proprietor: Tim Cox.
In business since 1979.
Registered by BHPA.
Hang gliding and paragliding courses on the Sussex Downs. Paragliding weekends £105, hang gliding weekends £120. Courses offered up to Club pilot standard. Professional instructors.
Ages: 14-75 years.

WILTSHIRE HANG GLIDING & PARAGLIDING CENTRE
The Old Barn, Rhyls Lane, Lockeridge, Marlborough, Wiltshire SN8 4EE (tel 01672-861555).
Proprietor: M Atkinson.
In operation since 1974.
Holidays for around 500 arranged annually.
All year round hang gliding and paragliding holidays on the Wiltshire downs. Prices from £50 per day including all equipment and expert tuition. Accommodation can be arranged locally (list supplied).
Ages: 16+ years.

Scotland

CAIRNWELL MOUNTAIN SPORTS
Gulabin Lodge, Glenshee, Perthshire PH10 7QE (tel/fax 01250 885255).
Member of BHPA.
Basic two or four-day courses available (£100 and £195) between May and November. Beginners courses are conducted on gentle slopes at first, but once trained the sky is the limit. Experienced flyers can experience the Cainwell at 3000 feet for superb launches and views. Various activities on offer if the weather is unsuitable for flying. Accommodation can be arranged in local hostels. Insurance required for the course duration.
Minimum age: 16 years.

Wales

PARAMANIA
15 Broad Street, New Radnor, Powys LD8 2SP (tel 01544-350375; fax 01544-350234).
Sole traders: Mr and Mrs Campbell-Jones.
In business since 1991.
Holidays for about 200 arranged annually.
Member of British Hangliding and Paragliding Association.
Hang gliding and paragliding holiday courses from September to April in the Welsh Borders. Two-day introductory course (£117); upgrade to student pilot (20+ flights) £95; Beginner to student pilot (within three months of starting) £145. Bed and breakfast accommodation available locally from £15 per night.

WELSH HANG GLIDING CENTRE
Bryn Bach Park, Tredegar, Gwent NP2 3AY (tel 01873-832100).
Proprietor: Paul Farley.
In operation since 1975.
BHPA registered.

Holidays arranged for around 300 each year.
Hang gliding holidays operating from Bryn Bach Park near Tredegar in Gwent. April to October all week (closed Friday); after October, weekends only. Prices range from £45-£200 including all equipment. Bunkhouse/self catering accommodation available though not included in price. Additional expense of £29 (three months)/£10 (weekend) for membership of the BHPA to obtain third party insurance.
'An energetic day out in beautiful countryside participating in the most natural form of aviation available, and, of course, also good fun'.
Ages: 16-55 years (if fit).

Parachuting and Parascending

Worldwide

SKYDIVE UNLIMITED
618a Thorne Road, Netheravon, Salisbury, Wiltshire SP4 9QG (tel & fax 01980-670100).
Sole Trader: Andy Parkin.
In business since 1997.
Holidays for 30+ arranged annually.
Accelerated Freefall Courses located in Florida, Spain, Germany and the U.K. Courses available all year round for a minimum of one week. Two highly specialised instructors accompany you for the first 3 levels of the course, followed by only one for the next 4 levels, finally leading to a solo graduation jump. Prices include equipment, flights, accommodation and instruction. Prices: U.K £1100, Spain/Germany £1500, Florida £1800. Meals are not included in the prices. Individuals, and groups of up to 6 catered for (trip lengths can be extended for groups).
Also available in the U.K: Tandem Skydives (£180) and Static Line Courses (£160). No experience required.
Minimum age: 16 years (unaccompanied).
Maximum age: 40 years.

England

BLUE SKIES PARACHUTE TRAINING SCHOOL
4 Shalford Terrace, Whitford, Axminster, Devon EX13 7P (tel 01297-553300).
Parachute training. Two-day beginners' courses on square-type canopies (which enable stand-up landings) held throughout the year. Bed and breakfast can be arranged locally. Courses include documentation, orientation and equipment, aircraft and exit drills, canopy control and how to steer the parachute, parachute landing falls, use of the reserve parachute and collapsing the canopy after landing. Introductory and more advanced instruction up to competition standard. Equipment supplied. The first jump will take place when the surface wind is less than 15 mph, usually in early morning or late evening. Price about £145.
Minimum age: 16 years.

BORDER PARACHUTE CENTRE
Brunton Airfield, Chathill, Northumberland NE67 5ER; tel 01665-589000.
Chief Instructor: T Andrewes.
In operation since 1983.
Member of BPA.
Holidays for around 1000 arranged annually.Parachuting weekends for beginners at Brunton Airfield, Northumberland all year round.
Ages: 16-50 years; (exceptions can be made to upper limit).

BRITISH PARACHUTE SCHOOL
The Control Tower, Langar Airfield, Langar, Nottinghamshire (tel 01949-860878).
Directors: D Hickling and D Turner.
In business since 1980.
Member of BPA.
Holidays provided for 1000 annually.
Parachuting weekends and weeks, all year round. Individuals and groups of up to 12 may be catered for. No experience is required. First jump square parachute course costs £165 and £30 per jump thereafter. Tandem skydives are £165, video and stills extra. Meals and accommodation available in a bunkhouse or camping. All

equipment is included in the price. Unaccompanied young people accepted from 16 years.
Maximum age: 40-50, with a medical certificate.
Physically and visually challenged people catered for.

FLY HIGH PARASCENDING/PARAGLIDING
101 Heath Road, Barming, Maidstone, Kent ME16 9JT (tels: 01622-728230, 0860 351130; 01580-211045).
Chief Instructor: B Clark.
In business since 1972.
BHPA.
Holidays for 1000 arranged annually.
Paragliding, powered paragliding and hang gliding courses lasting two to seven days offered all year round. Individuals and groups of up to 12. Prices: £40 per day or £200 a week. Accommodation can be bunkhouse and half board, or self catering and camping. Clients have to provide their own ankle-supporting boots and overclothes.
Minimum age: 14 years (accompanied).

HEADCORN PARACHUTE CLUB AND SLIPSTREAM ADVENTURES
The Airfield, Headcorn, Kent TN27 9HX (tel 01622-890862).
Established in 1979.
Parachuting all year round weather permitting. Static Line courses run four times weekly. Groups catered for. Prices from £105-£195. Tandem jumps available daily. Freefall from 10,000 feet with your own personal instructor. Price £180. Freefall Square Course. Make your first descent from 11 000 feet with two instructors holding on to you. Price for a full course is £1250.
'Come and enjoy the thrill of a lifetime'.

IPSWICH PARACHUTE CENTRE
Ipswich Airport, Nacton Road, Ipswich, Suffolk IP3 9QF (tel 01473-710044; fax 01473-440630).
Proprietor: A G Knight.
In business since 1981.
Recognised by BPA.
Parachute courses throughout the year. Two days, midweek or weekend. Courses cost from £95 and include all training and equipment to the first jump. Subsequent jumps from £25 each.
Age range: 16-55 years.

Scotland

STIRLING PARACHUTE CENTRE
Thornhill, Nr. Stirling FK8 3QT (tel 01786-870788; fax 01786-870748).
Chief Instructor: Rob Noble-Nesbitt.
Approved by BPA.
Two-day parachute courses throughout the year, midweek or weekend. Courses from £79 which includes all training and equipment to the first jump. Subsequent jumps £20 each. Camping on airfield or accommodation available locally.
Ages: 16-49 years. Older, by individual assessment.

Wales

SKYDRAGONS PARAGLIDING
Ruthin, North Wales LL15 1LB (tel 01824-707171).
Foot-launched paragliding from hills in North Wales. Instruction for individuals or groups up to 12 people. Courses operate all year round and last between one and four days. One-day 'Taster' involves practical and theoretical tuition and gives an introduction to the sport with an emphasis on flying. Price £59 (one-day). Four-day course takes you from beginner to Elementary Pilot Rating (EPR) which features high flights over 100 feet, accurate flight control and stand-up landings. Price £200 (4 days). Club Pilot Rating course, available once you have gained EPR, allows you to fly without an instructor present. Prices from £30-£50 per day.
Course fees include all equipment but not accommodation which is available locally in B&B, camping, farmhouses, hotels, Youth Hostels and college campus. No experience required, but need to join BHPA.
Minimum age: 16. Maximum age: 55.
'Self launch paragliding is the new exhilarating aviation sport. The wing, weighing only a few pounds, unpacks from a rucksack, inflates in seconds and with just a few steps down a hillside, you are walking on air'.

Northern Ireland

WILD GEESE SCHOOL OF ADVENTURE TRAINING
Movenis Airfield, 116 Carrowreagh Road, Garvagh, Coleraine, Co Londonderry (tel 012665-58609; fax 012665-57050).
Proprietor: David Penny.
In operation since 1978.
Recognised by the Northern Ireland Tourist Board.
S/L round and square parachute training courses. Progression through the free-fall system.
Tandem sky-diving, for both disabled and able-bodied.
Open seven days a week. Accommodation, camping facilities, games room and assault course available.
Minimum age: 16 years.
'The only air sports centre in Ireland to offer everything all of the time'.

Australasia

SKYDIVE TANDEM
P.O. Box 554, Queenstown, New Zealand (tel +64 21-325-961; fax +64 3 442 8869).
E-mail: paqitd@voyager.co.nz
Internet:
http://nz.com/queenstown/skydivetandem
Managing Director: Lindsay Williams.
Established 1990.
Tandem skydiving offered all year round. Dropzone is located 15 minutes from town centre, at the base of the Remarkables mountain range. Courtesy transport provided. Skydive includes all instruction (no experience needed). Twenty minute flight, 30 second freefall and 7 minutes ride under parachute canopy. Optional photo and/or video packages are available. Tandem skydive costs $245 per person. Reservations direct or through accommodation or information offices.
No minimum age (written consent required under 16 years).

Power Flying and Microlighting

England

BEDFORDSHIRE SCHOOL OF FLYING
Cranfield Airfield, Cranfield, Bedfordshire (01234-751403).
Flying training and aircraft hire for individuals. Private Pilot's Licence course from £5250.

BIGGIN HILL SCHOOL OF FLYING
Biggin Hill Airport, Biggin Hill, Kent (tel 019595-73583; fax 019595-570770).
Flying training and aircraft hire for individuals. Private Pilot's Licence from £4,750.

BLACKBUSHE SCHOOL OF FLYING
Blackbushe Airport, Blackbushe, Surrey (tel 01252-870999).
Flying training and aircraft hire for individuals. PPL course from £5,250.

CABAIR FLIGHT TRAINING
Redhill Aerodrome, Redhill, Surrey (tel 01737-822166).
Flying training and aircraft hire for individuals, Private Pilot's Licence course from £4,990 including 40 hours flying, club membership, ground lectures and exams, radio telephonic licence, flight case and equipment. Introductory lesson price available price £125.
Also, Helicopter Private Pilot's Licence course £8250. Introductory lesson available from £125.
NVQ tax relief available as above.

CABAIR HELICOPTERS LIMITED
Elstree Aerodrome, Borehamwood, Herts, WD6 3AW (tel 0181-953 4411).
Flying training and aircraft hire for individuals. Helicopter charter service, sight-seeing tours of London and venture days. The following flying schools in this section are all part of the Cabair Group (Cabair Flight Training, Bedfordshire, Biggin Hill, Blackbushe, Denham and Kingair).

DENHAM SCHOOL OF FLYING
Denham Aerodrome, Denham, Uxbridge, Middlesex (01895-833327).
Flying training and aircraft hire for individuals. Private Pilot's Licence course from £5250.

KINGAIR FLIGHT CENTRE
Biggin Hill Airport, Biggin Hill, Kent (tel 019595 75088).
Flying training and aircraft hire for individuals. PPL course from £4,750.

LEJAIR
8 The Watlings, Scarning, Dereham, Norfolk NR19 2LW (tel/fax 01362-687000; mobile 0585 328297).
Directors: A Webb, R Webb.
In business since 1984.
A five-day course in Norfolk for beginners to elementary pilots. Price £375. Accomodation extra from £15 per night B&B. Also dual flights with an instructor. One-day courses also available.

LONDON SCHOOL OF FLYING
Elstree Aerodrome, Borehamwood, Herts WD6 3AW (tel 0181-953 4343).
Flying training and aircraft hire for individuals. Private Pilot's Licence course from £5250 including 40 hours flying, club membership, ground lectures and exams, radio telephonic licence, flight case and equipment. Introductory lesson available, price £125.
NVQ tax relief (i.e. 23% or 40% reduction) on the price of a private pilot's course for those eligible for private pilot training.
Also Helicopter Pilot's Licence: trial lesson from £125; full course from £8250.
No experience needed.
Minimum age: 17 years.

NORTHERN MICROLIGHT SCHOOL
2 Ashlea Cottages, St Michael's Road, Bilsborrow, Preston PR3 ORT (tel 01995-641058).
Proprietor: G C Hobson.
In business since 1982.
Member of British Microlight Aircraft Association.
Holidays provided for 100 annually.
Microlight flying training in Lancashire throughout the year. Groups of up to 30 may be catered for. No experience is required. Prices: £30 for a 20 minute trial lesson, £65 for an hour. Accommodation available locally in pubs and B&B's.
Unaccompanied young people accepted from 12 years.

The ultimate jump *Skydive Tandem*

Cycling

Cycling is an activity which is more accessible than many other adventure holidays. Since almost everybody learned to ride a bicycle when young, the prospect of a cycling holiday is less daunting than one which involves windsurfing or camel caravanning. It may sound less adventurous than taking to the sea or the desert, but freewheeling down a mountain road can be as exhilarating (and dangerous) as sailing or micro-lighting.

Ten years ago, the vogue was for racing machines sporting ten or fifteen gears. Now 'mountain bikes' or ATBs (all-terrain bikes) are all the rage: tough enough for a mountainside but often too cumbersome for a city street. In North America it is rare to see an adult riding an 'ordinary' bicycle, and bells and baskets-on-the-front bikes are unknown. But it is not necessary to own the sportiest or toughest machine to enjoy town or country cycling: the so-called hybrid or town-and-trail bike which is lighter than a mountain bike and has fewer gears than a tourer, is the latest addition to the cycling stable. The Dutch are avid cyclists and yet because of their terrain don't need fancily-geared bicycles. After enjoying some gentle cycle touring, you might be inspired to emulate Dervla Murphy, the traveller and author who cycled from her home in Ireland to India on a boneshaker in the mid-sixties. Alternatively mountain bikers might like to follow in the wheelmarks of Richard and Nick Crane whose book *Bicycles Up Kilimanjaro* has sold thousands of copies since publication in 1985.

Most organisers of cycling holidays offer sturdy, three-speed bicycles equipped with rack, panniers and repair kit for touring, though some do hire out sports cycles with up to 21 gears. Some holidays described in this chapter are designed for the independent cyclist; maps and route suggestions are provided, but it is up to the individual to decide whether to stay in a tent or a hotel. Other operators organise the accommodation along a set route, and still others arrange group cycling with a leader who is knowledgeable both about bicycles and about the area. Often a support vehicle accompanies the group, to carry luggage and ease the problems of repairing the inevitable mechanical mishaps and punctures. You may wish to devise your own tour; in this respect, the annual *CTC Handbook* contains valuable information in addition to accommodation listings. For cycling holidays abroad, it is relatively easy to take your own bicycle by air, rail or sea. Many national tourist offices now provide free booklets about cycling with advice on routes and maps.

So whether it is the Isle of Wight, Cuba or China you wish to explore, consider taking to the back roads on a bicycle. One of the biggest organisers of charity bike rides is Bike Events of Bath (tel 01225-310859). The annual London to Brighton bike ride, held on the the third weekend in June, has now been taken over by The British Heart Foundation as a major part of their fund-raising. For those with even more stamina, Bike Tours (01225-480130) organise various bike trips in the UK and abroad. Some of the annual ones include: the Cotswolds, Portugal, Costa Rica, Budapest to the Adriatic, Bordeaux to Barcelona, Prague to Venice via Bohemia, Cuba (two weeks in March, November and over Christmas and New Year), Ireland and trips around Normandy and Brittany. Contact Bike Tours and Bike Events in January for free programmes and application forms for one-day bike rides and tours respectively.

The Cyclists' Touring Club (see entries below) is the oldest cycling organisation having been founded in 1878, and can be contacted for all cycling information for both Britain and overseas. Annual membership costs £25 per year for adults, half for the under eighteens and the unwaged and £16.50 for senior citizens. There is also a family membership (for three or more in a family living at the same address) for £42. Membership includes a cycling magazine *(Cycle Touring & Campaigning)*, free third party insurance and legal aid, and the opportunity to join one of 200 local CTC groups in Britain.

As the number of cycling enthusiasts increases so do the number of local clubs and groups they can join. You can contact other cyclists through the governing body of cycling, the British Cycling Federation (0161 2302301/0500 525676) which has about 14,000 members. Membership of the BCF costs £21 annually (half if you join after June) and includes insurance and entitlement to discounts (usually 10%) on a range of cycling gear and literature sold in member bike shops and special cycling insurance at a competitive rate. Members also receive an annual handbook and three to four issues of the BCF magazine *Slipstream*.

Useful publications for cyclists include the Ordnance Survey *Cycle Tours Guides* (O/S Hamlyn £9.99 each) on a range of about 24 on and off road cycle routes that can be done in a day. The series so far includes *Devon and Cornwall*, *Kent, Surrey and Sussex* and *Buckinghamshire, Berkshire and Oxfordshire.* The National Cycle Network routes are sponsored by the cycling organisation Sustrans and so far their maps (based on O/S surveys) include Carlisle to Inverness in Scotland (maps 7b and 7c), Padstow to Bristol/ Bath (map 3a), Hull to Harwich is covered by maps 1a and 1b while Chepstow to Holyhead is covered by 8a and 8b. National Cycle Network maps costs £5.99 each by mail order from Sustrans (0117-926 8893) and postage is a minimum of £1.50. These maps are also available from bookshops and other outlets. If you are planning your own cycling trip in France the French equivalent of Ordnance Survey maps are the *IGN* series.

Sustrans, the cycle route charity, is committed to developing a 6,500 mile national cycle network in the UK which will include a route from Inverness to Dover. There are already 55 traffic-free routes in the UK and the most popular is probably the Camel Trail (tel 01208 813050) in Cornwall. For further details and a range of leaflets and newletters on all the Sustrans routes call 0117-987 4585.

A new family cycling magazine *On Your Bike* appeared last year.

Worldwide

BIKE TOURS LTD
PO Box 75, Bath, Avon BA1 1BX (tel 01225-480130; fax 01255-480132).
Director: John Potter.
In business since 1985.
AITO, AITO Trust 1075, ATOL: 2943.
Holidays for around 800 annually.
A wide variety of cycling holidays in various parts of Europe and worldwide. Mileages and accommodation to suit everyone from the easy-going hedonist to those with a sense of challenge. Large groups, small groups and individual tours. Detailed route sheets and maps provided. Luggage transported. Pick up service. Prices from £275 for five days in France, half board in hotels, to £985 and airfare for two weeks in Costa Rica, full board in luxurious hotels.
Minimum age: 13 years (accompanied).
Visually challenged cyclists travelling on tandems with a sighted friend welcome.

England

ACORN ACTIVITIES
P O Box 120, Hereford, England HR4 8YB (tel 01432 830083; fax 01432 830110.
Two to seven-day holidays with farmhouse accommodation and bicycle hire in Shropshire (also Herefordshire and Wales). Luggage is transported ahead each day. £120-£420. Mountain bikes available.

ALSTON TRAINING & ADVENTURE CENTRE
High Plains Lodge, Alston, Cumbria CA9 3DD (tel/fax 01434-381886).
Mountain bike breaks in the Heart of the North Pennines. Ideal location for group holidays. Overnight accommodation or camp site. Flexible packages offered.

ANGLIA CYCLING HOLIDAYS
87 Perth Street, Blairgowrie, Perthshire PH10 6DT (tel 01250-876100; fax 01382-202507).
Established 1978.
Specialists in gentle self-led vacations on a network of traffic-free byroads in flat terrain around East Anglia, England. Shortbreak and Stayput holidays at base with heated pool, tennis, fishing and sailboarding facilities. Baggage transfers and tailor-made tours possible. Fully equipped touring cycles for hire or bring own. Large and small groups catered for. Seven nights b&b, including cycle, £210.

BICYCLE BREAKS
71 High Street, Colchester, Essex C01 1VE (tel 01206 868254; fax 01206-844484).
Proprietor Mr J R Edwards.
In business since 1995.
Holidays for up to 200 arranged annually.
Self-led themed cycle tours in rural Essex and Suffolk from March to November. Themes include smuggling, history, natural history and real ale. Tailor-made and bed and breakfast options available. Weekend or longer breaks. Costs about £45 per night for bed and breakfast accommodation and about £80 per night for half board hotel accommodation. Children's interests can be catered for. Hire of bicycles is included in the cost. Luggage transfer and emergency pick-up and repair service at no extra cost.

CALSHOT ACTIVITIES CENTRE
Calshot Spit, Fawley, Southampton SO45 1BR (tel 01703-892077).
Cycling on the only indoor cycling velodrome track in the south of Britain. Available for groups and individuals, adventure holidays and specialist coaching courses. All specialist equipment is provided.
Minimum age: 13 years.

COMPASS HOLIDAYS
48 Shurdington Road, Cheltenham, Glos GL53 OJE (tel 01242-250642; fax 01242 529730; US tel 800 4661713). E-mail: compass.holidays@bigfoot.com
Partners: Don Muir, Steve Short.
Established 1991.
Holidays for 300+ arranged annually. Singles or groups, guided or self-guided.
Cycling holidays in the Cotswolds arrange all year round from £50 per day including accommodation and breakfast. Bicycles can be hired as an extra. Walking holidays also arranged.

CYCLISTS' TOURING CLUB
69 Meadrow, Godalming, Surrey GU7 3HS (tel 01483-417217; fax 01483-426994).E-mail: cycling@ctc.org.uk Internet: http://www.ctc.org.uk
Established 1878.
The CTC offers more than 60 organised tours, led by experienced CTC Tour Leaders. Meander through quiet Norfolk, the Cotswolds, Welsh Borders or tackle a classic 'coast-to-coast' ride from Land's End to John O'Groats. Tours cater for experienced cyclists seeking high mountain passes or high daily mileages or newcomers, young people, families or 'potterers', offering low daily mileage with plenty of tea stops and sight-seeing. Accommodation ranges from camping to luxury hotels or even a castle, with fixed-centre or moving-on tours.
A CTC Tour guide can be obtained from the Touring Department with an s.a.e.
Alternatively, plan your own adventure holiday using the CTC's extensive files of information and routes for Britain and countries around the world. Information includes itineraries, recommended accommodation, bike transportation by air, sea and rail. Information leaflets available on request.

HF HOLIDAYS LTD
Imperial House, Edgware Road, London NW9 5AL (tel 0181-905 9556).
One week tours based at HF Country Houses and hotels. Cycling is at a leisurely pace with time to visit places of interest or more strenuous mountain biking. Price around £169 for four nights full board. Children under 17 receive a 30-50% reduction depending on age if they share room with parents. Reduced rate rail travel available. Call for a Special Interest Holidays brochure.

HOLMHEAD FARM
Hadrian's Wall, Greenhead-in-Northumberland, via Carlisle CA6 7HY (tel 0169977-47402; fax 016977-47402).
Proprietors: B Staff and P Staff.
In business since 1983.

Cycle (or walk) Hadrian's Wall or the Border Country. Night stops en route or circular from farm. Accommodation booked in advance along the 73½ miles of Hadrian's Wall. B&B at Holmhead, £24.50 per day; half board £41. Discounts for groups or longer stay. Cycle hire £12 per day. Guided walks; maps/guide books provided. No smoking policy. No experience required.

THE IMAGINATIVE TRAVELLER
14 Barley Mow Passage, Chiswick, London W4 4PH (tel 0181-7423113 ; fax 0181-7423045).
Cycling touring holidays in Devon, Cornwall and Oxfordshire lasting 7-8 days. Travel the coast from Plymouth to Padstow, from Bodmin to Land's End, or from Oxford to Bath on the 'Cotswold Explorer'. Prices from £395-£595 including luggage transfers, technical support, maps, routes, meals and accommodation in hotels and guesthouses.

OFFSHORE SPORTS
2-4 Birmingham Road, Cowes, Isle of Wight (tel/fax 01983-290514)
Mountain biking on the Isle of Wight all year round. Non-residential, bike hire, guide service, trail maps. Mountain bike obstacle course.

OUTDOOR ADVENTURE
Atlantic Court, Widemouth Bay, Bude, Cornwall EX2 30DF (tel 01288-361312)
RYA, BCU, BSA, BAHA approved.
This seafront centre offers mountain biking as part of a week's, three-day and weekend adventure sports holiday. Other activities include windsurfing, surfing, sailing, canoeing and climbing. Accommodation in twin rooms and lively bar in centre. Prices: weeks from £297 and weekends £127. Equipment, local transport and experienced, qualified instruction included. All abilities. Vegetarians and special diets catered for.
Minimum age: 16 years.

PEDALS & BOOTS
Cobblestones, Causeway End, Nr Haverthwaite, Ulverstone, Cumbria LA12 8JW (tel 015395-31391).
Partners: D M Brown, H J Brown.
In business since 1995.
Self-guided cycling tours in the Louth Lakeland region of the Lake District. Tours last three to seven days; available all year round. Freedom to travel at a pace that suits. Individuals and groups of up to six catered for. Accommodation in country inns and guesthouses; bed and breakfast included. Price for one week Multi Centre Holiday: £320 per person, including baggage transfer, route suggestions, OS maps and bikes. Two or three day 'taster' weekends available.
Minimum age: 14 years (16 unaccompanied).
'Stunning views, exhilarating descents, quality equipment and accommodation.'

ROCK LEA ACTIVITY CENTRE
Station Road, Hathersage, Hope Valley S32 1DD (tel 01433-650345).
Adventure Activity Licence.
Weekend, mid-week and week-long mountain biking breaks for beginners as well as enthusiasts, all year round. Weekends from £99, four nights from £199, six nights from £250. All prices include half board. Non-resident day trips can also be organised for parties.

SUFFOLK CYCLE BREAKS
PO Box 82, Needham Market, Suffolk, IP6 8BW (tel 01449-721555; fax 01449-721707). E-mail: info @cyclebreaks.co.uk
Proprietor: Andrew Patton.
In business since 1991.
Set tours of Suffolk, Essex and Norfolk borders. From three days/two nights, starting any day of the week. Individuals, large groups and families welcome (reductions for under 15's). Prices from £94 includes quality B&B, hire of Claud Butler cycles (ATB, Hybrid or Sports Tourers), luggage transport, rescue service and route planning (includes OS 1:50 000 maps and detailed route notes). Accommodation available in three price bands. Colour brochure available on request.

WHEELY WONDERFUL CYCLING
Petchfield Farm, Elton, Ludlow, Shropshire SY8 2HJ (tel 01568-770755).
Proprietor: Kay Dartnell.
In business since 1993.
Cycling holidays and short breaks around the English Marches and border country. Shropshire Castle Tour, Welsh National Cycle Route and Cider Orchard Tours all year round. Cycle back in time through Shropshire's Castle country or spend a weekend at a historic hunting lodge — wildlife watching by bike. All along quiet country lanes, pre-tested routes with plenty of time to picnic, paddle or rest. For individuals and groups up to ten. Prices

from £55-£350 including quality accommodation in B&B farmhouses or youth hostels. Luggage transported.

Scotland

HUNTLY NORDIC SKI CENTRE
Hill of Haugh, Huntly, Aberdeenshire AB54 4SH (tel 01466-794428; fax 01466-792180).
Bike touring from March to September from a purpose-built centre in Huntly. Accommodation can be arranged locally. Bikes can be hired.

SCOTTISH BORDER TRAILS
Drummore, Venlaw High Road, Peebles EH45 8RL (tel 01721-722934 ; fax 01721-723004). E-mail: arthur@trails.scotborders.co.uk
Proprietor: Arthur Phillips.
In business since 1985.
Member of Scottish Activity Holiday Association.
Cycling and walking holidays in southern Scotland and a range of bikes for hire for downhill cycle fun. No experience required. Prices range from £10 for day to £899 for 14 days inclusive of food, bicycle, accommodation and supported touring. Helmets are not included but may be hired.
Minimum age: eight years, if accompanied.

SCOTTISH CYCLING HOLIDAYS
87 Perth Street, Blairgowrie, Perthshire PH10 7NJ (tel 01250 876100).
E-mail: 106412.3500@compuserve.com
Established 1979.
Gentle or strenuous self-led vacations throughout Scotland and Western Isles. Short break, stayput, tailor-made (any length) holidays and for large or small groups. Fully equipped, suitably geared touring cycles or bring your own. Airport collection and baggage transfers arranged. Seven nights including bed and breakfast accommodation and cycle from £215. Short breaks from £65 (2 nights, 3 days hire).

SCOTTISH YOUTH HOSTELS ASSOCIATION
7 Glebe Crescent, Stirling FK8 2JA (tel 01786-891400).
Seven-day Island-hopping around Arran, Islay and Jura. Price around £165, including all ferry fares. Cycles not included but may be hired at a cost of £42.
Minimum age: 14 years.

Wales

BICYCLE BEANO
Brynderwen, Erwood, Builth Wells, Powys, Wales LD2 3PQ (tel 01982-560471).
E-mail: bicycle@beano.kc3.co.uk
Proprietors: J Barnes, R Green.
In business since 1982.
Member of the London Cycling Campaign and Cyclists' Touring Club.
Holidays for 300 arranged annually.
Week and weekend holidays in mid-Wales, west Wales coast, Shropshire and Herefordshire from Easter to September. Prices of £95-£350 include vegetarian and wholefood breakfast and evening meals, teas, camping and/or inns and hostels. Bike hire available.
All ages.
Physically challenged people who can cycle catered for.

CLIVE POWELL MOUNTAIN BIKES
Somerset House, East Street, Rhayader, Powys LD6 5DS (tel 01597-810585).
Guided off-road cycling holidays arranged in Wales from May to September. Approximate prices: 'Dirty Weekends' £106; 'Wild Wales Week' £258; day rides £25 or with own bike £15. Prices include half-board at The Mount guest house or local B&Bs.
Minimum age: 12 years.

PRESELI VENTURE
Parcynole Fach, Mathry, Haverfordwest, Pembrokeshire SA62 5HN (tel 01348-837709).
Partners: Sophie & Nick Hurst.
In business since 1988.
BCU/WCA Approved, Wales Tourist Board Accredited Centre.
Mountain biking holidays in the Pembrokeshire Coast National Park all year round. On and off-road routes, easy to follow route maps and local information. Holidays are centre-based and the accommodation is in comfortable Welsh cottages. Combine kayaking and 'Coasteering' for an adventure weekend you'll never forget. Guided rides or mountain bike hire. Prices from £89 for weekend.

RED KITE ACTIVITIES
Neuadd Arms Hotel, Llanwrtyd Wells, Powys, Wales, LD5 4RB (tel 01591-610236).
In business since 1983.
Member of WTB.
Holidays for around 300 annually.
Mountain bike holidays based in Llanwrtyd Wells, the smallest town in Britain, with riding in the Southern Cambrian Mountains, all year round. For individuals and groups up to 32 people. Prices from £64 for a weekend and from £230 for a week, including full-board hotel accommodation and a guide. Mountain bikes can be hired. No experience required, just a reasonable level of fitness.
Minimum age: 18 years (unaccompanied). No minimum if accompanied and with bike riding ability.

SWALLOW TANDEMS
The Old Bakery, Market Street, Llanrhaeadr-Ym-Mochnant, Oswestry SY10 0JP (tel 01691 780050). E-mail: info@swallow-tandems.co.uk
Internet: http://www.swallow-tandems.co.uk
Proprietors: Pete & Lorraine Bird.
In business since 1991.
Manufactureres of custom built tandems and sole distributors of key US production models. Tandem hire/framebuilding courses/ recycled tandems. Tandemania in the Tanat Valley — a tandem event for everyone with or without a tandem.

The Tanat Valley is superb cycling country with flat or hilly areas to choose from. Possibility of combining with other activities (walking, canoeing, paragliding etc.) nearby.
Physically, mentally and visually challenged people welcome.

Ireland

IRISH CYCLING SAFARIS
7 Dartry Park, Dublin 6, Ireland (tel +353 1 2600749; fax +353 1 7061168).
Directors: Eamon Ryan, Marion Ryan & Mary Ryan.
In business since 1989.
Dublin and West Cork Tourism member.
Holidays for 1100-1300 people annually
Guided cycling tours of small Irish country backroads in scenic, out-of-the-way areas all the way along the western coastline, from May to September. Individuals and groups of 12-20. All tours are priced at I£295 which includes bed and breakfast in a mixture of guest houses and small, family run hotels. Lunch and evening meal not included. Bicycles, rain gear, repair equipment, pannier bags are provided free as part of the package.
Unaccompanied young people accepted from 16 years.

KILLARY TOURS
Killary Tours, Derrynasliggaun, Leenane, Co Galway, Ireland (tel +353 95 42302; fax +353 95 42314). E-mail: Killary@iol.ie Internet: http://www.iol.ie/killary/
Specialist in cycling tours especially self-guided cycling for the independent. Gentle tours with luggage transfered to lighten the load, in some of Europe's most amazing countryside — Connemara and Kerry on the West coast of Ireland. Several options to choose from and any start date possible. Other activities (see *Multi Activity*).

SLATTERY'S TRAVEL AGENCY
1 Russell Street, Tralee, Co Kerry, Ireland (tel +353 66 24088; fax +353 66 25981).
Rambling With a Donkey Holidays. Ramble the hills and dales of Kerry in the company of your donkey friend. You stay with Irish people in their homes, reaching the real Irish hospitality; you get a bed while your donkey gets a field. Your donkey carries the luggage in two specially designed holdalls (capacity approx 30kgs). Prices from £35 per person, based on two sharing for two days (one night). Prices available for any length of stay. Full instruction and maps provided. Support vehicle on call.

Europe

ALP ACTIVE
Unit 9, Chesterton Mill, French's Road, Cambridge CB4 3NP (tel 01223-568220).
Mountain bike holidays in the Portes du Soleil area of the French Alps. One and two week packages including guiding, travel and either catered chalet or self-catered (chalet and apartment) accommodation. Some of the best biking in Europe, with 23 bike carrying ski lifts (operating during July and August) and over 500km of unrestricted mountain bike trails. Cross country and downhill only weeks available, as well as

bike testing opportunities. Prices from £185 per week including return Dover/Calais ferry crossing, self-catering apartment for 4 and 2 days guiding. Holidays run June to September.

ALPS MOUNTAIN BIKE TOURS

Tengstr. 1, D-80798 Munich, Germany (tel +49 89 895427880; fax +49 89 54290118).

Directors: S Rey, A Peters, H Rey, K Bach.
In business since 1989.
Cycling tours including a Tuscany and Umbria Tours of Italy, a Malta & Gozo Tour, La Gomera Tour of Spain, Alsace Tour in France and hut-to-hut tour in the Alps. Prices from US$500 to US$850. English-speaking guides and luggage transfers are included. Groups of three to twelve people. No experience needed, tours are for all skill levels. Accommodation in hotels with local cuisine.
Children under 13 must be accompanied.
'Personal groups, panoramic views, much more than just mountain biking'.

ANGLO DUTCH SPORTS

30a Foxgrove Road, Beckenham, Kent BR3 5BD (tel 0181-289 2808; fax 0181-663 3371).

Directors: W M & KC Brickley.
In business since 1976.
Gentle cycling holidays with luggage transported for all standards on cycle paths throughout the Netherlands, Denmark and along the Danube. Individuals and small groups of friends. Locations as various as Prague and Budapest, The Netherlands, Austria, Germany, Belgium and Southern England. Mainly April to the end of October but outside these months also available. Prices from £300 include dinner, bed and breakfast. Additional costs for cabin on ferry crossing if travelling on night ferry.
No minimum age if accompanied by parents; otherwise 18 years.
Physically challenged people will be accommodated if at all possible, on request.

BELLE FRANCE

15 East Street, Rye, East Sussex (tel 01797-223777; fax 01797-223666).

Proprietors: V R Sumner, P L Sumner.
In business since 1984.
Member of AITO and ATOL no 2382.
Cycling and walking holidays for individuals in France from April to October. Prices from £435. Includes bike hire, meals, travel and hotel accommodation.

BENTS BICYCLE & WALKING TOURS

The Blue Cross, Orleton, Ludlow, Shropshire SY8 4HN (tel 01568-780800; fax 01568-780801).

Proprietor: Stephen Bent.
In business since 1987.Member of AITO.
Holidays for 500-600 arranged annually.
Self-led cycling and walking holidays in Bavaria and the Black Forest, Germany from May to September lasting eight, ten and 12 days. Holidays are of the gentle potter rather than the Tour de France type and suit all ages from children to fit grandparents. Prices from £599 to £819 include flights, bed and breakfast accommodation in small Bavarian hotels and guest houses, bicycle hire, comprehensive information pack and the transportation of luggage between stops. Special child seats are provided for those aged two to five years and bicycles for children from eight years.

BRETON BIKES

14 Grande Rue, 22570 Plelauff, France (tel +33 296-248672).

E-mail: bretonbikes@compuserve.com
Internet: http://ourworld.compuserve.com/homepages.bretonbikes
Proprietors: Kate & Geoff Husband.
In business since 1990.
Holidays for around 200 annually.
Cycling holidays all over Brittany in France for individuals and groups up to 20 from May to September. Wide range of cycle-camping tours for 1998 to suit all abilities. Prices from £210 (one week) to £300 (two weeks). If hotel accommodation is required add £180 for B&B and evening meal or £100 for room only in small, family-run hotels. Detailed routes, full back-up and equipment provided. The range of quality bikes used are specifically designed for loaded cycle-touring. Choose from tourers, hybrids, recumbents (fast 'deck chairs') and tandems. Baby seats, trailer bikes and small mountain bikes available for all sizes of children.
Minimum age: 16 years unaccompanied.
Tandems are available for the visually challenged.
For a brochure phone 01579-350379 or write to : The Walled Garden, Metherell, Callington, Cornwall PL17 8BJ (tel 01579 350379).

CORPO VIVO, ACTIVIDADES RECREATIVAS
Rua do Pinhal, no 1, 7645 Vila Nova de Milfontes, Portugal (tel +351 83 997198; fax +351 83 997139); US agent: Experience Plus, 1925 Wallenburg Drive, Fort Collins, CO 80526, USA (tel 800 685-565).
Director: Ronald Sigmann.
Operating since 1992.
Holidays arranged for about 300 people annually.
Specialists in guided and self-guided off-road and road biking in Portugal and Spain. Off-road programmes in southern Portugal (Alentejo) and road rides cover almost the whole Iberian Peninsula including Mallorca. Operates all year round. Group sizes: off-road four to twelve; on-road six to 20. Price range: £595 for Trails of the Alentejo (eight nights) a centre based off-road programme; £1400 Galicia and The Minho (ten nights) luxury point to point programme. Bicycle rent included on on-road programme. Mountain bikes can be rented from Corpo Vivo.

CYCLISTS' TOURING CLUB
69 Meadrow, Godalming, Surrey GU7 3HS (tel 01483-417217; fax 01483-426994).
E-mail: cycling@ ctc.org.uk
Internet: http:www.ctc.org.uk
The CTC organises a number of cycle tours in Europe each year, covering Mediterranean islands, the undiscovered byways of Eastern Europe, the fjords and glaciers of Scandinavia or Europe's mountain ranges. Accommodation varies from camping, hostels, B&B to hotels. For all types of experience.
Further details can be obtained from the free CTC Tour Guide, with an s.a.e.

EUROPEAN BIKE EXPRESS
c/o Cyclists Touring Club, 69 Meadrow, Godalming, Surrey GU7 3HS (tel 01483-417217; fax 01483-426994).E-mail: cycling@ctc.org.uk
Internet: http://www.ctc.org.uk
Travel aboard the European Bike Express, a joint venture between the CTC and Bolero International Holidays. Designed to take the hassles out of getting to and from the start of your holiday with a bicycle. No more worrying about your bike ending up at a different train station to its rider, no need to brave busy roads around airports, or leave your bike to the mercy of baggage handlers. Your bike travels with you on the EBE and you can be picked up from 16 points around England.
The CTC provides recommended destinations and routes and suggests places for accommodation.

EXPLORE WORLDWIDE LTD
1 Frederick Street, Aldershot, Hants GU11 1LQ (tel 01252-344161).
Cycling in France's Loire Valley from Montrichard to the castle town of Saumur, visiting châteaux and vineyards en route. Hotel accommodation included. A support vehicle carries the luggage. 13 days from around £630.
Minimum age: 17 years.

FREEDOM HOLIDAYS
30 Brackenbury Road, Hammersmith, London W6 OBA (tel 0181-741 4471/4686; fax 0181-741 9332).
Moutain biking holidays on the Greek Island of Lefkas and in the French Alps

FREEWHEELING CYCLING
Alternative Travel Group, 69-71 Banbury Road, Oxford OX2 6PE (brochure tel 01865 315665; tel 01865 315678; fax 01865 310299).
Self-led, customised bicycle tours in Italy and France. Can be tailored to suit all budgets. Clients are met on arrival and all arrangements are dealt with by the staff in Italy and France. Luggage is transported ahead.

GRAHAM BAXTER SPORTING TOURS LTD
21 Manor Gardens, Pool-in-Wharfedale, Nr Otley, West Yorkshire LS21 1NB (tel 0113-2843617; fax 0113-2843588).
Directors: Mr G Baxter & Mr J Baxter.
In business since 1989.
Holidays for 2000 arranged annually.
Mountain biking and cycling holidays in France and Spain offered all year round. Price for one week half board: £350 including flights. Basic mountain biking skills required.
Ages: 16-80 years.

HEADWATER HOLIDAYS
146 London Road, Northwich, Cheshire CW9 5HH (tel 01606-48699).
Cycling holidays for independent travellers in France and Italy from April to October. Price for six nights half-board £329 including travel. All equipment included. Bags moved. No experience required.
Physically challenged people catered for.

THE IMAGINATIVE TRAVELLER
14 Barley Mow Passage, Chiswick, London W4 4PH (tel 0181-74323113; fax 0181-7423045).
Cycling holidays in France, Holland and Belgium, Italy, the Czech Republic, Switzerland, Spain, Greece and Turkey. Prices include hotel and guesthouse accommodation, some meals, luggage transfer and technical support.

INNTRAVEL
Hovingham, York YO6 4JZ (tel 01653-628862).
Cycling holidays in France (Dordogne, Loire, Lot, Provence and Tarn) and Switzerland. Price of around £449 includes daily cycle hire, transportation of luggage, inn accommodation and return ferry crossing.

JERSEY CYCLE TOURS
2 La Hougue Mauger, St. Mary, Jersey, Channel Islands JE3 3AF (tel 01534-482898; fax 01534-484060).
Partners: Daniel & Anne Wimberley.
In business since 1991.
Member of the National Trust, Societé Jersiaise, Cyclists Touring Club and Jersey Cycling Group.
Explore Jersey along traffic-free roads and country lanes. Guided rides include 'Treasures of the East' and 'Cider and Black Butter' — coast to coast through the heart of Jersey. Quality cycle hire with advice and delivery anywhere on the island.
Helmets for toddlers in child seats are available. Group holidays can be arranged.

MOSWIN TOURS
Moswin House, 21 Church Street, Oadby, Leicester LE2 5DB (tel 0116 271 9922; fax 0116 271 6016).
9-day, 11-day and 13-day self-led cycling tours in Bavaria on a network of safe cycle paths. The Dawes bicycles used can be equipped with child seats on request. Lightweight bicycles can be provided for the over eights. Representatives move the cyclists luggage to the next small hotel or family-run guest house on the route. Clients can book a package with flights to Germany or take the self-drive option arriving at an agreed meeting point in Germany.

PEAK INTERNATIONAL
15 Moor Park, Wendover, Aylesbury, Bucks. HP22 6AX (tel/fax 01296-624225).
Finland: self-guided tours from £195 for eight days or guided tours from £395.
Switzerland: four to six-day self guided tours with hotel based itineraries from £285.

PLUS TRAVEL (JET TOURS LTD)
9 Eccleston Street, London SW1W 9LX (tel 0171-259 0199; fax 0171-259 0190).
Cycling without luggage tours in Switzerland from May to October. Aare trail begins at Meiringen and following the river Aare as far as Koblenz where the Aare joins the Rhine. 300 km cycled over six days; three-day version also available. Three to five hours cycling per day. The other itinerary, the Jura trail, begins at Basel and ends at Lausanne. Luggage is transported between stops. Price from £450 includes hotel accommodation.

ROUGH TRACKS
6 Castle Street, Calne, Wilts. SN11 ODU or FREEPOST (SN2051), Calne, Wilts SN11 OSZ (tel 07000 560749).
Director: David Goodey.
In business since 1992.
Holidays for 500 annually.
Mountain biking adventures in the UK, France (Auvergne, Pyrenees, Normandy), Portugal and Turkey from April to October, Easter and Christmas/New Year. For individuals and groups of up to ten, beginners to experts. Professional, high-quality tours with a genuine personal touch. Example of price is about £398 for eight days in the Pyrenees including all food and wine, accommodation in gîte d'étape (adults' hostels) or hotels, travel, support vehicle and a guide who will also teach you techniques to help you enjoy your biking to the full. Mountain bikes and helmets can be hired. Clients should be reasonably fit or regular cyclists.
Regular introductory biking weekends throughout the UK.
'The ideal way to see unspoilt countryside in the company of like-minded people.'
Minimum age: 12 years (accompanied). Unaccompanied young people from 14 years.

SUSI MADRON'S CYCLING FOR SOFTIES
2 & 4 Birch Polygon, Rusholme, Manchester M14 5HX (tel 0161-248 8282; fax 0161-248 5140).
Directors: Susan Madron, Roy Madron.
In business since 1981.
Holidays for over 3000 arranged annually.

Cycling holidays in rural France for one or two weeks, May-September. Hotel accommodation pre-arranged on cycling circuits. Bicycles and equipment provided. Participants proceed at their own pace without group leaders. Price from approximately £650 per week; includes all travel and bed, breakfast and evening meal.
All ages.

TONY DOYLE PURSUITS
Victoria House, Victoria Street, Basingstoke, Hants RG21 7EQ (tel 01256-471616/471016; fax 01256-471018).
Managing Director: Austen Gravestock.
Director: Mike Gratton.
In business since 1992.
ATOL licence.
Holidays for 5,000 arranged annually.
Cycling holidays, training camps and race prepartion throughout Europe all year round. Club La Santa in Lanzarote hosts training camps by the famous cyclists Bjarne Riis and Mick Ives, offering seminars, lectures, coaching and racing. Prices from £280 (one week) to £1215 (two weeks) including flights, self-catering accommodation and full use of all facilities. Other destinations include Majorca, Spain, France, Switzerland and Munich. Also available is the opportunity to ride a stage of the Tour de France, from Pau to Loudonville. Prices: £389 (7 days, 2 star hotel, half board) or £589 (3 days, 3 star hotel, half board).

Americas

ADVENTURE CYCLING ASSOCIATION
PO Box 8308PP, Missoula, MT 59807, USA (tel +1 406-721 1776).
In operation since 1976.
Holidays provided for around 400 annually.
America's largest bicycle touring organisation.
Bicycle Touring and mountain bike adventures throughout the US, Alaska and Canada, from seven to 93 days from May to November, run by a non-profit organisation. For intermediate to advanced cyclists. Prices range from $500 to $2800. Bikes are not provided. Choose from the TransAmerica Tour, Yellowstone Loop, Great Parks North, Teton National Park Mountain Bike Tour or Denali Adventure. Maps are available for independent bicycle tourists with access to 20,000 miles of American backroads that make up the National Bicycle Route Network. Also free to members is the *Cyclists' Yellow Pages*, a comprehensive resource guide for bicyle touring.
Minimum age: 18 years.

CYCLISTS' TOURING CLUB
69 Meadrow, Godalming, Surrey GU7 3HS (tel 01483-417217; fax 01483-426994).
The CTC offer a number of tours in the USA and South America as well as Australia, New Zealand, Asia and Africa. Previous locations have included: Jamaica, Chile, Colorado, The Rockies, Nova Scotia and New England. Destinations vary from year to year. For current details write to the CTC for a free guide, enclosing a s.a.e.

PEAK INTERNATIONAL
15 Moor Park, Wendover, Aylesbury, Bucks. HP22 6AX (tel/fax 01296-624225).
Special tour of Andean Altiplano on the Chilean/Peruvian border. For experienced cyclists. Self contained expedition during November and December. Price: £1285 for three weeks or £1585 for four weeks, includes most meals, accommodation, guide, strategic support and internal flights but not international airfare.
Also 14-day cycle tours in Ecuador (£785); Chile (for experienced cyclists) two to three weeks (£1,585) with vehicle support.

Africa

CYCLEACTIVE
4 Bermondsey Mews, Otley, West Yorkshire, LS21 1SN (tel/fax 01943-462105).
Managing Director: C J Ford.
In business since 1996.
Holidays for 120 arranged annually.
Two-week long mountain biking holidays in Malawi, Zimbabwe and Lesotho all year round. Features of the Malawi tour include cycling through the plantations, mountains and plains of the Mulanje Massif, riding along the shores of Lake Malawi and viewing the elephants and big game of the Vwanza Marsh Reserve. The Zimbabwe tour begins in the capital, Harare, ends at Victoria Falls and visits the Nyandazi Hot Springs, Matobo Hills and Hwange National Park. Tours consist of groups of four to ten

people. No experience necessary, although a reasonable level of fitness is required. Prices from £1000-£1500 including accommodation (from hotels to luxury camping) and all meals. Bike hire is available but is not included in the holiday price.
Ages: 8-80 years (15 years unaccompanied).

Asia

HIGH PLACES
Globe Works, Penistone Road, Sheffield S6 3AE (tel 0114-2757500; fax 0114-2753870).
Journey through Kerala in southern India by bike, boat and foot. Price for 18 days between £1540 and £1670. Accommodation in hotels in town, forest lodge and rest houses elsewhere. Maximum group size of 12.
'An unhurried adventure for people of all abilities'.

TIKOTA TOURS
16 Main Street, Tingewick, Bucks. MK18 4BJ (tel/fax 01280-847209).
Proprietors: A B & T F Webb.
Arranging tours since 1992.
Twice-yearly cycling tours to various destinations in India (different place visited each time). Tours last two to four weeks, travelling 30-40 miles each day. Maximum group size of 20 people. Prices from £1000 including flight, accommodation in good hotels, some meals, bottled water and back up vehicle.
No minimum age if accompanied; 16 years if unaccompanied.

Australasia

PEAK INTERNATIONAL
15 Moor Park, Wendover, Aylesbury, Bucks. (tel/fax 01296- 624225).
Two mountain bike tours of the coast and beaches of New Zealand's North Island. Cycling through woodland on open tracks. Seven-day tour round the Coromandel Peninsular, £325 or nine-day tour around the more secluded East Cape, £385. Beach side camping with refreshing swims at any time of the day. Prices include bikes, meals, accommodation, all camping equipment, guide and vehicle support. Available throughout the year. Run to order for groups of three or more

Cotswold Cycling Company

Hiking and Rambling

The rediscovery of the skill of walking appears to spring from two main modern causes: the public's growing awareness of the importance of the countryside as an antidote to city life, and secondly of the advantages of keeping fit. Walking is one of the easiest and safest ways to improve health. As so many more people are walking — there are an estimated 800,000 hill walkers in the UK — it is important that walkers help to maintain the countryside. The Countryside Commission provides a good common sense guide: *Out in the Country*. For a free copy send a stamped, addressed envelope to the Countryside Commission, Postal Dept. PO Box 124, Walgrave, Northampton NN6 9TL; tel 01604-781848. The guide emphasises the need to guard against fire hazard, fasten all gates, keep to paths across farm land, avoid damaging fences, hedges, etc., leave no litter, and respect the plant and animal life of the countryside. The Countryside Commission postal department (see above). Other leaflets from the same address include one on showing all the National Trails and long distance routes. There are also separate leaflets for each National Trail. Similar leaflets are available for the National Parks of England and Wales.

National Trails and National Parks. Britain has over 135,000 miles of public footpaths and bridleways, in some of the most varied and beautiful landscape to be found in such a small area of the world. The Countryside Commission (John Dower House, Crescent Place, Cheltenham, Gloucester GL50 3RA tel 01242-521381) has played a leading part in promoting the most scenically outstanding long distance routes under the name of National Trails of which there are now ten. The most recent of these is the Thames Path opened on the 24th July 1996. Other routes likely to become National Trails are Hadrian's Wall and the Pennine Bridleway while the Cotswold Way is also under consideration to be upgraded to a National Trail. The Commission's mammouth project currently in progress is to ensure that all 120,000 miles of public rights of way are fully open, waymarked and legally defined by the year 2000. The latest report on the project was published in October 1996.

The Ramblers Association, 1-5 Wandsworth Road, London SW8 2XX (tel 0171-582 6878), plays a prominent part in the campaign to protect places of natural beauty and preserve public rights of way. An ordinary individual annual membership costs £17 and reduced membership for the unwaged, students, pensioners and disabled people is £8.50. Joint membership is £21 with a reduced rate of £10.50 for the same categories as above. Members receive a copy of *The Ramblers Association Yearbook and Accommodation Guide* and quarterly issues of the Association's magazine *Rambling Today*.

Clothing and Equipment. Even for guided hikes when the route is known and planned, it is important to be suitably and comfortably equipped. Walkers should have a wind and waterproof jacket or anorak, loose fitting trousers and depending on the terrain, a pair of good quality, well broken-in boots, a size larger than normal shoe size to be worn over two pairs of woollen socks. On dry, lowland areas boots are not usually essential and training shoes may be adequate. A reasonable pair of walking boots will cost at least £35 and should have one-piece leather uppers, a waterproof outside tongue and thick moulded rubber soles with a deep tread of the 'Vibram' type which will give up to 1000 miles of service before resoling becomes necessary. Also popular are the composite type walking boots which resemble trainers but which have a waterproof lining and a walking boot sole. Prices start at around £80. Continental walkers have been using aluminium walking poles to unload some of the pounding and stress inflicted on the hips, knees and ankles of serious walkers. These body saving poles are now available in the UK from shops specialising in mountaineering equipment and cost from about £40 a pair. They are telescopic and easily stowed. A compass, torch, whistle, spare woollens, waterproof cape, bivouac bag and high calorie provisions are advisable for mountain hiking. It is a good idea to carry a first aid kit containing elastoplast, gauze, a selection of bandages, antiseptic, antihistamine cream and aspirins. If you are hiking in the midge or mosquito season, don't forget insect repellent.

Rucksacks and Pack Frames. Whether you are carrying a small day pack, a weekend sack or an internal frame rucksack weighing 30 kg or more, the weight needs to be carried high on the back with the heaviest objects at the top close to the body. Many leading manufacturers have recognised that women need a different design of rucksack to fit comfortably on a shorter back, wider hips and a more pronounced bottom. Problems such as straps that get twisted or are too widely spaced make all the difference to your hiking comfort. A well-padded hip belt is highly recommended for carrying heavy loads.

Maps and Publications. Detailed maps such as the Ordnance Survey/Jarrold *Pathfinder Guides* (1:25,000 scale) show selected walking routes and all rights of way and are essential when hiking. The *Pathfinder* series includes the *Brecon Beacons, Isle of Wight, Chiltern and Thames Valley* and *Perthshire.* Aurum and Ordnance Survey co-publish the *National Trail Guides* of which two of the most popular are *The Ridgeway* and *Offa's Dyke Path South*. The map on page 74 shows both the National Trails and National Parks of England and Wales. An additional long distance route, Glyndwr's Way, a circular route in the Welsh mountains is under consideration for upgrading.

The Countryside Commission also publishes a free, quarterly magazine *Countryside* as well as other useful publications, a catalogue of which can be obtained from their Northampton (see above) address.

Scotland. Scottish Natural Heritage advises on the National Scenic Areas of Scotland. The head office is in Edinburgh (12 Hope Terrace, EH9 2AS; tel 0131-447 4784) and there are also regional offices of the SNH throughout Scotland. Scottish National Heritage can supply basic information leaflets on the long distance paths. For more detailed information on the long distance paths of Scotland contact the Regional Scottish Tourist boards whose numbers can be obtained from the main Scottish Board in Edinburgh (0131-332 2433). The tourist boards should also be able to provide information on accommodation along the routes. Other information about long distance paths can be obtained as follows: for the West Highland Way contact the Rangers Service of Loch Lomond Park (01389 758216); for the Speyside Way contact Murray District Council (01343-543451) and for the Southern Upland Way contact Dumfries and Galloway or Borders Regional Councils (01387-261234).

In 1996 Heather Connon and Paul Roper devised an alternative route to the West Highland Way and the result was The Highland Way which goes from Loch Lomond, north to Fort William (about 105 miles). Their aim in devising the route was to stay as high as possible for as long as possible. *The Highland Way* is published by Mainstream Publishing and costs £9.99.

Wales. The Countryside Council for Wales (Plas Penrhos, Ffordd Penrhos, Bangor, Gwynedd LL57 2LQ tel 01248-370444) is the Government's statutory advisor on wildlife, countryside and maritime conservation matters in Wales. It is the executive authority for the conservation of habitats and wildlife. Through partners it promotes the protection of landscape, opportunities for enjoyment and the support of those who live and work in, and manage the countryside. It enables partners, including local authorities, voluntary organisations and interested individuals to pursue countryside management projects through grant aid. The Countryside Council is accountable to the Secretary of State for Wales who appoints it and provides its annual grant.

Members of the public can contact the Countryside Council for free leaflets including *Offa's Dyke Path* and *Out in the Country.* Another publication free on request is *Managing Public Access* produced jointly with Farmers' Union of Wales.

Orienteering. The sport of orienteering was introduced into Britain during the 1960's. Orienteering is a running sport where competitors navigate their way at their own pace between features marked on a specially drawn, coloured map. Courses vary in length from 2km for the inexperienced, to 16km for the experienced or adult orienteer. Orienteering takes place on a wide range of outdoor sites from town parks to countryside, forest, woodlands and moorlands. Top class competitors require stamina, and there is the unique challenge of using their map reading skills whilst running at speed on the longer courses. The sport originated in Sweden in 1918, and World Championship events are held there in alternate years. Orienteerers' ages range from about ten years to over 70. Details of local clubs, award and training schemes and a list of publications may be obtained from the British Orienteering Federation, Riversdale, Dale Road North, Darley Dale, Matlock, Derbyshire DE4 2HX (tel 01629-734042). The national magazine is *Compass Sport, The Orienteer* published six times a year at £17.50 (£16.50 for BOF members) and available from the subscription department (25 The Hermitage, Eliot Hill, London SE13 7EH; tel 0181-852 1457).

Hiking Abroad. Travelling on foot is arguably the most rewarding way to see a foreign country. A reasonable level of fitness is often the one requirement for joining a group of travellers in the Alps, the Himalaya or the Andes. It is said that there are tracks in the Annapurna and the Mont Blanc massifs which are as crowded as Oxford Street on the last Saturday before Christmas. But there are also magnificently remote areas throughout the world for the adventurous hiker. Some of the more recent and exciting possibilities for hikers to explore include South America with Colombia and Argentina the current leading destinations. Russia too, is opening up wilderness areas like those of of Kamchatka. The Karakoram Mountains which straddle the Sino-Pakistan border have not been a great success for hikers because of the political situation in the area. Kashmir which is beset by disputes between Kashmir and Pakistan over who owns it, has become notorious for the kidnapping of tourists. Among the hostages taken during several years at least two have been killed. Kashmir is on the whole best avoided for the time being. Because of the relaxation of tourist restrictions in China, a few tour organisers have obtained permission to escort parties of walkers into these hitherto inaccessible regions. Other up and coming destinations nearer home include the Picos de Europa in northern Spain and remote northern Portugal.

Worldwide

ABOVE THE CLOUDS TREKKING INC
P O Box 398, Worcester, MA 01602-0398, United States of America (tel +1 508 799-4499; fax +1 508 797-4779).
President and Director: Steve Conlon.
In business since 1982.
Holidays arranged for about 500 annually.
Hiking holidays in remote, off-the-beaten-path places in Asia (Nepal, Bhutan, Ladakh), the Americas (Patagonia, Argentina and Costa Rica), Europe (Britain, Ireland, Italy, Norway, France), and Madagascar. Trips last one to four weeks all year. Prices from US$650-6,750 or US$130 per day including most meals (varies according to destination).

ARC JOURNEYS
102 Stanley Road, Cambridge CB5 8ZB (tel 01223-779200; fax 01223-779090).
Sole Trader: David Halford.
In business since 1992.
Holidays for 40-50 arranged annually.

Treks of all grades (from strolls to climbs) in many destinations worldwide including the Himalayas, Southeast Asia, Australasia and the Americas. Prices from £500 per week including twin rooms with en suite facilities and breakfast. Flights not included.
Also available: cycling tours in Australia, Bali, Thailand, India and Ecuador. Horse and camel safaris in India. Dog sledding in Canada.

England

ACORN ACTIVITIES
P O Box 120, Hereford HR4 8YB (tel 01432-830083; fax 01432-830110.
Self-guided and guided walking holidays in Herefordshire, Shropshire and Wales all year round. Walking Offa's Dyke, walking Wye Valley and walking the Pembrokeshire Coastal Path with luggage transported ahead. Three nights £160. A week's walking based at hotels £350.

ADVENTURELINE
North Trefula, Redruth, Cornwall TR16 5ET (tel/fax 01209-820847). E-mail: adventureline@virgin.net
Internet: http://www.chycor.co.uk/adventureline
US agent: Above the Clouds Trekking, Worcester, Massachusetts. Free phone: 800 233 4499.
Partners: Martin & Elizabeth Hunt.
In business since 1988.
Holidays for 200 arranged annually.
Guided exploration and walking holidays on the north and south tips of Cornwall, concentrating on the Cornwall coastal path, the moors and wooded estuaries. From late March to November. Singles, couples and groups of up to eight. Special attention is paid to the geology, ancient history and flora and fauna of the area. Typical price for a week with full board (picnic lunches) and accommodation is about £420. Prices also include transport by Adventureline's own personnel carrier to various locations in Cornwall.
Minimum age 8 years (accompanied); 11 years (unaccompanied). Maximum age: 78.

COLD KELD GUIDED WALKING HOLIDAYS
Fell End, Ravenstonedale, Cumbria CA17 4LN (tel/fax 015396-23273).
Proprietors: Ken & Kathy Trimmer.
In business since 1988.
Holidays for 120-140 annually.
A relaxing holiday of guided walks to suit the abilities of guests, all year round in Cumbria. Prices: £175 (five days), £245 (one week), £35 (weekend, no guided walks). Discounts for groups of eight to 15 people. En suite accommodation in a 300-year-old farmhouse, with some meals dining out in local restaurants, with mini bus service.
Age range: 18 to approximately 80 years.
Visually challenged people welcome.

COMPASS HOLIDAYS
48 Shurdington Road, Cheltenham, Glos GL53 OJE (tel 01242-250642; fax 01242-529730; in the US tel 800 4661713). E-mail: compass.holidays@bigfoot.com
Walking holidays in the Cotswolds arranged all year round from £40 per day including accommodation and breakfast. Cycling holidays also arranged.

COUNTRYWIDE HOLIDAYS
Grove House, Wilmslow Road, Didsbury, Manchester M20 1LH (tel 0161-448 7112; fax 0161 448 7113).
Company Chief Executive C Doyle.
In business since 1893.
Member of several regional Tourist Boards.
Holidays for 20,000 arranged annually.
Comprehensive selection of escorted and independent walking holidays in Britain. Accommodation in comfortable country guest houses. Prices from £210 per person per week, full board (all year).

DRYSTONE WALKING HOLIDAYS
1A Town Head Avenue, Settle, North Yorkshire BD24 9RQ (tel/fax 01729-825626).
In business since 1993.
Member of BTA and YHTB.
Holidays for 100+ annually.
Walking holidays in the unspoilt countryside of the Yorkshire Dales, all year round. Prices from £209-359 including en suite half-board or full board accommodation in local guesthouses, inns and country houses. Luggage transported.
Minimum age: 12 years (accompanied).

ENGLISH WANDERER
6 George Street, Ferryhill, Co. Durham DL17 0DT (tel 01740-653169; fax 01740-657996).
Directors: T Harrison, I Robertson and P Scriver.
In business since 1979.

Holidays for 1,500 arranged annually.
Walking holidays in Great Britain all year round including special New Year tours. Also in Ireland. Weekends and short breaks from £96. Otherwise prices from £180-£1400 including accommodation, all meals, guide and transport.
Minimum age: 18.

FIELD STUDIES COUNCIL
Head Office, Preston Montford, Montford Bridge, Shrewsbury SY4 1HW (tel 01743-850674; fax 01743-850178).
Rambling the FSC Way — enjoyable breaks which include learning about the countryside as well as walking. Led by experienced naturalists they are based at the FSC's seven centres in England: in the Lake District, Yorkshire Dales, Shropshire and the Welsh borders, Exmoor and south Devon, Constable Country and the North Downs. The choice includes: Rambling through the Dales at Malham Tarn in July and Exploring Offa's Dyke at Preston Montford in August. Prices from about £255 a week, £100 for a weekend inclusive of accommodation, all meals, tuition and transport.
Minimum age: 16 years, except on courses arranged for families.

GINA & VAL'S HOLIDAYS
10 Laurel Gardens, Aldershot, Hants GU11 3TQ (tel 01252-342789).
Proprietor: Gina Dando.
Formerly Bob Sloan's Holidays (in business since 1984).
Walking holidays in the UK including South West Way, Arran, Cleveland Way, Coast to Coast, Southern Ireland, Southern Upland's Way and Christmas 'Getaways'. Walkers are taken to the start of the walk, met during the day, and returned each evening to accommodation which is usually Youth Hostels (membership necessary). Walk at your own pace. Prices £180-£240 for seven to nine days, including hostel accommodation, transport and all meals.

GREENHOLME HOLIDAYS AND TOURS
Bewcastle, Carlisle, Cumbria (tel/fax 016977-48630).
Partners: G Price, R Price.
In business since 1989.
Member of Cumbria Tourist Guides, Association of Group Tour Operators.
Guided walking tours in the Yorkshire Dales, Lake District and The Borders from May to September. Individuals and groups of up to 12. Trail Breaks last five to eight nights and cost from £430. Flexi-breaks for groups of four or more three to six nights from £240 to £445. Prices include full board and accommodation. Eight to 14 miles per day. Choice of fixed base daily walks or long distance trails with two and three star accommodation and daily luggage transport. Tailor-made holidays can be arranged for groups of four or more.
Minimum age: 16 (unaccompanied).

GREENSCAPE (UK)
Milkaway Lane, Croyde, North Devon EX33 1NG (tel 01271-890677).
E-mail: walkbrit@greenscape.co.uk
Internet: http://www.greenscape.co.uk
Managing Director: Andrew Bull.
In business since 1985.
Guided walking holidays for about 400 arranged annually.
'Inn-to-inn' tours in the Cotswolds, Devon, Lake District, Exmoor, Dorset and Yorkshire Dales (also Highlands of Scotland and Wales), from May to September. Price of £750-£800 per week includes accommodation in three-star hotels.
No experience necessary.
Minimum age: 12 years (16 if unaccompanied).

HF HOLIDAYS LTD
Imperial House, Edgware Road, London NW9 5AL (tel 0181-905 9556).
Walking along long distance footpaths and in areas of scenic beauty throughout Britain. Holidays available all year round. Food and accommodation are provided in HF's own Country House and hotels in the Lake District, the West Country, the Isle of Wight, the Cotswolds, Northumberland, Yorkshire, Scotland and Wales. Many grades of walks are arranged, from the leisurely to the strenuous, walking five to 17 miles and ascending 300-4500 ft per day). Walk with competent and informal leadership, stopping at places of interest.
Prices: seven nights full board, from £280 with en suite rooms available for a supplement. No extra charge for single rooms. Special Interest holidays are often available for non-walkers accompanying walking friends on holiday. Call for a *Walking Holidays in Britain* brochure.
Reduced rate rail travel available.

INSTEP LINEAR WALKING HOLIDAYS
35 Cokeham Road, Sompting, Lancing, West Sussex BN15 OAE (tel/fax 01903-766475). E-mail: Walking@Instep.Demon.co.uk
Proprietors: A & M Hartley.
In business since 1987.
Member of the South East Tourist Board.
Instep specialises in self-guided walks, at any time of year from a few days to 14 days or longer if required. Walks include Coast to Coast, Offa's Dyke and the South Downs Way. Prices from £253 per person for five nights including accommodation, free guide book and personalised itinerary. There is also a separate luggage carrying service (White Knight) on the Coast to Coast, door to door for those who wish to plan their own accommodation. There is also a passenger link from Robin Hood's Bay back to the car or station.

MOUNTAIN GOAT HOLIDAYS
Victoria Street, Windermere, Cumbria LA23 1AD (tel 015394-45161).
In business since 1972.
Member of Cumbria Tourist Board.
Provides walking holidays and walking breaks based at Windermere or Keswick with accommodation and transport to and from the start of walks. Walks are led by experienced guides/leaders from the National Park Ranger Service recognised walking holiday companies. Day, short breaks (two to five nights) and week-long holidays. Prices from £85 (two nights including bed and breakfast), £299 (five nights including accommodation breakfast and dinner and £395 (seven nights).
Also off-the-beaten-track minicoach touring to places not accessible by large vehicles. Most trips are of educational interest following a planned itinerary.
All ages.

OUTWARD BOUND TRUST
Watermillock, Cumbria CA11 0JL (tel 0990-134227).
Trans-lakeland journeys for 16-24 year olds and 25 + . For more information phone for a free brochure.

PATHWAYS: Mountain Journeys
Coal Ash, Grisebeck, Kirkby-in-Furness, Cumbria LA17 7XU (tel 01229-889400; fax 01229-889400).
Six-day hikes and scrambles in the Lake District and Snowdonia (April to October). Routes include Scafell Pike (England's highest peak), and Snowdon (Wales's highest peak). Prices from £445 include six days' guided walking, six nights' half board accommodation in inns and guest houses (shared twin/double rooms), packed lunches, information pack, and baggage transfer to the next accommodation each day.

PEDALS & BOOTS
Cobblestones, Causeway End, Nr Haverthwaite, Ulverstone, Cumbria LA12 8JW (tel 015395-31391).
Self-guided walking holidays in the South Lakeland region of the Lake District. Tours last three to seven days; available all year round. Baggage transfers and pre-booked bed and breakfast accommodation included in the price. Individuals and groups of up to six catered for. Price for one week Multi Centre Holiday: £240.
Minimum age: 14 years (16 unaccompanied).

RAMBLERS HOLIDAYS
Box 43, Welwyn Garden City, Herts. AL8 6PQ (tel 01707-331133).
One-week walking holidays ranging from gentle rambling to more strenuous hill and mountain walking in the Lake District. Prices from around £195 include accommodation and the services of a Rambler leader.

ROCK LEA ACTIVITY CENTRE
Station Road, Hathersage, Hope Valley S32 1DD (tel 01433-650345).
Adventure Activity Licence.
Led-walks with friendly, experienced guides over moorland, craggy ridges, high wilderness peaks and green dales. Explore a wide variety of scenery on weekend, four-day or week-long walking breaks. Choose hard or less-strenuous walks to suit your ability and mood. Full minibus support to make the most of the varied landscape. Weekends from £65. Weeks from £180. Individuals, small parties and clubs, etc. catered for. 'Homely atmosphere'.

STEP BY STEP
(Inc. Wight Walking Holidays), The Hambledon Hotel, Queens Road, Isle of Wight PO37 6AW (tel 01983-862403/863651).
Proprietor: N Birch.
In business since 1986.
Holidays for 800 arranged annually.
Guided walks in Spring and Autumn. Rambling on the Isle of Wight with over 8000

The National Parks and National Trails of England and Wales

National Park, The Broads and the New Forest
National Trail - existing
National Trail - approved but not yet open

Northumberland
Hadrian's Wall Path
Cleveland Way
North York Moors
Lake District
Yorkshire Dales
Wolds Way
Pennine Bridleway
Pennine Way
Peak District
Snowdonia
Offa's Dyke Path
Peddars Way & Norfolk Coast Path
The Broads
Pembrokeshire Coast Path
Pembrokeshire Coast
Brecon Beacons
Thames Path
Ridgeway
Thames Path
Ridgeway
North Downs Way
Exmoor
New Forest
South Downs Way
South West Coast Path
Dartmoor
South West Coast Path
0 50km

miles of walking experience, in groups of up to 16 people. Prices range from £70 for two nights to £98 for three nights accommodation and include two full days walking.
We also specialise in unescorted walking holidays throughout the island, stopping at specially selected hotels, with full information on the best walks freely available. Contact Norman Birch for full details and a walking brochure.

WHEELY WONDERFUL WALKING
Petchfield Farm, Elton, Nr Ludlow SY8 2HJ (tel 01568-77055).
The Mortimer Trail is a new, waymarked walk linking historic Ludlow with Offa's Dyke. Plenty of castles and spectacular views. Accommodation in farmhouses, an historic hunting lodge and a riverside inn. Circular short break walking tours or walk the whole Mortimer Trail in one three day short break. New for 1998, walking tours along Offa's Dyke. Luggage transported. For individuals and groups of up to ten. Prices from £89.

WINETRAILS
Greenways, Vann Lake, Ockley, Dorking RH5 5NT (tel 01306-712111; fax 01306 713504).
Wine and walking weekends in September and October in the Wye Valley and in Surrey including a visit to the private wine estate of Denbies. Prices: Wye Valley £239; Surrey £249. Early booking essential.

YHA NORTHERN REGION
P O Box 11, Matlock, Derbyshire DE4 2XA (tel 01629-825850).
Guided walking holidays in the England and Wales. Coast-to-coast, White Peak Way, Herriot Way, Pembrokeshire Coast, South Downs Way and Cumbria Way. Centre-based walking weekends in the Peak District. Qualified, experienced guides with luggage transported by minibus.
Minimum age: 16 years.

Scotland

AVALON TREKKING SCOTLAND
Bowerswell Lane, Kinnoull, Perth PH2 7DL (24-hour tel/fax 01738-624194).
Proprietor: Mr T S Sandford.
In business since 1988.
Member of Perthshire Tourist Board and Scottish Activity Holidays Association.
Holidays for 200 annually.
Guided walking holidays in Scotland and Northern England for individuals and groups from April to November. A wide range of graded walks and programmes for experienced walkers covering up to 15 miles a day or shorter walks with climbs, to gentle-paced walking with limited ascent covering six to nine miles a day. Prices from £380 to £815 including guest house and hotel accommodation, all meals, guide and luggage transportation where necessary.
Minimum age: 18 years (unaccompanied).

CALEDONIAN DISCOVERY
The Slipway, Corpach, Fort William PH33 7NN; tel 01397 772167; fax 01397-772765).
Rambling weeks based aboard a large (126 ft) Belgian barge cruising the Great Glen with its canal section linking the spectacular highland lochs including Loch Ness and Loch Lochy. Clients can also just relax on the barge and enjoy the scenery of the Caledonian canal. In summer and winter the barge offers comfortable accommodation for walkers and skiers and well as for winter mountaineering courses. £290-£350 for six days. Price includes full board and accommodation in comfortable double cabins. Central heating, hot showers, spacious saloon. Individuals and groups catered for and all levels from beginnner to expert. No age limits.

C-N-DO SCOTLAND
77 John Player Building, Springbank Road, Stirling FK7 7RP (tel + fax 01786-445703). E-mail: cndo.scotland@BTinternet.com
Directors: Margaret Porter, Dorothy Breckenridge.
Established 1984.
Member of STB, SAHA, AMI and BAEML. Adventure Activity Licence.
Holidays for 1500 arranged each year.
Walking holidays throughout Scotland for individuals, families or groups (maximum ten people). Mountain walking holidays, vehicle-supported rambling tours for novice or experienced walkers, winter walking weeks, wilderness backpacking treks, climbing, abseiling, navigation and technical courses. Some equipment is available for hire. Own boots essential. 'Savour Scotland's hidden beauty under the guidance of experienced Scottish walking leaders'.
Minimum age: Varies with activity.
Physically challenged people can be catered for.

CRAIGOWER LODGE OUTDOOR CENTRE

Outdoor Centre, Golf Course Road, Newtonmore, Inverness-shire PH20 1AT (tel 01540-6733190.

Low-level rambles, hill walking, scrambling, introduction to mountain safety, navigation, orienteering and overnight expeditions in the Cairngorms and Central Highlands. Prices from £210 for six days includes accommodation, meals, activities, instruction, use of equipment. Weekend packages also available. Discounts for groups of ten or more.
Minimum age: eight years.

GLENCOE OUTDOOR CENTRE

Glencoe, Argyll PA39 4HS (tel 01855-811350).

Hillwalking courses in the Glencoe and Ben Nevis area for walkers of all standards and experience. Qualified instruction. Price from £70 for a weekend, including full board and accommodation. Hillwalking also available as part of a multi activity course.
Minimum age: ten years accompanied, 12 years unaccompanied.

GREENHOLME HOLIDAYS AND TOURS

Bewcastle, Carlisle, Cumbria (tel/fax 016997-48630).

Guided walking tours from fixed bases in the Scottish Highlands and trail walks such as the West Highland Way from Glasgow to Fort William. May to September. Three days or more for the stay-put holidays and up to nine nights for the trail walks. Prices for example from £480 for six nights in the Trossachs and £780 for the West Highland Way include quality accommodation, full board and baggage transport. Tailor-made tours for a minimum of three guests.

HF HOLIDAYS LTD

Imperial House, Edgware Road, London NW9 5AL (tel 0181-905 9556).

Walking excursions based at three country houses in Scotland — Isle of Arran, Loch Leven and Pitlochry. Holidays available March-October and at Christmas and New Year. Meals and accommodation provided in HF Country House and hotels. Itineraries include Glencoe and peaks, as well as gentler routes for the less experienced. Walking under competent and informal leadership. Prices from £279 for seven nights full board; reduced rate rail travel available. Reductions for children under 18 years old sharing a room with parents. Call for a Walking in Britain holiday brochure.
All ages.

HIGHLAND ACTIVITY HOLIDAYS

Norheim, Church Street, Dufftown, Glenfiddich AB55 4AF (tel + fax 01340-820892).

Proprietor: Geoffrey Armitage.
In business since 1985.
Member of Grampian Highlands Tourist Board, Scottish Activity Holidays Association.
Holidays for approximately 200 arranged annually.
Hillwalking holidays in the Grampian foothills during summer. Individuals and groups of up to 15. Prices of £210-£325 (guest house),or £430 (en suite hotel) per week. A reasonable standard of physical fitness required.
Minimum age: eight years (accompanied) or 18 years (unaccompanied).

MOUNTAIN CRAFT

Professional Mountaineering Services, Glenfinnan, Fort William, Scotland PH37 4LT (tel 01397-722213 24 hrs; fax 01397-722300).

E-mail: mail@mountaincraft.co.uk
Director: N Gregory MIC.
Member of AMI, BMC and SSC approved courses.
Walking and climbing in the Ben Nevis and Glencoe regions as well as Skye. Variety of accommodation. Private instruction and guiding possible.
Minimum age: 16 years.

NORTH WEST FRONTIERS

18A Braes, Ullapool, Ross-Shire IV26 2SZ (tel/ fax 01854-612628). E-mail: 101717.451@compuserve.com http://ourworld.compuserve.com/homepages/NWF

Proprietor: Andrew Bluefield.
In business since 1985.
Member of Scottish Tourist Board.
Holidays provided for 150+ annually.
Walking and trekking in the North West Scottish Highlands and Ireland. Bases: Ullapool, Gairloch, Skye, Harris, Lochcarron, Cape Wrath and more. Available May to October for weekly treks. Groups of up to ten people catered for. Prices £295-£495 for B&B or hotel accommodation, guide and transport. Personal walking gear not provided but waterproofs can be hired. Normal fitness and some hill walking experience

needed depending on trek grade. Walks vary from moderate to strenuous.
Minimum age: 14 years (accompanied), 18 years (unaccompanied).

OUTWARD BOUND TRUST
Watermillock, Cumbria, CA11 OJL (tel 0990-134227).
Outward Bound expedition programmes including a Mountain Journey, Skye Trek and Highland Rover. For more information phone for a free brochure.

PILGRIM ADVENTURE
120 Bromley Heath Road, Downend, Bristol (tel 0117-9573997).
Proprietors: David Gleed, Maguerita Carrington.
Member of the National Assoc of Christian Communities and Networks, and the National Association for Outdoor Education.
Christian based Pilgrim journeys for people of all ages mainly in Britain, Spain and Ireland. Pilgrims share the challenge and excitment of travelling through primitive landscapes to places that are often well off the beaten track and usually have a story to tell.

Destinations include the islands of Fetlar (Shetland), Inishbofin (Co Galway), Skellig (Co Kerry) and Iona. Pilgrim journeys vary from five to 21 days. Prices from £50 including full board, campsite/hostel/guest-house accommodation.

Average of six to eight miles hill or mountain walking most days.

RUA REIDH LIGHTHOUSE HOLIDAYS
Rua Reidh Lighthouse, Melvaig, Gairloch IV21 2EA (tel 01445-771263).
Partners: Fran Cree and Chris Barrett.
In business since 1989.
Members of Highlands of Scotland Tourist Board, Scottish Activity Holiday Association, Highland Hostels and Independent Backpackers Hostels Scotland.
Guided and self-guided walking holidays in the North-West Highlands and Western Isles of Scotland. Various programmes offered to suit all tastes and levels of fitness. Holidays based at the Rua Reidh Lighthouse. Prices from £150 (three nights) and £320 (seven nights) all inclusive. Pick up is from Inverness airport or rail station.

SCOT-TREK
9 Lawrence Street, Glasgow G11 5HH (tel/fax 0141-334 9232).
Proprietor: Fred Chatterton.
In business since 1994.
Member of Greater Glasgow Tourist Board.
Hill-walking and long distance trekking in the Scottish Highlands all year from one day, weekends or longer. Prices from £150-£300 per week with B&B and hostel accommodation. General fitness required. A series of six-day West Highland Way Charity Walks held throughout the year as are a series of historical walks e.g. the 'Braveheart', 'Robert the Bruce' and 'Rob Roy' treks.
Minimum age: ten years (no maximum).
Unaccompanied young people accepted from 14 years.
Physically, visually and mentally challenged people welcome.

Wales

BLACK DRAGON OUTDOOR EXPERIENCES
7 Ethelbert Drive, Charlton, Andover Hampshire SP10 4EP (tel 01264-357313).
Mountain walking, navigation, mountain safety and scrambling, in the Black Mountains of the Brecon Beacons and Snowdonia National Parks. Summer in the Austrian Alps and winter in the Scottish Highlands. Individuals and groups catered for. Experienced and qualified leaders. Prices from £140. Wide range of accommodation and catering options. No experience required. Courses can also be organised in other areas.

DINEFWR TREKS
Caban Cwmffynnon, Cefn Gorwydd, Llangammarch Well, Powys, LD4 4DW (tel 01591-610638 24 hours).
Owner: E Bryan Jones.
In business since 1991.
Member of Welsh Tourist Board.
Holidays arranged for around 100 annually.
Guided walking and birdwatching holidays in Mid/West Wales all year round. Guided and independent walks through Twm Sion Catti country, around the mystic Lady of the Lake area and the Kingdoms of the Welsh Princes. Prices from £300 per week. Accommodation is full board in peaceful guest houses, set in rural locations. Maximum group size of ten.

Also, a converted century-old stone barn provides an ideal base for group field study trips, Youth Training Projects or Management Courses. Easy access to the Brecon Beacons and Elenydd Range of hills, activities include hill-walking pony-trekking, mountain biking, expedition training, canoeing, painting and fishing. Accommodation is in two dormitories sleeping eight and twelve, with full kitchen facilities, barbecue area and drying room.
No mimimum age, (unaccompanied young people accepted from 16 years).

FIELD STUDIES COUNCIL
Head Office, Montford Bridge, Shrewsbury SY4 1HW (tel 01743-850674; fax 01743-850178).
Rambling the FSC Way — enjoyable breaks which include learning about the countryside as well as walking. Led by experienced naturalists they are based at the FSC's three centres in Wales in Pembrokeshire and Snowdonia. The choice includes Exploring the Pembrokeshire Coast at Orielton and Tearoom Trails at Dale Fort in August. Prices from about £255 for a week, £100 for a weekend inclusive of accommodation, all meals, tuition and transport.
Minimum age: 16 years, except on courses arranged for families.

FOCUS HOLIDAYS AT 'ARGOED'
Argoed Guest House, Crafnant Road, Trefriw, County of Conwy LL27 0TX (tel 01492-640091).
Proprietors: P Booth and K A Booth.
In business since 1987.
Member of Wales Tourist Board.
Mountain walking in the high peaks of Snowdonia. Weekends and weeks from March to October. Prices range from £70 for a weekend to £220 for a week including accommodation and all meals.
Unaccompanied children not accepted.

HEAD FOR THE HILLS
Garth, Builth, Powys LD4 4AT (tel 01591 620388).
Sole Proprietor: Laurence Golding.
In business since 1976.
Holidays for about 100 people arranged annually.
A programme of walking journeys through exceptional landscapes of the U.K. Trips vary in length and cost £36 per day. Two staff travel ahead with the luggage and erect a camp in a beautiful and wild spot. They prepare the cuisine (vegetarian) while the rest of the party are guided along a fully researched route. Groups number up to 12 (mostly adults). Walk at a relaxed pace, 8-14 miles a day. Personal tents and all equipment provided. Participants provide their own sleeping bags.

HIGH TREK SNOWDONIA
Tal y Waen, Deiniolen, Caernarfon, Gwynedd LL55 3NA (tel 01286-871232).
E-mail: high.trek@virgin.net
Partners: A Whitehead, I Whitehead.
In business since 1986.
Association of Mountaineering Instructors.
WTB accredited.
Holidays for 200 arranged annually.
Walking, scrambling and hillcraft holidays in North Wales from January to October. Three, four, five and seven night holidays. Prices: £189 (three nights) and £355 (seven nights) include full board accommodation and the services of an experienced and qualified guide. Individuals and groups of up to six. Treks include Castle-to-Castle, TransSnowdonia, Bank Holiday specials and navigation, scrambling and climbing courses. Some breaks are designed for experienced mountain walkers, others for anyone with a reasonable level of fitness. Also self-guided holidays, price: £355 for seven nights in pre-arranged hotels/guest houses, luggage transportation, consultations with walking expert, timetables and maps etc.
Minimum age: 18 years (unaccompanied).

HILLSCAPE
Blaen-y-Ddol, Pontrhydygroes, Ystrad Meurig, Dyfed SY25 6DS (tel 01974-282640).
Partners: Richard & Anne Wilson.
In business since 1984.
Holidays for 150 arranged annually.
Self-guided walking holidays for individuals and groups of up to eight, in mid-Wales from March to October. O.S. Maps and regularly updated directions for 40 walks of eight to 20 miles possible. Walks vary from coast paths to mountains and open moorland. Experience not essential but guests should be reasonably fit. Holidays cost £186 for six nights including guesthouse accommodation and full board including a packed lunch.
Minimum age: 11 years (accompanied). Unaccompanied: 16 years.
'Self-guided walks for those to whom large organised groups do not appeal and who prefer to explore at their own pace'.

KEVIN WALKER MOUNTAIN ACTIVITIES
74 Beacons Park, Brecon, Powys LD3 9BQ (tel/fax 01874-625111).
Proprietor: Kevin Walker.
In business since 1978.
Recognised by MLTB.
Holidays arranged for 500 annually.
Based in Crickhowell in the Brecon Beacons National Park and Betws Y Coed in Snowdonia offering a variety of mountain activities. One, two and five-day courses available: Hillwalking & Mountaincraft, Practical Mountain Navigation, Hillwalkers' Confidence Course, Scrambling etc. A wide range of accommodation is available locally. Prices from £50. No experience necessary. Individuals can have private guiding/personal tuition. Minimum age: 18 years.
Also professional teambuilding services to commerce and industry and leadership and teamwork training organisations, and MLTB courses.

OUTWARD BOUND TRUST
Watermillock, Cumbria, CA11 OJL (tel 0990-134227).
Walking 'Rover' expeditions from Wales. No experience needed.
Ages: 16-24 years. For more information phone for a free brochure.

PUFFIN CYCLE TOURS & WALKING HOLIDAYS
Middle Walls Lane, Penally, Tenby, Dyfed, South Pembrokeshire SA70 7PG (tel 01834-843057).
Proprietor: June Howell.
In business since 1992.
Holidays for 20-30 annually.
Walking holidays within the Pembrokeshire National Park, full of castles, wildlife and spectacular coastal scenery, on well researched routes, all year round. Prices from £125 (three days), £228 (seven days) to £288 (ten days) including B&B accommodation in selected farm and guest houses and luggage transportation. For individuals and groups up to eight. No experience necessary.
Minimum age: 18 years.

RHIWIAU RIDING CENTRE
Llanfairfechan, Gwynedd, North Wales LL33 OEH (tel 01248-680094).
Walking and rambling holidays available all year round, except school holidays. Also riding holidays in Snowdonia National Park.

SNOWDONIA GUIDED WALKS
Maesteg, High Street, Llanberis, Gwynedd LL55 4HB (tel 01286-871187).
Proprietor: Hillary O'Reilly.
In business since 1993.
Estimated 100 holidays arranged in first year of business.
Explore a region steeped in myths and legends with small and friendly tailor-made guided walks and scrambling, all year round. Walks are led by knowledgeable local leaders who can take you to some of the more remote parts of the National Park. Maximum group size of six. Prices from £300 per week. Accommodation is in a B&B, with a packed lunch, but other types of accommodation can be arranged. Own boots, waterproofs (mountain walking gear) required.
Minimum age: 16 years.
Maximum age: 70+.

WELSH WAYFARING HOLIDAYS
Neuadd Arms Hotel, Llanwrtyd Wells, Powys, Wales, LD5 4RB (tel 01591-610236).
Guided walking holidays based in LLanwrtyd Wells, the smallest town in Britain where the pace of life has changed little since the drovers used to drive their flocks of sheep across the nearby Southern Cambrian Mountains. Choose from walks such as the Drovers Walk, Welsh International, Real Ale Ramble, New Year Walk-In and more. For individuals and groups up to 32 people. Prices from £64 for a weekend and from £330 for a week, including full-board hotel accommodation and a guide.
Minimum age: 18 years (unaccompanied).

Ireland

KILLARY TOURS
Killary Tours, Derrynasliggaun, Leenane, Co Galway, Ireland (tel +353 95 42302; fax +353 95 42314). E-mail: Killary@iol.ie
Independent walking in Connemara and other areas of Ireland. Wide range of routes for gentle and relaxed walking holidays. Accommodation is pre-booked in selected B&B's. All transport during the holiday is arranged and the luggage is transferred. Other activities (see *Multi Activity*).

PILGRIM ADVENTURE
120 Bromley Heath Road, Downend, Bristol (tel 0117-9573997).

Proprietors: David Gleed, Maguerita Carrington.
Member of the National Assoc of Christian Communities and Networks and the National Association for Outdoor Education.
Christian based Pilgrim journeys for people of all ages mainly in Britain, Spain and Ireland. Pilgrims share the challenge and excitment of travelling through primitive landscapes to places theat are often well of the beaten track and usually have a story to tell.

Destinations include the islands of Fetlar (Shetland), Inishbofin (Co Galway), Skellig (Co Kerry) and Iona. Pilgrim journeys vary from five to 21 days. Prices from £50 including full board, campsite/hostel/guest-house accommodation.

Average of six to eight miles hill or mountain walking most days.

Europe

ABERCROMBIE AND KENT
Sloane Square House, Holbein Place, London SW1W 8NS (tel 0171-730 9600; fax 0171-730 9396).
Guided walking holidays in Andalucia, Spain. Groups of no more than 14 people. March to November (excluding July and August). The walks take you through exceptionally beautiful, mountainous and wooded country, amongst green fields and wild flowers, ancient Arab towns and villages and all under a canopy of blue sky. Two to six hours of relatively easy walking per day accompanied by mules to carry refreshments such as chilled Fino as well as weary walkers. Luggage is transported by back-up vehicle. There are two itineraries which include time in the cities of Ronda, Arcos and Jerez de la Frontera and Sanlucar de Barrameda. Accommodation is in private houses, hotels, hunting lodges and a few days in a luxurious private tented safari camp.

ALTERNATIVE TRAVEL GROUP
69-71 Banbury Road, Oxford OX2 6PE (tel 01865-315678; fax 01865-310299).
Directors: Christopher Whinney.
In business since 1979.
Member of AITO, CAA and ATOL.
Holidays for 3000 arranged annually.
Wide range of routes for gentle and relaxed walking holidays in Europe. Choose from Path to Rome, Tuscan Trail, Way to Assisi, Unknown Umbria, Verona and the Dolomites, Sierras of Catalonia, Portugal — The Alto Minho and more. Around five hours of walking a day in small compatible groups, with an hour and a half for lunch, a siesta and arriving at the next hotel about 4.30pm in the afternoon. Back up vehicle and luggage transportation. Experienced tour leaders as guides. Prices from £800-£2000 including all meals and the best available local accommodation.
Minimum age: 12 years (accompanied).

ALTO ARAGON
Stilehouse Yard, Deddington, Banbury, Oxfordshire OX15 0SR (tel & fax 01869-337339). E-mail: 106604.3242@compuserve.com
Partners: Nicola Forsyth, Richard Cash & Susan John.
In business since 1994.
Holidays for 100+ arranged annually.
Experience the wonders of an outstanding mountain range with guided walking holidays in the Spanish Pyrenees. For individuals and groups of up to 11 people. Some walking experience an advantage. Prices: £500-£850 for two weeks include accommodation in a range of full-board hotels. Flights are not included but can be arranged at an extra cost.
Minumum age: 16 years accompanied; 18 years unaccompanied.

BELLE FRANCE
15 East Street, Rye, East Sussex (tel 01797-223777; fax 01797-223666).
Walking holidays in France from April to October. Prices from £346 include half board hotel accommodation, luggage transfer and travel.
'Our independent walking and cycling holidays introduce you to areas off the beaten track and quite ungeared to mass tourism. You travel as individuals and are located so as not to overburden the local environment'.

BENTS BICYCLE & WALKING TOURS
The Blue Cross, Orleton, Ludlow, Shropshire SY8 4HN (tel 01568-800; fax 01568-780801).
Proprietor : Stephen Bent.
In business since 1987.Member of AITO.
Holidays for 500-600 arranged annually.

Self-led walking (and cycling) holidays in Bavaria and the Black Forest, Germany from May to September lasting eight, ten and 12 days. Holidays suit all ages from children to fit grandparents. Prices from £599 to £819 include flights, bed and breakfast accommodation in small Bavarian hotels and guest houses, comprehensive information pack and the transportation of luggage between stops.

COLLINEIGE
30-32 High Street, Frimley, Surrey GU16 5JD (tel 01276-24262; fax 01276-27282).
Summer and Winter adventure holidays including walking in the mountains around Chamonix. Bed and breakfast and catered accommodation, from £25 a night. Tailor-made packages, flexible to suit clients wishes.
Minimum age: 16 (unaccompanied).

DISCOVER THE PYRENEES
Encounter Travel, 14 East Street, Ashburton, Newton Abbot, Devon TQ13 7AZ (tel 01364-652374).
Directors: D Lyndale & A Glanville.
In business since 1989.
Member of the British Union of European Mountain Leaders.
Guided walking holidays and scrambles in the fabulous Mediterranean Pyrenees and French Alps. Stunning scenery, great food and wine. Full board, free transfers from around £400 per week. Also walking and adventure activity holidays in the U.K.

EXODUS EXPEDITIONS
9 Weir Road, Balham, London SW12 0LT (tel 0181-675 5550 or 0181-673 0859 24 hrs).
A large choice of trekking holidays in: France, Switzerland, Spain, Mallorca, Madeira, Greece, Italy, Portugal, Poland, Bulgaria, Cyprus, Romania and Turkey. Stay in hotels, campsites, mountain refuges or local tavernas while exploring the Pyrenees, Alps, Picos de Europa, Sierra Nevada, Sierra Chaparral, Pindos, Dolomites, Polish Tatras, High Balkans, Transylvanian Alps, Kackar and Taurus Mountains. Some of the trips involve light backpacking with vehicle support and others have donkey porterage. All are run with bilingual staff and leaders and are graded according to difficulty. Departures all year round, prices ranging from £385 to £1095.

EXPLORE WORLDWIDE LTD
1 Frederick Street, Aldershot, Hants GU11 1LQ (tel 01252-344161; fax 01252-343170).
A wide range of easy walks, village to village hikes and major treks throughout Europe, including the following examples: 16-day Cretan expeditions May-September, exploring villages, beaches and gorges and staying in small hotels and tavernas. Trekking through the Samaria Gorge and in the Ida Mountains. Price from around £549 includes flights, local transport by bus and ferryboat and guide.
Trekking in the Alps (Mont Blanc, the Matterhorn, Jungfrau and Eiger) for 15 days from June to September. Price of around £598 includes flight from London, accommodation in tents and Alpine huts, and services of support vehicle to carry baggage.
Minimum age: 17 years.

FINNISH TOURIST BOARD
30-35 Pall Mall, London SW1Y 5LP (tel 0171-8394048; fax 0171-3210696).
National Tourist Office.
Agent for many Finnish companies offering hiking and trekking tours in the National Parks. Detailed information on campsites, firelighting places and fishing areas is also available. Brochures available on request.

FOOTLOOSE WALKING
Alternative Travel Group, 69-71 Banbury Road, Oxford OX2 6PE (tel 01865 315678; fax 01865 310299).
Self-led, customised walking tours in Italy and France. Can be tailored to suit all budgets. Clients are met on arrival and all arrangements are dealt with by the staff in Italy and France. Luggage is transported ahead.

HEADWATER HOLIDAYS
146 London Road, Northwich, Cheshire CW9 5HH (tel 01606-48699).
European walking programme with independent and guided options all year round. Price from £356 which includes ferry crossing, seven nights hotel accommodation, private bathroom, dinner, bed and breakfast

and luggage transport. No experience required.
Physically challenged people welcome.

INNTRAVEL
Hovingham, York, YO6 4JZ (tel 01653-628862).
Independent walking holidays in France (Alsace, Alpes Maritimes, Auvergne, Basque Pyrenees, Cerdagne, Cévennes, Dordogne, Loire, Lot, Normandy, Provence, Savoie, Tarn, Vercors), Switzerland, Austria, Spain, Italy and Norway. Accommodation in family-run hotels with luggage being transported from hotel to hotel. Prices from £299 including return, self-drive journey. Guided walks also available in the Cerdagne (Pyrenees) and in Norway.

MARMOT TRAILS
12 Hazeldon Road, London SE4 2DD (tel/fax 0181-469 0127).
Owner & Director: Franco Bertocchi.
Ten day guided walking holidays in the Italian Dolomites from June to October. Holidays are based in traditional 3 star hotels. Daily walks can be as short as two hours or as long as all-day hikes, depending on preference. One week guided walking holidays in Andalucia from February to May. Extra activities include golf, horse riding and tennis. Prices include return flights, accommodation, all meals and wine, insurance and safety equipment.

MOSWIN TOURS
Moswin House, 21 Church Street, Oadby, Leicester LE2 5DB (tel 0116-271 9922; fax 0116 271 6016).
Carefree rambling without luggage amongst the well-signed and maintained footpaths of Germany's Black Forest and Bavaria. Accommodation is on a bed and breakfast basis and luggage is transferred from door-to-door for the overnight stops. An example of an active rambler holiday might be 9 days covering 28 miles.

PATHWAYS: Mountain Journeys
Coal Ash, Grisebeck, Kirkby-in-Furness, Cumbria LA17 7XU (tel 01229-889400; fax 01229-889400).
Two-week guided treks in the Pyrenees and the Mont Blanc massif (in July and August), suitable for experienced hillwalkers. Prices from £895, including return flights from UK, road transfers, baggage transfer each day, and all meals and accommodation.

PEAK INTERNATIONAL
15 Moor Park, Wendover, Aylesbury, Bucks. HP22 6AX (tel/fax 01296-624225).
High Tatras Trek: backpacking trek, nine days ex Vienna £345.
Switzerland: from tough mountain trail to easy valley walks. The former using huts and the latter using hotels. Self-guided. From £420 for an eight-day adventure (excluding travel to and from Switzerland).
Finland: Hike the 'Bear's Path' in central Finland or trek along the Russian border. Many wilderness hikes, easy to hard, from £485.
Provence: relaxed easy walks with English guide from a private villa based in Provence. Swimming pool, half-board £395 per week.

PLUS TRAVEL (JET TOURS LTD)
9 Eccleston Street, London SW1W 9LX (tel 0171-259 0199; fax 0171-259 0190.
Hiking without luggage tours in the Swiss mountains. Choice of trails graded easy to advanced in the Bernese Oberland, Romanche and Italian-speaking Switzerland. Self-guided and three and six-day treks offered. Prices from £430 include B&B and three-star accommodation.

RUSSELL HAFTER HOLIDAYS
26 The Square, Ashfield, Dunblane FK15 0JN (tel/fax 01786-824515).
Proprietor: Russell Hafter.
In business since 1986.
Holidays for 100-130 annually.
Discover the Black Forest, Bavaria, Franconia, the Eifel, the Rhine and Mosel Valleys and many other parts of Germany, also Alsace in France through self-guided walking holidays. Suitable for the long distance walker or the after-dinner stroller. See fairytale castles and legendary forests, historic architecture and wildlife or sample the beer and plentiful food. Prices from London by Eurostar £365-£645 including rail B&B accommodation in pensions, inns and guest-houses. Some half-board available.
Rail/sea travel from Hull or Newcastle. Self-drive travel via Le Shuttle. Air travel also possible.
Holidays may be added on to business trips to Germany or nearby countries, stopovers in France, Belgium or elsewhere in Germany while en route to or from your holiday also possible.
All ages from 8-80 years.

SOVEREIGN SCANSCAPE
First Choice Holidays, Peel Cross Road, Salford, Manchester M5 2AN) (tel 0990-768373; fax 0161 742 4542).
In business since 1986.
Member of ABTA (no V1549).
Hiking and rambling tours in Norway and Iceland from May-September. See the towering beauty of endless fjords and travel across the vast highland tracks of Sprengisandur in Iceland and, experience the mysticism of the Midnight Sun. Accommodation varies from 4 star hotels to family run pensions, farmhouses and tents. Tours are escorted by enthusiastic and knowledgeable guides.
Minimum age: approx. 12 years (accompanied); unaccompanied young people not accepted.
Physically challenged people catered for on some tours.

SUOMEN LATU RY
Fabianinkatu 7, FIN-00130 Helsinki 13, Finland (tel +358 9- 170 101; fax +358 9-663 376).
Wilderness hikes and walking holidays in Lapland and south and east Finland. Eight days, 100 km. All personal gear is carried by each individual participant. The tours take place in Urho Kekkonen National Park. Accommodation is in wilderness huts. The meals consist of freeze dried foods.

TENERIFE TRACKS & TRAILS
Los Quemados 2, La Escalona 38614, Tenerife (tel/fax +34 22 72 53 58).
Proprietor: Mr R W Carless.
In business since 1993.
Guided walking holidays for groups of not fewer than eight people, all year round at a centre situated in peaceful farming countryside, midway between the south coast and Las Cañadas National Park in Tenerife. The volcanic landscape provides a wide range of different terrain and walking conditions. Price: £199 for a week includes full board accommodation but not flights and insurance.
Self-catering apartments and individual guiding also available.
Age range: 16-70 years.

TREKKING HELLAS
7 Filellinon Street, Syntagma Square, 10557 Athens, Greece (tel +30 1 3310323; fax +30 1 3234548).
Trekking holidays in various Greek locations including Mount Olympus, Crete, Cyclades, North and South Pindos range, Peloponnisos and the Ionian Sea. Treks last three to eight nights, operating all year round. Minimum of six people per trek. Prices from around 146,000 drachma (about £340) for seven nights, including accommodation in village guesthouses or hotels, meals (full or half board) and tour leader services. Not included are international fares, transportation to meeting points, drinks and other personal expenses.
'Discover remote communities and traditions, and take the opportunity to swim in the sea, river gorges or mountain pools along the way.'
Tour guides speak fluent English and are experts on the local culture and landscape. Treks are graded Introductory to Challenging and require a reasonable level of fitness.
Minimum age: 8 years (accompanied); 16 years (unaccompanied). No maximum age limit.

WAYMARK HOLIDAYS
44 Windsor Road, Slough SL1 2EJ (tel 01753-516477).
Walking holidays in Austria, Poland, Cyprus, France, Germany, Greece, Ireland, Italy, Norway, Portugal, Romania, Spain, Switzerland, Turkey, Canada, Argentina and the USA. One to three weeks including return flights, half or full board accommodation and guides.

WINETRAILS
Greenways, Vann Lake, Ockley, Dorking RH5 5NT (tel 01306-712111; fax 01306 713504).
Gentle walking holidays through spectacular wine regions throughout Europe and also in North America, Australasia and Madeira. Prices from about £479 for six nights full board. Flights extra.

Americas

THE ADVENTURE TRAVEL CENTRE
131-135 Earls Court, London SW5 9RH (tel 0171-370 4555).
Directors: M Mack D Jack.
Specialist trekking holidays in South America.

ALPINE HELICOPTERS LTD
91 Bow Valley Trail, Canmore, Alberta T1W 1N8 (tel + 1 403 6784802; fax +1 403 6782176).
Directors: P Aldous, H Aldous and D Whyte.
In operation since 1988.
Member of National Tourism Association, Alberta Tourism Partnership, Calgary Convention & Visitors Bureau.
Heli-hiking tours of the alpine landscapes and mountains of the Canadian Rockies. Scenic helicopter flights to secluded areas above the Bow Valley followed by guided hiking. Explore the wildlife, geography, flora and fauna with knowledgable and helpful guides. Prices range from C$200-C$400 for half or full day trips (lunch included on full day excursions). Accommodation and other facilities available locally (5 minute drive).
'The only way to witness the majesty of the Canadian Rockies. Glaciers, alpine lakes and mountains as far as the eye can see'.

AMERICAN WILDERNESS EXPERIENCE INC
P O Box 1486, Boulder Co 80306, USA (tel +1 303 444 2622; fax +1 303 444 3999).
Walking and hiking trips in Utah (Bryce), Backside of Hawaii (three islands adventure), Copper Canyon (Mexico), Llama trek in New Mexico (llamas carry the luggage), and a journey to Choquiquirao (Peru). Trips last four to 18 days . Prices from $530 for a four-day trip not including flights.

ANDEAN TRAILS
47 Eskbank Road, Dalkeith, Midlothian, Scotland EH22 3BH (tel 0131-6634063; fax 0131-6638676).
Partners: Chris Hooker and Kathy Jarvis.
In business since 1997.
Two-three week trekking and mountain biking tours in Peru, Chile and Argentina from May-October and January-March. Treks are graded and supported by porters or pack animals. Small groups of four to eight people. Prices from £700-£1400 including accommodation, fully supported treks and bike trips, guides, support vehicle, cook and all equipment. Flights not included. Fitness level is more important than experience.
Minimum age; 18 years.

ANDES
Andes, 93 Queen Street, Castle Douglas, Kircudbright, Scotland DG7 1EH (tel/fax 01556-503929). E-mail: andes@dial.pipex.com
Internet: http://dialspace.dial.pipex.com/andes
Mountaineering and trekking in all areas of the Andes including Sajama (6542m) in Bolivia, Ojos del Salado (6893m) in Chile, Aconcagua (6960m) in Argentina and trekking in Bolivia, Peru and Patagonia. Prices from £1090, excluding flights. Accommodation: camping and mountain huts while on expedition; hotels in the cities.
Minimum age: 18 years.

AUSTRAL TOURS
120 Wilton Road, London SW1V 1JZ (tel 0171-233 5384; fax 0171-233 5385).
Directors: Richard Brass, Elena Gattinara.
Established 1994.
Member: LATA (Latin American Travel Assoc.), ATOL 3616, IATA accredited.
Trekking and horse riding in South America (Argentina, Chile, Peru, Bolivia, Brazil, Ecuador, Venezuela) year round. Typical price for a holiday is £2000 including full board and accommodation during treks.

EXODUS EXPEDITIONS
9 Weir Road, Balham, London SW12 0LT (tel 0181-675 5550 or 0181-673 0859 24 hrs).
Walking in the Venezuelan Andes or the Peruvian Andes with extensions to Macchu Picchu and Cuzco. Trekking in Argentina and Chile, visiting the Moreno glacier and the Towers of Paine with extensions to the Iguassu Falls. Climbing volcanoes on Isabela Island in the Galapagos and trekking to Lake Titicaca and Apolobamba Mountain in Bolivia. All trips are graded according to difficulty. No experience needed but participants should be reasonably fit. Departures all year round, prices ranging from £1150 to £2375 for 15-22 days. Camping, hotel, lodge and yacht accommodation.

EXPLORE WORLDWIDE LTD
1 Frederick Street, Aldershot, Hants GU11 1LQ (tel 01252-344161; fax 01252-343170).
Treks in small groups in Peru, Patagonia and Venezuela lasting 15 to 24 days. Peru trek from Lima including trekking the old

Inca Trail from Cuzco to Machu Picchu in small groups. All equipment provided. Price including air fare from London around £1200. Moderate hikes in Argentina's Fitzroy and Paine National Parks, plus a visit to Tierra del Fuego. 22 days from £2095. Venezuela trek includes a four-day river trip to Angel Falls and six-day Mt Roraima hike.
Also walking in Alaska, California and the Canadian and American Rockies.
Minimum age: 17 years.

GUERBA EXPEDITIONS
Wessex House, 40 Station Road, Westbury, Wilts. BA13 3JN (tel 01373-858956/826611; fax 01373-858351).
Directors: M Crabb, J Dunn, A Hicks, L Munro.
In business since 1977.
ATOL/AITO.
Guided walking/trekking and discovery holidays throughout South and Central America. Adventure holidays from one week to 95 days. Individuals and groups. Maximum group size normally 15. Prices £520 including all transport, accommodation and some meals.
Minimum age: 15 (accompanied) otherwise adults only.

HIGH PLACES
Globe Works, Penistone Road, Sheffield S6 3AE (tel 0114-275 7500; fax 0114-275 3870).
Directors: R Lancaster, M Lancaster.
Trekking and walking holidays to Ecuador, combining ascent of peaks and volcanoes of the Andes with trail walking through dense forest at the headwaters of the Amazon. Special trips combine hiking in Ecuador with nature watching in the Galapagos Islands. Prices for 26 days on the volcanoes and jungle trip £1920; for Ecuador and Galapagos 19 days is £2450. Walking experience needed. Groups size, 12 people maximum.

INCREDIBLE ADVENTURES
PO Box 77585, San Francisco, CA 94107, USA (tel +1 415 759 7071; fax +1 415 759 7072; Toll Free: 800 777 8464). E-mail: info@incadventures.com
http://www.incadventure.com
Hiking and camping expeditions in California. Adventurous four day and three night camping trip to Yosemite National Park. Packed full of swimming, hiking, campfires, good food and good laughs. Off the beaten path to the wilder side of Yosemite. Price: $169 includes food, camping equipment, transportation, park entrance fee and tax. Departs downtown San Francisco every Wednesday and Sunday afternoon. Also available for those with less time on their hands, one day trip for $75.

PEAK INTERNATIONAL
15 Moor Park, Wendover, Aylesbury, Bucks. (tel/fax 01926-624225).
Andes Mountain Trek in Central Chile. El Plomo (5400m) and Volcan San Jose (5800m) are summit objectives during a series of treks visiting lakes, glaciers and high passes. Accompanied by *huasos* (cowboys) and mules carrying equipment you will walk and camp in the high valleys around these mountains, over which the great Andean Condors soar. A high level tour suitable for adventurous walkers. Price for 22 days, (five hotel/17 camp), Dec-Jan, £1485.
Also, a range of treks in the Canadian Rockies from the easy six-day Mount Assiniboine trek in July and September (£395) to the Rockies Adventure Hike for experienced walkers, eight days (£435). See the valleys, mountains and lakes of Banff, Kootenay or Yoho National Parks you leave behind the modern world to find an environment untouched by 'civilised' society as you trek accross the ever changing scenery of snow-fields, steep rock ramparts and warm alpine meadows.
Also tours based on mountain biking, riding, canoeing, ski touring and whitewater rafting in Ecuador and Chile. Also available, trekking in Peru and Bolivia.

TUCAN SOUTH AMERICA
c/o Adventure Travel Centre, 131-135 Earls Court Road, London SW5 9RH (tel 0171-370 4555).
Trekking in Latin America which can be part of overland tours of Latin America. Hike the Inca Trail for three/four days across three main passes to Machu Picchu. Climb up Tungurahua volcano. Prices from under £40 per day. Groups of up to 21.
All ages.

WORLD CHALLENGE EXPEDITIONS
Black Arrow House, 2 Chandos Road, London NW10 6NF (0181-961 1122; fax 0181 961 1551.
Directors: C R Rigby, R Macaire, P Jenks and C Barrow
In business since 1987.
Expeditions arranged for 1000 annually.

Month-long expeditions involving mountain and jungle trekking to Ecuador, Bolivia, Peru, Guyana, Belize, Brazil and Venezuela. Groups of 16-20. Operates in July and August. Mostly school groups but some individuals accepted. No experience necessary but participants must be motivated and physically fit. A unique feature is the provision for team members to develop management and leadership skills by taking charge of day-to-day planning of an expedition under qualified supervision. Activities include trekking, mountaineering, safari, cultural exchange and selected project work. The ethos behind the expeditions is participation, challenge and environmental research. Prices from £2000 include flight, accommodation, transport, food and pre-expedition training, but not equipment such as rucksacks, clothing and footwear. All expeditions are lead by experienced leaders.
Age range:16-20 years.

WORLDWIDE JOURNEYS AND EXPEDITIONS
8 Comeragh Road, London W14 9HP (tel 0171-381 8638; fax 0171-381 0836).
Trekking holidays in Chile, Patagonia and Ecuador and the Galapagos Islands. Tailor-made tours for small groups and individuals. No previous experience necessary. Fully inclusive packages.

Africa

THE ADVENTURE TRAVEL CENTRE
131-135 Earls Court Road, London SW5 9RH (tel 0171-370 4555).
Specialist trekking holidays in Africa.

ADVENTURELINE
North Trefula, Redruth, Cornwall, TR16 5ET (tel/fax 01209-820847). E-mail: adventureline@virgin.net
Internet: www.chycor.co.uk/adventureline
Winter trekking holidays in Morocco in the remote mountain range between Atlas and Sahara. Treks operate between February and March, costing £500 for two weeks.

AFRICA EXCLUSIVE
66 Palmerston Road, Northampton NN1 5EX (tel 01604-28979; 01604-39879).
Directors: J Burdett, S Burdett,T Bygraves, P Ranken, W Hoffman.
In business since 1990.
Southern African Tour Operators Association.
Holidays for 1000 arranged annually.
Walking in Zimbabwe, Botswana, Namibia, Zambia, Tanzania, South Africa and Kenya all year round. Prices from £2350 including flights and accommodation in high quality tented camps, safari lodges and four or five star hotels on a fully inclusive basis. Activities include walking, canoeing, horse riding and extended white water rafting.
Minimum age (accompanied): 12 years.

EXODUS EXPEDITIONS
9 Weir Road, Balham, London SW12 0LT (tel 0181-675 5550 or 0181-673 0859 24 hrs).
Wildlife walking tours in the game parks of Tanzania, Kenya, Uganda, Malawi, Zambia, Swaziland, Lesotho, Botswana and Zimbabwe to include Kilimanjaro, Mount Kenya and Uhuru Peak. Trips explore the circuit of the Ruwenzori, the Mulanje massif and the eastern highlands and visit Lake Manyara, Ngorongoro crater, Pygmy villages, hot springs, Lake Malawi, Okavango delta, the Drakensburgs, Lake Kariba etc. Also Victoria Falls. Hotel, supported camping, park lodge and mountain hut accommodation. Also trekking in the Atlas and Jebel Sahro mountains of Morocco with opportunities to ascend Toubkal Mountain (13,833 feet). Departures all year round. Prices ranging from £1195 to £2095 for 15-25 days.

EXPLORE WORLDWIDE LTD
1 Frederick Street, Aldershot, Hants GU11 1LQ (tel 01252-344161; fax 01252-343170).
Fifteen days hiking in Morocco's High Atlas Mountains from May to September. Average altitude of walk is 10,000 feet. Accommodation in alpine huts and Berber houses. Price from £395 including flights, transportation, mule hire and all equipment. 15-day camping trek through the Jebel Sahro region, £420.
Fifteen-day Morocco Winter Breaks in the Anti-Atlas, October-April. Escorted walks to Berber villages from Tafraout. Price from £465 including flight to Marrakesh. Also foot safaris in Tanzania and Uganda.
Minimum age: 17 years.

KUMUKA EXPEDITIONS
40 Earls Court Road, London W8 6EJ (tel 0171-9378855; fax 0171-9376664; brochure tel 01223-211666).

Conquer Africa's highest peak, Kilimanjaro (5895m). It's not a technical climb, but certainly a formidable exercise and success is one of Africa's greatest rewards. Seven-day trips depart from Nairobi and cost from £655.

LET'S GO TRAVEL
P O Box 60342 Nairobi, Kenya (tel +254 2 213033/340331; fax +254 2 214713 & +254 2 336890).
Walking safaris in Kenya, Tanzania, Uganda and Zaire.

NATURETREK
Chautara, Bighton, Nr Alresford, Hampshire SO24 9RB (tel 01962-733051).
Sole Proprietor: David Mills.
In business since 1986.
Holidays provided for 500 annually.
Trekking and wildlife (birdwatching and botanical) holidays in Africa. Tours include: the High Atlas mountains of Morocco; Botswana; Zambia's parks and the Victoria Falls and The Bale Mountains of Ethiopia. Groups of up to 15 catered for. Prices £790-£3490. Accommodation is fully serviced camping or luxury hotels and lodges in cities. Sleeping bags and outdoor clothing not included but can be hired. Some meals, airport taxes and drinks not included.
Age range 15-80 years.
'Adventurous natural history tours and treks, each led by a leading botanist and/or ornithologist. Specialists in Himalayan trekking and African camping safaris'.

PEAK INTERNATIONAL
15 Moor Park, Wendover, Aylesbury, Bucks. HP22 6AX (tel + fax 01296-624225).
A variety of East African adventures available, in particular a two-week bush walking and trekking adventure safari in Kenya's remote North West. Trek through the mountain hilltops, tracking animals on foot, gold panning and visits to national game parks. Price: £895 ex Nairobi.
For experienced hill walkers, try a trekking ascent of Mt. Kenya (three to seven days, £195-£495) and Mt. Kilimanjaro (eight-day Machame route £595), or a two mountain walk, Mt Meru & Mt Kili, (11 days £895). Both treks explore quiet routes transversing the mountains. Combine both and add a short safari for £1285 for 15 days. Other treks available include walking safaris, Ngorongoro and the Highlands £795 or the adventurous Ruwenzori trek on the Uganda/Zaire border, with a chance to ascend Mt. Stanley (16,763 ft), £895. (Flights to Nairobi currently available from £325).
Ethiopia: wilderness trek on Ras Deshen (4620m).

WORLDWIDE JOURNEYS AND EXPEDITIONS
8 Comeragh Road, London W14 9HP (tel 0171-381 8638; fax 0171-381 08360.
Tailor-made trekking holidays for individuals or small groups at Mount Kenya and Kilimanjaro and walks in the Luangwa Valley in Zambia. Fully inclusive packages.

Arctic

ARCTIC EXPERIENCE LTD
29 Nork Way, Banstead, Surrey SM7 1PB (tel 01737 218800; fax 01737-362341).
Escorted 14-night hiking tour in Iceland from around £1090 including accommodation in tents and all meals. Also available is a less strenuous trip, designed for those who enjoy an active holiday but prefer the comfort of a solid roof over their heads. Price from around £849 for seven nights for an escorted walking tour with guesthouse accommodation.

DICK PHILLIPS
Whitehall House, Nenthead, Alston, Cumbria CA9 3PS (tel 01434-381440).
In business since 1960.
Holidays for 300 arranged annually.
Hiking tours in Iceland. Two to three weeks May-August. Maximum of 13 miles walking per day in the mountains of the South. Rucksack and sleeping bag needed. Prices from £760 including return air fare from Glasgow.
'We are genuinely concerned to avoid the tourist routes. We still have parties who walk for ten days without seeing another person'.

HIGH PLACES
Globe Works, Penistone Road, Sheffield S6 3AE (tel 0114-275 7500; fax 0114-275 3870).
Backpacking and trekking tours in North and East Iceland based in the fjord mountains of the East coast and the glaciers, volcanoes and waterfalls of the North. Nordic skiing trips also available at Easter. Price for seven days, £890 and for 14 days, £1350. Maximum group size: 12. Walking experience needed.

Asia

BUFO VENTURES LTD
3 Elim Grove, Windermere, Cumbria LA23 2JN. (tel/fax 015394-45445).
Directors: Diana Penny Sherpani, Ang Zangbu Sherpa.
In business since 1986.
Holidays provided for 100 annually (200 in Everest Marathon years).
Trekking in Nepal for private groups and individuals, using tents or tea shops depending on area. Also special interest treks, expeditions and other activity holidays Arrangements can be made to include flights from London or just Nepal arrangements. Send £7 for trekker's guide *Adventure Nepal.* Other activities include river rafting, jungle safaris, mountain biking, and the biennial Everest Marathon; next race March 1999.
Special arrangements can be made for the physically challenged.

CHANDERTAL TOURS
20, The Fridays, East Dean, Nr Eastbourne, East Sussex BN20 ODH (tel & fax 01323-422213).
Partners: S P Baker, R Newbury.
In business since 1985.
Member Government of India Tourist Board.
Trekking, jeep safaris and wildlife holidays in India and Thailand, including the Himalayas and wildlife parks. Also wildflower treks in Sikkim. Treks for two to eight weeks May-November, January-March. No experience required, treks to suit all. Prices £950-£1750 include return flight to London, accommodation, meals, tours, guides and equipment including sleeping bag if required. Accommodation in five star hotels in cities and lodges and tents on treks and safaris. Groups of no more than eight. Assistance also given to university departments for field trips and expeditions.
Minimum age (unaccompanied): 16 years.
Chandertal tours also has its own company in India — Himalayan Folkways for visitors to Manali wanting to go trekking.
'An opportunity to get off the beaten track and experience the real culture and wilderness of India, whether on top of a mountain in the remote Himalayas or on a camel in a tribal camp in the desert'.

CLASSIC NEPAL
33 Metro Avenue, Newton, Alfreton, Derbyshire DE55 5UF (tel 01773-873497; fax 01773-590243). E-mail: classicnepal@compuserve.com
Directors: A Brooks and N Walshe.
Member of ATOL licence no. 3022.
Trekking holidays in Nepal, India and Tibet. Treks include Everest Base Camp, the Annapurna Circuit, Langtang Valley, remote West Nepal, Kanchenjunga, Sikkim, Garhwal and Mt. Kailas in Tibet. Some treks include the optional climb of a 6000m 'trekking peak', guided by western climbing guides. Visits to Chitwan Wildlife Park, river rafting and private tours also arranged. Holidays last 15-31 days. Arrangements can be made for schools, colleges, private groups and individuals. Prices from £1500 to £2995 all inclusive. General fitness and robust health required.
Minimum age: 18 years unaccompanied, otherwise 15 years.

ECOSUMMER EXPEDITIONS
1516 Duranleau Street, Vancouver, B C Canada VH6 3S4.
Internet: http://www.ecosummer.com
Three-week trek in a remote section of Nepal from Barabise to Namche Bazaar crossing the Rolwaling Valley and through a high alpine pass, the Taschi Lapcha (5750m). For those who wish there will be an opportunity to climb to the summit of Parchama (6273m).

25-days trekking (July or August) on the Tien Shan to Samarkand route passing through several northeastern central Asian republics on The Silk Route. The only other humans you are likely to see are the colourfully dressed nomads grazing their sheep in the high valleys. Trip includes three days on horseback and a helicopter flight to the Pamir-Alai for a week's trekking in the pristine pastures. Cost $3550 including flights from the USA.

ENCOUNTER OVERLAND
267 Old Brompton Road, London SW5 9JA (tel 0171-370 6845).
Directors: W K Burton, J C Clarke.
In operation since 1963.
Treks in Nepal in the Annapurna region and to Everest Base Camp. Sherpa guides and porters carry all luggage and equipment, and prepare the campsites and meals. Cost includes all camping equipment and food.

EXODUS EXPEDITIONS
9 Weir Road, Balham, London SW12 0LT (tel 0181-675 5550 or 0181-673 0859 24 hrs).
Small group trekking holidays in the Himalaya and Karakorum regions to Nepal, Bhutan, Garwal, Himachal Pradesh, Sikkim, Pakistan, West China, Tibet and Ladakh. Other walking explorer trips to Indonesia and Malaysia. Prices £995-£2390 for 17-28 days. Also special treks in Nepal to Mustang, Jugal Himal, Everest, Manaslu, Dolpo, Mera Peak, Rolwaling and Ramdung (19, 550 ,feet). In China there are pioneering treks to Mount Tomuer, Karta Valley and Muztagh Ata and Bogda. All trips are graded according to difficulty and are led by experienced guides.

EXPLORE WORLDWIDE LTD
1 Frederick Street, Aldershot, Hants GU11 1LQ (tel 01252-319448; fax 01252-344161).
Treks and expeditions in Asia for small groups. An 18 or 22-day river journey and hilltribe walk in Thailand, or Borneo throughout the year from about £930. Prices include flights from London, accommodation and all guides and equipment. Also treks in the Himalayas of India and Ladakh, and a range of Nepalese treks in the Everest or Annapurna regions.
Minimum age: 17 years.

FIVE VALLEY TREKS
2 Somerset Cottages, Stoke Village, Plymouth, Devon PL3 4AZ (tel 01752-567617; fax 01752-567617; mobile 0467-220289).
Partners: Richard & Shari Ravensdale.
In operation since 1972.
Himalayan trekking holidays in Nepal. Trans-Himalaya, April, Mustang and Tibet May and June, Annapurna Sanctuary, March and October; Annapurna Circuit, November; Langtang, November with birdwatching tours for 17 and 24 days in February and March combining Phulchowki, Godaveri, Gokarna, Chitwan, Pokhara, Begnas Tal and Langtang. Specialising in custom-designed treks for groups of two to 14, clubs and Services expeditions all individually planned. Price around £1300, including flights and accommodation in B&B guest houses in Kathmandu and Pokhara, three sightseeing tours, full catering on treks with UK food supplies, dome tents, service of a company partner as trek leader, Sherpa guides & porters, sleeping bags and trek equipment. Suitable trek clothing can be hired cheaply from local Kathmandu expedition outfitters.
Minumum age: 14 years.
Maximum age: 70 + (with fitness note from GP).
Physically, visually and mentally challenged people welcome, including deaf clients.

GUERBA EXPEDITIONS LTD
Wessex House, 40 Station Road, Westbury, Wilts. BA13 3JN (tel 01373-858956/826611; fax 01373-858351).
ATOL and AITO.
Guided walking/treking holidays in Himalaya, India and South East Asia. From trekking off the normal tourist trails in the Himalaya to jungle treks in Indonesia visiting Orang Utan sanctuaries.

HIGH PLACES
Globe Works, Penistone Road, Sheffield S6 3AE (tel 0114-275 7500; fax 0114-275 3870).
Trekking tours through Ladakh, an ancient Buddhist kingdom in the Indian Himalayas. Treks run from July to October and include the classic traverse across Ladakh to Zanskar (£1960); peak ascents in Markha Valley £1870 and a trek into the remote Rupshu region £1740. Also trek through Garhwal Himalayas following an ancient pilgrim trail to the holy Hindu temple at Kedarnath, 24 days (£1540). Also treks in Sikkim towards Kanchenjunga range, 22 days (£1860). Maximum group size of 12.

HIMALAYAN KINGDOMS
20 The Mall, Clifton, Bristol BS8 4DR (tel 0117-923 7163).
The UK's leading Expedition organisers and premier trekking company, specialising in the Greater Himalaya and other mountain ranges of the world including the Seven Continental Summits. Many and varied treks, graded from easy (Christmas Adventure in Nepal) to strenuous (The Hidden Kingdom in Bhutan). For private individuals, groups and schools. Prices include flights, accommodation and food. Full colour brochure available on request.
'The first British company to guide clients to the top of Mt. Everest'.

JASMINE TOURS
53-55 Balham Hill, London SW12 9DR (tel 0181-675 8886; fax 0181-673 1204).
15-day holiday in Nepal includes seven days trekking four to six hours per day. Tours of Kathmandu at the beginning of the holiday

and whitwater rafting option after trek. £1168 to £1375 all inclusive.

MOUNTAIN TRAVEL NEPAL PVT LTD
Lazimpath, PO Box 170, Kathmandu, Nepal (tel +977 1-411225; fax +977 1-414075). E-mail:tiger@mtn.mos.com.np Internet: http://www.tigermountain.com
Directors: AVJ Edwards and Steve Webster.
In business since 1965.
Trekking in the Himalaya all year round from Kanchenjunga in the far east through the entire Nepal and Indian Himalaya, Tibet and the Karakoram mountains in Pakistan. Wide range of treks from short walks in Kashmir to more strenuous and demanding expeditions in Ladakh and Island Peak lying below the massive south wall of Lhotse. Fully trained Sherpa staff for guides. Tailor-made treks for individuals, small groups, families or larger parties. All treks are graded. Also special interest treks focusing on anthropology, ornithology, botany, entomology or photography with expert guides in each field. 'Pioneers of environmentally sensitive adventure holidays in Nepal'.
Book direct or through: ExplorAsia Ltd (tel 0171-973 0482); Abercombie & Kent Travel (tel 0171-730 9600) or Worldwide Journeys & Expeditions (tel 0171-381 8638).

NATURETREK
Chautara, Bighton, Nr Alresford, Hampshire SO24 9RB (tel 01962-733051).
Trekking and wildlife (bird watching and botanical) holidays in Nepal's Rara Lake (28 days, £1990); Mount Everest and the Gokyo Lakes of Nepal (22 days; £1890); Kanchenjunga, Nepal (30 days; £1990); The Indus Valley and Vale of Kashmir (22 days, £1690) and Zanskar Range in the Himalaya (27 days, £1690). Tours led by experienced botanist and/or ornithologist. Groups of up to 15 catered for. Prices range from £690-£3,490. Accommodation is fully serviced camping or luxury hotels and lodges in cities. Sleeping bags and outdoor clothing not included but can be hired. Some meals, airport taxes and drinks not included.
Age range; 15-80 years.

PEAK INTERNATIONAL
15 Moor Park, Wendover, Aylesbury, Bucks. HP22 6AX (tel + fax 01296-624225).
Uzbekistan/Kyrgyztan/Kazakhstan/CIS
Adventurous treks throughout Asia, Papua New Guinea and Iran. Tien Shan, Pamirs, Funsky mountains, Siberian Altai and more. Most trips last 12-17 days. Arranged upon request for two or more people from £425 ex Tashkent.
Nepal
Treks to order from one person or more — Annapurna and Khumbu/Everest regions. Treks from seven to 24 days easy to strenuous from £295 for 18 days ex Kathmandu.
Tibet
Mount Kailash, cultural tour and trek 18 days. May to September £1485 ex Kathmandu.
India
Many treks into the superb Indian Himalaya. Sikkim 'Gocha La' trek 20 days ex Delhi £875. Markha Valley trek 19 days £845. 'Valley of Flowers' ten days £685. Nubra Valley 15 days £785 . . . plus many others.

RAMBLERS HOLIDAYS
Box 43, Welwyn Garden City, Herts AL8 6PQ (tel 01707-331133).
Established 1946.
Member of ABTA, IATA.
Holidays for over 15 000 arranged annually.
Trekking holidays in Nepal lasting two to four weeks. Camping and accommodation. Treks to Everest base camp and to Annapurna. Also an easier *Introduction to Trekking* tour for those who have not trekked before. Hotel-based trips to Swat and Gilgit, and to Kali Gandaki and Annapurna regions.

ROAMA TRAVEL
Larks Rise, Shroton, Blandford, Dorset DT11 8QW (tel 01258-860298).
Directors: W Norman, E Norman.
In business since 1979.
Holidays provided for about 150 each year.
Trekking holidays in the Himalaya throughout the year. Individuals and groups of up to ten may be catered for. Prices range from £1268 to £1928 including hotel bed and breakfast accommodation. Airport taxes are included. No experience is necessary but you should be reasonably fit.
Minimum age: 12 years, if accompanied; maximum age: 75 years.

SHERPA CO-OPERATIVE TREKKING (P) LTD
PO Box 1338, Durbar Marg, Kathmandu, Nepal (tel +977 1 224068; fax +977 1 227983).
Managing Director: M L Pradhan.
Expert trekking holidays in the hills and mountains of Nepal, covering the Kumbbu (Everest Region), the Dhaulagiri Range, the Kali Gandaki Valley, Annapurna Sanctuary, Langtang, Manang, Marsyandi Valley, Dolpo and Mustang. Also river rafting and safaris for groups or individuals at reasonable prices.
Other tours in Tibet, Sikkim and Bhutan.

SITA WORLD TRAVEL (India) LTD
4 Malcha Marg Shopping Centre, Diplomatic Enclave, New Delhi-110 021, India (tel +91 11 611 1122; telex 31-72141 or 31-72263 SITA-IN; fax +91 11 687-0123). E-mail: sitaind@sita.sprintrpg.ems.vsnl.net.in
Recognised by the Indian Government.
Trekking holidays in the Himalayas for five to 27 days between April and mid-November. Also opportunities for camel and horse safaris in Rajasthan, Himalayan jeep safaris over some of the world's highest road passes on the Indo-Tibetan Plateau and other adventure activities. Prices/programmes on application.

STEPPES EAST
Castle Eaton, Cricklade, Wilts SW6 6JU (tel 01285-810267; fax 01285-810693. E-mail: sales@steppeseast.co.uk
Directors: NAG Laing, M Bullough, W Gascoigne.
In business since 1989.
ATOL licensed.
Holidays for 1000 arranged annually.
Trekking in Central Asia, Pakistan, India, Nepal, Bhutan and Sikkim, all year round. Cost of £1000 to £2500 includes flights, meals and hotels.

WEXAS INTERNATIONAL
45 Brompton Road, Knightsbridge, London SW3 1DE (tel 0171-589 3315).
Trekking holidays in the Himalaya and walking tours of Nepal and Northern India. Also treks to visit hill tribe communities in the North of Thailand. Trips last one to four weeks and are fully escorted by experienced guides.

WORLD CHALLENGE EXPEDITIONS
Black Arrow House, 2 Chandos Road, London NW10 6NF (tel 0181-961 1122; fax 0181-961 1551).
Month long leadership development expeditions in mountain and jungle trekking to India, Pakistan, Malaysia, Borneo, Nepal and Thailand. Trips are in July and August, and are led by experienced leaders. Expeditions for school groups of 16-20 people, though individuals are also accepted. No experience necessary but participants must be motivated and fit. Prices from £2000 which includes hostel accommodation, flights, transport, food and pre-expedition training, but not equipment such as rucksacks, clothing and footwear.
Minimum age: 16 years, if accompanied; maximum : 20 years.

Middle East

MAGIC CARPET TRAVEL
Sun House, 125 Ryston Road, London SW6 7HP (tel 0171-381 2304; fax 0171-381 23040).
15-day trek in Iran staying in tents and hotels. Itinerary begins with Tehran and includes Shiraz, Persepolis, Isfahan, Khor, Nayband, Birjand Golestan and Reneh. Packages cost around £1575. Separate flight cost is £400-£480.

New Zealand

HIGH PLACES
Globe Works, Penistone Road, Sheffield S6 3AE (tel 0114-275 7500; fax 0114-275 3870).
Trekking, 'tramping' and biking in the South Island: Abel Tasman beaches; west coast rainforest and glaciers; Aspiring and Mount Cook National Parks; Fiordland and Milford Sound; Tongariro National Park. Open-jaw itineraries and DIY. From 21 days at £1960, 27 days £2685.

Mountain Pursuits

MOUNTAINEERING

There was a fashion in the late eighteenth century to find mountains grotesque and distasteful. But today mountains are a very popular destination for adventurous travellers, and the post war period has seen the establishment of many new climbing centres in the Scottish Highlands, the Canadian Rockies, the Himalayas and elsewhere. The most popular areas have schools and guiding/teaching facilities.

It is not necessary to be a technical rock climber to enjoy moving among mountains. Conversely it is possible to become an expert rock climber without going above 30 metres. The British have distinguished themselves as rock climbers principally because there is no indigenous range of towering mountains but plenty of challenging crags from Cornwall to Skye. Whereas some relish the challenge of climbing steep and difficult cliffs, others are intimidated not only by the feeling of exposure but by the cumbersome hardware necessary for rock climbing. There are opportunities for people of either persuasion to learn new skills and explore new areas of the world.

Safety and Equipment. When practised with the appropriate equipment and precautions, climbing can be less dangerous than it may seem to the uninitiated. However, there has been concern in recent years at the increasing number of walkers and climbers who have met their deaths in the Highlands of Scotland. In 1993, 54 were killed, about 30 of them walkers. It is essential when venturing into the mountains to have a map and a compass and know how to use them, as well as a survival kit which should include spare high calorie food, a flask containing a hot drink, a whistle or bleeper to attract attention and an ice axe. Navigational errors and poor climbing skills played a large part in the majority of fatalities. Underestimating the harshness of the conditions in the Grampians and Cairngorms was another factor. Attention to weather forecasts and local advice is particularly important.

Most accidents abroad — such as the spate of disasters on Mont Blanc in August 1986, when over a dozen climbers died — are also the result of inexperience, inadequate equipment or an error of judgment. However even very experienced climbers also come to grief yearly in the Alps. Twenty people died as a result of mountaineering accidents in the Alps during the months of July and August alone in 1997. As one expert puts it, 'Experience limits but does not eliminate dangers'. Even easy hills can be dangerous when the weather changes unexpectedly and the climbers are caught unprepared. Warm and waterproof clothing (nowadays made of synthetics) should be carried even in summer (see wind chill chart on page 98) and boots with tough rubber soles which minimise slipping should be worn.

At least one member of a mountaineering party should have a working knowledge of maps and compass navigation, survival and rescue procedures and first aid. A sample equipment checklist for an ascent of Mont Blanc (the highest peak in the Alps) might include crampons, ice axe, a rope for every three climbers, glacier cream, sunglasses and three layers of special synthetic clothing. Bivouac gear, which consists of a light waterproof body-length bag, is necessary when there is a high chance of not being able to complete a climb during daylight. Afternoons in the Alps are generally more dangerous than dawn. Often it is best to climb in the dark when it is cold and stable underfoot.

CLIMBING AND ABSEILING

Most holiday organisers will provide or hire out the specialised equipment needed for the purpose. Climbing and the related activity of abseiling are included as part of almost all multi activity holidays. Abseiling involves 'walking' down a rock face with your weight borne by a rope attached to a secure anchor at the top. Organisations such as the Sports Council, the Youth Hostels Association and the Outward Bound Trust offer introductory and specialist courses in most aspects of mountaineering.

The British Mountaineering Council (BMC) is the representative body for climbers and mountaineers and can provide details of clubs and courses. The BMC produces a wide range of publications including the booklets *Safety on Mountains* (£1.90) and videos such as *The Complete Winter Experience* (£10). Information on all aspects of climbing and mountaineering can be obtained from the BMC, (177-179 Burton Road, West Didsbury, Manchester M20 2BB; tel 0161 445 4747; fax 0161 445 4500). The monthly magazine *High* carries the official newspages of the BMC and an annual subscription including BMC membership costs £36.

SKIING

Second only to sunning oneself on the Mediterranean, skiing is the most popular type of holiday. Because so many travel companies organise ski-packages abroad and information about such holidays is so easily obtainable from travel agents or the media, we include mainly those holidays which are more unusual or adventurous: such as summer skiing, or being transported by helicopter to ski down remote mountains and glaciers in the Rockies of Canada.

Cross-country skiing, sometimes called *langlauf,* or nordic skiing, does not have the glamour of downhill skiing or slalom skiing; but it offers much pleasure to the adventurous, especially those who wish to see more of the countryside and its wildlife. Special light skis and bindings that leave the heel free are needed but can usually be hired in a resort. It is not necessary to travel to Lapland or the Rockies to participate in the sport. There are opportunities in Snowdonia and in Scotland for cross-country skiing during the winter but for hut-to-hut trips the best circuits are likely to be found in Scandinavia or Austria.

Ski touring can be done in Europe where there are some well-known routes such as the Haute Route in the Alps which takes six days, or a three-day tour in the Gran Paradiso National Park in Italy, also has a steady following. Tours are suitable for intermediate skiers upwards. Special non-slip skins are attached to the skis for going uphill where necessary. Ski touring can be very strenous and at an advanced level overlaps with winter mountaineering.

Telemarking is a style of skiing that has made a big comeback in recent years. Essentially an elegant way of skiing it involves special turns and skis.

Essential clothing for snow skiing is a warm and waterproof suit or jacket and trousers (often these are one-piece salopettes), strong leather or plastic gloves, a woollen hat, goggles and of course ski boots. Skis with bindings, poles and boots can usually be hired.

Helicopter skiing or heli-skiing allows the skier who has had at least three years of skiing experience the chance to descend thousands of feet of deep powder snow on untouched mountainsides. It is not without its risks, since avalanches and sudden blizzards are ever-present hazards. But accidents are rare, partly because of the guides trained to spot crevasses, and because skiers are equipped with an electronic bleeper for signalling in an emergency. Special fat skis about double the width of normal skis have made this sport more accessible to less expert skiers in recent years.

Further information and details of resorts and companies in Britain can be obtained from The Ski Club of Great Britain, The White House, 57163 Church Road, Wimbledon, London SW19 5DQ; tel 0181-410 2000). Some multi activity holidays include skiing, especially at mountain centres which remain open throughout the winter; see the first chapter for details.

A valuable preliminary to any skiing holiday is to train for a spell on a dry ski slope before starting on the snow. Complete novices are able to get the feel of boots, poles and skis, and reduce the aching muscles from which many beginners suffer. Intermediate and advanced skiers find that they regain their skills after a year's lapse very quickly, which enables them to pick up immediately on the piste. Many skiing holiday operators offer cut-price sessions at artificial ski slopes to their clients.

Snow skiing is familiar to everyone, but grass skiing is a lesser known derivative sport. It was started in Germany over 25 years ago, but was not recognised by the National Ski Federation of Great Britain as a separate discipline until 1979. Grass skis are very short with rollers or a caterpillar track and can be attached to ordinary ski boots. A good grass skier can move up to 50 mph and race around slalom posts.

Snowboarding. Over thirty years ago American surfers invented snowboarding which is the alpine equivalent of surfing or skate boarding, ie. you stand sideways on the single board. In the past couple of years snowboarding has become the fastest growing winter sport in the European Alps and an ever increasing number of resorts, especially in Europe and North America now have their own snowboarding parks. A good snowboard costs around £400 including bindings. Boots can be either soft (for freestyle) or hard (for racing). Ski boots are not suitable. In Britain one can learn to snowboard in Scottish ski resorts or at some dry ski slopes including Hillingdon and the Ackers Trust in Birmingham. Such is the growing recognition of snowboarding as a serious discipline it is possible to go on snowboard instructor courses on both dry ski slopes and on the Kaprun Glacier in Austria. The representative body for snowboarding in the UK is the British Snowboarding Association BSA, (01494-462225). Further details on all aspects of the sport and courses can be obtained by calling the above number. Plans are currently in the pipeline to link the British Association of Ski Instructors (BASI) with the BSA and to make the snowboarding instructors' course part of the BASI qualification.

General

England

FIELD STUDIES COUNCIL
Head Office, Montford Bridge, Shrewsbury SY4 1HW (tel 01743-850674; fax 01743-850178).
Mountain pursuits in England include Exploring Mountains in Winter at the FSC's newest centre at Blencathra in the Lake District. Prices from about £255 a week, £100 for a weekend inclusive of accommodation, all meals and tuition.
Minimum age: 16 years except on courses arranged for families.

Scotland

C-N-DO SCOTLAND
77, John Player Building, Springbank Road, Stirling FK7 7RP (tel + fax 01786-445703). E-mail: cndo.scotland@BTinternet.com
Established 1984.
Backpacking, mountaineering and ridge walking treks throughout the mountains of Scotland for individuals and groups during summer and winter. Some walking experience necessary. Rucksacks, sleeping bags, mats and waterproofs available for hire. Own boots essential.

Minimum age: Variable depending on activity.

CUILLIN GUIDES
Stac Lee, Glenbrittle, Isle of Skye IV47 8TA (tel 01478-640289).
Proprietor: Gerry Akroyd.
In operation since 1970.
Recognised by Skye Tourist Board.
Mountaineering and rock climbing courses in the Cuillin Mountains of Skye and backpacking holidays on the West Coast of Scotland for individuals and groups. Five days, throughout the year. Price from £80 (day) to £275 (week), not including accommodation. Winter courses throughout Scotland also available.
Hill walking experience and physical fitness essential.
Ages: 16-65 years.

GLENCOE OUTDOOR CENTRE
Glencoe, Argyll, PA39 4HS (tel 01855-811350).
Winter mountaineering, skiing, hillwalking and rock climbing courses. Individuals and groups of up to 35. Prices from £70 for a weekend. Prices include bunk-bed accommodation, all activities and full board.
Minimum age depends on activity; for some six years. For unaccompanied children: 12 years.

HUNTLY NORDIC SKI CENTRE
Hill of Haugh, Huntly, Aberdeenshire AB54 4SH (tel 01466-794428; fax 01466-792180).
In operation since 1992.
Member: Aberdeen & Grampian Tourist Board, Assoc. of Ski Schools in GB, Cross-Country Ski Areas Association.
Holidays arranged for 500+ annually.
Cross-country skiing (track and telemark) from December to April from a purpose-build centre in Huntly, using the excellent natural facilities in the area. Typically one, two and five-day courses. Prices from £30 to £115; weekend £65. Accommodation is not included but can be arranged at special rates locally. Ski equipment can also be hired. Insurance is recommended. Ski tracks are maintained by a track cutting machine. Fully qualified BASI instructors.
All ages and abilities.

OSSIAN GUIDES
Sanna, Newtonmore, Inverness-shire PH20 1DG (tel/fax 01540-673402).
Partners: Aileen Bulmer and Dig Bulmer.
In business since 1988.
Recognised by Aviemore and Spey Valley Tourist Board.
Holidays provided for 450 annually.
Trekking, climbing and photographic holidays throughout the Scottish Highlands. Treks last from one to 14 days throughout the year. Groups of up to 12 catered for. Price £349 per week, including hotel and guest house accommodation and all meals. No experience is necessary and all equipment is supplied. More strenuous treks are also provided for the seasoned hiker.
Minimum age: 18 years.

Wales

ACORN ACTIVITIES
P O Box 120, Hereford HR4 8YB (tel 01432-830083; fax 01432-830110).
Climbing, abseiling, caving and survival in Wales, Herefordshire and Shropshire. Can be pursued on a daily, or consecutive days basis. Individuals, families and groups. Prices from £40 per day with a choice of farmhouse and hotel accommodation. Can be combined with other activities (see entry in *Multi Activity Holidays* section.

BARRY SKINNER (TRAETH)
Turnpike Cottage, Traeth, Beddgelert, Gwynedd LL55 4YF (tel 01766-890283).
Proprietor: B Skinner.
In business since 1986.
Member of Welsh Tourist Board.
Mountain walking, scrambling, climbing, abseiling, cross-country skiing and navigation in Snowdonia throughout the year. Days, weekends and weeks to your own specifications. Individuals and small groups of up to eight may be catered for. Prices vary according to accommodation, which can be arranged for you in local hotels, bed and breakfasts or bunkhouses. Daily rate for walking (up to six people) is approximately £75. Camping facilities are available locally. Boots, wet weather gear and other personal equipment is not supplied, but all other equipment is provided. School and youth groups welcome. Fully qualified and insured instruction.
Minimum age: 18 years, unless accompanied.

FIELD STUDIES COUNCIL
Head Office, Montford Bridge, Shrewsbury SY4 1HW (tel 01743-850674; fax 01743-850178).
Mountain First Aid and Mountain Leadership Assessment courses at the FSC's Snowdonia Centre (Rhyd-y-creuau). Prices from around £255 a week, £100 for a weekend inclusive of accommodation, all meals and tuition.
Minimum age: 16 years.

KEVIN WALKER MOUNTAIN ACTIVITIES
74 Beacons Park, Brecon, Powys LD3 9BQ (tel 01874-625111).
Recognised by the MLTB.
Holidays provided for 500 annually.
A wide range of courses in climbing, abseiling, caving, potholing, mountain walking and mountaineering in Wales throughout the year, with qualified instructors. Groups catered for. No experience required. Prices from £50 for an individual to £200+ for a group, including all equipment. A wide range of accommodation is available.
Minimum age: 18 years.

Europe

ADVENTURE WORLD INTERLAKEN
P O Box 645, 30080 Interlaken, Switzerland (tel +41 36 234 363; fax +41 36 267715).
A centre for a whole range of mountain activities including climbing, hiking, paragliding, rafting, canyoning, flying fox, fun yak and bungy jumping from the Schilthorn cable car.

COLLINEIGE
30-32 High Street, Frimley, Surrey GU16 5JD (tel 01276-24262).
Directors: C Gerrand, A Torr, A M J Savage.
In business since 1980.
Member of the SCGB.
Holidays for 1000+ arranged annually.
Mountain hiking, glacier walking, touring and climbing in the Chamonix valley France during summer. All levels catered for. Guides and instructors come from the Compagnie des Guides in Chamonix. Holidays can be off-the-peg or tailor-made for varying durations from a weekend to two weeks or longer. Other sports including parapente and hang-gliding also available. Winter skiing including heliskiing, also offered. Prices according to programme chosen. Luxury chalet accommodation on a fully catered or, self catering bed and breakfast basis.
Minimum age: 16.(Unaccompanied).

COMPAGNIE DES GUIDES DE CHAMONIX MONT-BLANC
190 Place de l'Eglise, 74400 Chamonix, France (tel +33 4-5053 90 88; fax +33 4-5053 48 04).
A renowned organisation (also in Argenti'ere, Les Houches and Servoz) for nearly all mountain sports and activities in summer and winter. Winter activities include: snowshoeing, ice climbing, off-piste skiing, ski mountaineering, heli-skiing, ski mountaineering/treks. Summer activities include: Alpine mountaineering, rock climbing, ice climbing, mountaineering, glacier treks, hikes and treks, canyoning and many more. Most activities are bookable on a daily basis, on a several days' course basis or three to seven days for ski-mountaineering/treks. Prices can be quoted on a daily or longer basis and for individuals or for groups. Example: 870 francs (about £94) per day snowshoeing for a group of ten; one-day ice-climbing course 540 francs (£58) per person; off piste skiing in the Vallée Blanche 340 francs (about £37) per person per day; six-days 4200 francs (about £456) per person all inclusive except personal drinks. The Compagnie des Guides de Chamonix also organises treks and expeditions worldwide.

Americas

KARAKORAM EXPERIENCE TRAVEL
32 Lake Road, Keswick, Cumbria (tel 017687-74693; fax 017687-73966). E-mail: keadventure@enterprise.net
US Office: Karakoram Experience, PO Box 10538, Aspen, Colorado 81612.
Directors: T Greening, G Rowley.
In business since 1984.
Holidays for 600 arranged annually.
Trekking and climbing holidays on the volcanoes of Ecuador and the Cordillera Blanca in Peru, 22 days. Also trekking and mountain biking in Bolivia and Peru. Land prices: £1545 (Ecuador), £1395 (Bolivia)

include accommodation in local hotels and tents and local and western food.

WORLD CHALLENGE EXPEDITIONS
(Black Arrow House, 2 Chandos Road, London NW10 6NF (tel 0181 961 1122; fax 0181-961 1122).
Month-long leadership development expeditions in Central and South America for young people aged 16-20. The unique feature is the provision for team members to develop management and leadership skills by taking charge of day-to-day planning of an expedition under qualified supervision. Activities are designed to be fulfilling and enjoyable, with emphasis on full participation, environmental awareness and challenge. These include trekking, mountaineering, jungle exploration, cultural exchange and selected project work. Prices from £2200 per person.

Africa

LET'S GO TRAVEL
P O Box 60342 Nairobi, Kenya (tel +254 2 213033/340331; fax +254 2 214713 & +254 2 336890).
Mountain climbing in Kenya and Tanzania including Mts. Kiliminjaro and Kenya.

WORLD CHALLENGE EXPEDITIONS
Black Arrow House, 2 Chandos Road, London NW10 6NF (tel 0181-961 1122; fax 0181 961 1551).
Month-long leadership development expeditions in Africa for young people aged 16 to 20. The unique feature is the provision for team members to develop management and leadership skills by taking charge of day-to-day planning of an expedition under qualified supervision. Activities are designed to be fulfilling and enjoyable, with emphasis on full participation, environmental awareness and challenge. These include trekking, mountaineering, safari, cultural exchange and selected project work. Prices from £1450 per person.

Asia

KARAKORAM EXPERIENCE TRAVEL
32 Lake Road, Keswick, Cumbria (tel 017687-73966; fax 017687-74693). US agent: Karakoram Experience, PO Box 10538, Aspen, Colorado 81612.
Trekking, mountaineering and mountain biking in the Karakoram mountains of Pakistan, China, Nepal and Bhutan. Various departure dates and durations from 21 to 37 days. Land only prices start at £1,315. Insurance costs £60-£70.

WORLD CHALLENGE EXPEDITIONS
Black Arrow House, 2 Chandos Road, London NW10 6NF (tel 0181-961 1122; fax 0181-961 1551).
Month-long leadership development expeditions in India and South-East Asia for young people aged 16-20 years. The unique feature is the provision for team members to develop management and leadership skills by taking charge of day to day planning of an expedition under qualified supervision. Activities are designed to be fulfilling and enjoyable, with emphasis on full participation, environmental awareness and challenge. These include trekking, mountaineering, jungle exploration, cultural exchange and selected project work. Prices from £2000 per person.

WORLDWIDE JOURNEYS AND EXPEDITIONS
8 Comeragh Road, London, W14 9HP (tel 0171-381 8638; fax 0171-381 0836).
Climbing and mountaineering holidays in the Himalayas. Climb a 22 000, feet trekking peak in the Himalayas. Climbs of Mera, Parchamo and Nyakanga have been arranged in the Nepal Himalaya. Fully inclusive packages.

Climbing and Mountaineering

England

BOWLES OUTDOOR CENTRE
Eridge Green, Tunbridge Wells, TN3 9LW (tel 01892-665665).

Climbing courses throughout the year. Weekend 'taster' course in the basics and more advanced courses also available. Price from £74 per weekend.
No experience needed.
Minimum age: nine years.Unaccompanied children accepted.

CALSHOT ACTIVITIES CENTRE
Calshot Spit, Fawley, Southampton SO45 1BR (tel 01703-892077).
Climbing courses throughout the year using specialist indoor walls (new indoor climbing wall). Evening and weekend courses are available from beginner to Instructor training. All specialist equipment is provided. The climbing walls are also available to individuals and groups of climbers at evenings and weekends.

HF HOLIDAYS
Imperial House, Edgware Road, London NW9 5AL (tel 0181-905 9556).
Winter Hill Walking and Mountaineering in the Lake District for beginners and in Scotland for the more experienced. Experienced, enthusiastic leaders offer tuition and guidance. Prices from £314 for seven nights full board. Call for a walking holidays in Britain brochure.

HIMALAYAN KINGDOMS EXPEDITIONS
45 Mowbray Street, Sheffield S3 8EN (tel 0114-2763322; fax 0114-2763344).
ATOL licence no 4019.
U.K. and Scotland based mountaineering and rock climbing courses. Scottish Winter Courses, introductory rock climbing in Snowdonia and the Peak District and private guiding anywhere. Qualified instruction offered. Full colour brochure on request.

THE OUTDOOR TRUST
Belford, Northumberland NE70 7QE (tel 01668-213289; fax 01668-213289).
Offers the following courses in rock sports: introduction for beginners; intermediate which covers lead climbing, gear placement, belaying and rope work; introduction for extreme climbing and advanced rope work; specialist training regimes for rock sports. Sports take place on Northumberland sandstone crags. Mountain walking holidays and scrambling available on request.

Wind Chill Chart

As wind has an important effect on the temperature it is most advisable to use a tent or bivouac shelter when sleeping in cold weather or at high altitude in windy weather.

ESTIMATED WIND SPEED IN MPH	ACTUAL THERMOMETER READING (°F)										
	50	40	30	20	10	0	−10	−20	−30	−40	−50
	EQUIVALENT TEMPERATURE (°F)										
calm	50	40	30	20	10	0	−10	−20	−30	−40	−50
5	48	37	27	16	6	−5	−15	−26	−36	−47	−57
10	40	28	16	4	−9	−21	−33	−46	−58	−70	−83
15	36	22	9	−5	−18	−36	−45	−58	−72	−85	−99
20	32	18	4	−10	−25	−39	−53	−67	−82	−96	−110
25	30	16	0	−15	−29	−44	−59	−74	−88	−104	−118
30	28	13	−2	−18	−33	−48	−63	−79	−94	−109	−125
35	27	11	−4	−20	−35	−49	−67	−82	−98	−113	−129
40	26	10	−6	−21	−37	−53	−69	−85	−100	−116	−132
(wind speeds greater than 40 mph. have little additional effect)	LITTLE DANGER (for properly clothed persons)				Increasing DANGER			GREAT DANGER Danger from freezing of exposed flesh.			

OUTWARD BOUND TRUST
Watermillock, Cumbria, CA11 OJL (tel 0990-134227).
Outward Bound rock-climbing and mountain leader courses. For more information phone for a free skills brochure.

ROCK LEA ACTIVITY CENTRE
Station Road, Hathersage, Hope Valley S32 1DD (tel 01433-650345).
Adventure Activity Licence.
Comprehensive weekends and longer courses in climbing, abseiling and mountaineering. Weekends all year, weeks Easter and summer. More than 12 BMC qualified instructors available. Full insurance cover. Adults — weekends from £99, £299-399 for one week in summer. Tuition from £25 per person per day. Also available follow-up weekends and mountain rescue team exercises for individuals or groups. All courses have a programme of alternative activities in the event of bad weather.
Usual ages: 18+ but school groups and younger guests on separate dates by prior arrangement.

YHA ACTIVITY CENTRE
Rowland Cote, Nether Booth, Edale, Derbyshire S30 2ZH (tel 01433-670302).
Climbing courses for all levels in the Peak District or North Wales. Learn and develop techniques and skills, plus evening lectures. All under the guidance of experienced instructors. Prices from £84 (weekend) including full board and equipment.
Minimum age: 16 years.

Scotland

ABERNETHY TRUST
Nethy Bridge, Inverness-shire PH25 3ED (tel 01479-821279).
Rock climbing and Mountain craft courses in the Cairngorm Mountains for individuals and groups. One week, or weekends, from May to October. £205-£240 includes qualified instruction, equipment, accommodation and meals. Mountain craft involves navigation skills, safety on steep ground, river crossing, abseiling, survival techniques, bivouacs. Rock climbing involves belays, rope work, route finding, leading on local crags and sea cliffs.
'The staff are committed Christians and enjoy sharing their faith with visitors to the Centre'.
Minimum age: 16 years.

ASSOCIATION FOR ADVENTURE SPORTS
Tiglin, The National Adventure Centre, Ashford, Co Wicklow, Ireland (tel +353 404-4016; fax +353 404-40701). E-mail: mail@tiglin.le
Winter mountaineering in the Ben Nevis and Glencoe regions. Five-day courses in February/March for those with previous rock experience and a knowledge of ropework.
Minimum age: 16 years.

CLASSIC NEPAL
33 Metro Avenue, Newton, Alfreton, Derbyshire DE55 5UF (tel 01773-873497; fax 01773-590243).
Winter mountaineering courses in the Cairngorm area of Scotland. Weekend and 5 day courses from January to March, for individuals and groups. Introductory snow and ice climbing, instruction in winter walking, ascent and descent of grade 1 gullies, equipment use techniques, survival skills and navigation. Intermediate/advanced winter snow and ice climbing for those with some winter experience.

GLENCOE OUTDOOR CENTRE
Glencoe, Argyll PA39 4HS (tel 01855-811350).
Winter and summer climbing and mountaineering courses in Glencoe, Ben Nevis and the surrounding area for individuals and groups of up to 35. Qualified instruction. Full board and accommodation at the Centre. Price from around £70 for a weekend.
No experience needed.
Minimum age: 15.

HIGHLANDER MOUNTAINEERING
Highlea, Auchnarrow, Glenlivet, Banffshire AB37 9JN (tel 01807-590250).
Partners: P Hill MIC.
In business since 1989.
Member of Moray Tourist Board and AMI.
Adventure Activity Licence.
Rock climbing and summer and winter mountaineering courses around Tomintoul in the Grampian. All year round except October and November. No experience is need for most courses. Guided walking

tours also arranged. Prices from £75-£395. Various types of accommodation available eg. bed and breakfast, full board.
Minimum age: 16 years.

MARTIN MORAN MOUNTAINEERING
Park Cottage, Achintee, Strathcarron, Ross-shire IV54 8YX (tel/fax 01520-722361).
Proprietor: Martin Moran.
BAMG, UIAGM.
In business since 1986.
Holidays for 300 arranged annually.
Hillwalking, scrambling and climbing courses in Skye and Torridon in North West Scotland. Beginners to advanced. January to June, and October. Individuals and groups of up to ten. Prices for five days, including full board and lodge accommodation starting at £325. Some previous walking experience is essential for beginners courses.
Minimum age: 14 accompanied, 18 unaccompanied.

MOUNTAIN CRAFT
Professional Mountaineering Services, Glenfinnan, Fort William PH37 4LT (tel 01397-722213; fax 01397-722300). E-mail: mail@mountaincraft.co.uk
Mountaineering and climbing courses in the Scottish Highlands. Private guiding and instruction. Variety of accommodation.
Minimum age: 18 years.

SKYE MOUNTAIN GUIDES
4d Wentworth Street, Portree, Isle of Skye IV51 9ES (tel 01478-612682).
Proprietor: A H Evans.
In business since 1993.
Member of Skye Tourist Organisation.
Private guiding throughout the year on Skye's mountains and in neighbouring areas. Classic rock climbs such as The Cioch, Window Buttress and Basteir Tooth featured. Walks and scrambles also available. Accommodation in hotels, self-catering, campsites or guesthouses available locally. Prices from £55 (day) to £190 (week). Most courses are for groups of up to ten.
Minimum age: 17 years.

Wales

BLACK DRAGON OUTDOOR EXPERIENCES
7 Ethelbert Drive, Charlton, Andover, Hampshire SP10 4EP (tel 01264-357313).
Mountain safety, navigation and rock climbing in the Black Mountains in the Brecon Beacons and Snowdonia National Parks, for days and weekends all year round. Prices from £140 per weekend including accommodation and all technical equipment. For individuals and groups up to 24. Climbing can be organised in other areas as well.
Minimum age: 11 years (accompanied).

KEVIN WALKER MOUNTAIN ACTIVITIES
74 Beacons Park, Brecon, Powys LD3 9BQ (tel/fax 01874-625111).
Rock climbing and caving based in the Brecon Beacons and Snowdonia National Parks. Novice, intermediate and advanced courses. Wide range of accommodation available locally. Prices from £50. Personal service with small groups, led by enthusiastic and qualified professional instructors.
Minimum age: 18 years.

OUTER LIMITS
Pwll-y-Garth, Prenmarhno, Gwynedd LL25 OHJ (tel/fax 01690-760248).
Rock climbing, mountaineering and sramblng courses in North Wales all year round. One to five-day courses, with introductory programmes teaching basic techniques, equipment and procedures. Groups and individuals catered for. Prices from £20 per day for instruction only. Weekends from £80. All equipment provided. Accommodation available locally, or in the bunkhouse (£8.50 per night including breakfast).
Minimum age: 14 years (accompanied); 16 years (unaccompanied).
Physically, visually and mentally challenged people welcome.

Ireland

ASSOCIATION FOR ADVENTURE SPORTS
Tiglin, The National Adventure Centre, Ashford, Co. Wicklow, Ireland (tel +353 404-40169; fax: +353 404 40701). E-mail: mail@tiglin.le
Rock climbing courses. Weekends and weeks based at the National Adventure Centre at Tiglin. Instruction by experienced and qualified staff. All specialist equipment provided. Prices from IR£70 approximately.
No experience needed.

Europe

ALPINE ADVENTURES/MOUNTAIN REALITY
P O Box 6490 Andermatt, Switzerland (tel +41 44 67770; +41 8871770; fax +41 887 17 37.
Recognised Mountaineering School.
Director Alex Clapasson.
In business since 1980
Rock and ice climbing weeks in Switzerland, France, Italy and Austria. Also a range of other mountain-based activities including ski touring, biking and hiking weeks. Weekends and weeks. Prices from 800-1800 Swiss francs for a week including accommodation in mountain huts/guesthouses/3 star hotels. Minimum age: 12 years accompanied; 16 years unaccompanied.

ASSOCIATION FOR ADVENTURE SPORTS
Tiglin, The National Adventure Centre, Ashford, Co. Wicklow, Ireland (tel +353 404-40169; fax +353 404-40701). E-mail: mail@tiglin.le
Rock climbing courses based around Ireland and Spain. Weekends and weeks. Instruction by experienced and qualified staff. All specialist equipment provided. No experience needed.

HIMALAYAN KINGDOM EXPEDITIONS
45 Mowbray Street, Sheffield S3 8EN (tel 0114-2763322; fax 0114 2763344).
Guided ascents of Mt Blanc, other Alpine peaks, of Europe's highest mountain, Elbrus in the European Caucasus. Tailor made guiding services also available, plus rock climbing holidays in Spain. Full colour brochure on request.

MARTIN MORAN MOUNTAINEERING
Park Cottage, Achintee, Strathcarron, Ross-shire IV54 8YX (tel 01520-722361).
Mountaineering courses in the Swiss Alps (including the Matterhorn) June to August based near Arolla. Novices to advanced. Individuals and groups of up to eight. Some previous hill walking and climbing experience necessary. Price of £900 for twelve days includes full board and chalet accommodation, helmets and harnesses. Ice axes, hammers and crampons may be hired. Travel ex-UK is not included, also cable-car and hut fees which cost around £40 per week.
Minimum age: 18 years (unaccompanied).

Americas

HIMALAYAN KINGDOMS EXPEDITIONS
Adjacent The Foundry, 45 Mowbray Street, Sheffield S3 8EN (tel 0114-274 3322; fax 0114 276 3344).
Guided climbs of McKinley in Alaska, Aconcagua in Argentina and other mountains in Bolivia, Ecuador and Peru. Prices start from £2,095 from London. Tailor made expedition arrangements available for private groups. Full colour brochure on request.

WORLD CHALLENGE EXPEDITIONS
Black Arrow House, 2 Chandos Road, London NW10 6NF (tel 0181-961 1122; fax 0181-961 1551).
Month-long leadership training expeditions in Central and South America for young people aged 16-20 years. The unique feature is the provision for team members to develop management and leadership skills by taking charge of day-to-day planning of an expedition under qualified supervision. Activities are designed to be fulfilling and enjoyable, with emphasis on full participation, environmental awareness and challenge. These include trekking, mountaineering, jungle exploration, safari, cultural exchange and selected project work. Prices from £2000 per person.

Africa

EXODUS EXPEDITIONS
9 Weir Road, Balham, London SW12 0LT (tel 0181-675 5550).
Climb the major peaks and rock areas of the Atlas and Jebel Sahro ranges in Morocco.

Eight to 22 days from £530. Also climb Kilimanjaro in Tanzania in eight days from £510, Mount Kenya and the Aberdares 17 days from £1,780. Also a chance to climb Jebel Mousa in Egypt's Sinai Desert.

HIMALAYAN KINGDOMS EXPEDITIONS
45 Mowbray Street, Sheffield S3 8EN (tel 0114-2763322; fax 0114-2763344).
Guided ascents of Kilimanjaro and Mt Kenya. Rock climbing holidays in South Africa and Namibia. A variety of routes are available on Kilimanjaro on which the company has a good track record. Tailor-made arrangements for private groups available. Full colour brochure available on request.

WORLD CHALLENGE EXPEDITIONS
Black Arrow House, 2 Chandos Road, London NW10 6NF (tel 0181-961 1122; fax 0181-961 1551).
Month-long leadership development expeditions in Africa for young people aged 16-20 years. The unique feature is the provision for team members to develop management and leadership skills by taking charge of day-to-day planning of an expedition under qualified supervision. Activities are designed to be fulfilling and enjoyable, with emphasis on full participation, environmental awareness and challenge. These include trekking, mountaineering, safari, cultural exchange and selected project work. Prices from £2000 per person.

Arctic

TANGENT EXPEDITIONS INTERNATIONAL
10 Stockdale Farm, Moor Lane, Flookburgh, Cumbria LA11 7LR; tel 015395-59087; 015394-59088.
Partners: Paul & Lucy Walker.
In operation since 1990.
Member of BMC.
Holidays for approximately 50 people arranged annually.
Mountaineering, ski touring and ski mountaineering expeditions in Greenland and Iceland for 3-5 weeks during March to August. Previous winter mountain experience needed. Expedition involves camping and sleeping bag accommodation in transit. Personal climbing/skiing gear can be hired if needed. Groups of four to 20 possible.
Ages: 18 to 60+.
'First ascents of remote virgin summits in Arctic Greenland'.

Asia

BUFO VENTURES LTD
3 Elim Grove, Windermere, Cumbria LA23 2JN (tel + fax 015394-45445).
Climbing and scientific expeditions plus trekking and wildlife holidays in Nepal.

CLASSIC NEPAL
33 Metro Avenue, Newton, Alfreton, Derbyshire DE55 5UF (tel 01773-873497; fax 01773-590243). E-mail: classicnepal@compuserve.com
Directors: A Brooks and N Walshe.
In business since 1986.
ATOL bonded, no 3022.
Holidays for 150-200 arranged annually.
Walking, climbing and mountaineering in Nepal, India and Tibet, escorted by western leaders. Climb Island Peak and Mera Peak in the Everest region, Naya Kanga in the Langtang and Chulu East in the Annapurna area. Climbing camp in the Himalaya organised annually. Arrangements can be made for schools, colleges, private groups and individuals. Prices from £1500 to £2995, all inclusive. General fitness and robust health required.
Also available are winter mountaineering courses in Scotland from January to April.
Minimum age: 18 years (unaccompanied), 15 years (accompanied).

EXODUS EXPEDITIONS
9 Weir Road, Balham, London SW12 0LT (tel 0181-675 5550).
Support an expedition to climb Brikhuti Peak in Mustang, Nepal. 29 days from £2,450. Opportunities to climb Ramdung Peak (19,550 ft) and Mera Peak (21,288 ft) for those with basic knowledge of crampon and ice-axe techniques.
Other trekking peaks and climbs include Gondogoro (Pakistan) Stok Kangri (Ladakh) Pangre and Pokalde in Nepal.

HIMALAYAN KINGDOMS EXPEDITIONS
Adjacent The Foundry, 45 Mowbray Street, Sheffield S3 8EN (tel 0114-276 3322; fax 0114-27933 44.

A pace-setting expedition company with ten years experience of providing guided climbs in the Himalaya, Karakoram and Tien Shan. Trips suitable for novice to expert, from trekking peaks to Everest. Tailor made expedition arrangements available for private groups. Full colour brochure on request. Call Steve Bell or Simon Lowe for details.

MARTIN MORAN MOUNTAINEERING
Park Cottage, Achintee, Strathcarron, Ross-shire IV54 8YX (tel/fax 01520-722361).
Mountaineering expeditions and trekking peaks in Indian Garhwal Himalaya in May/June and September. Price: £2500-£2700. Preparatory training courses offered.

PEAK INTERNATIONAL
15 Moor Park, Wendover, Aylesbury HP22 6AX (tel/fax 01296 624225).
Himalaya
Stok Kangri, excellent first Himalayan summit — 20-day trek and ascent from £695 ex Delhi. Island Peak, a superb 20,000ft summit requiring only basic alpine experience — 19 days £575 ex Kathmandu. Mera, stunning panorama of Everest, Kanchenjunga, Makalu, Lhotse, Ama Dablam and Cho Oyo. 19 days ex Kathmandu £575.
Also available Kang Yissay, Nun/Kun with others upon request. 18 days ex Delhi £895.
Trekking Peaks: Select from three 6000m+ peaks, Lobuje, Island and Mera. Non-technical ascents in the heart of the Everest region. Full instruction given. September to June. 19 days from £560.

ROAMA TRAVEL
Larks Rise, Shroton, Blandford, Dorset DT11 8QW (tel 01258-860298).
AITO fully bonded.
Alpine climbing treks in Himalaya, all year round. Prices £1268-£1928 including hotel bed and breakfast accommodation. Some climbing equipment is not included in the price but may be hired.

WORLD PEACE TREKKING (P) LTD
PO Box 550, Thamel, Kathmandu, Nepal (tel UK 01424-220892).
E-mail: worldpeace@dial.pipex.com
Internet:
http://www.pavilion.co.uk/website-designs/world — peace/
Directors: K L Tamang and A Tamang.
In business since 1992.
Member of Nepal Rafting Association. Nepal Tourist and Trekking Government Licence.
Holidays for 150 arranged annually.
Trekking and mountaineering in Nepal and Tibet available all year round. Tours last from five to 60 days. Extensive mountaineering experience required for climbing expeditions. Individuals and groups of any size catered for. Prices from \$200-\$6000 including camping and all meals. Flights, hotel in Kathmandu, personal clothing and climbing gear not included in the holiday price. Bookings taken on the internet only (see website address details).
Minimum age: 16 years unaccompanied. No maximum age limit.
'We specialise in off-the-beaten-track trekking and rafting. We are not a soft option'.

Australasia

ALPINE GUIDES LTD
Main Road, Mount Cook 8870, New Zealand (tel +64 3 4351834; fax +64 3 4351898).
In operation since 1962.
Member of New Zealand Mountain Guides Association.
Holidays for 6000+ arranged annually.
Mountain guiding and climbing instruction located in Mount Cook National Park all year round. Small groups of less than 10 catered for. Price: NZ\$2200 (about £920) for ten days including accommodation and all meals. Heli-skiing available, NZ\$600 (about £250) per day. Some previous hiking or skiing experience required.
Minimum age: 16 years (unaccompanied); maximum age: 70 years.

Middle East

MAGIC CARPET TRAVEL
125 Rylston Road, London SW6 7HP (tel 0171-385 9975; fax 0171-381 2304).
Nine and ten-day mountain climbing trips in Iran. Nine days includes Tehran, Tabriz, Ardabil, Sabalan Peak, Anzali, Isfahan and Shiraz. Ten-day trip includes Gousfand Sara, Reneh and Chalus. Also tailor-made trips. Accommodation includes, tent, shelter and hotel. Prices do not include flights

(currently about £400-£480 round trip to Tehran) or visas (about £90).

WORLD CHALLENGE EXPEDITIONS
Black Arrow House, 2 Chandos Road, London NW10 6NF (tel 0181-961 1122; fax 0181-961 1551.
Month-long leadership development expeditions in India, Pakistan and South-East Asia for young people aged 16 to 20. The unique feature is the provision for team members to develop management and leadership skills by taking charge of day-to-day planning of an expedition under qualified supervision. Activities are designed to be fulfilling and enjoyable, with emphasis on full participation, environmental awareness and challenge. These include trekking, mountaineering, jungle exploration, safari, cultural exchange and selected project work. Prices from £2000 per person.

Skiing

England

BOWLES OUTDOOR CENTRE
Eridge Green, Tunbridge Wells TN3 9LW (tel 01892-665665).
Skiing courses for beginners, intermediate and advanced skiers. Instruction given on a 250 ft long artificial ski slope with ski tow. Also 150 ft long nursery slope available. Winter courses in the Alps also offered. Courses from £19.
No experience needed.
Minimum age: eight years.

CALSHOT ACTIVITIES CENTRE
Calshot Spit, Fawley, Southampton SO45 1BR (tel 01703-892077).
Recognised by the English Ski Council.
Ski and snowboarding courses for all levels from complete novice to Artificial Ski Slope Instructors award. The centre runs short evening courses, and coaching days at weekends. Fully qualified staff offer expert tuition and advise on all aspects of the sport. The 100 ft slope is the largest indoor ski slope in the country and with its fixed tow provides an ideal learning environment. Weekend Ski Workshop £40 (one day) equipment and instruction included.
Minimum age: six years (13+ for weekends).

Scotland

ABERNETHY TRUST
Nethy Bridge, Inverness-shire PH25 3ED (tel 014798-21279).
Skiing courses for all standards in the Cairngorm Mountains, for seven nights January-April. Prices from £245 including accommodation, meals, instruction, equipment, ski pass and transport; £20 discount for under 18's. Cross-country ski courses are also available. No experience needed.
'The staff are committed Christians and enjoy sharing their faith with visitors to the Centre'.
Minimum age: six years accompanied; 16 years unaccompanied.

CAIRNWELL MOUNTAIN SPORTS
Gulabin Lodge, Glenshee, Perthshire PH10 7QE (tel & fax 01250-885255).
Member of British Association of Ski Schools.
Professional ski instruction for all levels and abilities. Courses include beginner packages, childrens classes, race training and timing, nordic and telemark skiing, heliboarding and snowboarding. Private lessons available for groups and individuals. Five-day ski holiday package from £145 including B&B, hire and instruction. Ski hire available. Achievement certificates awarded on course completion.

COMPASS CHRISTIAN CENTRE LTD
Glenshee Lodge, by Blairgowrie, Perthshire PH10 7QD (tel 01250-885209; fax 01250-885309).
Adventure Activities Licence.
Skiing holidays at Glenshee. No experience necessary. Weekend and mid-week breaks available for individuals and groups. Price from £61 including accommodation and full board (packed lunch), ski hire and instruction. Dormitory accommodation. Interdenominational Christian Centre with experienced and qualified staff. Open all year. Self-catering accommodation also available.

GLENCOE OUTDOOR CENTRE
Glencoe, Argyll PA39 4HS (tel 01855-811350).
Dual centre skiing holidays at White Corries, Glencoe and Nevis Range, Fort William, for individuals and groups of up to 35. Qualified instruction by Glencoe Ski

School. Various packages including two-day, five-day and full week breaks from January to early May. Full board and accommodation at the Centre. Price from around £70 for a weekend. All equipment included. No experience needed.
Minimum age: six years; unaccompanied children: 12 years +.

Europe

A.A.K. EUROPE LTD
4 Earl Street, Oxford OX2 OJA (tel/fax 01865-245077).
Director: Nick Hills.
In business since 1990.
Cross country, mountain touring and telemark ski instruction based at a renowned mountain centre in the stunning Romsdal Valley in Norway. Other mountain pursuits available from rope work to snow scooters. Complete package, including travel, full board, equipment hire and instruction or any part(s) of the package as required can be arranged.

ALPINE ADVENTURES/MOUNTAIN REALITY
P.O. Box 6490 Andermatt, Switzerland (tel +41 887 17 70; fax +41 887 1737).
Powder snow weeks, off-piste safari weeks. Beginners and intermediates. Ski touring includes the hautes routes for very experienced ski mountaineers only. Arranged in Switzerland, France, Italy and Austria from December to May. Weekends 290-400 Swiss francs (about £126-£173), weeks 800-1800 Swiss francs (about £350-£780). Includes accommodation in mountain huts/guesthouses/3 star hotels.
Minimum age: 12 years (accompanied); 16-18 Unaccompanied.

CHALLENGE ACTIV LTD
49 Eastwick Road, Walton-on-Thames, Surrey KT12 5AR (tel 01932-254501).
Directors: Mr S C Allen and Mrs A L Allen.
In business since 1993.
A flexible range of activities including skiing, mountain biking, rafting, mountain walking, canoeing, wind surfing, horse riding, tennis, ice skating, fishing, archery and others in Morzine in the French Alps. Skiing December-April; other activities April to October, Prices from £300-£360 per week. A mixture of half board and B&B accommodation in a luxury chalet sleeping 23. Plenty of restaurants and supermarkets locally.
Minimum age: 18 unaccompanied; maximum age: 68 years.

CRYSTAL HOLIDAYS
The Courtyard, Arlington Road, Surbiton, Surrey KT6 6BW (tel 0181-2415128).
Skiing holidays throughout Europe (including Scandinavia) and North America. Winter skiing (December-April) in Austria, France, Italy, Switzerland, Romania, Bulgaria, Andorra, Norway, Sweden, the USA and Canada. Summer skiing holidays in Austria from May to September.Learn to ski and snowboarding weeks. Groups, couples, singles and families catered for. Prices from £75 for seven nights' self-catering, self-drive based on five people. Accommodation also available in bed and breakfast, half board or catered chalets. Equipment not included but available locally. No experience needed.

ECLIPSE OUTDOOR DISCOVERY
Cragwood House, Windermere, Cumbria LA23 1LQ (tel 015394-44033; fax 015394-42145).
High Alpine Ski Tours in the Swiss/French Alps for those with experience of downhill skiing who wish to progress to off-piste skiing and touring. Courses offered are: Introductory Ski Touring, High Level Route, Chamonix Off-piste and Bernese Oberland. Prices from £570 (seven nights) includes hotel/pension/chalet or mountain hut accommodation and all meals. All courses are led by fully qualified UIAGM Mountain Guides. Travel from the UK, insurance and Alpine Club Membership are not included.

HEADWATER HOLIDAYS
146 London Road, Northwich, Cheshire CW9 5HH (tel 01606-48699).
Cross-country and downhill skiing in France, Switzerland, Italy and Norway for independent travellers from November to April. Price from £346 including ferry travel, hotel accommodation, private bathroom, dinner, bed and breakfast. No experience required.
Physically challenged people catered for.

HUSKI CHALET HOLIDAYS
63a Kensington Church Street, London W8 4BA (tel 0171-9384844; fax 0171-9382312). E-mail: sales@huski.com
Internet: http://www.huski.com
Partners: Mr & Mrs T C Newman.
In operation since 1985.
Member of BASI. Affiliated to Ski Club of Great Britain.
Specialist Alpine and Telemark ski courses located in Chamonix, France from December to May. Individuals and groups of up to 20 catered for. Prices range from £305-£410 per person including fully catered accommodation in a converted alpine farmhouse. Unaccompanied young people not accepted.

MERISKI LTD
The Old School, Great Barrington, Burford, Oxon OX18 4UR (tel 01451-844788; fax 01451-844799).
Directors: C Mathews and D Holmes.
In business since 1984.
Member of SCGB, ATOL and AITO.
Skiing holidays in Méribel, France. Opportunities for skiing, snow-boarding, ski touring, hang gliding, parapenting and cross-country skiing. Available December to May. Prices range between £399 and £1019 and include half board, flight and transfer. Ski equipment not included. Mainly groups of six to 20 catered for.

MOUNTAIN EXPERIENCE
Pike View Barn, Whitehough Head, Chinley, Stockport, Cheshire SK12 6BX (tel/fax 01663 750160.
Ski mountaineering packages based in Chamonix, France but also in the Swiss, Austrian and Italian Alps. Courses are held from December to mid-May and include Introduction to Ski Touring and week long tours in Dauphine (from La Grave), Gran Paradiso, Haute route, Zermatt and the-Bernese Oberland. Private guiding is also available for powder, off piste, glacier and ski touring days. Only fully qualified (UIAGM) mountain guides lead the courses. Prices from £595, includes half-board chalet or hotel accommodation. Ski and other equipment hire is extra, as are travel to Chamonix and insurance. Clients should be intermediate level or higher.Minimum age: normally eighteen but possibly younger by arrangement and depending on ability.

NEUCHATEL TOURISM
Hôtel des Postes, 2001 Neuchâtel, Switzerland (tel +41 38-251789; fax +41 38-251789; fax +41 328896296).
Winter holidays in the Neuchâtel region. Area boasts high quality cross-country ski trails among the finest of the Jura and the incomparable beauty of the Neuchâtel Mountains. Also downhill skiing, snow shoe tours and dog sled tours. Illuminated slopes for night time skiing.
Choose from five hotel categories. Wide selection of cultural, sporting and discovery activities (one per day included in package). Half board and breakfast included. Prices from 199 Swiss francs (about £86) per person for 3 nights/4 days.

RAMBLERS HOLIDAYS
Box 43, Welwyn Garden City, Herts AL8 6PQ (tel 01707-331133).
Cross-country skiing in Austria, the Czech Republic, Italy, Switzerland and France, for one or two weeks from December to March. Family-run pensions or hotel accommodation. Resorts suited to beginners, intermediate and advanced skiers.

SKI CLUB HOLIDAYS
The White House, 57-63 Church Road, Wimbledon, London SW19 55B (tel 0181 410 2000).
Organised by the Ski Club of Great Britain.
Skiing holidays tailored to different standards/ages led by SCGB leaders. All levels catered for from beginner to expert. Specialised groups include (qualified) instruction holidays, learn to ski powder, off-piste weeks, ski safaris and tours. Also families, unaccompanied teenagers and over 50's specially catered for. All off-piste holidays led by qualified mountain guides. The hire of autophons (avalanche transceivers) is included in the off-piste holiday cost.
Membership of the SCGB is needed, join when you book for a reduced membership subscription.

SKI GOURMET
Greenways, Vann Lake, Ockley, Dorking RH5 5NT (tel 01306-712111; fax 01306 713504). E-mail: steve.dallyn@winetrails.co.uk
Internet: www.winetrails.co.uk
Gourmet award winning chefs in exclusive private chalet with a 20 years experienced ski guide in Austria. Similar programmes in

Italy and the French Alps. Possibilities for boarding, walking and snow walking.

SKIWORLD
41 North End Road, London W14 8SZ (tel 0171-602 4826; fax 0171-371 4904).
In business since 1982.
Member of ABTA and AITO.
Holidays for 17,000 annually.
Skiing in top resorts in France, Italy and Switzerland from December to April, for beginners, intermediates and experts. Accommodation in catered chalets, chalet hotels, self-catering apartments and hotels. Flights from seven UK departure points, snowtrain and self drive. Prices from £189. 'Great value holidays in snowsure resorts.'

SUOMEN LATU RY
Fabianinkatu 7, FIN-00130 Helsinki, Finland (tel +358-9 170 101; fax +358-9 663 376).
General Secretary: Mr Tuomo Jantunen.
Skiing tours and treks in Lapland, South and East Finland and to the Arctic ocean. Eight to ten day tours between January and May. Distances range between 100km and 200km. Accommodation ranges from hotels and holiday homes to wilderness huts. Short trek participants carry their personal gear in backpacks, whilst luggage transportation is provided on the longer distance treks. Experience uninhabited regions and beautiful, unspoilt nature. Bookings through Suomen Latu or any local Finnair office.

UCPA
Action Vacances, 30 Brackley Road, Stockport, Cheshire SK4 2RE (tel 0161-442 6130).
UCPA (Union nationale des Centres sportifs de Plein Air) is a non-profit organisation which provides activity holidays at over 90 centres in France, 28 of which are in well-known ski resorts. Skiing holidays and instruction in La Plagne, Val d'Isere, Tignes and Val Thorens. Accommodation is in purpose built UCPA centres. Prices from £337 a week are *tous compris* which means there are no extras as all the following are included: accommodation, full board, lift pass, ski equipment, instruction if needed, après ski programme. Individuals and groups.

WAYMARK HOLIDAYS
44 Windsor Road, Slough SL1 2EJ (tel 01753-516477).
Cross-country skiing holidays in Austria, Germany, Italy, France, Norway, Finland, Poland, Switzerland, Sweden and Canada. Suitable for beginners through to advanced skiers. Centre holidays and tours. Seven to ten days, from Christmas through to Easter. Prices from £435 for a week in Italy. Packages include flights, half or full board accommodation, instruction and equipment hire.

Americas

ANDES
Andes, 93 Queen Street, Castle Douglas, Kircudbright, Scotland DG7 1EH (tel/fax 01556-503929). E-mail: andes@dial.pipex.com
Internet: http://dialspace.dial.pipex.com/andes
Skiing and ski-mountaineering holidays in Chile and Argentina.

CHALET SNOWBOARD
31 Aldworth Avenue, Wantage, Oxon OX12 7EJ (tel/fax 01235-767182).
Snow boarding in Lake Tahoe ski area in the USA. Prices £700-785. Individuals and parties of up to 20 people. No experience required.

FRONTIER SKI
21 Panton Street, London SW1Y 4DR; tel 0181-7768709; fax 0181-778 0149).
Directors: T Bakewell, P Snell, A Dunlop D Briggs.
In business since 1989.
AITO, ABTA, IATA.
Holidays for 1000 arranged annually.
Skiing holidays in Canada from December to April at all the main resorts including Whistler, Jasper, Banff, Mont Tremblant and Lake Louise. Downhill, snowcat skiing, heli skiing, cross-country, snow mobiles, alpine touring/telemark skiing, dog-sledding. Mixed itineraries possible eg: three nights at Kananaskis, five nights at Lake Louise, four nights dog-sledding at Nordegg (13 days total). Prices from £550-£1500 not including ski hire or 4WD vehicle hire (from £60 per week). Children get free skiing (age limit varies from seven to 12 years depending on the resort) and discounts on accommodation.

KOOTENAY HELICOPTER SKIING
P.O. Box 717 Nakusp, British Columbia VOG 1RO Canada (tel +1 250-265-3121; fax +1 250-265-4447).

In business since 1976.
Helicopter skiing in the Selkirk and Monashee Mountains, British Columbia from the beginning of January to the middle of April. Three, four and seven-day packages. Airport collection for clients on seven-day packages only. Skiers are shuttled up by a jet-powered helicopter for the ultimate skiing experience. Four groups of nine skiers per week so the service is very personalised. Prices from C$2250 (about £1000) for three days, to C$5250 (about £2,330) for seven days. Included in the price are double occupancy of rooms, all meals, guide service, use of special skis, a dip in the hotsprings every day after skiing and a guaranteed vertical footage.

LAURENTIAN INTERNATIONAL COLLEGE

221 Tour Du Lac, Ste Agathe Des Monts, Québec J8C 2Z7, Canada (tel +1 819 3268400; fax +1 819 3268403).
Skiing courses in the Laurentian Mountains of Québec. Courses last three months (12 January-26 March). Individuals and groups catered for. Students enter for the CSIA (Canadian Ski Instructors Alliance) awards. Cost of £4,350 includes airfares, instruction, French conversation classes and half board accommodation. Ski equipment not included. Approximate cost of ski exam, £150 extra.
Minimum age: 18 years.
'More than just a skiing holiday as the group works towards an Instructors Award in the heart of francophone Québec. Who knows, you may also get to build an igloo'.
UK booking agent: Catherine Ferree (tel 0181-780 2547) or book direct.

PISTE ARTISTE

1874 Champéry, Switzerland (tel +41 2-47 493489; fax +41 2-4 4973344).
E-mail: ski@pisteartiste.com
Internet: http://www.pisteartiste.com
In operation since 1987.
Holidays for 500 arranged annually.
Ten-day ski safari across the Canadian Rocky, Selkirk, Monashee and Coastal Mountains of British Columbia, Canada. Sample the skiing at five ski resorts including Whistler and Lake Louise. Travel by Snow Cat vehicle to acre upon acre of virgin snow for the ultimate powder skiing. Knowledgable and friendly guides accompany the safari. Trips available in January and February. Prices from £1223 including accommodation (hotels and Inns), some meals, ground transportation, two days Cat skiing and eight days lift passes.
Also available in Champéry, Switzerland: skiing, snowboarding and telemark (winter), mountain biking, climbing, hiking (summer). Reservations taken on 0171-436 0100.

SKI CLUB HOLIDAYS

The White House, 57-63 Church Road, Wimbledon, London SW19 55B (tel 0181 410 2000).
Organised by the Ski Club of Great Britain.
Skiing holidays tailored to different standards/ages led by SCGB leaders. All levels catered for from beginner to expert. Specialised groups include (qualified) instruction holidays, learn to ski powder, off-piste weeks, ski safaris and tours. Also families, unaccompanied teenagers and over 50's specially catered for. All off-piste holidays led by qualified mountain guides. The hire of autophons (avalanche transceivers) is included in the off-piste holiday cost.
Membership of the SCGB is needed, join when you book for a reduced membership subscription.

SKI INDEPENDENCE

Broughton Market, Edinburgh EH3 6NU (tel 0990 550 555; fax 0990 50 20 20).
Directors: J B Bennett, W Millar.
In business since 1994.
AITO, ABTA, SCGB affiliated.
Holidays for 4000 arranged annually.
Skiing, snowboarding, plus heli-skiing and wilderness snow cat skiing in the USA and Canada from November to April. Up to 28 days. Prices from £399 for seven nights (low season); average spend is £1200 per person. Not included are the ski lift pass and instruction (if required. A range of accommodation is available including catered chalets. Ski/snowboard equipment can be pre-booked.

SKIWORLD NORTH AMERICA

41 North End Road, London W14 8SZ (tel 0171-602 7444; fax 0171-371 1463).
Skiing in top resorts in the USA and Canada. Colorado, California, Utah and Wyoming in the USA and Whistler and Banff in Canada, from Nov-April, for beginners and experts. Extra and après ski activities: heli-skiing, snowmobiling, night skiing and back country snowcat skiing. Prices from £399 for a week fully catered, plus ski pass, equipment and insurance.

Accommodation in hotels, self-catering apartments or catered chalet rooms.

SMUGGLERS' NOTCH RESORT
Route 108, Smugglers' Notch, 05464-9513 Vermont, USA (tel toll free UK 0800-89-7159; toll free US & Can 800-451 8752; fax +1 802 644 1230). E-mail: smuggs@smugg.com
internet: http://www.smuggs.com
In business since 1956.
Holidays for 50,000 arranged annually.
Well known resort for families offering Alpine and Cross-country skiing, snowshoeing. Telemark skiing and children's adventure programmes at Smugglers' Notch resort, 30 miles north east of Burlington, Vermont. Prices from $445 (about £275) per person, double accommodation based on five night/five day programme. Prices do not include ex UK flights or ski rental equipment. Summer and Fall vacations. Family fun guaranteed.
Minimum age unaccompanied: 18 years.
Special 'Bold' winter programme for blind skiers.
Bookings direct or in the UK through: Ski the American Dream.

Arctic

ARCTIC ODYSSEYS
2000 McGilvra Blvd East, Seattle, WA 98112, USA (tel +1 206 325 1977; fax +1 206 726 8488).
Baffin Island Skiing Odyssey by Twin Otter aircraft (expert skiers only) 11-16 May ex Ottawa. Price $5,110 (about £3154).
Nordic Skiing Odyssey from hut to hut to Lake Baikal (Siberia) for intermediate skiers begins any Monday January to March. Ex Seattle. Ends second Wednesday (nine days, nine nights). Price $3,900 (about £2407).

ARCTURUS EXPEDITIONS LTD
PO Box 850, Gartocharn, Alexandria, Dunbartonshire G83 8RL (tel/fax 01389-830204).
Directors: K L Cartwright, L N Cartwright, R W Burton, J Burton.
In business since 1992.
Nordic ski tour of Baffin Island in Arctic Canada. Eighteen-day tour following the ancient inuit Itijjagiaq Trail from Iqaluit to Kimmirut. Expedition is supported by a dog-team allowing skiers to carry minimum gear. Accommodation in hotels and camping on route. Maximum group size of 8 people. Participants should be fit and have previous cross-country skiing experience. Price: £2650 including flights, accommodation and meals.

TANGENT EXPEDITIONS INTERNATIONAL
10 Stockdale Farm, Moor Lane, Flookburgh, Cumbria LA11 7LR (tel 015395-59087; 015394-59088).
Partners: Paul & Lucy Walker.
In operation since 1990.
Member of BMC.
Holidays for approximately 50 people arranged annually.
Mountaineering, ski touring and ski mountaineering expeditions in Greenland and Iceland for 3-5 weeks during March to August. Previous winter mountain experience needed. Expedition involves camping and sleeping bag accommodation in transit. Personal climbing/skiing gear can be hired if needed. Groups of four to 20 possible.
Ages: 18 to 60+.
'First ascents of remote virgin summits in Arctic Greenland'.

Asia

PEAK INTERNATIONAL
15 Moor Park Road, Wendover, Aylesbury, Bucks HP22 6AX (tel & fax 01296 624225).
Mustagata Ski Ascent
Trekking Ascent also available of this remote Chinese giant. 26 days, July 1998, £1985 ex Almaty.
Kedar Dome
Ski down the Kedar Dome in the Indian Himalaya. Great adventure for intermediate skiers. 30 days in May or October, £2285 ex Delhi.
Patagonia Ski Traverse
Traverse of the Southern Patagonian Ice Cap. June/July 1998. 20 days ex Rio Gallegors £1950.

Australasia

TREBLE CONE SKI AREA
Box 206, Wanaka, New Zealand (tel (+64) 03 443 7443; fax (+64) 03 443 8401). E-mail: tcinfo@treblecone.co.nz Internet: www.new-zealand.com/treblecone
In operation since 1969.
The biggest of the South Island's big five ski areas. Holidays for skiers, snowboarders and telemark skiers. Learn to packages start at NZ$40 all inclusive. Well-known area for off-piste action and the South Island's largest vertical and amazing views over Lake Wanaka. Season lasts 20 June to the beginning of October.

Snow Boarding

Europe

CHALET SNOWBOARD
31 Aldworth Avenue, Wantage, Oxon OX12 7EJ (tel/fax 01235-767182).
Director: Ian Charles Trotter.
In business since 1991.
Member of British Snowboard Association.
Holidays arranged for 400 annually.
Snow boarding in Les Deux Alpes and Avoriaz in France. Burton Snowboards Super Fly Test Centre, with full range of equipment. Guiding at all times if required and video camera recordings to check progress and spills. Prices £350-£475 per person per week including insurance, lift pass and lessons are extra. Individuals and parties of up to 20 people. No experience required. Unaccompanied people from 17 years.

CONTIKI
Wells House, 15 Elmfield Road, Bromley, Kent BR1 1LS (tel 0181-290 6777; fax 0181 225 4246).
Director: David Hosking.
In business since 1962.
60,000 holidaymakers dealt with worldwide annually.
Specialists in ski holidays for 18-35's. Ski/snowboarding holidays in Hopfgarten, Austria. Snowboard lessons last two hours daily. Prices £249 (one week) and £445 (two weeks) includes return coach travel from London and half board accommodation.

Northern Lights Alpine Recreation

Overland

For an increasing number of young people, the modern alternative to the 'Grand Tour' is the Overland Expedition. Travel may be by specially-modified coach or double-decker bus, three-ton truck, four-wheel drive vehicle or by public transport; under the leadership of a seasoned guide and organiser, overlanding can be an appealing and reasonably priced way of seeing new places and peoples. There are three great overland trips: the trans-Asia to Kathmandu, the trans-Africa to Kenya and across and around South America. On most overland trips, a food kitty is organised from which fresh food is bought *en route* and then prepared communally. Return travel from the destination is not always included in the prices quoted. Unlike many holidays, most expeditions require you to book several months in advance, to secure the necessary visas and facilitate detailed planning.

There seems, alas, to be an ever-growing number of places which are off limits to Western travellers. The capture by the authorities of Abimael Guzman, leader of the *Sendero Luminoso* (Shining Path) guerillas, in September 1992, made Peru less hazardous, for travellers but recently his followers have been making their presence felt again. The old trans-Asia route which crossed the Khyber Pass from Afghanistan to Pakistan and India remains closed because of the continuing internecine struggle between the Kabul regime and the Mujahidin. Jammu and Kashmir's protracted civil war between Muslim militants (who are rebelling against Indian control of the state) and the Indian security forces, continues and entry is very inadvisable as was shown by 1995's kidnapping of five hill-trekkers and the murder of one of them. The Pakistan/Indian border at Lahore has been open since March 1989, but could easily be shut again at any time if more Sikh disturbances flare up in the Punjab. The Sino-Pakistan border crossing via the Khunjerab Pass is open, whilst travel in Tibet remains officially the preserve of tour groups (but unofficially, some independent travellers too). In Turkey recent years have seen a spate of incidents involving western tourists travelling in the south-eastern part of the country and bomb attacks, attributed to the Kurdish Workers Party (PKK)in Istanbul and other places frequented by tourists. However, the situation now seems under control and Turkey's tourism levels look set to rise again in 1998. Meanwhile another Middle Eastern spot has become hazardous as indiscriminate arab suicide bombers have injured tourists as well as Jewish inhabitants in Tel Aviv and Jerusalem in 1997. Even nearer home, some popular Spanish resorts are still regarded as at risk from ETA (the Basque Separatists) some of whose bombs have been deliberately aimed at tourists in the last few years.

Algeria is definitely a no-go area as it is a hotbed of the Islamic Salvation Front, a fanatical organisation that wanted all foreigners out of the country by 1 December 1993. Not all foreigners complied and 29 of them including French and Croatians had been murdered by the ISF by mid-1994. By mid-1997 the total was nearing a hundred plus massacres totalling hundreds of fatalities by Algerians by fanatics running amok among their own citizens. About 280 Britons are still in Algeria, most of them employed by oil multinationals in the south of the country. The British Embassy in Algiers is protected by a special British military police unit and diplomats from all non-muslim countries travel in armoured vehicles with armed guards.

There is no change in the situation regarding the border from southern Sudan to Kenya which remains closed. However Kenya itself is proving increasingly dangerous to tourists who are at risk from attack (or worse) from local rebel groups and Ivory poachers. Tanzania has also seen an increase in problems as there have been a number of incidents involving armed police (or their impersonators) committing violent robberies against tourists. Zaire, Rwanda and Sierra Leone are also volatile.

Travellers are becoming more common in Indo-China as Vietnam gradually opens up to tourism but travel is still hazardous. The border with Laos and China is particularly dangerous. Cambodia is definitely an area to avoid, particularly after the coup in July 1997 which illustrates the political instability there. The Khmer Rouge guerillas are still in evidence and have taken to kidnapping western tourists. Some were snatched from the highway between Phnom Penh (the capital) and the coastal resort of Sihanoukville in April 1994 and according to the British foreign office all travellers are at risk if they travel across Cambodia by road.

Myanmar (Burma) continues to court tourists, but many potential ones off by the apparently authenticated accounts of slave labourers being used to build the necessary tourist facilities and the fact that the country is under military leadership which has breached the human rights of those who support the cause for democracy. The big new destination for Westerners on treks and tours is Iran. In the conflict between Iran's rulers loathing of corrupt western capitalists and their need for western currency the latter seems to have won. Women travellers have to be veiled even in restaurants.

Despite minor concessions to travellers the Istanbul to Delhi overland trip via the traditional route of Iran and Afghanistan remains closed for the foreseeable future. The opening up of the CIS (formerly the Soviet Union), has lead to a new route via the states of that country and also through China from Bejing to Pakistan.

The British Foreign Office has a travel advice unit (0171-238 4503/4 which operates weekdays from 9.30am to 4pm and is updated twice daily. It can give general advice on which areas of which countries are best avoided (at present there are over 80 such areas). Foreigh Office advice is also available on the Internet http://www.fco.gov.uk/ or on Ceefax, page 564 onwards.

The seventh edition of *The Traveller's Handbook*, published in 1997 by Wexas at £14.99, is an excellent source for those planning travels and expeditions of all kinds. It can be obtained from the publishers at 45-49 Brompton Road, London SW3 1DE (tel 0171-589 3315) or from bookshops, especially travel bookshops like Daunts (0171-224 2295), Stanfords (0171-836 1321) and The Travel Bookshop (0171-229 5260).

For expert advice would-be overlanders and independent women travellers can go to an independent travel agent/consultancy such as Marco Polo Travel Advisory Service (24A Park Street, Bristol BS1 5JA (0117-9294123; fax 0117-9292972). Their comprehensive service includes seminars for women travellers held in London and Bristol about three times a year and discounted flights.

Also of interest to women is the book *Women Travel* published by the Rough Guides which contains 100 personal accounts by women travellers and advice for their peers.

The organisation Women Welcome Women (88 Easton Street, High Wycombe, Bucks HP11 1LT; tel 01494-465441) bills itself as an organisation of international friendship. Membership, which costs £20 a year provides participants with worldwide lists of contacts for homestays and and exchanges.

Specialist publications for independent travellers include *Wanderlust* (P O Box 1832, Windsor, Berks, SL4 5YG; tel 01753-620426; fax 01753-620474) which costs £15 for a year's subscription (six issues). Also available from major book shops including Waterstones.

Anyone looking for a travelling companion for their odyssey may find them through the classified advertisements in *Traveller* magazine (published by Wexas Ltd. 45-49 Brompton Road, London SW3) or *Wanderlust.* An alternative source would be the *Globetrotters' Club* (c/o BCM/Roving, London WC1N 3XX). Founded over 50 years ago, Globetrotters aims to share information on adventurous travel by means of monthly meetings and a budget magagine, *Globe.*

Alternatively there are organisations that perform a similar function including Travel Mate (52 York Place, Bournemouth BH7 6JN; tel 01202-431520) and Travel Companions (110 High Mount, Station Road, London NW4 3ST; tel 0181 202 8478).

ADVENTURE SOUTH AMERICA
Head Office, Top Deck House, 131-135 Earls Court Road, London SW5 9RH (tel 0171-244 8641).
Directors: Pip Tyler, Liliana Tyler.
In business since 1991.
Holidays provided for 220 annually.
Overland trips in South America from 19 days to 24 weeks for groups of 22 all year round.'Andino' tour or sections from 19 days to 14 weeks, from Colombia to Rio de Janeiro, Brazil, following western Latin America, or reverse. 'Amazonia' tour from 31 days to ten weeks starts in Brazil and ends in Colombia following the eastern side of South America. Grand Circle (joins the two tours) 24 weeks. Prices: nine weeks £1100, plus US$700 (about £430) food fund to 23 weeks £2,300, plus US$1,700 (about £1049) food fund. Tent accommodation. Hotels and food in major towns not included in price.
'Amazonia trip is unique — travelling through the Amazonian wilderness to the Caribbean coast. Other highlights include Angel Falls, Machu Picchu, Rio Carnival, Volcano climb.'
Age range: 18-45 years.

THE ADVENTURE TRAVEL CENTRE
131-135 Earls Court Road, London SW5 9RH (tel 0171-370 4555).
Directors: M Mack, D Jack.
The Adventure Travel Centre is an agency for all the main overland and adventure companies.

AFRICA EXPLORED
Rose Cottage, Summerleaze, Magor, Newport, Gwent NP6 3DE (tel 01633-880224; fax 01633 882128).
Tours and safaris arranged throughout Africa. Tours range from two weeks in East Africa/Morocco to a 22-week Trans African Expedition.

AMERICAN ADVENTURES INC
64 Mount Pleasant Avenue, Tunbridge Wells, Kent TN1 1QY (tel 01892-512700).
Director: D Stitt.
In business since 1982.
Member of FIYTO, TIA and ABTA.
Adventure tours to the USA, Canada, Alaska and Mexico. Travel is in small groups from one to six weeks, with a Tour Leader and a maximum of 13 passengers. Prices start from £265 per person for a seven-day 'California Cooler' tour from Los Angeles to San Francisco. The tour includes camping equipment and transport. Food is on a kitty basis — $6 per day. Sleeping bags are not included, but may be hired. Participation in day-to-day running of the camping tours is expected.
No age limit, but most passengers are in the 18-38 age group.

ARCTIC EXPERIENCE LTD
29 Nork Way, Banstead, Surrey SM7 1PB (tel 01737-218800; fax 01737-362341).
Fly-drive and lodge jeep safaris in Iceland with the freedom to go as you please but with the security of pre-booked accommodation of your choice. Prices from £577 for flight, accommodation on a B & B basis, taxes and seven days unlimited mileage rental.

AUSTRALIAN PACIFIC TOURS
William House, 14 Worple Road, Wimbledon, London SW19 4DD (tel 0181-879 7444).
Directors:D Magris, G McGeary, R McGeary, P Sefton.
In business since 1927.
Member of PATA, ABTA.
Camping and four-wheel-drive tours in Australia. Coach-camping holidays for nine to 45 days include: ten to 13-day 'Outback

Adventure/Darwin' and 44-days 'Around Australia.' Prices between £50 and £60 per day with lodge style or tented accommodation and cook who prepares meals. All equipment provided except sleeping bags which are available at wholesale rates.
Minimum age: eight years.

BUKIMA AFRICA
55 Huddlestone Road, Willesden Green, London NW2 5DL (tel 0181-451 2446; fax 0181-830 1889). E-mail: 101732.7315@compuserve.com
Began trading 1990.
Holidays arranged for 650-700 annually.
Overland trips in Africa, South America and the Middle East. Tours run from 25 days to 30 weeks, costing from £445-£2045. Kitty contributions £67-£615. Long haul or short tours covering many exciting optional excursions like Gorilla visit (£115), Petra city ruins tour in Jordan (£33), Ruwenzori mountain climb in Uganda (£165), Red Sea diving at Sinai (£30), walking the Inca trail, exploring Marrakesh's place Djemaa el-Fna, whitewater rafting and many more. Transport is by specially adapted FWD vehicles.
Minimum age: 18.
'The right style in adventure travel'.

DISCOVER LTD
Timbers, Oxted Road, Godstone, Surrey RH9 8AD (tel 01883-744392). E-mail: info@discover.ltd.uk
Internet: http://www.discover.ltd.uk/net/
In business since 1976.
Tours to Morocco for small groups of up to 25 people. Considerable experience in school tours, particularly adventure and field studies. Prices include equipment, food, insurance, etc. Price around £555 per person.

DRAGOMAN LTD
28 Camp Green, Debenham, Suffolk IP14 6LA (tel 01728-861133; fax 01728-861127).
Overland trips across Asia, Africa and all the Americas in specially designed expedition vehicles. Long Transcontinental journeys. UK to Nairobi, Harare or Cape Town across Africa, 20 to 37½ weeks. UK to Kathmandu, 13 to 26½ weeks. Trans America expeditions including North and South and Central America up to 26 weeks from Anchorage to Tierra Del Fuego and 22 or 24 week circuits of South America.
Shorter journeys of three to ten weeks in Southern and East Africa. Two to ten weeks in India. Accommodation either camping or hotels. When camping groups prepare three meals a day on equipment supplied. Prices from £180 a week including fuel, equipment, vehicle, crew, plus kitty for food, gameparks, campsites, etc.
Minimum age: 18 years.

ENCOUNTER OVERLAND
267 Old Brompton Road, London SW5 9JA (tel 0171-370 6845).
Overland camping safaris from two to 32 weeks in Africa, Asia and South America. Wide range of shorter journeys of two to six weeks in East Africa, Southern Africa, Egypt, India, Pakistan, Nepal, Tibet, China, Bolivia, Ecuador, Venezuela, Peru and Mexico. Transcontinental journeys include London to Cape Town, London to Kathmandu and Quito to Rio via Lima. Travel is by specially-prepared safari truck with a group of 20 people. All camping equipment supplied (except sleeping bag). Prices from £135 per week including all meals.

EXODUS EXPEDITIONS
Exodus Expeditions, 9 Weir Road, Balham, London SW12 0LT (tel 0181-675 5550 or 0181-673 0859 24 hrs).
Long range overland expeditions from two to 30 weeks in Africa, SE Asia, South America, the CIS, China and Central America. Travel is by specially-constructed expedition truck, carrying 20-25 people. The emphasis is on exploring more remote regions, as well as sightseeing. Trans-Asia routes through Turkey, the Middle East, Pakistan, India and Nepal. Trips through Russia, Central Asia and along the Silk Route in China. Also and exploratory trip from Bangkok to Bali in South-East Asia. Trans-Africa routes across the Sahara to Western, Central and Eastern Africa, terminating in Zimbabwe. Also African overland trips via the Middle East, Egypt, Eastern and Southern Africa as well as West African Overland trips from Dakar to Nairobi. South American trips encompass the whole sub-continent from the Andes to the Amazon. Also shorter trips in Morocco, Namibia, India, Central America and Peru are also available. Overall cost from £130 per week with a supplement of £10 for food kitty.

EXPLORE WORLDWIDE LTD
1 Frederick Street, Aldershot, Hants GU11 1LQ (tel 01252-344161; fax 01252-343170).
Directors: T Cox, D Cook, P Newsom.

A wide range of shorter overland journeys utilising different modes of transportation from small buses to four-wheel drive desert trucks, riverboats, camels and trains. Areas of exploration include Alaska, Argentina, Australia, the Azores, Belize, Bhutan, Bolivia, Borneo, Botswana, Brazil, Bulgaria, Burma, Canada, Canary Islands, Chile, China, Costa Rica, Czech and Slovak Republics, Ecuador, Egypt, Eritrea, Ethiopia,France, Fiji, Greenland, Greece, Guatemala, Iceland, India, Indonesia, Israel, Italy, Jordan, Kenya, Madagascar, Malawi, Malaysia, Mali, Mexico, Mongolia, Morocco, Namibia, Nepal, New Zealand, Nicaragua, Norway, Pakistan, Philippines, Paraguay, Peru, Portugal, Romania, Russia, Scandinavia, Spain, Sri Lanka, Switzerland, Syria, Tanzania, Thailand, Tibet, Turkey, Tunisia, Uganda, USA, Uzbekistan, Venezuela, Yemen, Zambia and Zimbabwe. Most accommodation at small hotels; some camping (all equipment provided except sleeping bags). Length of trips varies from eight days to five weeks. All small group prices from about £300 to £3000.
Minimum age: 17 years.

GLOBAL GYPSIES PTY LTD
PO Box 123, Scarborough, Western Australia, 6019 Australia (tel/fax +61 8 9341-6727). E-mail: gypsies@andromedia.com.au
Directors: J Barrie & J Perks.
In business since 1997.
Self-drive, fully escorted safari tours from Perth to Sydney in Australia (operating April-November), and from Johannesburg to Cape Town in South Africa (operating all year). Tours last 20 days (covering 5000km) with clients driving themselves in well equiped vehicles (two people per vehicle), travelling in a convoy and camping along the way. Convoy is escorted by a professional guide acting as a mechanic, safari host and local expert. Prices from £3,102 (Austrailia) and £3,924 (Africa) for two people including vehicle hire, camping equipment, park entrance and camping fees, transfers from airport and guide services. Additional expenses include flights, fuel, vehicle insurance, food and drink. Driving experience and relevant licences necessary. 'Drive yourself through Africa or Australia for 20 wonderful days — independent but not alone.'
Ages: 25-70 years.

GUERBA EXPEDITIONS LTD
Wessex House, 40 Station Road, Westbury, Wiltshire BA13 3JN (tel 01373-826611).
Directors: M Crabb, A Hicks, L Munro and J Dunn.
In business since 1977.
Bonded member of AITO and ATOL.
Holidays for 3000 arranged annually.
Overland expeditions, safaris and adventure holidays in Africa. One to 33 weeks including Morocco, Egypt, West Africa, Kenya, Tanzania, Zimbabwe, Botswana, Namibia, South Africa and Madagascar. Departures all year round are fully escorted, mostly in Guerba's own expedition vehicles. All camping equipment supplied, but own sleeping bag required.

HINTERLAND TRAVEL
(Aimworld Ltd), 2 Ivy Mill Lane, Godstone, Surrey RH9 8NH (tel 01883-743584; fax 01883-743912).
Director: Geoffrey Hann.
Specialists in longhaul adventure 'experiences' for travellers in small groups. Overland expeditions across Eurasia via the Middle East, including the Lebanon to Kathmandu. Special train tours London to Delhi. Short adventures on the Silk Road

and in the Rain Forests of Madagascar. Trips to Central Asia including Iran, Turkmenistan, Uzbekistan and Afganistan. Plus trekking adventures in India, Nepal, Tibet and Madagascar.

JOURNEY LATIN AMERICA LTD
16 Devonshire Road, Chiswick, London W4 2HD (tel 0181-747 8315) (tours and admin); 0181-747 3108 (flights only); fax 0181-742 1312). E-mail: tours@journeylatinamerica.co.uk
Internet: http://www@journeylatinamerica.co.uk
Directors: J B Williams, C A Parrott, W Parrott, Mrs R Sanmugam, P Veloso, N Moman. O Hume.
In business since 1980.
Member of ABTA, IATA, AITO, ATOL.
Small group holiday journeys in Latin America. Departures throughout the year for groups of up to 20. Choice of 22 itineraries lasting nine to 46 days days starting in Lima, La Paz, Santiago, Quito, Rio de Janeiro, Buenos Aires, Guatemala, Mexico, Panama or San José. Highlights include hiking in the Andes, the glaciers of Patagonia, the Amazon and visiting pre-Columbian ruins. Accommodation ranges from first class hotels to budget hostels. Prices £645-£3000 including all group transportation on trains, buses, taxis, boats or planes, plus a tour leader who will speak Spanish and/or Portuguese. Allow £20-£40 per day for local expenses. Journey Latin America also deals with low cost flights, and is happy to advise clients who are buying air fares on the best way to travel independently in South America. The company also specialises in tailor-made travel arrangements to Latin America for those whose budgets are not so limited. Recent additions are a number of trekking, whitewater rafting and mountain biking trips.
Minimum age on small group tours: 18 years.

KUMUKA EXPEDITIONS
40 Earls Court Road, London W8 6EJ (tel 0171-937 8855; fax 0171-937 6664; brochure line 01233-311666).
Overland expeditions on 18-seater trucks in Africa, covering Kenya, Zimbabwe, Botswana, Malawi, South Africa, Tanzania and Namibia. Each truck is equipped with a water tank, stereo, cooking facilities, tent and camping equipment. Additions by creating your own safari and beach extensions. Opportunities for white water rafting, gorilla treks, hot air ballooning and horse safaris. Prices from £545 plus contribution to food kitty.
Also South America Overland Expeditions in a 26-seater customised Mercedes truck. Itineraries range from eight days to 24 weeks covering a diverse array of countries. Highlights include Macchu Picchu, Tierra del Fuego and the Amazon Jungle.
Age range: 18 to 40 years.

MAGIC OF BOLIVIA
182 Westbourne Grove, London W11 2RH (tel 0171-2217310; fax 0171-7278746).
Directors: Zoë Crawshaw, Humberto Barron Robles.
In business since 1996.
Holidays for about 120 annually.
Escorted jeep exploration tours of Bolivia with local guides. Tours last for 3 weeks between March and December. Visit places of ancient historical interest, including the pre-Inca ruins at Samaypata and the numerous Inca sites around Lake Titicaca. The highlight of the tour is possibly a trip to the fascinating desert of South-West Bolivia. The incredible scenery includes a cake of salt 10,000sq km, volcanoes, geysers and lagoons. Maximum group size catered for is 12. Accommodation in desert lodges, mud huts or good hotels. Prices of around £1800 for three weeks, inclusive of all meals but exclude international flights, insurance and alcohol.

MAGIC CARPET TRAVEL
Sun House, 125 Ryston Road, London SW6 7HP (tel 0171-381 2304; fax 0171-381 2304).
Fifteen-day adventure in Iran ex-Tehran and including desert, Yazd, Kerman, Shiraz and Isfahan. Travel by patrol car overland and accommodation is mostly in tents but also some hotels. Prices do not include flights (about £400-£480, visas (about £90).

OVERLAND LATIN AMERICA
13 Dormer Place, Leamington Spa, Warks CV32 5AA (tel 01926-332222; fax 01926-435567).
Director: David Gordon.
In business since 1990.
Holidays for around 100 arranged annually.
Small group overland journeys through Ecuador, Peru, Bolivia, Chile and Argentina. Travel is by train, bus, plane and company owned expedition vehicle. Itinerary includes an Amazon trip, Lake Titicaca, Torre del Paine and Tierra del Fuego. Prices: 19-day tour £685, 100-day tour

£1,995 (excluding camping, hotel accommodation and meals). Participation expected in day-to-day shopping and cooking duties.
Ages: 18-50 years.

PHOENIX EXPEDITIONS
College Farm, Far Street, Lymeswold, Leicestershire LE12 6TZ; (tel 01509-881818; fax 01509-881822).
Proprietor: B Moreton
Four to ten-week adventure camping safaris and expeditions with comprehensive itineraries throughout East and Southern Africa. Also 21 weeks expedition from Istanbul, via The Middle East, to Cairo and Nile route to Cape Town.

SAFARI DRIVE LTD
Wessex House, 127 High Street, Hungerford, Berks RG17 0DL (tel 01488-681611; fax 01488-685055).
Directors: Charles Norwood and Meregan Turner.
In business since 1993.
Holidays for about 150 arranged annually. Escorted, small group, safari tour adventures in Botswana, Namibia, Zimbabwe and South Africa for one to four weeks all year round. Trips arranged for simple family safaris or artistic, photographic or scientific projects. Short holidays or lengthy professional tours. Prices from £1800. Detailed daily itineraries and handbooks provided. Accommodation in pre-booked lodges or own tented camp. All food and equipment is stored on the landrover. Prices include fuel, camp food, game park entrance fees, airport transfers, flights and third party vehicle insurance.
New for 1997/98: Group escorted safaris including Zambia and the Central Kalahari.

STA TRAVEL
86 Old Brompton Road, London SW7 3LQ and 117 Euston Road, London NW1 2SX (tel Europe 0171-361 6161); worldwide 0171-361 6262; free copy of STA Travel Guide 0171-361 6166.
Complete range of overland tours to worldwide destinations — trekking in Nepal, safaris in Africa, outback adventures in Australia, houseboats in Kashmir, desert treks in Israel, etc. All available to independent and student travellers. Low cost flights arranged around the world on quality airlines. Expert advice from well-travelled sales consultants, from 33 offices in the UK, will point you in the right direction and worldwide offices will help you on your way.

STEPPES EAST
Castle Eaton, Cricklade, Wilts SN6 6JU (tel 01285-810267; fax 01285-810693). E-mail: sales@steppeseast.co.uk web site:http://www.steppeseast.co.uk
Tailor-made and semi-independent cultural, trekking and overland journeys in Russia, Central Asia, China, Tibet, Mongolia, Pakistan, India, Bhutan, Nepal, Sikkim, Burma, Vietnam, Laos and Indonesia. Cost from £1,300 to £2,500.

SUNTREK ADVENTURES
Greyhound International, Sussex House, London Road, East Grinstead RH19 1LD (tel 01342-317317).
President: D Hiltebrand Suntrek Tours Inc (USA).
In business since 1973.
Adventure camping tours in the United States, Canada, Mexico and Alaska. One to 13 weeks throughout the year. Individuals and groups of up to 13 may be catered for. Prices range from £199 up to 233376 plus flights. A typical three-week holiday costs £548 plus flights. This includes accommodation (mostly camping but some motels). There is a $30 (£18.50) per week food kitty. Help is expected with shopping and cooking. Sleeping bags are not included you may bring your own or hire one. New additions include 'Trek'n'Cruise' Adventures, combining trekking and cruising on Carnivals Fun ships.
No age restrictions.

TOP DECK TRAVEL
131-135 Earls Court Road, London SW5 9RH (tel 0171-244 8641).
Directors: M Mack, D Jack.
In operation since 1973.
Overland adventures from London to Kathmandu, India, South America and Africa from two to 24 weeks throughout the year. Escorted tours through the Middle East including Egypt, Jordan and Israel. Specialist tours in Australia and New Zealand. Extensive European Coach Camping and Coach Hotel tours from four to 60 days including Russia and Scandinavia. Also, ski holidays in Andorra, Austria and Switzerland.
Age limits may apply on certain tours.

TRACKS
Avegate Park Barn, Sneeth, Ashford, Kent TN25 6SX.

Camping tours through Europe (including eastern Europe), Scandinavia and Russia. Mostly in summer but a few winter tours operated. Independent groups can be arranged. Trip durations from 23 to 52 days from March to December. All camping, cooking and eating equipment supplied but participants must bring their own sleeping bags and participation is expected in daily tasks connected with camping. Travel is by modern coaches crewed by driver, tour manager and super cook. Emphasis on group participation. Professional guides used in major cities and throughout Russia. Mainly camping but also special stopovers in châteaux, pensions and the like. Prices from £495 plus £135 food fund; for 23-day trip visiting ten countries. Prices do not include visas. Also a range of shorter trips: Hogmanay (four days), Easter in Amsterdam (five days) Pamplona Running of the Bulls Festival (ten days), Munich Oktoberfest six to eight days, Edinburgh Military Tattoo etc. Age range: 18-38 years.

TRAILFINDERS
194 Kensington High Street, London W8 7RG (tel 0171-938 3939 Longhaul; 215 Kensington High Street, London W8 6BD (tel 0171-937 5400 Transatlantic & European. Also at 22-24 The Priory, Queensway, Birmingham B4 6BS (tel 0121-236 1234 Worldwide; 48 Corn Street, Bristol BS1 1NQ (tel 0117-929 9000 Worldwide); 254-284 Sauchiehall Street, Glasgow G2 3EH (tel 0141-353 2224); 58 Deansgate, Manchester M3 2FF (tel 0161-839 6969 Worldwide).
Directors: M Gooley, A Russell, M Bannister, P Fenwick, L Wood, G Dyer and A Pyper.
In business since 1970.
Member of ABTA no. 69701; ATOL no. 1458 and IATA.
Trailfinders is one of the UK's leading flight specialists, experts in discounted flights especially multi-stopover and round the world itineraries. Trailfinders also offers immunisation, a visa service where Australian tourist and business visas can be issued on the spot, a travellers' library and information centre and a bureau de change.

TREK AMERICA
4 Waterperry Court, Middleton Road, Banbury, Oxon OX16 8QG (tel 01295-256777; fax 01295-257399).
Sales Manager: Matt Berna.
In business since 1971.
Member of ABTA (no V0828).
Adventure holidays throughout the USA, Canada, Alaska, Mexico, Belize and Guatemala. Trek America offers over 45 itineraries, lasting seven days to nine weeks. Travel in small, international groups, with never more than 13. All levels of adventure are available for first-time visitors to experienced travellers. Winter and summer brochures are available.
Ages: 18 to 38.
Trek America has expanded the age limit of adventure holidays with 'Footloose', an open-aged adventure programme which offers active trips at a more leisurely pace.
Ages: 18-80.

TRUCK AFRICA LTD
37 Ranelagh Gardens Mansions, Fulham, London SW6 3UQ (tel 0171-731 6142; fax 0171-371 7445). E-mail: truckafrica@zambezil.demon.co.uk
Directors: G Marley, N Fisher & J Jordan.
In business since 1988.
Holidays for about 400 arranged annually.
Trans-Africa expeditions in specially converted overland trucks, providing a perfect balance between travelling independently and an organised tour. Tours operate from 3 weeks to seven months and are camping orientated. Visit Mountain Gorillas and raft on the Zambezi at Victoria Falls. Travel is often off-the-beaten-track.
Age range generally 18-40, but this is not a restriction.
'Not-so-easy-tours for those who want to get a taste of Africa without the hassle of visiting a Third World country for the first time'.

TUCAN SOUTH AMERICA
c/o Adventure Travel Centre, 131-135 Earls Court Road, London SW5 9RH (tel 0171-370 4555).
Partners: Pip Tyler, Liliana Cortes Tyler.
In business since 1987.
Holidays provided for 150+ annually.
Long and short overland tours throughout Latin America. Trips from two to 20 weeks all year round. Tours include:
'The Grand Tucan Adventure', Caracas to Rio, 15 weeks (or any section of the expedition). Optional Galapagos Islands Cruise if you leave or join in Quito.
'Equatorial Discoverer', Caracas to Quito, 33 days (including eight days in Galapagos), and Bogota to Quito, 22 days (including eight days in Galapagos).
'Andean Experience', Lima to Lima (Peru and Bolivia), 22 days. Experience the great diversity of desert, mountain and jungle

scenery and meet local Indians.
Groups of up to 21. Prices from £380 for 11 days to £2950 for 103 days. Hotel accommodation in mid-range hotels. Food not generally included. Equipment not included but can be hired. Local transport.
'We visit all the main sights of the continent plus some countries that few people visit. We are a small company that gives a very personal and knowledgeable service.'
All ages: 18 years.

UNITED TOURING COMPANY

Travel House, Spring Villa Park, Spring Villa Road, Edgware, Middx. HA8 7EB; tel 0181-905 7383; fax 0181-905 6947.
In business since 1966 in the UK.
Safaris, water rafting, mountain climbing and hot-air ballooning in Eastern and Southern Africa. All year round, depending on chosen sport. Prices from £1500, usually full board. For further information and booking contact any UK ABTA Travel Agency.

WEXAS INTERNATIONAL

45-49 Brompton Road, Knightsbridge, London SW3 1DE (tel 0171-581-8768).
Short overland expeditions by coach, minibus or truck in Egypt, Morocco, Turkey, Kenya, Tanzania, Malawi, Botswana, Madagascar and India. Tours last two to five weeks.

East African Safari *Transafrique*

Riding and Trekking

Hacking and trekking are very different activities, but enthusiasts of both activities are united by their love of and respect for the horse, and by their desire to learn to ride well. Throughout the world there are riding establishments which run holiday courses, many of them residential. The standard of teaching and horses varies tremendously, as does the emphasis of each riding centre. Some specialise in family activities, others cater for unaccompanied children, and yet others welcome only experienced adult riders. For those interested in riding in Britain, further information can be obtained from the British Horse Society (BHS), British Equestrian Centre, Stoneleigh Park, Kenilworth, Warwickshire CV8 2LR (tel 01203-414118). They publish *Where To Ride* which costs £5.95 plus £1 for postage, and which lists all the establishments approved by the BHS. The Association of British Riding Schools (Old Brewery Yard, Penzance Cornwall TR18 2SL 01736-369440) also supplies a list of approved schools which costs £5. Regional associations include: The Trekking and Riding Society of Scotland (tel 01887-830274; fax 01887 80606), the Wales Trekking and Riding Association (01873-858717) while for Ireland there is the Association of Irish Riding Establishments (+ 353 45 431584).

Prices of riding gear are as follows: long, rubber boots (from about £20), stretch jodhpurs (from about £20), hacking jacket (from £30 to £150) and hard hat (£30-£45). The two essential pieces of equipment: a BSI approved hat which should carry the stamp PAS015 or BSEN1384. The standard these stamps represent means they give maximum protection lower down all round the head than previous helmets and are designed for greater impact resistance. They also have a chin strap rather than a chin cup which is now considered too dangerous. These replace the older standards BS4472 (1988), or BS6473. From January 1st 1998 riding schools which offer to supply their clients with helmets will have to provide those of the new standards mentioned above, and not BS4472 or BS6473. Clients wishing to wear their own hats which are of the older sort will of course be allowed to do so. As a general recommendation, riding helmets should be renewed by the wearer every five years.

The other essential for riding are shoes or boots with a 2cm heel to prevent feet slipping from or through the stirrup.

Trekking can be a gentle if somewhat passive form of equestrianism, and is an excellent way of seeing areas of the countryside not easily reached by road. It also has the great advantage of needing comparatively little exertion from the human participant. It is however strongly recommended that clients prepare themselves by riding for an hour a week for about six weeks beforehand, especially if they have never ridden before. Generally the horses or ponies, often native to the locality, are tough yet gentle and the trek will be conducted at walking pace. Some holidays are based at a single centre from which daily excursions are made. Others involve 'post-trekking' which means moving on from place to place, intended mainly for experienced riders. Operators listed in this chapter offer trekking holidays in Europe and beyond. Iceland is becoming increasingly popular for post-trekking.

A useful organisation for anyone interested in equestrianism generally is EQUINET (website: http://www.EquiWorld.Net/) whose range of information includes all the UK riding and training centres and also provides a job-search and advice section for employers and young people.

Worldwide

EQUITOUR
Peregrine Holidays Ltd, 41 South Parade, Summertown, Oxford OX2 7JP (tel 01865 511642; fax 01865 512583); in the USA: P O Box 807, Dubois, Wyoming 82513 (tel 307-455-3363; fax 307-455-3363.
E-mail: 106357.1754@compuserve.com
Riding holidays in Europe (England, Wales, France, Greece, Iceland, Ireland, Italy, Portugal and Spain); Asia (India, Mongolia, Turkey, Bhutan/Nepal); Africa (Botswana, Egypt, Morocco, South Africa and Kenya Malawi, Namibia and Zimbabwe); North and South America (Argentina, Belize, Ecuador, Costa Rica, five US states, Canada, Australia and New Zealand. Prices range from £398 for seven nights, six half days riding, half board basis in Portugal to £3198 for 21 nights, 13 days riding, full board basis in India.

RIDE WORLD WIDE
58 Fentiman Road, London SW8 1LF (tel 0171-7351144; fax 0171-735 3179).
Partners: Ruth Taggart and Nigel Harvey.
Established 1995.
Holidays for 100-200 annually.
Riding holidays arranged in Europe (Spain, Italy, France), South America (Chile, Argentina, Equador), Africa (Botswana, Kenya, Tanzania, Malawi, South Africa, Zimbabwe), Pakistan, Mongolia, Jordan and Australia. Set date or tailor made trips. Maximum group size usually eight or ten. Generally prices include all riding, accommodation (tented, hotels lodges etc), food and drink (in many cases including wine); although on trips in Southern Spain, dinner on certain nights is not included. Prices do not include flights but Ride World Wide can help to arrange these. All rides require a reasonable level of competence (i.e. be secure and comfortable at all paces). Average of five to six hours in the saddle daily. Some rides for experienced riders only. African rides from £85-£190 per person per night; South America from £90 to £136 per person per night; Europe from £475 per person for eight nights camping; Pakistan from £1060 for 16 nights.

England

ACORN ACTIVITIES
P.O. Box 120, Hereford HR4 8YB (tel 01432-830083; fax 01432- 830110).
Riding holidays including: pony trekking, trail riding and riding instruction in Herefordshire, Shropshire and Wales. Choice of hotels, farmhouses, group accommodation and self-catering. Fully qualified instructors. Prices for accommodation from £22 per night and for activities from £40 per day.

ALBION RIDES
Duck Row, Cawston, Norwich, Norfolk NR10 4EZ (tel 01603-871725).
Director; Clementina Sutton.
In business since 1987.
Member of Ponies Association (UK).
Holidays arranged for 300 annually.
Riding weekend and week-long holidays and carriage-driving holidays in North Norfolk. Available throughout the year. Individuals and groups of up to six catered for. Ability to control horse at all paces required. Price range of £130-£290 including riding and full board. Accommodation in en suite single and double rooms. Personal riding gear not included.
Minimum age: 14 years (unaccompanied), 18 years (unaccompanied).

ARMATHWAITE HALL HOTEL
Bassenthwaite Lake, Keswick, Cumbria CA12 4RE (tel 017687-76551).
Directors: R V Graves, B J Graves, C J Graves and C E Graves.
Member of Cumbria Tourist Board.
Riding holidays in the Lake District all year round. Activities available include: riding tuition, country hacks, jumping and livery. Children must be accompanied by an adult.

CONTESSA RIDING CENTRE
Willow Tree Farm, Colliers End, Nr Ware, Herts. SG11 1EN (tel 01920-821496/792).
Proprietors: S Layton & T Layton.
In business since 1975.
Member of BHS & ABRS.
Instructional riding holidays all year round. Choice of four main types of course: general purpose, beginners, dressage and special dressage charged on a daily basis at

£25/£30/£32/£35 respectively. Tailor-made courses also provided. Choice of accommodation: on-site self catering (from £6.50 per night if shared), off-site self catering (from £65 per week), local guest houses (from £11 B&B in family guest houses) and hotels from £15 per night B&B.

ENDON RIDING SCHOOL
Coltslow Farm, Stanley Moss Lane, Stockton Brook, Stoke-on-Trent, Staffs ST9 9LR (tel 01782-502114).
Proprietors: D J & D k Machin, A W Asplin.
In business since 1977.
BHS and ABRS approved.
Children's horse riding holidays at Easter and Whitsun and July-September; children's and adults' residential holidays from October to June. Individuals and families. Groups catered by special arrangement.
Minimum age: nine years (unaccompanied).

EUROYOUTH
301 Westborough Road, Westcliff, Southend-on-sea, Essex SSO 9PT (tel 01702-341434; fax 01702 330104).
Riding courses at BHS or ABRS approved centres. Two weeks by arrangement.
Accommodation with families. No experience needed.
Minimum age: 14 years.
Unaccompanied teenagers: 16 years + .

EXMOOR RIDING HOLIDAYS
Combe, Luckwell Bridge, Wheddon Cross, Minehead, Somerset TA24 7EJ (tel 01643-841224; fax 01643-841628).
Proprietors: Jon and Biddy Trouton.
In business since 1972.
Riding holidays on Exmoor from May to September. Wild, beautiful and exciting riding country for competent adults and small groups. Tours with different overnight stops, or stay at the farm and ride daily from nearby stables. Riding attire not provided. Prices from £390 for B&B and riding.

HF HOLIDAYS LTD
Imperial House, Edgware Road, London NW9 5AL (tel 0181-905 9556).
Riding holidays based at one of the many HF country locations. Riding interspersed with training in grooming, horse care and saddling. No experience needed. Call for a Special Interest Holidays brochure.

KNOWLE RIDING CENTRE
Timberscombe, Minehead, Somerset TA24 6TZ (tel 01643-841342; fax 01643-841644).
Owners: John Richard Lamacraft & Kathlyn Mary Lamacraft.
Family business since approx. 1930s.
Member of BHS and ABRS.
Holidays for around 750 annually.
Horse riding holidays in Exmoor National Park, with its countryside mix of moorland, forestry and coastal scenery, all year round. Large indoor school and extensive cross country course and 100 acres to roam in plus a trout river and and lake. All standards welcome. Tuition available. For individuals and groups. Prices from around £327-£360 including full-board accommodation in country manor house (en suite available) with games rooms, indoor swimming pool, lounge and bar. Upkeep of own horse during stay is encouraged. Also opportunites for trout fishing, archery, golf and croquet.
Minimum age: 11 years (unaccompanied).

LYDFORD HOUSE RIDING STABLES
Lydford House Hotel, Lydford, Okehampton, Devon EX20 4AU (tel 01822-820347).
Principal: Claire Knight, BHSII.
In business since 1981.
Approved by BHS.
Riding holidays on Dartmoor. Prices from £390 per week include at least 18 hours of riding plus breakfast, dinner and two-star hotel accommodation. Daily rates available. Reductions for children. Non-residential riding and instruction also available. Walking, golf and fishing opportunities for non-riders. Residents can enjoy free admission to local leisure centre and tennis courts.
'Exceptional riding country with minimal road work. The ideal family holiday for non-horsey parents with horse-mad children.'
Minimum age: five years.

LYNCOMBE LODGE
Churchill, Somerset, BS19 5PQ (tel 01934-852335; fax 01934-853314).
Riding holidays in the Mendip hills in the heart of the West Country. Catering for beginners to experienced riders — Learn to Ride Holidays, Unaccompanied Children's Riding Holidays and Improve Your Riding. Fully qualified and individual instruction. Horses to suit all abilities. Own gymkhanas, jumping contests, all-weather

surface manège, cross-country and dressage. Prices: £250 for children, £300 for adults. Farmhouse and half-board accommodation.
Minimum age: seven years (unaccompanied).

NABURN GRANGE RIDING CENTRE
Naburn, York YO1 4RU (tel 01904-728283).
Proprietor: D Horn.
In business since 1962.
BHS approved training centre.
Riding holidays and courses in Yorkshire throughout the year for individuals and small groups. Prices £300 (children), £350 (adults) for a week, inclusive of full board and farmhouse accommodation. Indoor and outdoor schools qualified instruction novice/advanced level. Learn to ride, cross-country riding, jumping, dressage and hacking available individually or in combination. Stable management courses also provided. Novice to advanced level. Riding hats are provided free. Own horse/pony welcome. Exam training. Small groups of up to six people.
Unaccompanied young people welcome from eight years. Careful supervision provided.

NORTH HUMBERSIDE RIDING CENTRE
Easington, near Hull, East Yorks HU12 OUA (tel 01964-650250).
Proprietor: Mrs T Biglin.
In business since 1965.
Approved by BHS.
Riding holidays close to beach for unaccompanied children. Indoor school and cross country course. Price of £195 includes riding, instruction, accommodation and full board.
Ages: eight to 16 years. Separate courses for adults.

NORTHUMBRIA HORSE HOLIDAYS LTD
East Castle, Annfield Plain, Stanley, Co Durham (tel 01207-235354/230555).
Recognised by BAHA.
In operation since 1976.
Two to 14 days' horse riding holidays from April to November, prices from £149 inclusive. All grades catered for with 'learn to ride' and 'improve your riding' courses. Post trail riding, seven and 14 days long, prices include all meals and accommodation.
Also horse-drawn caravan holidays. Groups of up to 50 catered for. No experience needed.
Minimum age: six years (accompanied).

REDESDALE RIDING CENTRE
Soppitt Farm, Otterburn, Northumberland NE19 1AF (tel 01830-520276).
Proprietor: B J. Deniel-Rowe.
In business since 1987.
Northumberland Tourist Board, ABRS.
Riding holidays for adults, children and families all year round. Prices for one week: £225 (child) and from £380 (adult) include board and accommodation. No previous experience required but all riders are expected to help with tack cleaning and on children's holidays participants are expected to help tidy and wash-up. Now operating carriage driving holidays.
Minimum age: eight years (unaccompanied); six (accompanied).

ROBIN HOOD RIDING HOLIDAYS
Upper Broughton, Melton Mowbray, Leicestershire LE14 3BH (tel 01664-823686).
Directors: Ian and Amanda Jalland.
In business since 1992.
BHS approved training centre, East Midlands Tourist Board.
Holidays for 200 annually.
Horse riding holidays in Robin Hood's county, all year round. Combinations of riding out and tuition in the mornings with a choice of learning to drive a pony and trap, dressage lessons, hacking in Sherwood Forest, BHS lectures, cross country lessons, show jumping lessons as well as clay pigeon or rough shooting and fishing in the afternoons. Also Robin Hood Riding Camps for young people in the school holidays. Prices from £149 for five-day children's camp, £139 for an adult's weekend, to £299 for an adult's week with B&B accommodation. All camps are full-board. For individuals and groups up to 16. No experience necessary.
Minimum age: five years (unaccompanied).

SKAIGH STABLES
Belstone, Okehampton, Devon EX20 1RD (tel 01837-840429).
Proprietor: Mrs R Hooley.
Riding holidays on Dartmoor for individuals and groups of up to nine. Weekends or one week holidays Easter to October. Accommodation in chalets or local guesthouses with full board. Price from £250 per

week all inclusive. Warm waterproof clothing and rubber boots recommended. No experience needed, but preferable.
Minimum age: 12 years. Unaccompanied children accepted.

TM INTERNATIONAL SCHOOL OF HORSEMANSHIP
Sunrising Riding Centre, Henwood, Liskeard, Cornwall PL14 5BP (tel & fax 01579-362895.
Partners: E W R Moore and K M Tyrrell.
In business since 1982.
Approved by BHS as a training centre.
Riding holidays and courses on the edge of Bodmin Moor throughout the year. No experience necessary. Price from £250 (adults, £160 (juniors) for seven days includes riding instruction, accommodation and full board. You should provide your own personal equipment, though helmets may be borrowed.
Minimum age: six years (12 if unaccompanied).
Physically and visually challenged clients catered for.

WELLFIELD TREKKING CENTRE
Staintondale Road, Ravenscar, Nr Scarborough YO13 0ER (tel 01723-870182).
Owner: Mr M B Foulds.
Manager: Miss N Foulds.
In business since 1980.
Riding holidays in Scarborough from March to November, around the North Yorkshire Moors National Park. Moor beach and forest rides for all abilities. Prices from £150-£175 including rides, transport, bungalow accommodation and food. Outdoor entertainment also available, swimming, farm visits, shows, cross-country courses, gymkhanas, picnic/pub rides. Riders are expected to help with the feeding, brushing and care of the horses. Also pony-trekking £5 per hour.
Age range: five to 70 years.
Unaccompanied young people's holidays for eight to 16-year- olds.
Physically, visually and mentally challenged people welcome.

WELLINGTON RIDING
Basingstoke Road, Heckfield, Hook, Hampshire RG27 OLJ (tel 01734-326308; fax 01734-326661).
Directors: J Goodman, N Goodman, R Pickles.
In business since 1974.
BHS and ABRS approved.
Courses for beginners, improvers and experienced riders all year round. Specialises in children's courses but adult courses for over 16s also arranged. Individuals and groups of up to 40 children catered for. Price for five-day junior (six nights) holidays from £266 including dormitory accommodation in cabins, full board and full evening social programme. Adult holidays £83 (day), £310 (five days), are non-residential but various types of accommodation can be arranged locally.
Minimum age: eight years (unaccompanied).

WHEAL BULLER RIDING SCHOOL
Buller Hill, Redruth, Cornwall TR16 6ST (tel & fax 01209-211852).
Proprietors: Mrs J Dallimore.
In business since 1985.
Horse riding holidays in Cornwall throughout the year. Individuals and groups of up to 30 may be catered for. No experience is necessary. BHS qualified staff. Holidays feature beach, pub and picnic rides, hacking and cross-country riding, hunting with the Four Burrow Fox Hounds, side saddle lessons. Large outdoor arena, cross country course with water jump. There is an indoor school for lessons and jumping. Package deals include fully inclusive two weeks, with collection from Heathrow and Gatwick airports. Adult courses for BHS and NVQ exams from £500. Prices from £120 (children). Minimum age: seven years. Unaccompanied young people accepted.

ZARA STUD & TRAINING CENTRE
Highleigh Road, Sidlesham, Chichester, W Sussex PO20 7NR (tel 01243-641662).
Proprietors: Mr. & Mrs. P Brown.
In business since 1989.
English and western-style riding instruction holidays all year round. Arabians and Quaterhorses. Individuals and groups of up to four. Price for a weekend/week with two hours riding a day £96/£336 including half board accommodation. The Training Centre also has a western tack shop where saddles imported from the USA and other American riding accoutrements are on sale.
Minimum age: 12 years (accompanied); 16 years (unaccompanied)

Scotland

AYRSHIRE EQUITATION CENTRE
South Mains, Corton Road, Ayr KA6 6BY (tel 01292-266267; fax 01292-610323).
Kevin Galbraith.
In business since 1952.
Recognised by BHS, TRSS and ABRS.
Riding holidays at Easter, summer and early winter. Price: one week £295 includes meals, three hours of riding per day and accommodation. One-day, student, cross-country and showjumping courses also available.
Age range: five to 65 years.

BAREND PROPERTIES LTD
Barend, Sandyhills, Dalbeattie DG2 4NU (tel 01387-780663).
Director: F M G Gourlay.
Approved by BHS.
Riding holidays throughout the year in Dumfries and Galloway. Five-day courses for adults and children covering all aspects of horsemanship. Special courses for beginners aged six to ten. Trekking in Dalbeattie Forest also available. Accommodation in self-catering chalets or bed and breakfast in local farmhouse. Indoor swimming pool and sauna. Also mountain biking trails.

BORLUM FARM COUNTRY HOLIDAYS
Drumnadrochit, Inverness-shire IV3 6XN (tel/fax 01456-450358).
Partners: Capt A D MacDonald Haig, Mrs V MacDonald Haig.In business since 1963.
Member of ABRS, BHS, Riding for the Disabled Association, Association of Scotland's Self-Caterers.
Holidays provided for around 1500 annually.
Horse riding holidays overlooking Loch Ness throughout the year. Groups can be catered for. No experience required.
No minimum age, but unaccompanied young people not accepted.
Physically challenged people welcome.

HAYFIELD RIDING CENTRE
Hazlehead Park, Aberdeen AB1O 8BB (tel 01224-315703; fax 01224-313834).
E-mail: hols@equiworld.net
Internet: http://www.equiworld.net/
Proprietors: John & Sue Crawford.
In business since 1959.
BHS, ABRS, TRSS.
Holidays for 500 arranged annually.
Come and be part of the action on a variety of residential riding holidays from inexpensive beginners to special coaching and from leisurely to challenging executive weeks. Tuition available in all usual areas plus western riding, side-saddle riding and polo playing. Non-residential packages also available for those who wish to arrange their own nearby. Prices from £55 to £100 per day inclusive of accommodation.
For further details contact the Holiday Department, at the above address.

LOCH NESS RIDING CENTRE AND LOG CABINS
Drummond Farm, Dores, Inverness-shire IV1 2TX (tel 01463-751251; fax 01463 751240).
Partners: I Cameron and C Cameron.
In business since 1979.
Member of BHS, Scottish Tourist Board, Highlands of Scotland Tourist Board.
Riding holidays beside Loch Ness throughout the year for experienced riders only, on competition horses or bring your own. Specialists in endurance and marathon, but all the centre's horses also compete in dressage, showjumping and cross-country. Excellent hacking with wonderful views and top class facilities include indoor and outdoor arenas, showjumps and cross country course. Tuition available. Hacks from £15, lessons from £20. Self-catering accommodation available on site and guest house/B&B locally.
Minimum age: 16 years.

SCOTTISH YOUTH HOSTELS ASSOCIATION
7 Glebe Crescent, Stirling FK8 2JA (tel 01786-891400).
Pony trekking and riding holidays in the Scottish Borders using Exmoor ponies and based at Snoot Youth Hostel. Prices from around £150 per week.
Minimum age: 12 years.

Wales

CANTREF RIDING CENTRE
Cantref, Brecon, Powys LD3 8LR (tel 01874-665223).
Proprietor: M Evans.
In business since 1968.
Member of Wales Trekking & Riding Association.

Horse riding in the Brecon Beacons all year round in beautiful scenic countryside away from any crowds and traffic.Quality bunkhouse or farmhouse B&B accommodation. Minimum age: eight years (accompanied); ten years (unaccompanied).

PARC LE BREOS RIDING & HOLIDAY CENTRE
Parkmill, Gower, West Glamorgan SA3 2HA (tel 01792-371636).
Proprietors: J & D Edwards.
In business since 1963.
BHS approved, Wales Trekking & Riding Association, WTB accredited and AA Farmhouse.
Holidays for 1000 arranged annually.
Specialises in trekking holidays on the Gower Peninsula. No experience needed. For novices who wish to receive instruction there are basic horsemanship courses on certain weeks of the year. Also weekends. Prices for riding: from £15.50 (day); residential: from £76 (£70 child) per weekend; from £209 (£195 child) per week. B & B accommodation from £17, or £24 with evening meal or from £113.50 weekly B&B or from £158.50 with evening meal.
Minimum age: ten years (unaccompanied by arrangement).

RHIWIAU RIDING CENTRE
Llanfairfechan, Gwynedd, North Wales LL33 0EH (tel 01248-680094).
Proprietor: Ruth Hill.
In business since 1973.
Member of BHS.
Holidays provided for around 300 annually.
Riding holidays in the Snowdonia National Park throughout the year. Groups of up to 25 catered for. No experience required. Price £255 per week for adults, £235 per week for children and young people up to eighteen years, including accommodation and full board. Hats and boots can be borrowed.
'Excellent riding in beautiful surroundings, with no roads or traffic.'
Also walking and rambling holidays available all year except school holidays.
Ages: seven to 70 years.
Unaccompanied children accepted from nine years.
Physically or mentally challenged people catered for.

TY COCH FARM RIDING & TREKKING CENTRE
Ty Coch Farm, Penmachno, Betws-y-Coed, Gwynedd LL25 0HJ (tel/fax 01690-760248).
Proprietor: Cindy Morris.
In business since 1972.
Member of Welsh Tourist Board, Welsh Trekking and Riding Association.
Horse riding, trekking and trail riding holidays in and around the Gwydyr Forest of the Snowdonia National Park. Offered all year round. Individuals and groups of up to 25 can be catered for. Novices welcome, although some riding experience may be required for longer routes and trail rides. Price per day: £26.50 including bed, breakfast and evening meal, packed lunches and riding hats. Trail rides organised by arrangement. Refreshments and summer evening rides available.
Minimum age: 8 years (accompanied); 14 years (unaccompanied).
Facilities for physically, visually and mentally challenged people.

Ireland

ERRISLANNAN MANOR
Clifden, County Galway, Ireland (tel +353 95-21134).
Proprietors: Mr & Mrs Donal Brooks.
In business since 1965.
Riding holidays for individual children and young adults on Connemara ponies. Weekly during the summer. Supervised guest house accommodation with full board. Mountain, moorland and seaside riding on sure-footed and kind family ponies. Qualified teaching and ponycraft instruction. Price £350 per week. Hard hats can be bought or borrowed. Hourly riding also available.
No experience needed.

HORETOWN HOUSE RESIDENTIAL EQUESTRIAN CENTRE
Foulksmills, Co Wexford, Ireland (tel +353 51 565771; fax +353 51 565633).
Partners: Ivor J Young and Robert L Young.
In business since 1964.
Member of Irish Tourist Board, Restaurants Association of Ireland, Association of Riding Establishments and Irish Farm Holidays.

Holidays for 3000 annually.
Residential riding holidays situated in the South East of Ireland around an eighteenth century manor house surrounded by beautiful parklands and quiet countryside. Open all year round except for four days over Christmas. Tuition available for complete beginners, large indoor arena, dressage instruction, escorted ride-outs, opportunities for cross country and games of polocrosse for intermediate and experienced riders. All equipment provided. Prices: £415 (one week, half-board and 12 hours riding or tuition) to £520 (one week, full-board and 18 hours of riding or tuition). For non-riders £270-£310 for half or full-board, all with options to dine in the Cellar Restaurant of the manor house.
Ages: seven to 70 years.
Unaccompanied young people from 12 years.

STRACOMER RIDING SCHOOL
Bundoran, Co Donegal, Ireland +353 72-41787; fax +353 72-41002).
Terry and Aidan Fergus-Browne.
In business since 1985.
Member of Irish Tourist Board, BHS and Association of Irish Riding Establishments.
Residential horse riding in Bundoran and Dunfanaghy. Six-day trail rides for intermediate and experienced riders at both locations. Minimum number on a trail ride is four and the maximum twelve. Four to six hours riding a day covering approximately 25 miles (45 km) per day at all paces. There is also a trail ride for beginner riders who would like a gentle introduction to trail riding. Prices for a week start at IR£750 (April-May) up to IR£840 (June-September) all inclusive.

At Dunfanaghy there is also, casual riding for all ages and levels of experience through beautiful scenery.

Residential programmes for adults and unaccompanied children.

Europe

ASSOCIATION NATIONALE DE TOURISME EQUESTRE HIPPOTOUR
12 Rue du Tienne, 5140 Ligny, Belgium.
In operation since 1972.
Recognised by Belgian Ministry of Sport.
Holidays provided for 1500 each year.
A non-profit organisation which promotes equestrian tourism in Belgium. Holidays available from April to November. Riding experience is required. Prices from around £48 for a weekend, including accommodation, meals and equipment.
Unaccompanied young people accepted from 12 years.

CAMINHOS DO ALENTEJO (CDA)
Apartado 116 Milfontes, 7645 Alentejo, Portugal (tel +351 8399106; fax +351 8399206).
Proprietor: Robert Lee.
Established 1989.
Member of International Lusitano Horse Society, Portuguese Jockey Club, ABTA and ATOL with UK agent, Specialised Horse Trail Riding.
Organises 15 to 25 weeks annually of week-long trail programmes in South West Portugal. Groups of eight to ten riders per trail. Only suitable for experienced and regular riders capable of riding outdoors at all paces (walk, trot and canter). Prices from £395 to £1000 include modern three-star traditional hotel, breakfast and lunch.
Minimum age unaccompanied: 17 years; 14 with an adult.

Bookings can be made direct or with an agent in your country. Enquire for details.

CRUSADER TRAVEL
57 Church Street, Twickenham TW1 3NR; (tel 0181-744 0474; fax 0181-744 0574).
Varied horse riding itineraries into the Highlands and through farm settlements and lakelands, across open plains and desert. Accommodation in homely guest houses and holiday farms. Eight or ten days from June to August. Price from £1399.

FREEDOM HOLIDAYS
30 Brackenbury Road, Hammersmith, London W6 OBA (tel 0181-741 4471/4686; fax 0181-741 9332).
Horse riding courses and trekking at the Henri Cassagnes Riding Centre at La Sella on Spain's Costa Blanca.

GOURMET BIRDS
Birdwatching holidays, Windrush, Coles Lane, Brasted, Westerham, Kent TN16 1NN (tel 01959-563627; fax 01959-562906).
Proprietors: David & Janet Tomlinson.In business since 1984.
Holidays for 40-70 arranged annually.Birdwatching holidays on horseback in Andalucia and the Siera Gredos, Spain.
Minimum age: 12 years (accompanied).

INNTRAVEL
Hovingham, York, YO6 4JZ (tel 01653-628862).
Horse riding weeks in the Cévennes, Cerdagne, Corbières, Dordogne and Lot Valleys, Provence and Tarn areas of France and Corsica, also, Andalucia and the Sierras in Spain. Also weekend rides in Scotland or Normandy. Independent and accompanied trekking with accommodation in farmhouses or 2-star and 3-star hotels. Luggage transported between each stop. Prices: Normandy weekend £324; all inclusive week by air from £479.

ISHESTAR ICELANDIC RIDING TOURS
Baejarhraun 2, 220 Hafnarfjördur, Iceland (tel +354 565 3044; FAX +354 565 2113). E-mail: ishestar@itn.is
Internet: http://www.arctic.is/travel/ishestar
Director: Einar Bollason.
In business since 1982.
Member of the Icelandic Tourist Board.
About 5000 clients annually.
Riding tours of all lengths and types. All tours are guided and English/German/French is spoken. Holidays from nine locations around Iceland. Short tours (two hours), and day tours all year round. Eight to 12-day tours from June to August. Individuals and groups of eight to 20. All levels of ability are catered for. Prices: ten days (£1070); four to 12 days (£515-£1370). Prices include accommodation (mountain huts/farms/guest house/hotel) and full board.
Unaccompanied young people accepted from 13/14 years.
Age range of participants so far: seven to 82 years.

Americas

AMERICAN ROUND-UP
Oxenways, Membury, Axminster, Devon EX13 7JR (tel 01404 881777; fax 01404 881778.
Directors: Mrs S V Beecham, Mrs C Symington.
Member of Colorado Dude Ranches Association, AITO and ATOL no. 2921.
In business since 1984.
Tailor-made ranching, river-rafting and riding holidays in USA and Canada all year round. No experience necessary. Prices range from £900 to £2000 (typical holiday costs £1200) and generally include cabin accommodation, three meals daily and all equipment.
'Riders and non-riders alike have a chance to experience the western way of life; also the excitement and wilderness adventure of a whitewater expedition.'
No minimum age for ranches.
Minimum age for river-rafting: eight.
No maximum age.

AMERICAN WILDERNESS EXPERIENCE INC
P O Box 1486, Boulder, Co 80306, USA (tel +1 303-444-2622; fax +1 303-444 3999). Web site: http://www.gorp.com/awe
President: Dave Wiggins.
In business since 1971.
Member of the Dude Ranchers Association.
Holidays for 5,000 arranged annually.
Wide selection of horseback adventures in Wyoming, Colorado, New Mexico, Arizona, South Dakota, Utah, California and in Canada (Alberta). Arizona from April to October. Mostly three, four, five, six, seven, eight and nine day trips. Longest trip is 12 days (Lake of Lone Indian Ride). Prices from $335 (about £206) for three days) to $1300 (about £800) for twelve days. Daily rate works out at $75-$150 (about £46-£92) a day. No prior experience needed.

AUSTRAL TOURS
120 Wilton Road, London SW1V 1JZ (tel 0171-233 5384; fax 0171-233 5385).
Directors: Richard Brass, Elena Gattinara.
Established 1993.
Member: LATA (Latin American Travel Assoc.), ATOL 3616, IATA accredited.
Horse riding and trekking in South America (Argentina, Chile, Peru, Bolivia, Brazil, Ecuador) year round. Typical price for a holiday is £2000 including full board and accommodation at lodges or ranches.

BLUE GREEN ADVENTURES
2 Priory Cottages, Parsonage Lane, Lamberhurst, Kent TN3 8DS (tel/fax 01892-891071).
Partners: L A Haynes, A M Quevedo.
In business since 1997.
Awaiting membership of ABTOT.
Holidays for 100 arranged annually.
Ten-day horse riding and camping expeditions in South America. Chilean Patagonia available December-March. Pantanal (Brazil) from July-September. Trek through the spectacular Torres del Paine National Park witnessing granite peaks, mountain lakes,

glaciers and a diversity of wildlife, including condors and penguin colonies. Prices: Patagonia £1280-£1480, Pantanal £1000-£1400. All accommodation, meals and wine included. Camp under the stars, beginning each day with a cooked English breakfast. Flights, tips and sleeping bags not included. Some horse riding experience necessary (ability to walk, trot and canter comfortably). Individuals, and groups of up to 8 catered for. Bookings can be made direct or with a designated UK travel agent.
'An opportunity to experience the ultimate horseback adventure in one of the worlds last true wildernesses. Professional guides and good horses'.
Minimum age: 16 years unaccompanied.

PEAK INTERNATIONAL
15 Moor Park, Wendover, Aylesbury HP22 6AX (tel/fax 01296 624225).
Riding holidays in Canada: Rocky Mountains Ride, seven days including a Rodeo (£585). Kootenay Plains Ride, nine days touring the backcountry (£785). Ts'yl-os by horseback: Coastal alpine range north of Vancouver, eight days ex Chilko £675

WESTERN ENCOUNTERS
24 Birchfield Lane, Lander, Wyoming 82520, USA (tel/fax +1 307-3325434).
E-mail: dashley@wyoming.com
Proprietors: Skip and Vivian Ashley.
In business since 1993.
Holidays arranged for 220 people each season.
Week-long horseback riding and camping adventures throughout Wyoming from mid-May to mid-September. Visitors are met at Riverton airport and then transfered to a motel before receiving a welcome dinner to get everyone acquainted. Meet your horse the next day (following an early breakfast) and begin the trail ride. A farewell dinner is served on the final day of the ride, before transport back to the airport. Prices include transport to and from airport, welcome and farewell dinners, first and last night motel lodgings, camping equipment, all meals on the trail, horses and complete tack, and a qualified guide. Prices from $1295 for a Pony Express or Wild Horse/Mountain ride, $1345 for an Outlaw Trail ride and $1575 for a Cattle Drive. There are no age limits, but people must be able to ride for a minimum of five hours each day.

Africa

CAMPFIRE CLASSIC ADVENTURES
Lowlands, Homanton, Shrewton, Salisbury SP3 4ER (tel/fax 01980-620839).
Directors: A Kiff and F Kiff.
In business since 1994.
Holidays for 200 arranged annually.
Horse riding safaris in Botswana, Zimbabwe, South Africa, Namibia, Kenya and Malawi. An opportunity to experience untouched wilderness and wildlife. Prices range from £900 to £4,000 (all inclusive) depending on the destination. Individuals and groups catered for. Detailed information packs avilable on request.
Minimum age: 12 years (unaccompanied).
'Our horse riding safaris allow riders to become a part of the scene, landscape, environment and wilderness, as opposed to an intrusion when using vehicles'.

EQUUS HORSE SAFARIS
36 12th Avenue, Parktown North, Joannesburg 2193, South Africa (tel +27 11 788 3923; fax +27 11 880 8401).
Owner: Wendy Adams.
Established 1989.
Member: African Horse Safari Association and South African Tourism and Safari Association.
Horseback safaris in the Northern Province of South Africa. December to October. Safaris operate on Lapalala Wilderness, a private game reserve 3½ hours drive north of Johannesburg. Two types of safari are offered:
Bush Camp Safari: guests can book for as many nights as they please (there are no fixed departure dates). A minimum of three nights and a maximum of eight is recommended. Rides out into the bush daily for five to six hours to explore the bushveld and view game, returning to the camp for meals. Game walks available for non-riders.
Luxury Wilderness Safari: moving from camp to camp for nights accommodation in tented camps, log cabins, rock ledges and reeded river huts. Equipment is transported between camps by vehicle and back-up crew, while a chef ensures each camp is ready for arrival. May to September only for a minimum of four guests and a maximum of eight.

Prices from £100-£130 per person per night fully inclusive except drinks, transfers and gratuities.

Minimum novice rider. Not suitable for total beginners.

Age range: 12-75 years.

J & C VOYAGEURS
Buckridges, Sutton Courtenay, Abingdon, Oxfordshire OX14 4AW (tel 01235-848747).
Riding holidays for five days in the foothills of Mount Kilimanjaro, Kenya, in the Okavango Delta, Botswana, Nyika Plateau, Malawi. Groups of four to eight. Stay in tented or
cottage accommodation. Prices include flights from the UK.

LET'S GO TRAVEL
P O Box 60342 Nairobi, Kenya (tel +254 2 213033/340331; fax +254 2 214713 & +254 2 336890).
Horse back safaris in Kenya. E.g. ten days horse riding from the Loita Hills to the Masai Mara. Six to seven hours of riding each day with vehicles available for game drives. Price $3,100. Bookings direct to the above address.

OKAVANGO TOURS AND SAFARIS
Gadd House, Arcadia Ave. London N3 2TJ (tel 0181-343 3283; fax 0181-343 3287).
Horse safaris in the Okavango Delta region of Botswana. Sitting high above the reeds on horseback you will venture deep into the Delta where wildlife remains undisturbed by your silent approach. Accommodation is in twin-bedded tents and a hot bucket and pulley shower is available each evening! Available from March to October individuals and groups of up to eight maximum, are catered for. Five days minimum duration. Price: approx. £145 per person per day sharing, excluding flight.

Asia

BOOJUM EXPEDITIONS
14543 Kelly Canyon Road, Bozeman, Montana 59715, USA (tel +1 406-587-0125; fax +1 406-585-3474).
Director: Linda Svendsen.
In business since 1984.
Holidays provided for 100 annually.
Horseback tours in China (Xinjiang and Altai Mountains), Tibet and Outer Mongolia for three weeks from June to October. Horse riding experience is essential. Tours cover an average of 15 miles per day, with six hours spent in the saddle. Accommodation is in tents, so you should bring a sleeping bag. Groups of up to 15 can be catered for. Prices from $3950 to $4150. Horseback rides in Argentina and Venezuela (November and December) also available.
Minimum age for unaccompanied young people: 16 (14 subject to interview by trip leader).

STEPPES EAST
Castle Eaton, Cricklade, Wilts SW6 6JU (01285-810267; fax 01285-810693). E-mail: sales@steppeseast.co.uk. Web site: http://www.steppeseast.co.uk
Riding in Mongolia and India. Riding experience necessary in Mongolia. Trekking holidays in Morocco, Central Asia, Pakistan, India, Nepal, Bhutan and Sikkim. Cost includes flights, meals and accommodation.

PEAK INTERNATIONAL
15 Moor Park, Wendover, Aylesbury, Bucks (tel 01296-624225).
Horseback safari in the Aravalli Hills to Mount Abi in India.
Chance to see rare wildlife en route. Best in October and February.
Ride lasts fifteen days. Price of £985 does not include flights to and from India. Also, Nanga Parbat to Hunza riding through the wild valleys of the Karakoram, 14 days ex Islamabad £1060.

Middle East

J & C VOYAGEURS
Buckridges, Sutton Courtenay, Abingdon, Oxfordshire OX14 4AW (tel 01235-848747).
Riding holidays for five days in Cappadocia, Turkey. Move from village to village through the 'surrealistic' countryside of Cappadocia or through the Red River Valley of Kizil Irmak. Opportunities in May and June to see many wild flowers. Groups of four to eight. Prices from £675. Accommodation is in pensions and bed and breakfasts.
Minimum age: 12 years.

Specialist Activities and Courses

This chapter contains details of more unusual activities, such as cave studying in the Ardennes or going on a combined walking and winetasting tour. These offbeat adventures need not be expensive: spending time as a volunteer on a conservation project, an organic farm or archaeological excavation is perhaps the cheapest break you can have. Those who wish to learn or develop skill in a craft can go on a course at the end of which they will have made something useable like a guitar or pottery. Yet others may wish to tackle physical and mental challenges such as rally driving or a survival course. Perhaps the most esoteric activity in this section is to be an integral participant in a recreation of Tudor life in a mansion of the period.

Those who wish to meet like-minded companions prior to enrolling for such specialist activities and courses might wish to contact the friendship bureau *Natural Friends* of 15 Benyon Gardens, Culford, Bury St. Edmunds, Suffolk IP28 6EA (tel & fax 01284 728315), whose non-smoking members' interests include organic farming, all outdoor pursuits and the creative and performing arts as well as holistic and personal development philosophies and green issues.

Agriculture

FIELD STUDIES COUNCIL
Head Office, Montford Bridge, Shrewsbury SY4 1HW (tel 01743-850674; fax 01743-850178).
Farms and Farming in the Borderland weekend course at the FSC's Preston Montford centre in July. An opportunity to step through the farm gate to observe and discuss the changing agricultural scene as farmers respond to external pressures and policies. Price about £100 inclusive of accommodation, all meals and tuition.
Minimum age: 16 years.

WWOOF
Willing Workers On Organic Farms, 19 Bradford Road, Lewes, East Sussex BN7 1RB.
In operation since 1971.
Activities for about 2000 people arranged each year.
Weekend and midweek working breaks on organic farms throughout the British Isles and — through affiliated groups — worldwide. In return for their keep, members are expected to participate fully in farm chores. After successfully completing two organised weekends, members may obtain an International Directory for 'fix it yourself' arrangements. Annual subscription £10; send an s.a.e. to the Co-ordinator at the address above.
The only other expense is in travel to the farm.
Minimum age: 16 years.

Angling

Worldwide

ROXTON BAILY ROBINSON WORLDWIDE
25 High Street, Hungerford, Berkshire RG17 0NF (tel 01488-683222; fax 01488-682977).
Directors: M Firth, C Robinson, G Stephenson, D Reynolds, R Pilkington and C Orssich.
In operation since 1980.
Member of British Field Sports Society and Game Conservancy.

Holidays for around 700 arranged annually.
Tailor-made worldwide fishing tours. Destinations include Bahamas, Cuba, Mexico and Belize (for saltwater fly fishing), Alaska, Montana, Argentina, Chile, Iceland, U.K., Norway, Kenya and New Zealand (for salmon, trout or sea trout fishing), Madeira, Bom Bom, East Africa and Benguela (for blue water fishing). Holidays available throughout the year subject to destination. Typical prices from £1500-£3500 per person include full board and luxury accommodation in tents or small lodges. Individuals and groups catered for. Unaccompanied young people rarely accepted. Experience requirements are subject to choice of fishing.

WORLDWIDE FISHING SAFARIS
55 English Drove, Thorney, Peterborough, Cambridge PE6 OTJ (tel & fax 01733-849244).
Tailor-made angling holidays in Kenya, Moçambique, Madagascar, the Maldives, Mauritius, Seychelles, Tanzania, the Azores, Madeira, Venezuela, Guatemala, New Zealand, Canada (Québec, New Brunswick, Saskatchewan, Alberta, British Columbia). All the world's big game fish including Marlin, Great White Shark, Swordfish, Sailfish, Tuna and Atlantic Salmon can be battled with, then tagged and released. Some types may be boated.

England

FIELD STUDIES COUNCIL
Head Office, Montford Bridge, Shrewsbury SY4 1HW (tel 01743-850674; fax 01743-850178).
Introduction to Fly-fishing and Fly-tying course at FSC's Malham Tarn Centre in the Yorkshire Dales in August. Fishing techniques will be practised on Malham Tarn and some of the Dales' rivers. Prices about £255 for a week inclusive of accommodation, all meals and tuition.
Minimum age: 16 years.

Scotland

BOBSPORT (SCOTLAND) LTD
9 Craigleith Hill Crescent, Edinburgh EH4 2LA (tel & fax 0131-3226607).
Director: Robert Brownless.
In business since 1985.
Holidays for 1,000 arranged annually.
Salmon fishing holidays offered all year on the East coast of Scotland. Individuals, and groups of up to 200 catered for. No experience necessary. Choice of three or six-day holiday with fishing on the River Tay, Teith, Tweed or Spey. Prices range from £100-£1,000 depending on duration. Accommodation ranges from castles to cottages depending on the package taken and the area fished. Also included in the price: dinner, bed and breakfast, transfers and equipment (waterproofs and waders not included, but can be hired).
Minimum age: ten years (unaccompanied).
'Your ghillie will help you choose the deadliest lure and cast over the likeliest lies'.

Europe

FINNISH TOURIST BOARD
30-35 Pall Mall, London SW1Y 5LP (tel 0171-8394048; fax 0171-3210696).
National Tourist Office.
Detailed information available on companies offering fishing holidays and tours in Finland. Huge variety of fishing in the great lakes, gentle or fast flowing rivers or the sea. Brochures available on request.

Archaeology and History

Worldwide

FIELD STUDIES COUNCIL OVERSEAS
Montford Bridge, Shrewsbury SY4 1HW (tel 01743-850164/850522; fax 01743-850178).
Fully bonded: CAA (ATOL 3331), ABTOT (4059).
Organiser: Anne Stephens.
Fully escorted study tours with an archaeological theme to the Scilly Isles, Arran and the Outer Hebrides and the Channel Islands. Further afield archaeology features on courses to Andalucia, Malta and Guatemala. All abilities catered for, expert tuition

and guidance included. Courses vary in duration from one to four weeks.

Britain

COUNCIL FOR BRITISH ARCHAEOLOGY
Bowes Morrell House, 111 Walmgate, York YO1 2UA (tel 01904-671417; fax 01904-671384).
Director: Richard Morris MA, FSA.
Information Officer: Mike Heyworth BA(Hons), MA, PhD, MIFA.
Established 1944.
Details of excavations and other fieldwork projects are given in the Council's publication *CBA Briefing*, a supplement to the magazine *British Archaeology* The magazine appears ten times a year and is accompanied by *Briefing* every other issue (in March, May, July, September and November). An annual subscription to the magazine is £19, however it also forms part of an individual membership package which is available for £20 per year and brings many extra benefits. Having studied *Briefing*, you should apply to the director of the projects which interest you.
Minimum age for many field projects: 16 years.

FIELD STUDIES COUNCIL
Head Office, Montford Bridge, Shrewsbury SY4 1HW (tel 01743-850674; fax 01743-850178).
Medieval, industrial and rural archaeology courses based on the local history of the areas around several of the FSC's ten residential centres, with opportunities to explore Suffolk's medieval houses, find out about Stone Circles in the Lake District, and walk in the footsteps of Brother Cadfael in Shropshire. Prices from about £255 for a week, £100 for a weekend inclusive of accommodation, all meals and tuition.
Minimum age: 16 years, except on courses arranged for families.

FOCUS HOLIDAYS AT ARGOED
Argoed Guest House, Crafnant Road, Trefriw, County of Conwy, LL27 OTX (tel 01492-640091).
Heritage weekends and weeks including visits to Bronze/Iron Age settlements, Roman, mediaeval and Victorian sites illustrating the history of Wales. Groups of up to 12 catered for. From March to October. Prices from £70 (weekend) to £220 (week) including accommodation and all meals. Unaccompanied children not accepted.

Europe

ATELIER DE LA ROSE
Le Bourg, 46700 Montcabrier, France (tel +33 5-65 24 66 36; fax +33 5-65 36 59 97).
Owner & Director of Studies: Ed Herring.
Established in France since 1991.
Member of the National Soc. for Education in Art & Design (UK) & Société Internationale pour L'Education Artistique.
Creative holidays for 30-40 people a year.
Historical studies and tours in the Lot region of south-west France (between the Dordogne and Lot rivers). Prehistoric caves and dolmens, romanesque churches and abbeys and the Toulouse Lautrec museum can be included in your personal guided tour. Five days+. Open all year. Course only prices from 3,000-6,000 francs (about £325-£650) per person. Rooms available on site. A range of alternative accommodation from campsites to three-star hotel is available locally. Course leaders are English.

THE TRIREME TRUST
Pyrton Halt House, Watlington, Oxford OX9 5AN (tel 01491-612411; fax 01491-614061).
Directors: Peter Turner, John Quenby, Boris Rankov, Peter MacLeod, John Morrison, John Coates, Frank Welsh, Rosie Randolph and Timothy Shaw.
In business since 1987.
Holidays for 170 annually.
Available in 1999.
Help to row the 170-oared Greek Trireme *Olympias* on a voyage over the Aegean Sea, a reconstruction of a ship used by the ancient Greeks. Anyone who is 'physically fit, with a sense of humour and an appreciation of history' is welcome as long as they are under six feet two inches tall. A fitness test is usually compulsory, and rowing experience would be an advantage. Price: £175 plus airfare, plus food. Accommodation in a naval barracks is free. Plenty of local tavernas to eat in.
Age range: 18-50+ years.

Arts and Crafts

England

DEBORAH BAYNES POTTERY STUDIO

Nether Hall, Shotley, Ipswich, Suffolk IP9 1PW (tel 01473-788300; fax 01473-787055).

Sole trader: Deborah Baynes.
In business since 1971.
Committee member of Craft Potters Assoc. and E Anglian Potters Assoc.
Approx 100 would-be potters taught annually.
Long weekends and standard weekends (from April to October) and week-long pottery courses in July and August. £125 for a weekend to £290 for a week. Includes half-board accommodation in Nether hall (breakfast and lunch daily and dinner on the day of arrival). Raku firing the pots is the highlight as everyone stokes the wood-fired kiln and watching them mature into the final result. Each course consists of six to eight students.
Unaccompanied young people over 14 years accepted.

FIELD STUDIES COUNCIL

Head Office, Montford Bridge, Shrewsbury SY4 1HW (tel 01743-850674; fax 01743-850178).

A variety of craft courses at several FSC Centres in England. Choose from: Enamelling and Bookbinding at Flatford Mill in Suffolk, Stained Glass at Preston Montford in Shropshire or Calligraphy at Blencathra in Cumbria. Prices from about £255 for week, £100 for a weekend inclusive of accommodation, all meals and tuition.
Minimum age: 16 years.

LOWER ASTON HOUSE POTTERY AND PAINTING SUMMER SCHOOL

Aston Bank, Knighton-on-Teme, Tenbury Wells, Worcestershire WR15 8LW (tel 01584-781404).

Proprietors: M Homer and T Homer.
In business since 1981.
Holidays provided for 200 annually.
Pottery and painting courses in Worcestershire from April to October. Courses last from two days to three weeks. Individuals and groups of up to 18 may be catered for. No experience is required. Prices from £125 to £338, including all meals and accommodation. Potters should bring an overall and a hand towel, while painters should bring brushes and paints.
Age limits: 12-80 years.
Unaccompanied young people accepted from 14 years for painting and drawing, 17 years for pottery.

THE TOTNES SCHOOL OF GUITARMAKING

Collins Road, Totnes, Devon TQ9 5PJ (tel 01803-865255).

Proprietor: Norman Reed.
In business since 1985.
18 taken on courses annually.
Courses last 12 weeks and involve making instruments of the guitar family. Tuition is by a member of the Crafts Council Index of Selected Makers. Courses run from January-March, May-July, September-December. The tuition fees are £3130 including materials. This may be exceeded if the client wishes to purchase more expensive parts. Accommodation can be arranged with local families a few minutes walk from the workshop, for around £85 weekly for meals and bills.
Ages: 16 +
'Anyone who spends 12 painstaking weeks building a guitar will be imparting to it something of themselves. The highlight is the same for everyone — the sound of the finished instrument, at the start of its playing life'.

WENFORD BRIDGE POTTERY

St Breward, Bodmin, Cornwall PL30 3PN (tel 01208-850471).

Directors: S Cardew.
In business since 1939.
(First established by Michael Cardew a well-known English potter).
Pottery holiday courses in North Cornwall during the summer. Weekends or one to four weeks. Courses include all day tuition and wheel thrown pottery. Price: £195 per week (non residential), includes lunch and tuition; £300 includes six nights B&B, lunch and tuition.
Minumum age: 15 years unaccompanied.

WOLDS SILVER

Rothay Cottage, Leppington, Malton, North Yorkshire YO17 9RL (tel 01653-658485).

Sole Traders: V Ashworth and M Ashworth.
In business since 1986.
Association of British Designer Silversmiths.
Holidays for 50 arranged annually.

Courses in silversmithing, goldsmithing and jewellery for beginners or experts. Courses run each year from April-December. Small groups of four allow personal tuition. Price: £60 per day includes full board, accommodation and tuition. Additional expenses are for precious metals used.
Ages: 12+ (unaccompanied young people not accepted).

Wales

FIELD STUDIES COUNCIL
Head Office, Montford Bridge, Shrewsbury SY4 1HW (tel 01743-850674; fax 01743-850178).
Several weekend craft courses at the FSC's Dale Fort centre in Pembrokeshire. Choose from Calligraphy for Beginners and Nature in Sugarcraft. Prices from about £255 for a week, £100 for a weekend inclusive of accommodation, all meals and tuition.
Minimum age: 16 years,except on courses arranged for families.

Europe

ATELIER DE LA ROSE
Le Bourg, 46700 Montcabrier, France (tel +33 565 24 66 36; fax +33 565 36 59 97).
Owner & Director of Studies: Ed Herring.
Established in France since 1991.Member of the National Soc. for Education in Art & Design (UK) & Société Internationale pour L'Education Artistique.
Creative holidays for 30-40 people a year.
Design, drawing, painting, photography, creative writing and sculpture courses in the Lot region of south-west France (between the Dordogne and Lot rivers). Five days+. Open all year. Course only prices from 3,000-6,000 francs per person. Rooms available on site. A range of alternative accommodation from campsites to three-star hotel is available locally. Course leaders are English.

Cattle Ranching

AMERICAN WILDERNESS EXPERIENCE INC
P.O. Box 1486, Boulder, Co 80306 (tel +1 303-444-2622; fax +1 303-444-3999).
Old West dude ranch vacations year round. Options include working cattle ranches where guests can participate alongside professional cowboys working cattle, checking fences, roping cattle and taking part in the day-to-day running of a ranch in Arizona, Idaho, New Mexico, Oregon, Wyoming, Montana or Colorado and British Columbia. Prices $100 to $200 per day plus tax and tips.

HARGRAVE CATTLE & GUEST RANCH
300 Thompson River Road, Marion, Montana 59925, USA (tel+fax (+406) 858 2284).
Directors: Leo & Ellen Hargrave.
In business as ranchers for 30 years; commercial guests since 1988.
Member of National Cattleman's Association, Dude Ranches, Montana Outfitters and Montana Guides Association.
Working cattle ranch holidays in north west Montana all year round. Live the western legend on an historic 87,000 acre working ranch. Price: US$1100 per week including home cooked meals and accommodation in log cabins. Also opportunities for canoeing, rafting, fishing, trekking in the Cube Iron Wilderness and visits to the Glacier National Park or the National Bison Range with downhill skiing in Winter. Maximum of 15 guests per week. No experience required.
Minimum age: five years.

USA TAILOR-MADE HOLIDAYS
82a High Street, Tonbridge, Kent TN9 1EE (tel 01732-367711; fax 01732-367722).
Directors: P Read, P Lee, R Jenkins.
In business since 1995.
Over 50 working, dude and resort style ranch properties in Arizona, California, Idaho, Montana, Utah, Wyoming, Texas and Alberta in Canada. Working ranches include trail rides, cattle work, lessons and horseback games. Additional activities include white water rafting, wagon train adventures, hiking, biking and fishing.

Caving and Cave Studying

England

FREETIME ACTIVITIES
Sun Lea, Joss Lane, Sedbergh, Cumbria LA10 5AS (tel/fax 015396-20828).

Director: Paul Ramsden, Nationally qualified cave instructor (C.I.C.).
In operation since 1988.
Caving in the Yorkshire Dales all year round. Introductory half-day caving trips. 'A step beyond the show cave for the more adventurous who want to explore a unique and unknown environment'. Own waterproofs, boots and warm clothes needed. All specialist equipment provided. Groups of up to 24 catered for.
Also specialist caving courses, training and assessment for National Caving Qualifications.
Abseiling for groups.
Ages: 12-60 years.

MENDIP OUTDOOR PURSUITS
Laurel Farmhouse, Summer Lane, Banwell, Weston-super-Mare BS24 6LP (tel 01934-820518).
Caving days and weekends. Caving can be combined with other activities eg. climbing or abseiling, on an 'Underground and Overground' package. Tailor-made courses can be arranged for groups of six persons plus. Suitable for children and adults.
Minimum age: eight years unaccompanied. Physically challenged people can be catered for depending on the activity required.

ROCK LEA ACTIVITY CENTRE
Station Road, Hathersage, Hope Valley S32 1DD (tel 01433-6503450).
Adventure Activities Licence.
Adults only weekend and week caving and pot-holing holidays. All year (except Christmas). Weekend from £99; £299 for one week. Qualified staff. Special fixtures and dates can be arranged for Scouts, schools, clubs etc.
Complete beginners age 16+ (younger groups by arrangement).

YHA ACTIVITY CENTRE
Rowland Cote, Nether Booth, Edale, Derbyshire S30 2ZH (tel 01433-670302).
Explore the underground world of the Peak District or North Wales with experienced instructors. Beginners' courses include two contrasting underground trips, plus evening lectures. More intensive courses available to improve skills. Price of £81 (weekend) includes full board accommodation.

Europe

SOCIETE SPELEOLOGIQUE DE WALLONIE
93 Rue Belvaux, B-4030 Liége-Grivegnée, Belgium (tel +32 4 3426142; fax +32 4 3421156). Internet:http://www.itfm.be/ubs/ssw
Non-profit making organisation. Recognised by the Youth Council (Belgium).
Society founded in 1954.
Cave studying in Southern Belgium, all year round. Scientific study of caves (known as speleology), for people interested in their formation and structure. Youth hostel accommodation available in the Ardennes all year round.
Ages: 15-35 years.

Conservation

England

FIELD STUDIES COUNCIL
Head Office, Montford Bridge, Shrewsbury SY4 1HW (tel 01743-850674; fax 01743-850178).
Conservation courses at six of the FSC's centres in England. Topics include: Trees and Woodlands, National Vegetation Classification, Hedge Laying and Conservation Management. Prices from about £255 for a week, £100 for a weekend inclusive of accommodation, all meals and tuition.
Minimum age: 16 years.

THE NATIONAL TRUST WORKING HOLIDAYS
PO Box 84, Cirencester, Glos GL7 12P (tel 0891-517751 brochureline — calls cost 50p per minute).
Registered Charity.
In operation since 1967.
4000 volunteers needed annually.
Conservation working holidays in England, Wales and also Northern Ireland for two, three or seven day projects, year round. Enjoy an active week, with like-minded people in a beautiful corner of the UK's countryside. Over 450 different holidays covering dry stone walling, woodland path construction, downland management, botanical surveys, building construction and

archaeology, etc. Prices about £42 per week with hostel accommodation and all meals. Own sleeping bags, suitable footwear and waterproofs needed. For individuals and pairs.
Age range: 18 to 70 years.

Scotland

SCOTTISH CONSERVATION PROJECTS TRUST
Balallan House, 24 Allan Park, Stirling FK8 2QG (tel 01786-479697; fax 01786-465359).
Charitable organisation.
Director: Nicholas Cooke.
Operating since 1984.
Member of Scottish Tourist Board.
Holidays for about 500 arranged annually.
Practical conservation holidays (Action Breaks), offered all over Scotland including the Western Isles and Orkney and Shetland from March to November. Usually a week or two weeks, but sometimes longer. Prices start at £5 per day (adult), £4 (unemployed, student, retired people) covers training, insurance, basic accommodation and food. The latter is prepared by the participants on a rota basis. Individuals and pairs of friends accepted, but no groups. Participants need no previous experience but must be fit and healthy as the work is demanding e.g. restoring native tree cover, replacing stiles and footbridges, drystone dyking and fence-building. Volunteers will have the opportunity to learn new skills. Own warm and waterproof clothing essential. Participants pay their own travel costs to a published pick-up point.
Ages: 16 to 70 years. (18 years from overseas).

THISTLE CAMPS
National Trust For Scotland, 5 Charlotte Square, Edinburgh EH2 4DU (tel 0131-2439423; fax 0131-2439444).
Charitable organisation.
Holidays for 350 arranged annually.
Conservation working holidays on National Trust properties all over Scotland. Camps run for seven to 21 days, between March and October. Groups of up to 12 catered for. Prices: seven days £40, 21 days: £90. Concessions for unwaged volunteers. Accommodation in outdoor centres and base camps; all meals provided. Volunteers need to be fit and healthy, and are expected to help with meal preparation and other domestic duties.
'A chance to learn a practical conservation skill, meet new people, get fit and put something back into the environment.'
Minimum age: 16 years.

Wales

FIELD STUDIES COUNCIL
Head Office, Montford Bridge, Shrewsbury SY4 1HW (tel 01743-850674; fax 01743-850178).
Conservation courses at two of the FSC's centres in Wales. Choose from: Woodlands in Pembrokeshire and Environmental Projects in Snowdonia. Prices from about £255 for a week, £95 for a weekend inclusive of accommodation, all meals and tuition.
Minimum age: 16 years.

Northern Ireland

CONSERVATION VOLUNTEERS NORTHERN IRELAND
159 Ravenhill Road, Belfast BT6 OBP (tel 01232-645169; fax 01232 644409).
The Northern Ireland branch of the BTCV was started in 1984.
Takes 250 people on week-long and 200 on weekend projects annually.
Mostly conservation/environmental work. However, some working holidays include special interest activities such as caving and canoeing. Projects are organised year round but the majority take place during summer. Groups of ten to 12 people carry out various tasks including footpath construction and repair, pond building, tree planting and drystone walling. One weekend project involves building a kissing gate. Costs includes accommodation, meals, insurance and return transport from Belfast.
Training programmes are offered from July to December on a day, two/three day or six day basis.
Age range: 16-80 years.

Europe

SUNSEED DESERT TECHNOLOGY
Apdo. 9, 04270 Sorbas, Almeria, Spain (UK contact: 01865-721530).
Registered Charity No. 292511.
In operation since 1986.
Organises working holidays at a Desert Technology Research Station in Almeria, south-east Spain. Participation is available all year round and is part of a long-term search for ways to reclaim deserts and make life easier on their fringes. Working visitors are welcome for stays of at least two weeks. Opportunities also exist for longer term placement students (five week minimum stay). Summer project work may also be available in Tanzania. Residents work on projects such as tree nursery, tree planting, organic growing, hydroponics, solar ovens, solar stills and on community tasks (household, cooking etc). Cost to participate is £42 to £96 a week depending on season and type of work. (Send £1 for full details).
Minimum age: 16 (unaccompanied).
'They come for sun, good wholefood, challenge, and community life'.

The Americas

ONE WORLD WORKFORCE
Hands-on Conservation, Rt 4, Box 963A Flagstaff, Arizona 86001, USA (tel +1 520 779-3639; fax +1 800-451-9564).
One World Workforce offers trips for the general public to visit and work at environmental conservation projects in Baja and Jalisco, Mexico. Trips vary from year to year and have included protection of turtle nesting sites, preservation and care of captive turtles in tanks. Projects occur year round and cost $575-$650 per week. No air fares are included but simple accommodation at the camps, and food are provided.

There are no official age limits but ages 14 and under must be accompanied by an adult and ages 15-17 require written parental consent.

Historical Re-creation

KENTWELL HALL
Long Melford, Suffolk CO10 9BA (tel 01787-310207).
In operation since 1979.
Member of East Anglia Tourist Board, Historic Houses Association, Independent Tourism Consortium.
Holidays provided for 350-400 each year.
Historical re-creation of Tudor life during a three- or four-week period in late June and early July. There is no charge for participation. All food is provided and there is a meadow for camping as well as communal marquees. You will need to provide your own Tudor costume. Applications should be made between mid-January and mid-February. Send a S.A.E.
'Many who have participated in the past have discovered aspects of themselves which neither they nor their families or friends suspected existed'.
Unaccompanied young people accepted from 18 years; otherwise no mimimum age.

Just Women

England

SUNSAIL UK
The Port House, Port Solent, Portsmouth PO6 4TH (tel 01705 222224).
Dinghy sailing and yachting courses with ladies only weeks. Courses aim to make sailing rewarding, accessible and fun and are held in the sheltered waters of the Solent and the Clyde using dinghies, keelboats and yachts. No experience is necessary for a five-day course which is taught by qualified instructors. Prices start from £180.

OUTWARD BOUND TRUST
Watermillock, Cumbria, CA11 OJL (tel 0990-134227).
Call for a free brochure.

PENSHURST OFF ROAD CLUB
Grove Cottage, Grove Road, Penshurst, Kent TN11 8DU (tel 01892-870136; fax 01892-871187).

Director: Mike Westphal.
Established: 1993.
All instructors are qualified Association of British Cycle coaches.
Holidays for 300 + arranged annually.
Women on wheels courses cater for those with or without experience and cover all aspects of off-road biking including bike set up, posture, mechanics, cornering, braking, uphill and downhill technique, fitness, nutrition and route planning. Training takes place on a purpose built site with over 40 acres of tracks and trails. Courses run every month from March to October. Cost per weekend is £47 including VAT. Free camping or accommodation in B&B's and meals are extra. Bike hire available for those without their own. Nationwide courses.

Also women only cycle tours in Cuba.

WEEKEND ESCAPE
Fenelon, Hyde Lane, Marlborough, Wilts SN8 1JN (tel/fax 01672-511373).
Multi activity breaks for women with a choice of location (Dorset, Dartmoor, Pembrokeshire), activities (including rope course, hill walking, rock climbing, mountain biking and watersports) and accommodation (pub, hotel, activity centre). Prices from £160 for two full days of activities, two nights' accommodation and full or half board. Weekends start with arrival at 7pm on Friday ending late afternoon Sunday.

Europe

PEAK INTERNATIONAL
15 Moor Park, Wendover, Aylesbury, Bucks. HP22 6AX (tel/fax 01296-624225).
Ladies only cycle and canoe tour. Easy-going adventure exploring the culture and countryside of Karelia, Finland. 14 days ex Joensuu £655.

Management Courses

THE OUTDOOR TRUST
Belford, Northumberland NE70 7QE (tel/fax 01668-213289).
Management training courses arranged with each client to enable programmes to meet both general and specific training objectives. Courses range from one day 'now get out of that' team building challenges to fully residential course programmes. Courses prepared in direct negotiation with sponsoring training departments.

OUTWARD BOUND PROFESSIONAL
Eskdale Green, Holmrook, Cumbria CA19 1TE (tel 019467-23281).
Outward Bound programmes for management development.

ROCK LEA ACTIVITY CENTRE
Station Road, Hathersage, Hope Valley S32 1DD (tel 01433-650345).
Adventure Activity Licence.
Senior Training Director: Dr Iain Jennings FIPD.
Development Training Courses run by highly qualified trainers available for tailor-made outdoor development and adventure training for groups from industry and commerce. Choose from a very wide range of sports activities and tried and tested training modules. Highly professional service for quality-conscious clients. Various accommodation options available in and around the centre. Phone for a copy of the brochure or to discuss individual company requirements. Prices on application.

Motor Sports

ACORN ACTIVITIES
P O Box 120, Hereford HR4 8YB (tel 01432-830083; fax 01432-830110).
Motorsports activities include: car rallying, four wheel off-road driving, go-karting, quad-biking and motor racing. Individuals and groups catered for. Prices from £40 per session. £225 for car rallying, £250 for motor racing. Accommodation from £22 per night.

DOVEY VALLEY SHOOTING GROUND AND POWER TREK
Brynmelin, Llanwrin, Machynlleth, Powys SY20 8QJ (tel & fax 01650-511252).
Director: H D Jones.
In business since 1984.
WTB accredited.
Opportunities for clay pigeon shooting, quad biking, power treks and off-road driving in the Welsh Highlands. Based near the historic market town of Machynlleth overlooking the picturesque River Dovey. No experience necessary for any activity. Corporate entertainment packages available. All equipment provided. Prices: quad bikes and shooting lessons £15 per hour.

Full range of accommodation available locally.
Minimum age: 12 years.

THE FOREST EXPERIENCE AND RALLY SCHOOL
Carno, Montgomeryshire, Wales SY17 5LU (tel 01686-420201; fax 01686-420670).
Proprietors: Tony & Christina Higgins.
In business since 1985.
Holidays for about 1000 arranged annually.
Rally driving courses using RS2000 rear-wheel drive and Astra front-wheel drive rally cars based in a 900 acre forest. The holidays are centred on a small village in mid-Wales. Half-day, one- and two-day (residential) courses held all year round. Individuals and groups of up to 30 catered for. The instructors are expert in classic Scandinavian loose-surface rally driving. Techniques include the pendulum, handbrake turn and power slide. All-terrain quad bikes are provided for light relief. Clients must be competent drivers. Prices: £115 (half-day), £235 (one-day introductory) and £555 (two-day) residential). Off-road courses also available for individuals and groups using the school's or customers' vehicles.Accommodation can also be provided for non-participants at £20 per night for bed and breakfast.
Minimum age unaccompanied: 17 years.

JIM RUSSELL RACING DRIVERS SCHOOL UK LTD.
Donington Park, Castle Donington, Derbyshire DE7 2RP (tel 01332-811430; fax 01332-811422).
Director: John Kirkpatrick.
In business since 1957.
Member of RAC, Motor Sports Association.
Holidays for hundreds arranged annually.
Offers racing driving holiday courses throughout the year. Course covers training, and first race entry. Course fees range from £120 for a two-hour trial, to £2500 for a full week course with a race). Accommodation is not included but is available locally for £25-£50 + per night. Own soft flexible driving shoes and gloves essential. Other equipment included in course fee on full courses. Driving proficiency required.
Minimum age accepted: 16 years.
Minimum age for entering races: 17 years.
'A unique chance to drive a racing car round one of Britain's major racing circuits.'

Murder and Mystery Weekends

ACORN ACTIVITIES
P O Box 120, Hereford HR4 8YB (tel 01432-830083; fax 01432-830110).
'Play detective for a weekend and solve a brain teasing crime'. Hotel accommodation. Price per person £225 includes en suite accommodation and meals.

HF HOLIDAYS LTD
Imperial House, Edgware Road, London NW9 5AL (tel 0181-905 9556).
Murder Mystery weekends at the HF Country House or hotels located nationwide. Solve the grisly crime before breakfast on Monday or risk being 'murdered' yourself. Prices from around £130. Call for a Special Interest Holidays brochure.

THE WHODUNNIT COMPANY
Tanners Yard, 100 High Street, Crediton, Devon EX17 3LF (tel/fax 01363-774467).
Proprietor: Edward Holden.
In business since 1986.
Murder mystery evenings and long weekends in various hotels in the South of England and Europe, for individuals and groups up to 80. A unique brand of entertainment offering a sleuthing challenge in various themes and periods of history from Victorian times to the current day. Constant change of plots and individual murder mystery entertainment, also for corporate clients. Active participation by guests is positively encouraged and the actors are prepared at all times to be questioned and interrogated. Prices from £180 for Friday-Sunday including three-star accommodation, two nights B&B, dinner and Sunday lunch.
Minimum age: 14 years.
Certain venues cater for the physically challenged.

Orienteering

England

FIELD STUDIES COUNCIL
Head Office, Montford Bridge, Shrewsbury SY4 1HW (tel 01743-850674; fax 01743-850178).
A weekend learning basic navigational skills is on offer at the FSC's centre in

Shropshire. The course will help participants develop the skill and confidence to devise and follow their own routes. Price around £100 inclusive of accommodation, all meals and tuition.
Minimum age: 16 years.

YHA ACTIVITY CENTRE
Rowland Cote, Nether Booth, Edale, Derbyshire S30 2ZH (tel 01433-670302).
Introductory weekend courses including basic map and compass work, more advanced orienteering techniques, lectures and plenty of practice on the Hostel's own course. £81 including full board accommodation.

Ireland

ASSOCIATION FOR ADVENTURE SPORTS
Tiglin, The National Adventure Centre, Ashford, Co. Wicklow, Ireland (tel +353 404-40169; fax +353 404-40701). E-mail: mail@tiglin.le
Orienteering courses for novice and advanced students as well as training and assessment courses for instructors. Prices from £80.

Painting

England

FIELD STUDIES COUNCIL
Head office, Montford Bridge, Shrewsbury SY4 1HW (tel 01743-850674; fax 01743-850178).
The FSC's seven residential centres in England arrange landscape painting and drawing courses in a variety of media, as well as those on flower or fungi illustration and more specialist courses like Chinese brush painting or painting on silk. Flatford Mill in Suffolk offers the opportunity to live and work in the buildings featured in much of John Constable's work; all FSC centres are situated in areas of outstanding natural beauty. Courses for all levels. Prices from about £255 for a week, £100 for a weekend inclusive of accommodation, all meals and tuition.
Minimum age: 16 years, except on courses arranged for families.

Wales

FIELD STUDIES COUNCIL
Head office, Montford Bridge, Shrewsbury SY4 1HW (tel 01743-850674; fax 01743-850178).
Two of the FSC's residential centres in Wales offer a choice of painting courses, including Landscape Painting at Rhyd-y-creuau in Snowdonia, Botanical Illustration at Orielton, and the opportunity to draw Seascapes at Dale Fort in Pembrokeshire. Prices about £255 for a week, £100 for a weekend inclusive of accommodation, all meals and tuition.
Minimum age: 16 years.

Europe

FIELD STUDIES COUNCIL OVERSEAS
Montford Bridge, Shrewsbury SY4 1HW (tel 01743 850674; fax 01743 850178).
Based on the west coast of mainland Greece, Parga is the setting for a well-established and popular painting course. Its narrow streets, quaint houses, simple harbour, Venetian fortress and surrounding olive groves and citrus orchards provide plenty of inspiration for the artist. Expert tuition and trips to a nearby island included.

LSG THEME HOLIDAYS
201 Main Street, Thornton, Leicester LE6 1AH (tel 01509-231713).
Painting courses lasting one or two weeks in different regions of France from the Dordogne to Provence. Can be combined with other activities eg. cookery, rambling and conversational French. May to mid-October. Approximately 25 to 30 individuals on each holiday. Prices from £429 including single or twin rooms with en suite facilities and full board. Participants should provide their own materials.
Ages: 18 to 70+.

WINETRAILS
Greenways, Vann Lake, Ockley, Dorking RH5 5NT (tel 01306-712111; fax 01306-713504).
Painting holidays with expert artist and tutor Jackie Simmonds. Destinations to include French Alps, Provence, Southern

Spain, Switzerland and Madeira. Prices from around £690 per week, including tuition, transport to locations and most meals.

Photography

Worldwide

FIELD STUDIES COUNCIL OVERSEAS (AH)
Head office, Montfort Bridge, Shrewsbury SY4 1HW (tel 01743-850164/850522; fax 01743-850599). E-mail: 100643.1675@compuserve.com
Internet: http://www.soton.ac.uk/dace/fsco/index.htm
Specialist tuition available on photography and wildlife courses visiting destinations as far north as Spitzbergen beyond the Arctic Circle and as far south as the Falkland Islands, as well as the Swiss Alps, the Pyrenees, the White Mountains of New Hampshire and the Peruvian rainforest.

PHOTO TRAVELLERS
P O Box 58, Godalming, Surrey GU7 2SE (tel 01483-425448; fax 01483 419270).
Since 1980, Photo Travellers have been operating holidays designed for photographers by photographers. Destinations range worldwide from the Azores to Zanzibar and vary from year to year. Prices from £495 (Cypriot springtime) to Wildlife of the Falklands (£3295).

England

ACORN ACTIVITIES
P O Box 120, Hereford HR4 8YB (tel 01432-8300835; fax 01432-830110).
Two-day course on landscape, portrait and dramatic action photography in a fully-equipped studio and darkroom, and on location. On-site processing. Use of latest equipment. £120 for two days. Choice of farmhouse or hotel accommodation from £22 or £30 respectively.

FIELD STUDIES COUNCIL
Head Office, Montford Bridge, Shrewsbury SY4 1HW (tel 01743-850674; fax 01743-850178).
Weekend and week-long photography courses at several FSC centres in England. They include Landscape Photography at Blencathra in the Lake District, Nature Photography at Juniper Hall in Surrey, Photographing Fungi at Preston Montford in Shropshire and Black-and-White Photography at Flatford Mill in Suffolk. Beginners are welcome. Prices from about £255 for a week, £100 for a weekend inclusive of accommodation, all meals and tuition.
Minimum age: 16 years.

HF HOLIDAYS LTD
Imperial House, Edgware Road, London NW9 5AL (tel 0181-905 9556).
Photography holidays offered at a number of locations nationwide, mostly in areas of outstanding natural beauty. Practice your skills with a knowledgeable and enthusiastic leader. Opportunity for discussion, study and criticism of photographs in the evenings. No special skills needed, all abilities welcome. Bring a 35mm or medium format camera. Some walking involved. Prices from £169 for four nights, full board. Call for a Special Interest Holidays brochure.

PHIL PARISH PHOTOGRAPHY
Ravenscourt House, 138 Lynn Road, Wisbech, Cambs. PE13 3DP (tel 01945-585052).
Proprietor: Phil Parish.
In business since 1989.
Photographic one or two-day workshops, for the complete novice who wants to improve camera techniques or film and print processing, from £45. Accommodation available.
Physically disabled people welcome, depending on their capabilities.
Minimum age: 16 (accompanied); 18 (unaccompanied).

Wales

FIELD STUDIES COUNCIL
Head Office, Montford Bridge, Shrewsbury SY4 1HW (tel 0143-850674; fax 01743-850178).
Weekend and week-long courses at the FSC's Dale Fort centre in Pembrokeshire. They include: Black-and-White Photography and Nature Photography weekends and an Underwater Photography week in August. Prices from about £255 for a week,

£100 for a weekend inclusive of accommodation, all meals and tuition.
Minimum age: 16 years.

Powerboating

D V DIVING
138 Mountstewart Road, Newtownard, Co Down BT22 2ES Northern Ireland (tel 01247-464671).
RYA Powerboat instruction. Levels one and two, safety boat and advanced powerboat course.

ISLAND CRUISING CLUB
10 Island Street, Salcombe, South Devon TQ8 8DR (tel 01548-843481; fax 01548-843929).
RYA levels one and two and safety boat certificate using 5m and 6m Ribs and 20ft inboard launches. Two-day or longer residential or non-residential courses from £90.

PLAS MENAI NATIONAL WATERSPORTS CENTRE
Caernarfon, Gwynedd LL55 1UE (tel 01248 670964)
Powerboating courses for beginners to advanced level. Two, three and five day courses. RYA qualifications available. Prices: 2 day £140, 3 day £175, 5 day £295, including full board and accommodation, all instuction, equipment and personal protective clothing.
Minimum age: 14 years (unaccompanied).

Shooting

ARMATHWAITE HALL HOTEL
Bassenthwaite Lake, Keswick, Cumbria CA12 4RE (tel 017687-76551).
Clay pigeon shooting and archery holidays in the Lake District all year round.
Children must be accompanied by an adult.

BOBSPORT (SCOTLAND) LTD
9 Craigleith Hill Crescent, Edinburgh EH42 2LA (tel/fax 0131-3326607).
Director: R Brownless.
In business since 1985.
Tailor-made shooting breaks in Scotland's finest countryside and woodlands. Driven, mixed or rough shooting days available for a huge variety of game. Deer stalking arranged April-October. Carefully selected accommodation and a keeper always on hand to offer advice. Price quotes available on request.

DOVEY VALLEY SHOOTING GROUND AND POWER TREK
Brynmelin, Llanwrin, Machynlleth, Powys SY20 8QJ (tel/fax 01650-511252).
Director: H D Jones.
In business since 1984.
WTB accredited.
Opportunities for clay pigeon shooting, quad biking and power treks and off-road driving in the Welsh Highlands. Based near the historic market town of Machynlleth overlooking the picturesque River Dovey. No experience necessary for any activity. Corporate entertainment packages available. All equipment provided. Prices: quad bikes and shooting lessons £15 per hour. Full range of accommodation available locally.
Minimum age: 12 years.

Survival Courses

England

BREAKAWAY SURVIVAL SCHOOL
17 Hugh Thomas Avenue, Holmer, Hereford HR4 9RB (tel 01432-267097).
Proprietor: M Tyler.
In business since 1984.
Holidays for around 400 arranged annually.
Weekend and five-day management and management initiative team building courses. Enjoy the unspoilt beauty of the area. Individuals and groups may be catered for. Prices: £70 for individuals and £600 for a group of ten for a weekend course, £150 for individuals and £1500 for a group of ten for a five-day course. Participants must provide their own sleeping bags, boots and basic kit.
Minimum age: 18 years.Visually challenged people catered for.

WILD QUEST EXPEDITIONS
29 Kings Court, Bishops Stortford, Herts, CM23 2AB (tel 01279-658714).
Stone Camp course has been running since 1990. It teaches basic outdoor skills, designed for schools, expedition training, expedition selection, individuals and groups. The course starts with a training phase, and finishes off with small groups practising the skills taught earlier. Courses

can include team building and communications. Price £295 for a five-day course. Training phase includes shelter building, water collection and purification, fire lighting using no matches, different cooking methods and many more skills.
Minimum age: 14 years.

Scotland

JOHN BULL SCHOOL OF ADVENTURE
12 Littlethorpe Park, Ripon HG4 1UQ (tel/fax 01765-604071).
Survival course in the Scottish Western Isles during September. Learn to live off the land, build shelters and find your own food in a natural environment. Tour the isles by canoe paddling by day and camping on the shore each night. Also includes a Viking Weekend and City Challenge.

Winetasting

WINETRAILS
Greenways, Vann Lake, Ockley, Dorking RH5 5NT (tel 01306-712111; fax 01306-713504). E-mail: steve.dallyn@winetrails.co.uk
Internet: http://www.winetrails.co.uk
Proprietor: Stephen Dallyn.
In business since 1994.
Member of ATOL and ABTOT.
Gourmet, wine and walking holidays through spectacular wine regions. Also winetastings in the UK and wine trips and tastings in Europe and beyond: Italy, Spain, Madeira, France, Switzerland, California, the Cape Winelands of South Africa, South Australia, Cyprus, Bulgaria, Chile, Hungary and Portugal.

Winetrails also organise tailor made programmes virtually anywhere in the world with a wine industry, for walkers, cyclists, gourmet groups etc. Typical prices are £960 for ten days in Alsace; £1195 in the Veneto, Italy. Nearly all trips are full board.

Also wine and walking weekends in the UK and Ski Gourmet holidays in the European Alps.

JON HURLEY'S COUNTRY HOUSE WINEWEEKENDS
Upper Orchard, Hoarwithy, Herefordshire HR2 6QR (tel 01432-840649).
Owners: Jon and Heather Hurley.
In business since 1973.
Winetasting and walking weekends all year round provided for groups of up to 20 in the Herefordshire countryside. Mixes wine tasting with fresh air and delicious food. Prices from £195 includes accommodation, tastings and two dinners with wine.
Minimum age: 18 years.

Other

England & Wales

ACORN ACTIVITIES
P O Box 120, Hereford HR4 8YB(tel 01432-830083; fax 01432-830110).
Over 50 specialist pursuits including pottery, painting, drawing, cooking, woodturning, needlecraft, beautycare, calligraphy, sugarcraft, bridge, cider and wine tasting, cultural courses and murder mysteries in Herefordshire, Shropshire and Wales. Choice of hotels, farmhouses, group accommodation and self-catering. Prices for accommodation from £22 per night and for activities from £40 per day.

BOSWEDNACK MANOR
Zennor, St. Ives, Cornwall TR26 3DD (tel 01736-794183).
Proprietors: Dr E Gynn, Mr G Gynn.
In business since 1985.
Recognised by the West Country Tourist Board and RSPB.
Holidays for about 20 arranged annually.
One-week courses between May and October (not continuously). Natural history, birdwatching and archaeology around West Penwith, Cornwall (west of River Hayle). Guided walks also available daily. Groups of up to ten people catered for. Prices £250-£280, including board and accommodation.
Minimum age (accompanied): ten years otherwise 16 years.

BRITISH UNIVERSITIES ACCOMMODATION CONSORTIUM LTD
Box Number 1511, University Park, Nottingham NG7 2RD (tel 0115-9504571; fax 0115-9422505).
Executive Director: Carole Formon.
Study and activity holidays, self catering, bed and breakfast and full board available at over 60 venues. Facilities available for groups as well as individuals and families.

CHICHESTER INTEREST HOLIDAYS
14 Bay View Terrace, Newquay, Cornwall TR7 2LR (tel 01637-874216).
Proprietors: S R Harper & S J Hebdige.
In business since 1982.
Member of the ETB, West Country Tourist Board, Newquay Hotels Association, Cornwall Create Activity Network.
Holidays for around 150 provided annually.
Cornwall based week-long courses in mineral collecting and identification, Best of Cornwall Allsorts, archaeology and walking and from March to June and during September and October. Individuals and groups of up to ten adults catered for. Activities may also be sampled in combined programmes. No experience required. All courses cost £200 plus entrance fees, and include full board and transport.

COUNTRYWIDE HOLIDAYS
Grove House, Wilmslow Road, Didsbury, Manchester M20 1LH (tel 0161 448 7112; fax 0161 448 7113).
Walking and activity holidays based at country guest houses throughout Britain all year. All guest houses are based in areas of outstanding natural beauty. Guided walks, led by experienced leaders are available and are graded according to levels of strenousness for all ages and abilities. Also special interest holidays ranging from indoor activities such as bridge, country dancing and scrabble to outdoor ones such as British heritage, countryside appreciation and natural history and photography. Individuals, families and groups catered for. Prices vary depending on destination, duration and season but start at £31 per person, per day, full board including picnic lunch.

FIELD STUDIES COUNCIL
Head Office, Montford Bridge, Shrewsbury SY4 1HW (tel 01743-850674; fax 01743-850178).
Over 500 short special interest courses run throughout the year at 11 residential study centres in England and Wales, all chosen for the diversity and richness of their surroundings. There are short courses at every level, from introductory to specialised, in a wide range of natural history topics as well as arts and crafts like painting, photography and creative writing. Topics not covered in other sections include: Geology like 'Introducing Geology' weekend at Blencathra in the Lake District; gardens and gardening courses like the Horticulture weekend at Flatford Mill in Suffolk, Housman's Shropshire, at Preston Montford in Shropshire, Understanding Weather at Malham Tarn in the Yorkshire Dales, and Yoga at Rhy-y-creauau in Snowdonia. The standard of tuition, either by resident teaching staff (all fully qualified naturalists) or visiting tutors, is outstanding. Fees are from about £255 a week, £100 a weekend inclusive of accommodation, all meals and tuition.
Disabled people are catered for at some centres.
Minimum age: 16 years, except on courses organised for families and unaccompanied young people.

LOWER SHAW FARM
Old Shaw Lane, Shaw, Swindon Wilts. SN5 9PJ (01793 771080).
In business since 1976.
Holidays arranged for about 500 people annually.
Alternative holidays involving ecology, permaculture, communities, women's activities, men's activities, childrens and family activities, crafts, music and dance at Lower Shaw Farm all year round. The idea is to provide a friendly, supportive atmosphere. Some clients have commented that time spent at Lower Shaw turned out to be a catalyst for change in their lives. Individuals and groups of up to 25 catered for. Costs from £60 per weekend includes accommodation and vegetarian meals. Visitors are expected to help with washing up.

MARLBOROUGH COLLEGE SUMMER SCHOOL
Marlborough, Wilts SN8 1PA (tel 01672-892388).
Holidays for 1500 arranged annually.
A variety of active holiday courses at Marlborough College in July and August. A range of over 140 courses available, from art to wild flowers and bridge to wine appreciation. Weekly prices for residents around £330 for a private room; from £290 for dormitory accommodation: non residents pay £160 per week.
Minimum age: three years (accompanied); 13 years (unaccompanied).

OUTDOOR ADVENTURE
Atlantic Court, Widemouth Bay, Nr. Bude, Cornwall EX23 0DF (tel 01288-361312).
RYA, BCU, BSA, MLTB, BAHA Approved Centre.
Personal Development Programmes for careers outdoors. A 13-week course leading to four national governing body coaching

awards. Choice of activities includes windsurfing, canoeing, surfing, climbing, sailing, first aid, life saving and power-boat awards. NVQ levels two and three. Diploma in Outdoor Leisure Management after successful completion of the course. Price: £3750 with full board.

SUMMER ACADEMY
Keynes College, The University, Canterbury, Kent CT2 7NP (tel 01227-470402; fax 01227-784338).
Director: N Riding.
In operation since 1986.
Holidays for 2,000+ arranged annually.
Extensive range of study courses based at 15 of Britain and Ireland's finest Universities. Choose from four main themes: Arts, Countryside, Heritage and Personal Development. Courses operate for six/seven nights between June and September. Prices from £370-£460, including tuition, course related excursions and full board accommodation in University halls of residence.
'An excellent combination of academic and recreational activities'.
Minimum age: 16 years (unaccompanied); no maximum age.

Europe

ALTERNATIVE TRAVEL GROUP
69-71 Banbury Road, Oxford OX2 6PE (tel 01865-315678).
Walking and . . . holidays focus on the outstanding features of Europe. Choose from a range of holidays combining three to four hours walking a day with other specific interests. Walking and truffles, orchids, whale watching, painting, Piero della Francesca, Italian gardens, the painters of Provence and more. All are led by experienced guides in small compatible groups with back-up vehicle. Prices from about £800 to £1200 including all meals and comfortable hotel accommodation.

GRECO-FILE & FILOXENIA LTD
Sourdock Hill, Barkisland, Halifax, West Yorkshire (tel 01422-375999; fax 01422-310340).
Suzi & Oliver Stembridge.
In business since 1986.
ATOL no 2817, AITO.
Holidays for 1500 arranged annually.
Tailor-made specialist interest holidays eg. walking, archaeology, natural history, cookery, wine tours, art, painting, botany, railway and musical tours arranged mostly in Greece. Individuals and groups of any size. Prices £350-£800 but can adapt to most price ranges. Most holidays are during summer but winter also possible.

LSG THEME HOLIDAYS
201 Main Street, Thornton, Leicester LE67 1AH (tel 01509-231713).
May to October. One or two-week courses rambling in small groups in beautiful off-the-beaten-track France and walking in off-the-beaten-track Paris. Half-day and full-day rambles at a leisurely pace. Rambling runs in parallel with other courses including French, photography, regional cookery, painting and cultural discovery to enable spouses and friends with different interests to share the same holiday.

STIFTELSEN STJÄRNSUND
77071 Stjärnsund, Sweden (tel +46 225 80001; fax +46 225 80301).
A wide range of courses held at a spiritual development centre started in 1984. It is non-profit and based on the Findhorn Foundation of Northern Scotland. Courses include dance, yoga, tai chai, meditation, music, painting, tarot and healing. Some even more esoteric ones include a Course in Miracles. The course centre is a large timber building dating from the 1890s. There is accommodation for 25 overnight guests. Transport can be arranged from the nearest railway station. There are reductions for senior citizens. Rooms from Skr 275 (about £22) per night and meals from Skr 125 (about £10) per day.

You can also go to Stiftelsen as a working guest giving four hours of labour daily. For this you get free meals while there is a negotiated contribution for lodging.

TRIPS WORLDWIDE
9 Byron Place, Clifton, Bristol BS8 1JT (tel 0117 987 2626; fax 0117 987 2627).
Trips acts as agents for Heimvegen who offer traditional culture and wilderness courses in Hemsedal, Norway. Two courses are offered in autumn and winter with two departures in October and six in winter from January to March. Heimvegen's courses are based around living with nature (not survival technique) incorporating the philosophy of Friluftslive, using traditional mountain ways such as travelling on wooden skis in winter with Greenland huskies and fishing and sailing on the autumn courses.

Autumn courses cost about £350 per week; winter £380. Prices include full board and accommodation, mentoring and use of equipment. Flights start at about £150, return rail fare from Bergen or Oslo to Hemsedal is about £65.

Americas

INTERNATIONAL CENTRE FOR GIBBON STUDIES
PO Box 800249, Santa Clarita, CA 91380, USA (tel +1 805 296-2737; fax +1 805 296-1237). E-mail: gibboncntr@aol.com
Non-profit making conservation and education organization.
In operation since 1978.
Member of American Zoo and Aquarium Association.
Primate care centre in Southern California recruiting about 30 volunteers each year to help in feeding, watering, cleaning, behavioural observation, data recording and library research. Volunteers may even witness the birth of an infant. Expenses include transportation and food. Lodging is provided on the site with individuals responsible for their own meals and laundry. Application forms available at the above address or E-mail. No experience necessary although the work is strenuous and the climate can be extreme.

Africa

GAMBIA EXPERIENCE
Kingfisher House, Rownhams Lane, North Baddesley, Hants S052 9LP (tel 01703-730888; fax 01703-731122).
Year round programme of adventure holidays in the Gambia — birdwatching safaris with leading ornithologist, river, creek and sport fishing, plus bush excursions. Prices begin at £288 for seven nights and £396 for 14 nights including bed and breakfast and flights. Ten-night holidays now available.

PANORAMA TUNISIA
29 Queens Road, Brighton, Sussex BN1 3YN (tel 01273-206531; fax 01273 205338). E-mail: panorama@pavilon.co.uk
Internet: http://www.phg.co.uk
Specialist in Tunisian holidays. Can provide a range of accommodation types in many locations including Hammamet, Port El Kantaoui, Djerba, Skanes and Mahdia. Winter specialist activity holidays include (prices from) Fitness £299, Bridge £299, Painting £699 (two weeks) and Sequence Dancing £289.

Thornlands shooting centre

Special Tours and Expeditions

In this chapter we have included those tours which rate as the most interesting or unusual. Some are exotic: host based holidays in the Ashanti region of Ghana, Saharan camel trekking in Tunisia, or joining a coral conservation project in Belize. Many of the companies included here offer a range of special activities within one package from trekking and motor-sailing in the Chilean Fjords to seeing the Arctic by minibus and white water rafting. Yet other companies specialise in tours led by expert guides whether they be desert tours led by *Beduin* or battlefields led by historians.

As you would expect such tours can be pricey — up to £4000, but there are some less expensive alternatives: or a desert tour in Israel and Egypt from under £200 (land price).

Aid Expeditions

Americas

AMIZADE
1334 Dartmouth Lane, Deerfield, IL 60015, USA (tel +1 847 945-9402; fax +1 847 945-5676).
First programme 1995.
Amizade means friendship in Portuguese. This organisation takes groups of volunteers to the Brazilian Amazon to participate in service projects. Past projects include building a vocational training centre for children. Volunteers do not need any special skills. Other programme sites proposed are in Bolivia, Eastern Europe and the USA (Yellowstone and Chicago). While helping with community projects, volunteers are provided with food and board and an experience of the rich and exotic environment. Volunteers have the chance to explore the Amazon with a boat ride on the Amazon or Tapajos rivers, hike through the jungle etc. and spend one entire day at a quaint beach town 30 miles from Santarem.

Volunteer programmes run from June to August, last about two weeks and cost $2,600 which covers meals, lodging, the cost of running the programme and round trip airfare Miami/Santarem.

Anthropological

Africa

INSIGHT TRAVEL
6 Norton Road, Garstang, Preston, Lancashire PR3 1JY (tel 01995-606095).E-mail insight@provider.co.uk
Proprietor: R Ashworth.
In business since 1990.
Member of Tourism Concern.
Holidays provided for 10-20 each year.
Tailor-made host based holidays in the Ashanti region of Ghana, with opportunities for birdwatching, dance and music. Two to four weeks, all year round. Individual holidays catered for according to interests. Price £490 plus flights, including 14 nights half board and airport transfer to host. Local transport is extra.
'An opportunity to experience Africa with Africans'.
Minimum age: 16 years, if accompanied.
Physically challenged people catered for.

Archaeological and Historical

Europe & Worldwide

ARC JOURNEYS
102 Stanley Road, Cambridge CB5 8ZB (tel 01223-779200; fax 01223-779090).
Tailor-made cultural tours visiting the sites of the ancient civilisations of Asia and South America. Visit the temples and palaces of Java and Bali, the longhouses of Batak, tombs and Bugis boats in Sulawesi and pagodas in Nepal. Typical price: £500 per week including twin room with en suite accommodation, and breakfast. Flights not included.

CATHY MATOS MEXICAN TOURS
215 Chalk Farm Road, Camden, London NW1 8AF (tel 0171-284 2550; fax 0171-267 2004).
Tailor-made tours in Mexico with emphasis on Mexico's 3000-year-old archaeology and history. A trip of three weeks offers an itinerary of the great Mayan sites such as Palenque, tombs set in rainforest and the ruins of Bonampak and Yaxchilan and Monte Alban and Mitla near the city of Oaxaca. Price from £999 per person.

EXPLORE WORLDWIDE LTD
1 Frederick Street, Aldershot, Hampshire GU11 1LQ (tel 01252-344161; fax 01252-343170).
Specialist archaeological tours in Sicily and the Bay of Naples led by a guest lecturer. Accommodation in hotels. Eight days from £669.

HOLTS TOURS(BATTLEFIELDS & HISTORY)
15 Market Street, Sandwich, Kent, CT13 9DA (tel 01304-612248; fax 01304-614930).
Internet: http://www.battletours.co.uk
Directors: Sir G Brunton, Mr M Silver, Lt-Col M Martin, Mrs I Swan. Lt-Col DRB Storrie, Capt P Snook.
In business since 1976.
Member of AITO. Fully bonded through CAA.
Holidays arranged for 3000 annually.
Battlefield and military historical tours throughout Europe, USA & Canada, Far East, North Africa, South Africa, New Zealand, India, Falklands and the Middle East from Jan-Nov. Specialist group tours by arrangement.
Holts' span history from the ancient civilisations to the Falklands War. Individuals and groups up to 45. Prices: Europe from £265; Long range eg. S. Africa approx. £2300. Accommodation is mostly half-board in three-star or above hotels with en suite rooms. All tours accompanied by top calibre guides, many with military backgrounds.
Physically and visually challenged people catered for.
All ages.

MIDAS BATTLEFIELD TOURS
The Old Dairy, The Green, Godstone, Surrey RH9 8DY (tel 01883-744955; fax 01883 744967).
Directors: Alan Rooney, Ian Fletcher.
CAA; ATOL licence 3716.
Holidays for 700 arranged annually.
Battlefield tours in Europe, USA, South Africa,India, Crimea and the West Indies. Tours last two to 15 days from April to November. Tours are accompanied by leading experts in their field. Price range from £200 for a weekend to £1000 for a week including minimum 3 star half board with wine and coffee, guide, tour notes, lectures and transportation.
Minimum age unaccompanied: 14 years; 12 with an adult.

SUNVIL HOLIDAYS
7 & 8 Upper Square, Old Isleworth, Middlesex TW7 7BJ (tel 0181-847 4748).
Directors: N Josephides, Der Parthog, P Der Parthog.
In business since 1974.
ABTA, Licensed by the CAA, ATOL No. 808, IATA, AGTA.
Holidays for 200 arranged annually.
Archaeological tours of Cyprus and Sicily from April-October.
Individuals and groups welcome. Price range from £724-£789 per person includes half board hotel accommodation. Travel insurance not included.
Also year round individual fly-drives to Namibia, Zimbabwe, Thailand and Costa Rica from £1500-£2200.

Arctic & Antarctic Exploration

ARCTIC EXPERIENCE
29 Nork Way, Banstead, Surrey SM7 1PB (tel 01737-362321; fax 01737-362341).

Combined cruise and hotel-based tour in Greenland's Disko Bay. 11 nights in June, July and August for around £2614 which includes land accommodation, cabin on board the MS Disko, on full-board basis, flights and all excursions.
Husky sledge adventure in Greenland, six or ten days in spring. A unique opportunity to gain an insight into the lives of the Greenlanders by visiting tiny isolated settlements. Prices from around £1192 including return flights, hotel accommodation and the services of an Inuit (Eskimo) guide and a team of huskies.
Seven day, husky sledge tour in Swedish Lapland, for around £1398. Participants need to be reasonably fit and are required to drive their own dog team.
South Greenland Adventure Cruise, seven nights in Greenland, two nights Iceland for around £1604 in June, July and August. Price includes land accommodation, cabin on board, most meals, flights and all excursions.

ARCTIC ODYSSEYS
2000 McGilvra Blvd East, Seattle, WA 98112, USA (tel +1 206-325-1977; fax +1 206-453 4734).
Directors: Robin Duberow and Carol Murray.
In business since 1976.
Directors belong to the US Ski Association, Northwest Territories Tour Operators and Guides, Baffin Region Tour Operators and Guides, and Polar Society.
Journeys for 70-80 people arranged annually.
Arctic Odysseys specialises in Arctic oriented holidays including wildlife, cultural, scenic tours, dogsledding and nordic and alpine skiing aspects. Tour and holiday destinations include Arctic Canada including upper Hudson Bay, Baffin and Ellesmere islands and the Arctic Archipelago, North Pole, Greenland, the Russian Far East and Yakutia (Siberia). Trips last five to 17 days and tour season generally includes March through May, July and August. Individuals and groups of up to 13 depending on the tour. Prices from $2,975 to $11,950
North Pole and Greenland Odyssey. April. Ex Resolute. Seven days. Price $11,000.
Dog Sled Odyssey and Igloo building to Baffin Island. Departs weekly, March through May. Five or nine days. Price $2,975 to $3,475.
Discover the Worlds of the High Arctic Odyssey — tour of Baffin and Ellesmere Islands and the Arctic Archipelago. Ex-Ottawa. Ten days. Price $5,875.
Polar Bears at Wager Bay Naturalist and Wildlife Odyssey. Ex Winnipeg. 8 days. Price $4,350.
Russian Far East, Siberia, Lena River to the Arctic Ocean Odyssey. Ex Seattle. 13 days. Price $5,445.
Minimum age: ten years (accompanied); 14 unaccompanied. Any maximum assuming good health.

ARCTURUS EXPEDITIONS LTD
PO Box 850, Gartocharn, Alexandria, Dunbartonshire G83 8RL (tel & fax 01389-830204).
Directors: K L Cartwright, L N Cartwright, R W Burton, J Burton.
In business since 1992.
Holidays for 100 arranged annually.
Cruises, dog-sledging, nordic skiing, sea kayaking and walking tours in the Arctic (December-August) and Antarctic (November-March). Tours last 8-19 days. Sail in comfort to the remote Arctic islands on the research vessel *Professor Molchanov* exploring wildlife, geology, archeology and history. Accommodation available on other tours ranges from tents and huts to chalets and hotels. Groups of up to 12 catered for. Prices from £1500-£3000. Clients must provide their own skis. Unaccompanied young people not accepted.

THE CRUISE PEOPLE
88 York Street, London W1H 1DP (tel 0171-723 2450; 0800 526313).
Directors: K Griffin, B Gibson, J Lang.
Established 1992.
Member: Guild of Professional Cruise Agents, Cruise Lines International Association and Passenger Shipping Association Scheme.
Antarctic and Arctic expedition voyages. Overall sales agents for Marine Expeditions Inc. of Toronto, Canada. Antarctica November to March; Arctic June to September. No relevant experience required. Prices from £1500 to £5000 include full board on ship and B & B on land. Expedition gear, parkas not supplied. Highlights include wildlife, scenic beauty, landings on Zodiac and lecturers on all expeditions. Also worldwide freighter cruises.

FIELD STUDIES COUNCIL OVERSEAS
Head Office, Montford Bridge, Shrewsbury SY4 1HW (tel 01743-850164; fax 01743-850599). E-mail: 100643.1675@compuserve.com
Internet: http://www.soton.ac.uk/dace/fsco/index.htm
Specialist botanical and wildlife study tours to Iceland, Spitsbergen, and the Canadian Arctic accompanied by expert tutors. Opportunities to undertake individual projects if desired. Groups of ten to 15 people and fees cover travel, full board accommodation, tuition and guidance.

EXODUS EXPEDITIONS
9 Weir Road, Balham, London SW12 0LT (tel 0181-675 5550 or 0181-673 0859 24 hrs).
A 19-day journey exploring Alaska's arctic wilderness by minibus, ferry and plane with opportunities for fishing, riding, canoeing and whitewater rafting. Prices from £1990 for 19 days, June to August. A special project to see polar bears close up in their natural environment before the Hudson Bay freezes over. A ten-day trip from £1690 October/November. Also Beluga Whale Tours in the Summer.

POLAR TRAVEL COMPANY
Wydemeet, Hexworthy, Yelverton, Devon PL20 6SF (tel 01364-631470; fax (01634-631270).
Director: Mr Pen Hadow.
In business since 1995.
Member of AITO.
Holidays for around 100 arranged annually.
Organisers of the celebrated McVities Penguin Polar Relay — the first all women expedition to walk to the North Pole. Specialist tours and expeditions located in the Arctic and Antarctic regions including travel by foot, ski, dogsledge, kayak, boat and plane. Tours operate between February-May (Arctic Spring), June-August (Arctic Summer) and November-January (Antarctic Summer). Individuals and groups of up to 6 catered for. Experience requirements depend on activity undertaken. Prices range from £5,000-£15,000 all inclusive. Accommodation ranges from lodges to tents depending on tour. Clothing is not included in the holiday price although boots and down jackets can be hired.
'Most clients return deeply impressed by the sheer breadth and depth of their experience'.
Minimum age: 18 years (unaccompanied).

WEXAS INTERNATIONAL
45-49 Brompton Road, Knightsbridge, London SW3 1DE (tel 0171-589 3315).
Discovering the wild side of the Canadian Arctic, with itineraries in search of polar and grizzly bears, whales, harp seals, walrus and many other fascinating inhabitants of the north. Options include: hiking, rafting, canoeing, sailing, cycling and dog-sledging.

Camel Caravanning

Africa

EXPLORE WORLDWIDE LTD
1 Frederick Street, Aldershot, Hampshire GU11 1LQ (tel 01252-344161; fax 01252-343170).
Three-day Saharan camel trek in Tunisia, visiting the dunes of the Northern Sahara, during 15 day holiday. Price £635.
Age: over 17 years and fit.

LET'S GO TRAVEL
P O Box 60342, Nairobi, Kenya (tel +254-2 213033 & 340331; fax +254-2-214713 & +254-2-336890).
Camel treks in various districts of Kenya. Four to fourteen days. Prices from $570-$800.

Horse Drawn Holidays

BOWLAND BOWTOPS
Stubb Farm, Wigglesworth, Skipton, North Yorkshire BD23 4RH (01729 840382).
In business since 1990.
Holidays for 250 arranged annually.
Touring the Yorkshire Dales and the Forest of Bowland with one-horse-power Romany Bowtop caravan equipped with gas cooker, lighting, kitchen utensils and a tent. Overnight stops are at farms and pubs. April to October. Long weekends, week or two-week holidays. Prices £400 per caravan (for four people), per week and £230 for a long weekend.

SLATTERYS TRAVEL AGENCY
1 Russell Street, Tralee, Co. Kerry, Ireland (tel (+ 353) 066-24088; fax (+ 353) 066-25981).
Proprietor: David L Slattery.
In business since 1970.
Member of ABTA, IATA and ITAA.
Horse-drawn gypsy caravan holidays. Hire a beautiful Irish horse and a fully-equipped gypsy caravan and go roaming the rainbows of Co Kerry at your own pace. Each caravan sleeps five people and is equipped with blankets, a gas stove and cooking utensils. April to September. A week is recommended; shorter breaks also available. Prices from £150-£550 with additional expenses for overnight parking, insurance and horse feed. Full instructions given. Support vehicle on call.

Europe

MOSWIN TOURS
Moswin House, 21 Church Street, Oadby, Leicester LE2 5DB (tel 0116-2719922; fax 0116-2716016).
Holidays by genuine 19th-century mail-coach (pulled by four horses) in Bavaria. Holiday lasts six days including four days travel by coach and horses and costs £985. The price includes scheduled flights from Heathrow to Munich, five nights' bed and breakfast, transfers and services of an English-speaking guide/coachman. Other stage-coach journeys on request.

Husky Sledging

ARCTIC EXPERIENCE
29 Nork Way, Banstead, Surrey SM7 1PB (tel 01737 218800).
Offer a guide-driven husky sledding trip in Greenland for six or ten days departing on Fridays in March, April and May and a self-driven Husky trip in Swedish Lapland for seven days (£1475 fully inclusive).
In addition they offer a two week, dog-sledding course in Swedish Lapland in November.

ARCTURUS EXPEDITIONS LTD
PO Box 850, Gartocharn, Alexandria, Dunbartonshire G83 8RL (tel & fax 01389-830204).
Dog-sledging tours in Arctic Norway from December-April. Spend eight days over Christmas at the home of Odd-Knut Thoresen, experiencing Norwegian Christmas dinner and the thrill of driving your own dog team. Prices for 8-9 day tours from £1390-1690 including flights. Accommodation in mountain cabins, chalets, tents and hotels.

CAMPFIRE CLASSIC ADVENTURES
Lowlands, Homanton, Shrewton, Salisbury SP3 4ER (tel/fax 01980-620839).
Husky safaris in Finnish Lapland. Choice of three tours.
Frontier Husky Safari: 200km route along the Finno-Russian border of Karelia. Drive your own husky team through forests and over frozen lakes to famous battlefields. Accommodation in chalets and guesthouses.
Lapland Husky Safari: Leisurely safari to the ancient village of Tepasto and a reindeer farm. Week-long tour with hotel accommodation in the Sirkka ski resort. Cross-country and downhill skiing available.
Arctic Survival Safari: Introduction to ancient survival techniques and dogsledging in the Arctic Wilderness. Accommodation in log cabins and traditional shelters.
Detailed information pack available on request. Typical price: £2,000 (all inclusive).
Minimum age: 12 years (unaccompanied).

ECOSUMMER EXPEDITIONS
936 Peace Portal Drive, PO Box 8014-240, Blaine WA, USA (tel + 1 604 6997741; fax + 1 604 6693244).
Dogsledging tours in Northwestern Greenland following the routes of the Polar Inuit (two-weeks duration) in March and April. Beginning in Savigsivik, each member will travel with their own dog team and Inuit driver across Melville Bay to Kullorsuaq. Prices: $7495 and $8495, including guiding service, equipment, all meals and accommodation.

FINLANDIA TRAVEL AGENCY (NORVISTA)
3rd Floor, 227 Regent Street, London W1R 8PD (tel 0171-409 7334; 0171-409 7733).
Seven-day husky adventure across the fells of Lapland starting from Harriniva holiday village near Muonio. The first day is spent getting to know the dog teams, checking equipment and learning to drive a dog sledge. A distance of 20-35 km is travelled per day. Accommodation is in wilderness huts, without electricity and showers,

although some will have saunas. Price per person about £1015 all inclusive. Suitable thermal clothing for outdoors will be provided at no extra cost.
Lapland Winter Safari Week: Activities include snowmobile safari, reindeer rides and a two-day husky safari stopping overnight in a wilderness cabin. Cross-country skiing also available. Price: £1061 all inclusive (thermal clothing provided). Departures from January-April.

PEAK INTERNATIONAL
15 Moor Park, Wendover, Aylesbury, Bucks HP22 6AX (tel/fax 01296-624225).
Alaska: explore the Alaskan wilderness with your own dog team. Tuition and guiding by author and racer Mary Shields. Easy day trip options, local races or multi-day expeditions for the more adventurous. Trips tailored to your preferences. 12 days. Luxury lodge accommodation. £1985 ex Fairbanks.
Canada: Bowron Lakes Expedition. Based in the remote Caribou Mountains of British Columbia. Exploration with your own team of dogs. five days for £330, eight days for £575 ex Clearwater.
Finland: Husky safaris in Finland from luxury eight-day adventures in Lapland for £845 to tough ten-day expeditions near the Russian border for £1095.
Other tours include nights out in remote cabins using the Wells Gray Ranch as a base. Eight days ex Clearwater from £775. Travel across Baffin Island or an expedition to the worlds most northerly settlement, Thule in Greenland.

WINTERGREEN DOGSLEDDING LODGE
1101 Ring Rock Road, Ely, 55731 Minnesota, USA (tel +1 218 365-6022; fax +1 218 365 3088.
President: Paul Schurke.
In business since 1985.
Holidays for 500-600 arranged annually.
Four to six-day, lodge-to-lodge dog-sledding vacations in northern Minnesota December to April. Prices from about $150 (about £95) per day; $525 (£325) to $1,550 (£956). Included in the price are deluxe lodge accommodation and restaurant meals.
Also, introductory and advanced dog sled, ski and camping trips involving all winter camping and travel skills using 'Himalayan hotel tents', building an igloo or new Antartic sleeping systems. A Finnish sauna and feast at the Wintergreen lodge awaits clients on the last evening. Price $590-$695 (about £365-£470).
Advanced trips graded one to ten for difficulty and increasing distance cost from $300 to $750.
The 1998, really adventurous programme includes Arctic expeditions: Ellesmere Island Expedition May 10-25 $3900 (about £2407) from Edmonton, and a dogsled expedition to the North Pole. Also planned are dog sled trips in the Grand Tetons/ Yellowstone area.

Inland Cruising

Europe

BLAKES HOLIDAYS LTD
Wroxham, Norwich NR12 8DH (tel 01603-782141).
Executive Directors: T Howes, R Peverett, C Prentice.
In business since 1908.
Member of ABTA.
Cruising holidays in France, Brittany, Burgundy, Lorraine-Alsace and the South of France from 17 different starting points on the country's most attractive waterways. Groups of two to 12. Prices depend on numbers and duration. Also wide choice of sailing and cruising holidays in UK and Ireland.

FINLANDIA TRAVEL AGENCY (NORVISTA)
3rd Floor, 227 Regent Street, London W1R 8PD (tel 0171-409 7334; fax 0171-409 7733).
Four-day (three nights) cruise on the 125-year-old Gota Canal which links the cities of Gothenburg and Stockholm in Sweden. Accommodation is on renovated steamers nearly as old as the canal, with running hot and cold water in the cosy cabins and showers in the corridors. The only other innovation is a diesel engine which is more efficient than steam. Prices from about £553 which includes full board, excursions and tax.

GUILDFORD BOAT HOUSE LTD
Millbrook, Guildford, Surrey GU1 3XJ (tel 01483-504494; fax 01483-506318).
Directors: Robert Chase, Richard Chase, Russell Chase, Anne Chase, Wendy Copeland, Anne Murrell and John Hall.
In business since 1974.

Member of SEETB, STB, BMIF, THCA and APCO.
Holidays for 5000 arranged annually.
Narrow boat holidays on the River Wey, Royal River Thames and the Basingstoke Canal providing 170 miles of waterways to explore. Choice of three or four-day short breaks, one-week, ten-day or two-week cruises. Groups of up to 12 catered for. No experience necessary. Prices range from £120-£300 per person per week. Self-catering accommodation on board. Bookings taken direct or through Hoseasons Holidays.
Minimum age: 18 years (unaccompanied).

HOSEASONS HOLIDAYS
Sunway House, Lowestoft NR32 2LW (tel 01502-500505; fax 01502-500532). UK Boating (fax 01502-586781).
James Hoseason OBE (Chairman), Ken Gaylard, Richard Overy, Yvonne Borg, Paul Temple, James C Hoseason, Tim Fullam (Directors).
In business since 1944.
Holidays for over a million people arranged annually.
Self-drive boating holidays on inland waterways in England, Wales and Scotland, and canals and waterways throughout France and Holland. Boats from two to 12 berths. Prices from about £72 per person per week for a self-catering holiday afloat. All equipment and buoyancy jackets are provided, some boats include free TV, diesel, car parking and pets.
Minimum unaccompanied age: Usually 18 years.
Physically, visually and mentally challenged people and their carers welcome.

FRENCH COUNTRY CRUISES
54 High Street East, Uppingham, Rutland LE15 9PZ (tel 01572-821330; fax 01572 821072).
Ten or 11-day, self-drive canal boating holidays aboard *penichettes* (continental narrowboats), which sleep two to 12 people. Choice of 20 starting points in France, Holland and innovatively, on the waterways and lakes of Mecklenburg in the eastern part of Germany.

MOSWIN TOURS
Moswin House, 21 Church Street, Oadby, Leicester LE2 5DB (tel 0116-271 9922; fax 0116 271 6016).
Luxury river cruises on the Danube. There is a choice of eight-day cruises: Holland and Rhine (from Amsterdam to Basel); Berching to Budapest. Also eight-day Elbe Cruise and four-days Main, Rhine and Moselle (Frankfurt to Trier). Prices from £485 to £1529 including flights, transfers and full board accommodation.

RIVIERA SAILING HOLIDAYS
45 Bath Road, Emsworth, Hants P010 7ER (tel 01243-374376).
Motor cruiser holidays on the rivers and canals of France.

Asia

AIRWAVES
10 Bective Place, London SW15 2PZ (tel 0181-875 1188; fax 0181-871 4668.
China & Yangtze River Cruise. 17-day trip to China includes six days cruising on the Yangtze from Chongquing to Wuhan on a Regal China Cruise Ship. Prices from £2095 including flights andfull board during the cruise.

Motorcycling

Worldwide

H-C TRAVEL
The Old School, Red Lion Lane, Overton, Hampshire RG25 3HH (tel 01256-770775; fax 01256-771773).
Proprietor: David Grist.
In business since 1994.
Member of the Travel Trust Association.
Holidays for 100-200 arranged annually.
Worldwide motorcycle hiring and touring holidays offered all year round, from a day to a months' duration. Destinations include Mexico, Costa Rica, Peru, Australia, New Zealand, Thailand, India, Bhutan, South Africa, Zimbabwe, Morocco, Western Europe, UK and USA. Individuals and groups catered for. Full UK motorcycle licence required. Choice of motorcycles for hire. Prices from £99-£2,800 per person. Typical price for two people, for two weeks in the USA: £3,000. Riding gear and petrol not included in price. Tours are minimum board only, although some provide all meals.

'Offers the largest choice of tours and hire in the world. From Alaska to the Australian deserts, from the Himalayas to the Highlands of Scotland.'
Minimum age: 21 years. No maximum age limit.

Europe

BIKE & SUN TOURS INTERNATIONAL
42 Whitby Avenue, Guisborough, Cleveland TS14 7AN (tel 01287-638217).
Proprietor: S C Jenkinson.
In business since 1983.
Holidays provided for 100-150 each year.
Motorcycle tours throughout Europe, including France, Germany, Austria, Greece, Slovenia, Italy, Spain, Portugal, the Alps and the Pyrenees. Tours take place from late May until early October. Most last two weeks, although the Greek tour lasts for three. You will need a full driving licence. Prices range between £508 and £1472. This includes bed and breakfast accommodation. Own motorcycle required.

Americas

DUBBELJU MOTORCYCLE RENTALS,LLC
271 Clara Street, San Francisco, CA 94107, USA (tel +1 415 495-2774; fax +1 415 495-2803).
Directors: Wolfgang Taft, Wiebke Daniels.
In business since 1991.
American Soc. of Travel Agents, Deutscher Reiseburo Verband, SFCVB Chamber of Commerce.
Motor cycle rentals (BMW & Harley Davidson) and self-guided tours for individuals, pairs (one rider one passenger) and groups of up to twelve all year round excluding a couple of weeks in January. Starting off mainly from San Francisco. One way trips within the USA are available on request. Maps, travel information and touring recommendations provided, and if required personal advice with your itinerary. Models are the HD Heritage Softail Classic, HD FLHT Electra Glide, Hd Sportster and Hugger, and the BMW R850R.
Hirers must have valid motorcycle licence, international licence (for non US-citizens) and a minimum two years' experience. Daily rental rates from $92-$139 and weekly rates from $553-$882, depending on the motorcycle. Extras include gasoline, optional insurance, security deposit and hire of jackets and tankbags (BMW) only if needed.
Minimum age accepted for hirer: 24 years.
Bookings can be made direct or through the office in Germany: Weg am Sportplatz 25A, 22850 Norderstedt (tel +49 40 525 7887; +49 40 5257984.
'Enjoy exploring on your own with the most freedom and adventure possible'.

USA TAILOR-MADE HOLIDAYS
82a High Street, Tonbridge, Kent TN9 1EE (tel 01732-367711; fax 01732-367722).
Motorcycle rentals (Triumph Thunderbird and Honda) in the USA and Canada, in Los Angeles, Salt Lake City, Phoenix, Las Vegas, Orlando, Miami, San Francisco, Seattle, Chicago, Denver, Atlanta, Calgary, Toronto and Montreal. Various special deals available e.g. Route 66 special Chigaco to Los Angeles, Phoenix or Las Vegas with no one way drop fees and discounts for longer rentals. Harley-Davidson rentals from Los Angeles, San Francisco, Chicago and Orlando. Rates from $42 per day in low season (16 October to 31 December) for a Sportster to $86 per day for an Electra Glide in high season (1 April to 15 October). Renters must provide their own motorcycle gear and helmet. Clients are not permitted on 'logging' and other non-public roads, off road routes or entry into Mexico.
Minimum age for rental is 21 years.

Asia

HIMALAYAN ROADRUNNERS
14 Iveley Road, London SW4 0EW (tel & fax 0171-6272030). USA: PO Box 538, Lebanon, New Jersey, USA 08833 (tel +1 908 2368970; fax +1 908 236 8972).
Proprietors: Mr R Callender, Mr E Shuttleworth.
In business since 1992.
Holidays for 75 arranged annually.
Motorcycle tours and expeditions in India, Nepal, Bhutan and Thailand for two-three weeks throughout the year. Groups of ten to 20 people. Prices from £1500-£4000

including accommodation ranging from tented camps to five-star hotels, and most meals. Participants must provide their own motorcycle clothing and possess a recognised licence.
Ages: 17-75 years.

Photographic

HOSKING TOURS LTD
Pages Green House, Wetheringsett, Stowmarket, Suffolk IP14 5QA (tel 01728-861113; fax 01728-860222).
Directors; David Hosking, Martin Withers.
In business since 1986.
Holidays provided for 30 annually.
Photographic nature holidays in Asia, Africa and the Americas. Camera equipment and film not included. Clients are asked to attend a pre-tour meeting where they will be advised which equipment would be useful and where to get it from. Groups of up to 12.
'Close encounters with nature and being able to record this on film'.
Minimum age: 18 years.
See *Wildlife* section.

Rail Tours

AIRWAVES
10 Bective Place, London SW15 2PZ (tel 0181-8751188; fax 0181-8714668).
Trans-Siberian rail tour to Beijing, visiting Moscow, Omsk, Novosibirsk, Irkutsk, Lake Baikal (Siberia) and Ulan Bator (Mongolia). Price for 16 days £2595 including flights, all train travel and full board. optional arrangements include London to Moscow by rail and a 2-night extension to Xian.
Also available, 15-day journey through Zimbabwe, Botswana and South Africa, from Victoria falls to Cape Town.

REGENT HOLIDAYS
15 John Street, Bristol BS1 2HR (tel 0117-921 1711 (24 hours); fax 0117-925 4866).
Regent holidays are experts in booking the Trans-Siberian Railways covering the different routes: to China through Mongolia or Manchuria, or to Vladivostock and on to Japan. There is a choice of itineraries but no set departure dates. It is possible to travel out on one route and return on another, or to fly back from China or Japan. Prices vary from £291-£444 according to type of berth, the route and season and include one night in a Moscow hotel and full board during the train journey which lasts up to eight days. Flights are extra and can be arranged by Regent Holidays.

Research Expeditions

CORAL CAY CONSERVATION LTD.
154 Clapham Park Road, London SW4 7DE (tel 0171-498 6248; fax 0171-498 8447).
Internet: http://www.coralcay.org
Contact: Peter Raines.
Non-profit organisation founded in 1989.
Working holidays arranged for 350-400 annually.
Recruits teams of interntional volunteers to join major research expeditions to Belize, the Philippines, Indonesia and elsewhere. The aim of each expedition is to provide resources for the protection and sustainable use of coastal marine and forest resources. To date, CCC volunteers have helped create eight new Marine Protected Areas and an off-shore Marine Research Centre for the University College of Belize.

Volunteers spend from two to twelve weeks based on remote tropical islands. Expedition activities include (a) surveys of coral reefs and tropical forests (b) conservation education and training programmes for coastal-dwelling communities, and (c) construction of field centres for education and research. Volunteers are also expected to assist with every aspect of the expedition, from boat handling and equipment maintenance, to catering and logistics. All necessary training (including SCUBA diving tuition) is provided at the expedition base and no previous experience is required.

Expeditions depart monthly throughout the year. Prices (excluding flights) range from £650 (two weeks) to £2,850 (12 weeks) and include full training, equipment hire, and board and lodging. Travel and medical insurance can be arranged through CCC.

Regular talks and presentations about CCC expeditions are organised nationally throughout the year.
Age range: 16-65 + years.
'Since 1986 over 1,500 volunteers have joined CCC expeditions. They helped change lives — now it's your turn.'

DISCOVERY INITIATIVES
No 3, 68 Princes Square, London W2 4NY (tel 0171-229 9881; fax 0171-229 9883).
E-mail: CBP@discoveryinitiatives.com
Internet:
http://www.discoveryinitiatives.com
Director: Julian Matthews.
In business since 1993.
Member of ATOL.
An environmental support company. Discovery Initiatives aims to channel the skills, energies and resources of the travelling public and partnering corporations into 'hands on' projects and programmes of international and local NGO's that contribute to a better understanding of the world and a more sustainable approach to its natural resources.

Worldwide programme in 1998, under the Discovery Initiative banner, carries places for 250 people to join a host of conservation and environmental projects during their holidays, sabbatical or as part of a corporate training programme, for seven to 21 days. Projects are proposed and sourced through International and indigenous Non-Governmental Organisations and agencies working in conservation and sustainable development and funded by fee paying participants. Each project comes with add-on holiday options. Destinations include Canada, Bolivia, Zimbabwe, Pakistan, Mongolia and the Congo.

Ventures are graded according to levels of comfort provided, the physical aptitudes required and the interests and skills sought of fee paying participants.

Project fees will range from £995 including airfares, meals and accommodation.
Age range: 16-70 years.

EARTHWATCH EUROPE
57 Woodstock Road, Oxford OX2 6HJ (tel 01865-311600; fax 01865-311383).
Internet: http://info@uk.earthwatch.org
Over 160 research expeditions throughout the world needing team members for one week to one month. Teams consist of four to 20 members. The participants share the work as research assistants to prominent scientists. No special skills or experience required. Projects range from studying the complex songs of humpback whales off the Hawaiian islands; investigating the ecosystems of South American rainforests; the prey-predator relationship of wolves and stags in the mountains of south-eastern Poland; saving endangered leatherback turtles in the US Virgin Islands and excavating giant mammoth bones in Oxfordshire, to list just a few. Accommodation varies from tents to hotels, usually with homecooked local food. Participants share in the cost of the projects which range from £375 to £2000 per volunteer, not including air fare to location.
Scholarships are available for students and teachers.
For an information pack, write, phone or send a fax to the above address.

FIELD STUDIES COUNCIL OVERSEAS
Head Office, Montford Bridge, Shrewsbury SY4 1HW (tel 01743-850164/850522; fax 01743-850599).
E-mail: 100643.1675@compuserce.com
Internet: http://www.soton.ac.uk/dace/fsco/index.htm
Organiser: Anne Stephens.
A wide range of escorted study tours examining conservation and environmental issues worldwide. Some courses offer participants the opportunity to undertake their own research/survey work — from the Peruvian rainforest to the Canadian Arctic — accompanied by expert leaders. Courses include visits to specific environmental projects e.g. a conservation and reforestation programme led by a local Buddhist monk in Thailand or captive bat-breeding programmes in the Philippines

FRONTIER
77 Leonard Street, London EC2A 4QS (tel 0171-613 2422; fax 0171-613 2992).
E-mail: enquiries@frontier.mailbox.co.uk
Internet: www.mailbox.co.uk/frontier
Non-profit organisation.
Director: Eibleis Fanning.
Founded 1989.
Frontier conservation expeditions is looking for explorers to join expeditions conserving some of the world's most threatened wildlife and endangered habitats. Participants may be diving with dolphins on Frontier's marine conservation expedition in the Indian Ocean, tracking elephants with game guards in Uganda's wildlife parks or discovering new species and experiencing new lifestyles and cultures as they live with local people in the forests of Vietnam and Tanzania. By taking part in a Frontier conservation expedition you will be helping to protect precious habitats and wildlife.

Each project runs four times and year and last ten weeks. Volunteers are self-funding and raise between £2800 and £3000 which covers flights, insurance, local travel, food, accommodation, field equipment and a residential briefing weekend prior to deployment. Enthusiasm and tolerance are the most important qualities needed as all the work will be supervised by qualified scientific and logistic staff (most of whom are former volunteers). If you think you can rise to the challenge contact Frontier for an information pack.

MAYA MOUNTAIN LODGE
P.O. Box 46, San Ignacio Cayo, Belize (tel +501 92 2164; fax +501 92 2029).
Maya Mountain Lodge is an educational field station for cultural, archaeological and wildlife studies in Central America and has been offering inclusive packages in Belize for 12 years. Possibilities include jungle and reef expeditions including bird watching and hiking, canoeing and biking, horseback trail riding, scuba, fishing and snorkelling. Special features includes eco-expeditions to the national parks, Mayan ruins, jungle rivers, mountains, villages and more. Also study programmes at the Rainforest Institute.

MOUNTAIN TREKS & TRAINING
125 Coombes Lane, Longbridge, Birmingham B31 4QU (tel 0121-6803507; fax 0121-4402408).
Director: Jeff South.
In operation since 1996.
Six-week discovery and research expedition to Morocco, covering more than 200 miles from Tarroudant to Midelt. Research on route monitors the climatic change, terrain, and the flora and fauna of the region. Expedition departure date is planned for July 1998, with pre-expedition training weekends beginning in April 1998. Volunteers must apply before the end of November 1997. Price of £2000 includes flights, personal insurance, food, accommodation and tents, vehicle hire, training, post expedition report and reception, expedition sweatshirt and T-shirt. Expedition handbook received on payment of deposit. An informal selection process will determine team allocation. A reasonable level of fitness is required.

TREKFORCE EXPEDITIONS
134 Buckingham Palace Road, London SW1W 9SA (tel 0171-824 8890; fax 0171-824 8892).E-mail Trekforce@dial.pipex.com. Website: ds.dial.pipex.com/town/parade/hu15
In business since 1988.
Expeditions organised for about 200 people annually.
Trekforce is the expeditionary arm of the UK registered charity International Scientific Support Trust. Trekforce organise six-week expeditions to Indonesia, Belize and Kenya in support of science and conservation. Each expedition involves three phases: pre-expedition training, project phase and an adventurous trekking phase. Projects so far have included: the construction of a turtle hatchery, a scientific research station and an orangutan rehabilitation centre; the mapping of boundaries for a rhino and tiger sanctuary and Mayan Indian ruins using Global Positioning Systems. Future projects will also include working on the Barrier Reef in Belize and in the rugged regions of Northern Kenya.

All applicants are invited to attend an introduction weekend, held monthly, which provide an opportunity to learn all about the expeditions and how to become involved. Trekkers are asked to fundraise £2,750 towards the cost of the expeditions and extensive fundraising advice is given at the weekend.
Applicants should speak English and be able to swim.
Minimum age: 17 years.

WHALE WATCH AZORES
18a Harold Road, Deal, Kent CT14 6QH (tel/fax 01304-381110).
Holidays for small informal groups.
Operating since 1992.
Yacht-based whale and dolphin research holidays around the Azores Archipelago. Mainly sperm whales and several types of dolphin. An opportunity to help on the only long-term cetacean research project in the Azores. Seven to 12-day tours from May to October. Prices from around £750 to £1100 includes six to 12 nights' accommodation in two-person cabins and full board. The trips are often accompanied by students carrying out their own research projects.

Wine Tours

ARBLASTER & CLARKE WINE TOURS
Clarke House, Farnham Road, West Liss, Hants. GU33 6JQ (tel 01730 893344; fax 01730 892888).
Managing Director: L Arblaster.
In business since 1987.
ATOL,AITO.
Holidays for 1500 arranged annually.

Guided wine tours in France (Champagne, Sancerre, Pouilly and Chablis, Rhône, Bordeaux, Loire, Burgundy) Spain (Rioja and Northern Spain), Italy and Germany, Eastern Europe, South Australia, New Zealand, Chile, Argentina and South Africa. Year round, three to seven days. Small parties and groups of any size. Prices range from £199 (three days in Champagne) to £689 (six days in Portugal) Prices include air/coach travel and half-board (usually) accommodation and wine tastings. Tailor-made wine tours and gourmet weekends also organised.
Minimum age: 17 years (unaccompanied).

ARC JOURNEYS
102 Stanley Road, Cambridge CB5 8ZB (tel 01223-779200; fax 01223-779090).
Sole Trader: David Halford.
In business since 1992.
Holidays for 40-50 arranged annually.
Tours to the famous wine growing regions of Australia, New Zealand, South Africa and South America. Australian tours include accommodation at the wineries and gourmet food. Caters for groups of two to 20 people. Prices do not include flights.

Other

ASIAN JOURNEYS LTD
32 Semilong Road, Northampton NN4 6BT (tel 01604-234855; fax 01604-234866).
E-mail: mail@asianjourneys.com
Internet: http://www.asianjourneys.com
Director: C Burkinshaw.
In business since 1995.
Holidays for 550 arranged annually.
Escorted group and tailor-made tours of South East Asia including Vietnam, Laos, Cambodia, Thailand, Burma, Malaysia and Singapore. Group tours are led by an experienced western leader and can cater for groups of 18 to 40 people. Tour lengths range from nine to 22 days. Tailor-made tours range from two to seven days with various itinerary options available including cycling, trekking, scuba diving and beach extensions. Prices from £1400 per person including flights, accommodation (various options available) and breakfast.
Minimum age: 18 years (unaccompanied).
No maximum age limit.

ASIAN PACIFIC ADVENTURES
826 South Sierra Bonita Avenue, Los Angeles, CA 90036, USA (tel +1 213-935-3156; fax +1 213 935 2691).
E-mail: travelasia@earthlink.net
Proprietor: Tovya Wager.
In business since 1986.
Holiday adventures for 100-200 people annually.
Small groups of two to 12 people, and custom individual trips. Bike, hike, cultural, photography, textile, fertility, women's focus and ethnic holidays in China, Tibet, India, Nepal, Bhutan, Pakistan, Burma, Thailand, Malaysia, Vietnam, Laos and Cambodia all year round. Highlights include an Irian Jaya pig feast, a royal wedding in India, meeting a tiger in Nepal, tribal festivals and a fertility ceremony. Prices range from $400 to $5000 (about £250 to £3086), including accommodation, sightseeing with English-speaking guides, some or all meals.

AUSTRAVELS GREAT ESCAPE
125 Brompton Road, London SW3 1HX (tel 0171-5840202).
Managing Director: A Bathme.
In business since 1977.
Holidays for 2000 arranged annually.
Wide range of tours in Australia and New Zealand including Sydney to Cairns, Alice Springs to Darwin, Perth to Darwin, Auckland to Wellington, and Auckland to Christchurch. Tours last from two to 20 days, including opportunities to experience many adventure activities eg. white water rafting, bungee jumping, diving, tandem skydiving and ballooning. Prices range from £350-£1090 including accommodation, breakfast and dinner, and coach travel.
Average flight price: £630.
Minimum age: 18 years.

CEDARBERG TRAVEL
14 Belgrade Road, Hampton, Middlesex TW12 2AZ (tel 0181-9411717; fax 0181-9793893).
Director: G Fenton.
In business since 1995.
Member of SATSA, SATOA, AITO, IATA, ABTA.
Self-drive and walking safaris, wildflower, wine and golfing tours in Southern Africa all year round. Prices from £1800-£2000 including accommodation in country house hotels, guesthouses, bush camps and game lodges. Meals and camping equipment are not included in the price.
Minimum age: 21 years.

CUBAN CIGAR TOURS
Special Places, Brock Travel Ltd, 4 The White House, Beacon Road, Crowborough, East Sussex TN6 1AB (tel 01892 661157; fax 01892-665670).

One week cigar tours from January to March are designed to give clients a detailed knowledge of how cigars are produced from the seed to the factory and at the same time to introduce one of the world's most beautiful countries. As well as visits to cigar factories and tobacco plantations there will be opportunities to relax, sightsee, go fishing, ride horses and much more. Price £1195 (single supplement £150) includes return flights to Havana, transportation in Cuba, a day trip to the island of Cayo Jutias, accommodation and some meals.

CULTURAL PURSUITS
Box 128 4B, 1533 Estevan Road, Nanaimo, British Columbia, Canada V9S 3Y3 (tel +1 6250 758 5162; fax +1 604 758-516). E-mail: james@culturalpursuits.bu.ca Web: http://www/islandnet.com/-eco adv/cultural pursuits/htmt
Established 1996.
Group trips from October to April each year and customised trips yearly. Trips include visits to Guwahati (Assam), Kaziranga National Park, Assam tea plantations, Garo Hills, Khasi Hills (Meghalaya) and other parts of North East India. No more than 10 people per trip. Ten-day trips from $575 and 19-day trips from $1150, includes all accommodation (guest house, homestays and camping), ground transportation and half board per day. Cultural Pursuits philosophy is to promote the cultural diversity of North East India in an environmentally and culturally friendly manner.

ELDERTREKS
597 Markham Street, Toronto ON, M6G 2L7, Canada (tel (+1 416) 588-5000; fax (+1 416) 588-9839). E-mail: passages@inforamp.net
Director: T Mason.
In business since 1987.
Member of PATA and Better Business Bureau.
'Soft' adventures for the over 50's to worldwide destinations including Tibet, India, Nepal, Vietnam, Borneo, Sumatra, Java, Bali, East Africa, Belize, Costa Rica, Ecuador and the Galapagos, all year round. Trips have strong educational focus by putting travellers in close contact with the nature and culture of the countries visited, whether it be dinner with a local family, or sleeping in a tribal headman's home. Prices from £50-£100 per day with accommodation in small hotels or quality guest houses chosen for their charm and location and full-board. For individuals and small groups of up to 15 people. Moderate physical exercise is required and so clients must be in reasonable physical condition. Many trips include extra Adventure Options for which clients are required to fill out a medical questionnaire.
Minimum age: 50 years.

EXODUS EXPEDITIONS
9 Weir Road, Balham, London SW12 OLT (tel 0181-675 5550 or 0181-673 0859 24 hours).
Sail down the Nile in a traditional, single-masted, lateen-rigged felucca as part of a 16-day adventure trip in Egypt from £590. Other trekking and adventure trips in Eastern Europe with prices ranging from £615 to £715 and pioneering trips into little-known areas of the CIS, China, Indonesia and Vietnam as well as expeditions to North Yemen, Oman and the Emirates. Also opportunities to charter a Galapagos motor-yacht or to cruise around the Galapagos islands.

GALAPAGOS ADVENTURE TOURS
37-39 Great Guildford Street, London SE1 0ES (tel/fax 0171 2619890). E-mail: pinzon@compuserve.com
ATOL NO. 3760.
Proprietor: David Horwell.
In business since 1985.
Holidays for approx. 130 arranged annually.
Special adventure tours in South and Central America, especially Ecuador and Galapagos Islands available throughout the year but high season is Christmas and Easter. Tours can include walking, wildlife and bird watching and scuba diving. Highlights can include swimming with sea lions and seals, proximity to seabirds, tortoises and iguanas, watching turtles hatch and whale watching. Individuals and groups of up to 12 accepted. Tour lengths and itineraries vary, and incorporate a variety of transport as appropriate: plane, private yacht, minibus, jeep and dugout canoe. The Galapagos Tour includes an eight-day cruise around the islands. Expert naturalists join the tour in the Galapagos and Amazon jungle. In the Amazon the guide forges ahead with his machete and stops to point out anything of interest. Jungle fare includes the local alcoholic beverage *guayusa* prepared by witch doctors. Tailor-made tours also arranged for clients with particular interests eg. Inca cities, Chilean National Parks, Whale-

watching etc. Prices range from £861 (Galapagos eight-day cruise only) to £3779 for a 24-day tour including flights, full board and various accommodation. Weekly independent Galapagos motor cruise with local guide from £549 excluding flights.
Minimum age: seven years (accompanied).

GOODWOOD TRAVEL
St Andrew's House, Station Road, East Canterbury, Kent CT1 2RB (tel 01227-763336; fax 01227-762417).
Offers a wide range of imaginative tours by Concorde. Itineraries include great cities and famous events. Superior and luxurious ground arrangements are also part of the package. A fantasy flight on Concorde can celebrate a special occasion, be given as a present or be an act of pure self indulgence.

HIGH PLACES
Globe Works, Penistone Road, Sheffield S6 3AE (tel 0114-275 7500).
Wide range of special trekking tours in Africa including wildlife viewing, Rift Valley hikes, ascent of Mts Kenya and Kilimanjaro and Kenya, Tanzania, Malawi and South Africa.Walking experience necessary. Prices from £1690 to £1950 for 17 days.
Also adventure and trekking tours in Costa Rica. Ascent of Chirripo (12,550 ft). River rafting on Savegre river, Rain Forest Trek, Manuel Antonio and Corcovado National Parks. Prices from £1525 for 16 days.

HORSE RACING ABROAD
24 Sussex Road, Haywards Heath, W Sussex RH16 4EA (tel 01444-441661; fax 01444 416169).
In business since 1979.
Offers a programme of tours to the European classic race meetings (e.g. Prix de l'Arc de Triomphe) and others (e.g. Breeders' Cup USA, Dubai World Cup and Melbourne Cup) worldwide. Accommodation in very comfortable hotels and facilities for clients include a private grandstand at Longchamp. Very personalised service.

INDIA LINK
The Travel Company,Weavers Cottage, Westgate, Lapford, Crediton, Devon EX17 6QF (tel 01363-83487; fax 01363-83963).
Sole Proprietor: Pie Chambers-Sethi.
Travel in India by off the beaten track visiting tribal villages and wildlife reserves' from two to three weeks. Art and textile tours a speciality in Gujurat, Orissa and the South. Maximum number of people per trip is ten. Price for 15 days £1850 inclusive includes accommodation in converted palaces, safari lodges and family run guest houses, and internal travel. All rooms have bathroom facilities.
Also cultural holidays during May to September in Ladakh, Kashmir, Darjeeling and Sikkim.

INTOURIST TRAVEL LTD
Intourist House, 219 Marsh Wall, London E14 9PD (tel 0171-538 8600; fax 0171-538 5967). Glasgow: 29 St. Vincent Place, Glasgow G1 2DT (tel 0141-2045809). Manchester: Suite 2F Central Buildings, 211 Deansgate, Manchester M3 3NW (tel 0161-831 7865; fax 0161-831 7865).
Director: Mr Stephen Penney.
In business since 1938.
Holidays for 1000+ arranged annually.
Tailor-made overland Trans Siberian/Mongolian Railways holidays, in Russia and the former Soviet Union, also Hong Kong, Mongolia and China from Jan-Dec. Accommodation on a bed and breakfast, or half board basis, in local hotels.
No age restrictions.

MAGIC CARPET TRAVEL
Sun House, 125 Ryston Road, London SW6 7HP (tel 0171-381 2304; fax 0171-381 2304).
Trekking, mountain climbing and adventure tours in Iran. Staying in tents and hotels. Tours take place in March, April, May, September, October and November and last nine to sixteen days. Prices do not include flights (£400-£480) or visas (about £90). Price of a two-week package costs about £1,565 with flights. Tailor-made holidays also organised.

MARCO POLO EXPERIENCE
79 Dean Street, London W1V 6HY (tel 0171-7341059; fax 0171-7346460).
Managing Director: Anwar Saeed.
In business since 1994.
Member of ATOL and the Civil Aviation Authority.
Small group and tailor-made exploratory holidays including trekking, mountain biking, horse trekking, whitewater rafting and wildlife excursions. Holidays located in Bhutan, China, Uzbekistan, Mongolia, Pakistan, India, Borneo, Nepal, Tibet and Iran. Tours last ten to 24 days, catering for a maximum of 10 people per group. Experience white water rafting on the Trisuli river in Nepal, elephant treks in search of tigers in Royal Chitwan Park, mountain biking

down the Karakoram highway or trekking to K2, the world's second highest peak. Prices range from £1100-£2400 including accommodation in hotels, lodges or camping on trek and all meals. No experience necessary.
Minimum age: ten years (accompanied); 16 years (unaccompanied).
Special tours can be arranged to accommodate physically challenged people.

MOTOR RACING INTERNATIONAL
The Golden Key Building, 15 Market Street, Sandwich, Kent CT13 9DA (tel 01304 612424; fax 01304 614930).
Offers a programme of tours to Formula One races throughout Europe and North America and visits to Le Mans 24-hour Race. Sample prices: £179 for a day trip to the Belgian Grand Prix including specially chartered flight from Stansted to Liege and coach transfer to the race in Belgium; Some tours combine a relaxed holiday with the racing as the tour's highlight, e.g. £459 for three nights in Annecy followed by three nights in Nice from where there is a free coach to the practice and formula 3 event in Monaco. On the following day there is a full day's attendance at the Monte Carlo Grand Prix. There is also a day trip to the Monaco Grand Prix including flights for £249. Many other events similarly covered.

MULTITOURS (RUSSIA)
7 Denbigh Street, London SW1V 2HF (tel 0171-2338458; fax 0171-931 9980).
As well as destinations that have become familiar (Moscow, St. Petersburg) Multitours offer itineraries taking in smaller towns: Vladimir, Suzdal, Zagorsk, as well as the Baltic Republics. Can also arrange tailor-made and special interest tours.

OCEAN CONTACT LTD
Box 10, Trinity, Newfoundland, AOC 2SO Canada (tel +1 709 464-3269; fax +1 709 464-3700). E-mail: beamish@nf.sympatco.ca
Internet: http://www.nf.sympatico.ca/beamish
Directors: Dr Peter Beamish, Dr Vincent Rice, Sylvia Rice.
In business since 1979.
Under the direction of a renowned whale scientist, tours specialise in human/whale contact. Prices include accommodation at the Village Inn, meals and a three hour charter each day. All ages. Prices available on request.

OUTBACK UK
The Cottage, Church Green, Badby, Northants. NN1 3AS (tel 01327-704115; fax 01327-703883).
Sole Trader: Peter Brendling.
In business since 1997.
Holidays for around 150 arranged annually.
Two 14-day discovery tours of the UK travelling in specially adapted minibuses. Tour visits ten National Parks, castles, cathedrals, Jane Austen's Cottage, Dartmoor, smugglers' coves, Bath, Oxford, the Welsh Mountains, Liverpool and Edinburgh, with much more in-between. Activities available include horse riding in the Brecon Beacons, mountain biking in Yorkshire, night abseiling and walking in Snowdonia. Wet weather gear and walking boots required. Price for 14 days £490, or £35 per day, including youth hostel and B&B accommodation. Travel only prices available. Small groups of 12. Shorter itinerary tours can be combined.

J F PADWICK
The Garden Suite, Pinewood Studios, Iver Bucks SL0 ONH (tel 01753-650055; fax 01753-631008).
Own tours from 1993, but in the business since 1958.
Member: ABTA, IATA, PATA.
Specialists in up-market 'Palaces and Tigers' tours to India, recreating the days of the Raj. Small group, fully inclusive guided tours in India arranged and tailor-made. Tours last two to three weeks from October to June.

PAN ANDEAN TOURS
PO Box 454, Avenida Pardo 705, Cuzco, Peru (fax +51 84-228911).
Director: Thomas Hendrickson.
In business since 1980.
Member of Peruvian Adventure Travel Association.
Holidays for over 1000 arranged annually.
Trekking, wildlife, culture and archaeology tours in Peru, Bolivia, Ecuador and Chile, lasting five to 22 days all year round. Prices in every range from no-frills to deluxe, from US$70-120 (about £43-£75) per day, with accommodation and most meals included. On trekking tours camp staff put up the

tents. Clients must provide their personal gear, but sleeping bags can be hired on most trips. Amazon lodge stays and Galapagos cruises arranged in conjunction with highland programmes.
Mountaineering expeditions lasting 25 days in January-February on Mount Aconcagua, Argentina, for experienced mountaineers only.
Patagonia trips also available including trekking in Paine Towers National Park, river rafting and motor-sailing in the Chilean fjords.
'Active exploration beyond the well-trodden tourist paths'.
Minimum age: eight (accompanied), 16 unaccompanied.

PANORAMA TUNISIA
29 Queens Road, Brighton, Sussex BN1 3YN (tel 01273-206531; fax 01273 205338). E-mail: panorama@pavillon.co.uk Internet: http://www.phg.co.uk
Specialist in Tunisian holidays. Can provide a range of accommodation types in many locations including Hammamet, Mahdia and Djerba. Extensive range of excursions such as a four-day desert safari, including locations used in the film 'The English Patient'. Can also tailor tours for special interest groups including archaeology and sports.

PASSAGE TO SOUTH AMERICA
Fovant Mews, 12 Noyna Road, Tooting Bec, London SW17 7PH (tel 0181-7678989; fax 0181-7672026).
Directors: W R Stanton and A W Dunn.
In business since 1989.
Tailor-made tours throughout South America for two or more weeks, all year round. Activities include jungle and mountain treks, river rafting and skiing in the Andes. Typical price: £1750 for two weeks. This includes accommodation in lodges and Indian huts or under canvas and most meals.

QUARK EXPEDITIONS
980 Post Road, Darien, CT 06820, USA (tel +1 203 656-0499; fax +1 203 655-6623). E-mail: quarkexpeditions@compuserve.com Internet: http://www.quark-expeditions.com
President: Lars Wikander.
In operation since 1991.
Member of American Society of Travel Agents and the International Association of Antarctic Tour Operators.
Holidays for 1200 arranged annually.
Expedition cruising on board Russian icebreakers to various destinations including the Arctic, Antarctic, South Pacific, Indian Ocean and British Isles. Explore Polar regions beyond the reach of other expedition vessels; visit ice-blocked wildlife sanctuaries and cruise on one of the few ships able to reach 90° North. Ships operate all year round with voyages from ten to 27 nights. Individuals or groups of any size catered for. Prices from $2,950 (triple share, Antarctic) to $23,300 (suite, North Pole) including vessel accommodation, all meals on board and an overnight hotel stay in the city of embarkation. No experience necessary, only an adventurous spirit.
Minimum age: 12 years (unaccompanied).
'Reaching 90° North and celebrating with champagne; using helicopters to visit Emperor Penguin rookeries'.

QUASAR NAUTICA GALAPAGOS EXPEDITIONS
Penelope Kellie Worldwide Yacht Charter and Tours, Steeple Cottage, Easton, Winchester, Hants S021 1EH (tel 01962-779317; fax 01962-779458). E-mail: pkellie@yachtors.u-net.com
ASTA, Yacht Charter Association, Latin America Travel Association.
Charters for 1500+ annually
Seven to ten-day inter island cruises on eight to 18-berth luxury sail and power yachts with multi-lingual guides and high class cabin service. Both naturalist and historic cruises are available. Bespoke mainland tours to historic sites, haciendas and national parks accompanied by highly qualified guides, as well as tours to high class jungle lodges. Quasar Nautica can arrange your whole holiday in Ecuador.

QUEST AUSTRALIA
Quest Worldwide, 4/10 Richmond Road, Kingston upon Thames, Surrey KT2 5HL (0181-547 3322; fax 0181-547 3320).
A range of exciting tours in Australia, New Zealand, USA and Canada. These include a Cairns six-day Adventure package (white water rafting, Great Barrier Reef trip, Kuranda Train or Skyrail trip, hot air ballooning and sea kayaking); Seven-day diving expedition out of Townsville to Flinders Reef 130 miles offshore and considered Australia's top dive location and includes wreck diving. Coral Trekker Cruises comprising four or seven days on a traditional square rigger; The Flinders Ranges Camel Trek, a seven-day camping trek and The World's Longest Mail Run : a four-day tour flying

with the mail plane from Adelaide on route that includes Port Augusta, various cattle stations and settlements into Queensland, Boulia, and dozens more stops before returning to Port Augusta and catching a return flight to Adelaide. The trip covers vast distances over the outback. A truly once in a lifetime experience.

New Zealand tours feature a four-day Kiwi Adventure which includes the TransAlpine train, a helicopter flight to glacier walking on the Franz Josef Glacier, along with jet boating and rafting in Queenstown. New features in the South Pacific include a three-day sailing adventure around Fiji exploring Mamanuca and the South Yasawa Islands.

'Trek America' tours are featured in the USA and Canada.

REGENT HOLIDAYS
15 John Street, Bristol BS1 2HR (tel 0117-921 1711).

Directors: F Gottesman, A Lloyd, N Taylor.

In business since 1970.

Member of ABTA, IATA and ATOL no. 856.

Special interest group and individual holidays to unusual parts of the world. Rambling, fishing, geology, ornithology and cycling in Georgia, Laos, Cuba, Estonia, Latvia, Lithuania, Russia, Uzbekistan, Mongolia, China, Turkey, Vietnam and Cambodia.

'The chance to visit unusual places with the benefit of an experienced guide'.

Most holidays are unsuitable for children.

THE RUSSIA EXPERIENCE
Research House, Fraser Road, Perivale, Middx UB6 7AQ (tel 0181-566 8846; fax 0181 566 8843). E-mail 100604.764@compuserve.com.

Director: Neil McGowan.

Member of The Travel Trust Association.

Company relaunched 1995.

Holidays for approximately 1000 arranged annually.

Specialists in travel in Russia, the former USSR and Mongolia. Trans-Siberian adventure trips, trekking in Mongolia and Siberia and scuba and cross-country skiing in Siberia. Multiple options, flexible itineraries and tailor made tours. Trips last four, seven, ten, eleven, twelve days. The Turkestan-Siberian railway journey from Moscow to Beijing ('the greatest journey left on earth') incorporates a detour to Bokhara and Samarkand and lasts 30 days. Trip prices from £265-£1470 and include various accommodation in hostels, hotels, sleeper trains, Russian family homes and Mongolian felt tents. Flights, visas and vaccinations are not included in the price but can be arranged.

SILK STEPS LTD
PO Box 24, Bristol BS16 6JY (tel 0117-9402800; fax 0117-9406900).

Directors: D McCracken, J Thorne.

In business since 1995.

Member of the Travel Trust Association.

Tailor-made holidays to suit individual preferences, budgets and schedules no matter how elaborate or simple. Destinations include China, Vietnam, Laos, Burma, Thailand, Ethiopia and Cambodia. Suggested itineraries include trekking and boat trip opportunities, but remain entirely flexible. Individuals and groups of up to 25 catered for. Prices from £1000-£2000 including hotel, B&B, camping accommodation and all meals. Unaccompanied young people not accepted.

SOUTH AMERICAN EXPERIENCE
47 Causton Street, Pimlico, London SW1P 4AT (tel 0171-976 5511; fax 0171-976 6908).

Directors: A de Mendonca, D Gilmour.

Established 1987.

ATOL, LATA (Latin American Travel Association).

Operators of tailor made tours and expeditions for individuals. Whitewater rafting trips, Amazon Jungle trips, horse riding in Argentina and the Inca Trail in Peru are just some of the possibilities. Trips can be arranged all year for any duration. Flight only also possible.

SUPERSTAR HOLIDAYS
UK House, 180 Oxford Street, London W1N 0EL (tel 0171-9574300; fax 0171-9574399).

'Desert Trailblazer' tour along the Nabatean spice trails by air-conditioned jeep through the Negev Desert. Also available, exploration of the Ramon Crater and a Bedouin Feast in a Bedouin tent.

SYMBIOSIS EXPEDITION PLANNING
113 Bolingbroke Grove, London SW11 1DA (tel 0171-924 5906; fax 0171-924 5907). E-mail: 101456.2155@compuserve.com

Directors: Christopher and Michael Gow.

Established 1993.

Member of CERT (Campaign for Responsible Tourism).
Recruits paying volunteers for projects in S E Asia. Various projects, in different countries for various lengths of minimum stay. For War Project volunteers stay at least one month. For most projects no previous experience is necessary. However sometimes, as in Wild Animal Rescue Project in Thailand, veterinary experience was requested (but not essential). Depending on the project, there are opportunities for volunteers to dive, trek, surf, go on jungle survival courses, practise watersports and cycle.

THE TRAVELLERS'CLUB
Halnaker Park Cottage, Chichester, West Sussex P018 0QH; (tel /fax 01243 773597).
Travellers' Club holidays are designed and led by experts and are tailor-made for small groups and individuals. Escorted tours depart for India, Pakistan, Nepal, Sri Lanka, Mexico and Peru. Art and architectural highlights of Europe are also available. Holidays can be booked to suit your dates (and pocket). For couples, families, clubs or societies.

WIND SAND AND STARS
2 Arkwright Road, London NW6 (tel 0171-433 3684; fax 0171-431 3247).
Director: E Loveridge MA, FRGS.
Established 1991.
30-40 journeys arranged annually.
Journeys to the desert and mountains of Sinai, travelling with the Bedouin, and to Ethiopa. Pre-arranged and tailor made itineraries for individuals and groups incorporating a wide range of special interests and activities with experienced and knowledeable leadership. Activities include camel trekking and mountain walking with the Bedouin, jeep safari, climbing, mountain biking and Red Sea snorkelling. Special interests include history and archaeology, Christian sites and traditions, wildlife, art history, photography and study groups. Special arrangements for schools and youth groups.
Prices from £600 to £900 including flights, jeeps, guides, accommodation, food and equipment.

WORLD CHALLENGE EXPEDITIONS
Black Arrow House, 2 Chandos Road, London NW10 6NF (tel 0181-961 1122; fax 0181-961 1551).
Month-long leadership developement expeditions in South America, India, Africa, and South-East Asia for young people aged 16 to 20. The unique feature is the provision for team members to develop management and leadership skills by taking charge of day to day planning of an expedition under qualified supervision. Activities are designed to be fulfilling and enjoyable, with emphasis on full participation, environmental awareness and challenge. These include trekking, mountaineering, jungle exploration, safari, cultural exchange and selected project work. Prices from £2000 per person.
A new feature from this company is 'The Ultimate Challenge', an intense four-week adventure for 18-25 year old individuals to the world's most physically and culturally challenging destinations. Individuals make up small groups that complete stunning treks or projects with local communities, taking turns at team leadership. Destinations range from the humid jungles of Belize, the plains of Africa and the Himalayan or Andes mountain ranges. Prices start from £1995.

YOUTH TRAVEL BUREAU
1 Shazer Street, P O Box 6001, Jerusalem 91060, Israel (tel +972 2-655 84 00; fax +972 2-655 84 32).
In business since 1972.
Member of IYHF, FIYTO.
Holidays provided for 10,000 annually.
Desert and special interest tours throughout the year in Israel and Egypt.

Watersports

CANOEING

Canoeing is an ideal recreational activity, open to all ages and involving relatively little expense. It is also a highly competitive sport with world championships in all sections. The type of canoe used and the techniques involved are almost as diverse as the locations and types of water encountered.

Novices should first take a course to master the basic principles of embarking, disembarking, paddle control and righting the canoe after a capsize. More advanced courses include instruction in how to execute an Eskimo Roll, which is very important in whitewater canoeing. The majority of multi activity centres offer a basic introduction to canoeing and, in some cases, advanced tuition. Beginners can then practise the skills they have learned by touring on a wide variety of waters such as the gently flowing Wye and Dordogne rivers or the placid lake networks in the wilderness areas of Sweden or the south-east USA. The more advanced canoeist can experience the thrills of shooting rapids or racing in turbulent whitewater in the Cairngorms, Rockies or Andes. In the UK kayaks are used for this type of canoeing. Kayaks are derived from Eskimo canoes and are lightweight, very stable and easily portable. In North America touring canoes are used which have larger cockpits and can accommodate luggage.

Coastal or sea touring is to the canoeist what mountain expeditions are to the rock climber, combining planning, skill and stamina. The kayak is adapted for the sea by adding a rudder and sometimes inflatable buoyancy bags to provide stability when swamped. Surf canoeing is for those who have mastered the basic skills and is best done from coasts with a gently shelving beach and reasonably sized waves; an offshore breeze also helps. Slalom canoeing is another variation which consists of manoeuvring the canoe through a series of suspended posts and requires special techniques. A fairly recent innovation is canoe polo similar to water polo, but using small easily manoeuvrable kayaks.

Many holidays abroad feature a rafting expedition as well as hiking, riding, cycling, etc. River rafting outfitters allow adventure-seekers to enjoy the thrill of turbulent waters without having to master the finer techniques of canoeing themselves. Rafting expeditions, often known as Float Trips, are particularly popular in North America but can be practised on the rivers of Chile, Nepal and other exotic places. One operator warns 'you will get real wet, so bring a change of clothes and prepare to have a blast'. The rafts are generally made of inflatable rubber or neoprene and are powered by oars or a motor. At the other extreme, you can build your own log raft (ropes and instruction provided) and float gently through central Sweden at a sedate 1 mph.

There is also a new French variation to the rafting theme, known as hydrospeeding. This involves launching yourself into white water, protected by a reinforced buoyancy aid, and riding the rapids on a *luge de torrent*, effectively a floating toboggan. Flippers provide extra propulsion to help you avoid obstacles. Hydrospeeding is gaining in popularity.In Sweden, a similar sport is called river-boogying.

Another daredevil innovation is 'squirt canoeing' where a low-volume canoe which sinks easily is used mainly for whitewater stunts such as disappearing under the water and reappearing further down the rapids. This should not be attempted by inexperienced canoeists.

Canyoning. Canyoning is the latest European river sport in which participants launch themselves down smooth-sided alpine gorges with swiftly flowing streams or cascades which are just wide enough for the average body to pass through; in short it is like water sliding on a natural water slide with very hard sides. It is organised everywhere in the Alps where there are suitable gorges. Canyoners wear skin-tight neoprene wet suits, including booties and an overvest. A helmet is essential, and a climbing harness (canyoners abseil from pool to pool in the mountains). A kind of padding like a baby's nappy, is worn to further protect the body from knocks. The sport is believed to have been launched in France where it is called *un baptême* (baptism). Needless to say canyoning can be dangerous if not performed with adequate safeguards. So far there are only a handful of centres for instruction including in France at Cautérets (tel +33 5-6292 5027) where a week's course from FF2,000 including room and board. In Austria try BAC (Berg und Abenteuer Club) in Solktäler, near Schladming (+43 3685 22245).

Safety and Equipment. The majority of canoeing courses will stipulate that you be able to swim at least 50 metres and that you wear a buoyancy aid. Use only those which are made to British Standards Specifications. It is inadvisable to go out alone; indeed canoeing in a group of three is ideal. In addition to the basic canoe and paddle, a waterproof cover which fits around the cockpit called a spray deck is required. A wetsuit and plastic sandals are ideal for canoeing but a shirt, shorts, waterproof anorak and gym shoes are usually sufficient. In cold weather a jersey is necessary as this will keep you warm even when wet. Special dry cagoules that seal around the wrists and trousers that seal around the ankles are becoming increasingly popular. A new canoe costs from £200, paddles £30-£100, spray decks £15 and buoyancy aids £28. A well-fitted helmet is vital for white water stunts and sea canoeing.

The British Canoe Union (BCU, John Dudderidge House, Adbolton Lane, West Bridgford, Nottingham NG2 5AS tel 0115-982 1100) is the governing body of canoeing for sport or recreational purposes. As well as a source of information and advice, the BCU can provide a list of BCU approved centres and private clubs nationwide. The BCU also oversees courses, competitions and publications. Basic adult membership £17 which includes the BCU Licence fee which entitles the holder to use all British Waterways Board waterways. The BCU can also provide contacts for licences for privately-owned waterways. BCU membership details can be obtained from the above address.

Canoeing proficiency tests have been established by the BCU to set standards for the sport within Britain. The Supervisor Award is the basic qualification for group instructors and is recognised by the Department of Education as the minimum requirement for teachers and youth leaders on very sheltered waterways.

The BCU publications output includes handbooks and maps for canoeists, including the essential reference book for anyone planning a canoe journey in the UK: *the Canoeing Handbook* (£16.95 including post and packing). A series of waterways guides for individual regions is also available. Prices vary depending on the region. A list of BCU publications can be obtained from BCU publications distributors Mobile Adventure Ltd. (Bridge Works, Knighton Fields Road West, Leicester LE2 6LG tel 0116-283 0659) who will also supply them by mail order.

SAILING

The first boat to be used purely for recreation was the yacht which Charles II brought back from Holland in 1661. It was not until the Victorian era, however, that sailing and racing for pleasure became popular. The most important and longest established of all racing events is the America's Cup which was first sailed in 1851 (the oldest international trophy for any sport) and was consistently won by the USA until 1983 when the Australians managed to capture it. The subsequent races in Fremantle, Western Australia in 1986-87, when the Americans regained their Cup, received massive media publicity around the world.

Despite its venerable history and glamorous image, sailing is not necessarily a rich person's sport. Yachts are expensive to purchase, but residential sailing holidays and courses are often accessibly priced. Dinghy sailing holidays are available almost wherever there is a stretch of water. They can be ideal for a family with children old enough to swim (about seven years upwards) and to endure what can be a fairly wet and cold experience. For unaccompanied young people, dinghy sailing features in many multi activity holidays.

Dinghies can be very fast and exhilarating, with stability sacrificed for speed. Because a dinghy reacts more quickly than a larger boat to the slightest movement of wind and tide, a practical knowledge of seamanship is essential. Before setting out it is important to find out about local conditions, the direction and strength of currents, the times of high and low water and the weather forecast. In addition to life jackets, distress signals and a bailer, it is advisable to carry some means of propelling the boat if there is no wind.

Cruising means touring by boat. Originally cruising was always under sail, but nowadays almost all cruisers are equipped with an auxiliary engine. The yachts used for estuary, coastal and ocean cruising are usually capable of looking after themselves in rough seas because of their size and the electronic equipment they carry. People who are seeking a gentle introduction to sailing may choose to charter a skippered yacht, where the crew offer instruction as desired. Coping with the cooking and sanitary facilities in a small cabin may prove to be enough of an adventure for some. 'Bare boat' charters are available only for skilled sailors who have the appropriate qualifications. The Cruising Association (0171-537 2828) runs a service whereby would-be crew can be put in touch with skippers looking for hands. Crew members usually expected to make a weekly contribution towards expenses and possible something for the passage. The amount is usually negotiable. Surprisingly perhaps, previous experience of crewing is not necessarily essential.

In Britain the Yacht Charter Association Ltd admits only those companies who satisfy high standards of maintenance, service, safety equipment and insurance and who have been inspected by the YCA. Any member who falls below the acceptable standards is subject to cancellation of their YCA membership. A list of the approved charter members may be obtained from the YCA, c/o Michael Brown (01703-338400).

Legislation introduced four years ago means that all charter boats have to have a Marine Safety Agency Certificate. In practice this does not mean much as the MSA inspect only five percent of boats passed and boat insurance is not a prerequisite. If the charterer is a YCA member it will have been inspected to higher standards than the MSA and will be insured. Furthermore YCA members are bonded so customer's money is protected. The YCA membership is therefore the most important assurance for anyone chartering a boat.

Flotilla cruising is gaining in popularity from the Hebrides to the Sporades. The idea of sailing in a flotilla appeals to those who may not be confident enough sailors to set off on their own, or who are attracted by the social benefits. Usually about six yachts cruise together accompanied by the Captain's yacht which is equipped with spare parts and acts as a navigator for the group. The Royal Yachting Association, founded in 1875 is the governing body for all forms of sailing, and caters for all those who go afloat in small boats whether propelled by power or sail. It encourages a sensible approach to safety and proficiency and runs many coaching schemes. Apart from about 800 sailing schools in Britain, which have the approval of the RYA, there are 939 shore-based schools which run evening, intensive and correspondence courses in navigation and seamanship. The publication *Dinghy Sailing and Keelboat Courses* free from the RYA (RYA House, Romsey Road, Eastleigh, Hants S050 9YA; tel 01703-627400; fax 01703-629924) lists mosts of the recognised RYA schools and learning establishments and shows which offer residential courses or can book accommodation locally.

The RYA also organises a training scheme in yachts which leads from the basic course, Competent Crew, to Yachtmaster. The courses can be taken on yachts ranging from 30 ft to large sail training vessels. Details and a list of schools are available from the RYA.

Young people aged 14-23 years with dinghy sailing or sailing training experience can apply for The Young Skippers Scheme which involves training in a flotilla and taking turns at being skipper. Older, more experienced members who have previously taken part in YSS cruises may, at the discretion of the group leader, act as senior skipper (a sort of Admiral of the flotilla). Further details from the Southampton Institute of HE, c/o A Moat, RM.043, East Park Terrace Southampton, Hampshire (tel 01489 576161 ext. 210).

For disabled sailors RYA Sailability scheme (tel 01703 627400; minicom 01703-627432) runs dinghy and yacht courses for those with special requirements. On some boats audio compasses facilitate navigation for the visually impaired.

SCUBA DIVING AND SNORKELLING

The term scuba is an abbreviation of self-contained underwater breathing apparatus. Such apparatus consists of a cylinder of compressed air, a breathing regulator and an integral harness/buoyancy device. According to water temperature, either a wetsuit or a drysuit will be necessary and other accessories include weightbelt, instruments and of course, mask, fins and snorkel tube. Suits provide both thermal insulation and protection against abrasion. It costs about £1000 to buy a full set of quality equipment, but diving apparatus can often be hired at holiday resorts, or from Diving Schools.

Since the introduction of a relatively simple, low-cost diving lung by Emile Gagnan and Jacques-Yves Cousteau in 1943, scuba diving has become available to more and more people throughout the world. Previously untouched areas such as the Red Sea and the South Pacific are opening up as excellent sites for diving holidays. Some holidays require experience which can be gained by attending a course at a British Sub-Aqua Club (BS-AC) School. These offer two levels of training: *Novice Diver Novice Diver II* and *Sports Diver* qualifications. The instruction takes place initially in a swimming pool while you learn the principles and how to use the equipment, then progresses to open water diving. It is not necessary to become a member of the BS-AC to obtain the Novice Diver qualification. If you simply wish to sample the sport this standard is sufficient for you to continue diving under the supervision of a qualified diving instructor.

To go further and qualify as a Sports Diver you should join the BS-AC through one of its branches. These offer regular diving programmes, progression to more advanced diving qualifications and all the benefits of an active social group. Membership costs £55 for the first year and then £32 annual membership after that and includes a copy of *Sport Diving Manual* and *Diver* magazine each month, liability insurance and the opportunity to take part in courses and events. The address is: Telfords Quay, Ellesmere Port, South Wirral, Cheshire L65 4FY (tel 0151-350 6200). *The Diver Videos (1&2)* which are sponsored by BS-AC act as an introduction to the sport and can be obtained from: *Diver* magazine, 55 High Street, Teddington, Middlesex TW11 8HA (tel 0181-943 4288). An annual subscription for the monthly *Diver* magazine costs £33 including postage or for a single issue the cover price is £2.75.

Snorkelling provides a good introduction to underwater swimming, especially for those who are too young or unfit to be able to cope with the equipment. Basic snorkelling equipment consists of a mask with breathing tube and water exclusion device for diving. The old-style mask with one piece of glass at the front and a 'ping-pong ball' water excluder have been virtually phased out in favour of a mask with two eye pieces and a nose pocket. The snorkel tube curves around the head with the end being almost on top of it, rather than a straight tube that sticks out at the back. There is also an orthodontic variation snorkel which fits the mouth rather than the other way around and claims to avoid snorkellers' jaw cramp. A top of the range mask can set you back £40 and fins cost £28+. The BS-AC is the governing body of snorkelling (see address above) and they publish a guide *Snorkelling for All*. A well-known guide for scuba-divers and snorkellers is *Classic Dives of the World* published by Oxford Illustrated Press (£14.95). Other publications dealing with specific diving areas are beginning to appear on the scene, e.g. *Underwater Indonesia* published by Periplus (£9.95). It is worth asking at a specialist bookshop like, The Travel Bookshop, The Travellers Bookshop and Daunts (all in London) for the lastest diving guides.

SURFING: It's one thing to grow up in Southern California or Australia and become a surfer, but quite another to take up the activity in Britain. To acquire some experience and improve your technique requires many winter weekends of clambering into a cold wetsuit and braving the waters. But enthusiastic surfers forget the occasions when their hands turned blue, and remember only the sunshine and the two metre breakers. Both Scotland and Cornwall have some of the best surfing conditions in Europe (but not the weather the go with it). Brimms Ness and Thurso test even the most thermal of wetsuits but surfers are now even venturing as far north as the Outer Hebrides though this is recommended only for very experienced surfers. It is possible to surf intuitively and try to ride whatever wave is available. But it also appeals to the more scientifically minded who weigh such factors as the tidal position, the wind direction, underwater shelves, etc. The experienced surfer develops a fairly acute meteorological eye. There are a number of surfing schools in Britain and the best source of information on them is the British Surfing Association (Champions Yard, Penzance, Cornwall TR18 2SS; tel 01736 360250).

Many multi activity holidays offer windsurfing or surfing as part of their adventure attractions. Or look in the following chapter under *Windsurfing and Surfing* for details. The only equipment needed is a wetsuit for North European waters and the board. The advanced surfer may have a custom-built board made. However the average surfer can obtain a reasonable board for around £75. The beginner may want to hire a board before committing himself.

WHITEWATER RAFTING

Earlier river explorers were continually thwarted by stretches of rapids which they were forced to circumnavigate by foot. It was not until the early 1960's, when Americans discovered that by lashing together inflatable World War II bridge pontoons, it was possible to produce a raft that could ride the fiercest of rapids. Raft technology has moved on considerably since that time, and purpose-designed hyperlon or PVC rafts are self-bailing, whereby water drains quickly through the base after a rapid.

Commercial rafting trips have become increasingly popular in the last ten years. Where ever there are rapids (in France, Switzerland, Australia, New Zealand, Nepal, Zimbabwe and Colorado, USA to name but a few),it seems there are local rafting companies offering one-day trips that provide a taste for the whitewater adrenaline rush. There are also a limited number of short runs in the UK. A few companies offer extended multi-day trips (notably in Turkey, Zimbabwe, Ethiopia, Uganda, Nepal, Chile, Ecuador, New Zealand and the USA),where a team of rafters spend seven to 31 days on the river and are completely self-supporting. This is the ultimate river journey and allows rafters to experience exotic and remote locations around the world that would be completely inaccessible by any other means. No previous rafting experience is necessary as guides will instruct clients. There are two rafting styles: 'paddle' rafting describes a guide directing a team of up to nine individuals, each with their own paddle and seated on each side of the raft. In 'oar boating' the guide sits in the middle of the raft and rows while while the other participants are carried as passengers. Rafting trips usually involve two to three rafts with guides and up to 20 passengers. Rivers are graded according to difficulty on an internationally recognised scale from one to six. One is a slow moving current while six is not considered safe to run commercially.

WINDSURFING

Windsurfing, also known as boardsailing and sailboarding, became popular over 25 years ago in California. It originated from the simple expedient of attaching a mast and sail to a surf-board; it has since become a very widespread participant sport. There are now more than one million windsurfers on European waters alone, and it was accepted as a new sport for the 1984 Olympic Games. In Hawaii, a new freestyle has evolved which requires that the windsurfer sails fast into the surf and uses the wave as a ramp from which to take off.

In the UK there are around 220 approved windsurfing schools which offer courses for beginners. A full list of schools is available from the RYA, (RYA House, Romsey Road, Eastleigh, Hants SO5 4YA tel 017036-29962). Instruction progresses from a dry land simulator (basically a windsurfer mounted on springs), to a moored windsurfer to learn about balance and control and finally to freesailing and the principles of tacking and gybing. Most people can learn to balance and experience the thrill after just an hour or two of practice. The schools provide the equipment: you need only to be able to swim. Anyone from eight to eighty can learn to windsurf, and the RYA have a special Junior Windsurfing Scheme for children. If you enjoy the sport you may wish to purchase your own board. A basic board costs from around £450 although you can find second-hand boards for about £250; a top racer can cost £1000 plus. There is an inflatable windsurfer that packs up to the size of a golf bag, for around £499. For cooler climates a wetsuit costing £80-£200 is also required.

General

England

ACORN ACTIVITIES
P O Box 120, Hereford HR4 8YB (tel 01432-830083; fax 01432-830110).
Watersport holidays in Herefordshire and Wales. Activities include sailing, windsurfing, waterskiing, scuba diving, kayaks, Canadian canoeing, white-water rafting and surfing. Beginner and intermediate courses. Hotels, farmhouses, group and self-catering accommodation. All equipment provided. Prices for accommodation from £16 per night and for activities from £40 per day.

ADVENTURE SPORTS
Carnkie Farm House, Carnkie, Redruth, Cornwall TR16 6RZ (tel 01209-218962). Internet: http://www.adventure-sports.co.uk.
Proprietors: L & J Cruse.
In business since 1982.
Member of West Country Tourist Board, ETB, BHPA with RYA & BSA Instructors.
BHPA & BSA registerd schools.
Holidays for 400 arranged annually.
Multi activity watersport holidays featuring surfing, waterskiing, windsurfing, paragliding, sailing, snorkelling, jet skiing, climbing, abseiling, and coastal touring, based near Redruth. April to October. Individuals and groups of up to 25 people. Prices from £150-£250 include self-catering accommodation in farmhouse, chalets, caravans or camping, tuition and equipment. Action is guaranteed and arranged to suit the prevailing weather conditions.Ages: 16-50.

BRADWELL ENVIRONMENTAL & OUTDOOR EDUCATION CENTRE
Bradwell Waterside, Southminster, Essex CMO 7QY (tel 01621-776256; fax 01621-776378).
Education Authority run.

In operation since 1964.
RYA member.
Holidays for approx. 3000 arranged annually.
Courses in offshore sailing, dinghy-sailing, archery, abseiling and canoeing at Bradwell waterside and the Blackwater Estuary in Essex. Also land activities e.g. archery. Individuals and groups. Prices from £17.50 per day (residential), £12 daily (non-residential). Prices include dormitory accommodation and full board. Clients are expected to participate in with clearing tables at mealtimes.
Minimum age: ten (accompanied); 13 (unaccompanied).

GALLOWAY SAILING CENTRE
Loch Ken, Castle Douglas, Kirkcudbrightshire DG7 3NQ (tel 01644-420626).
Principal: Richard Hermon.
In business since 1988.
RYA Recognised (for dinghy sailing, power boating and windsurfing) and Member of Dumfries & Galloway Tourist Board. BCU recognised for canoeing.
Holidays for about 1000 arranged annually.
Watersports tuition and boat hire from Easter to the end of October. Accommodation is not included in course fees, but residential courses are available. Special adventure courses for groups of up to 35 people, £75 to £175 including camping on site and catering in the Clubhouse.
Minimum age: eight years.

HF HOLIDAYS LTD
Imperial House, Edgware Road, London NW9 5AL (tel 0181-905 9556).
Watersports holidays for all the family on the Isle of Wight and the Lake District based at the HF Country House and hotels. Canoeing, sailing, gorge walking and windsurfing available in various combinations. Prices from around £390 seven nights full-board. Reduced rate rail travel and children's discounts of 30-70% available. No experience needed. Call for a Special Interest Holidays brochure.

MENDIP OUTDOOR PURSUITS
Laurel Farmhouse, Summer Lane, Banwell, Weston-super-Mare, Avon BS24 6LP (tel 01934-820518 & 823666).
Tailor-made watersports courses including canoeing, windsurfing and sailing. One day or longer. Prices on application and depending on activities but start at £8 for a half-day.
Minimum age depends on activities but usually eight years.

WIGHT WATER ADVENTURE SPORTS
19 Orchardleigh Road, Shanklin, Isle of Wight PO37 7NP (tel/fax 01983-866269).
Partners: I D Williams and C R Williams.
In business since 1985.
RYA, BCU, BSA approved. Adventure Activity Licence.
Watersports and landsports holidays in Sandown Bay on the Isle of Wight from April to September. Sample windsurfing, sailing, canoeing, wave skiing, surfing and body boarding. Individuals and groups of 40+ may be catered for. No experience is required. Courses are non-residential but a variety of accommodation is available locally. All equipment is provided.
Physically challenged clients welcome.

WINDSPORT INTERNATIONAL
Mylor Yacht Harbour, Falmouth, Cornwall TR11 5UF (tel 01326-37691; fax 01326 376192).
Partners: B & C Phipps.
In operation since 1985.
RYA, BAHA and West Country Tourist Board recognised.
Holidays for 2000 arranged annually.
Sailing, windsurfing and multi watersport holidays for children, families and adults. Tuition and hiring facilities available on a day, weekend or weekly basis from March to October. Prices from £95 for watersport courses, all equipment included. Residential or non-residential. Bed and breakfast available from £15 per night.
Minimum age: eight years (accompanied).

Scotland

ABERNETHY TRUST
Nethy Bridge, Inverness-shire PH25 3ED (tel 01479-82279).
RYA sailing and windsurfing courses run on Loch Morlich. Price includes tuition up to RYA level two, equipment and full board accommodation. £240. No prior experience required, but you must be able to swim 50 metres.
Ages: 12+ if accompanied; 16+ unaccompanied.

LOCH INSH WATERSPORTS AND SKIING CENTRE
Insh Hall, Kincraig, Inverness-shire, PH21 1NU (tel 01540-651272; fax 01540-651208).
In business since 1970.
Recognised by RYA and BCU.
Two- and five-day courses in sailing, windsurfing, canoeing and 'Sport-a-day'. Situated on the shores of Loch Insh with en suite accommodation for 90. TV lounges, pool table, darts, table tennis, full tennis, sauna, mini-gym, washing/drying room, also mountain bikes, archery, fishing, dry slope skiing, interpretation trail and adventure area. Self-catering log chalets available all year. Licensed restaurant.
December-April winter skiing packages.
No experience needed.
Minimum age: 12 years (unaccompanied).

PORT EDGAR SAILING SCHOOL
Shore Road, South Queensferry, Edinburgh EH30 9SQ (tel 0131-331 3330; fax 0131-331 4878).
Member of the Edinburgh Tourist Board, RYA and BCU.
Holidays for up to 7000 annually.
Watersports holidays in the Firth of Forth, eight miles from Edinburgh situated beside the Forth Bridges, from April to October. High quality equipment, high safety standards, caring and experienced instructors. Prices from £25-£103. Wide variety of accommodation available locally. No experience necessary. All equipment provided.
Minimum age: eight years (unaccompanied).
Good facilities for disabled people.

Wales

WEST WALES WINDSURF & SAIL
Dale, nr Haverfordwest, Dyfed SA62 3RB (tel/fax 01646-636642).
Proprietor: Peter Bounds.
In business since 1984.
Memnber of RYA, BSA and WTB accredited.
Holidays for 800 arranged annually.
Watersports holidays in Pembrokeshire, all year round. For individuals and groups up to 20. Prices from £59 per full day to £469 for one week with full-board accommodation in guest houses. No experience necessary.
Minimum age: eight years (accompanied); 14 years (unaccompanied).

Europe

MARK WARNER
20 Kensington Church Street, London W8 4EP (tel 0171-393 3131 Reservations).
Fully inclusive watersports holidays provided in Corsica, Sardinia, Italy, Greece and Turkey from May to October for seven or 14 nights. Free waterskiing, windsurfing and dinghy sailing with tuition offered at all Mark Warner clubs. Also tennis with coaching at selected clubs. Full board hotel accommodation in rooms with private facilities.
Minimum age unaccompanied: 18 years.

PELIGONI CLUB
UK Booking agent: Tarific Holidays, P.O.Box 88, Chichester, West Sussex PO20 7DP (tel 01243-511499; fax 01243-513132).
Opened in 1989, the Peligoni Club is a centre mainly for sailing and windsurfing but waterskiing, wake boarding and kneeboarding are additional popular sports. Rock face and cave scuba diving is also offered at approx. £20 per accompanied dive (for holders of current diving certificates only). Snorkelling and canoeing can also be practised. Sports, including tennis and table tennis, and socialising take place at the Club but accommodation is arranged locally in a range of buildings from a studio to a converted olive press. Some are within a few minutes walk for those who choose not to hire a car or moped. Many buildings are British-owned and are situated at the rural end of the island . Prices are based on the number sharing the accommodation. Available May to October. Price of the holiday includes accommodation and watersports tuition and equipment. Not included are flights and meals.
Yacht charters also arranged.

SUNWORLD SAILING HOLIDAYS
120 St George's Road, Brighton, E Sussex BN2 1EA (01273-626284 — reservations; 01273-626283 — brochure line).
Member of Royal Yachting Association, ABTA, ATOL, ABSC.
Dinghy sailing, windsurfing and yachting holidays and crewed yacht charters with instruction at all levels in Greece, Turkey and Spain. Summer or winter. Prices include

flights, accommodation, equipment and tuition. No experience needed. Mountain biking also available. Families welcome.
Any age.

Worldwide

SPORTIF INTERNATIONAL
Fleets, Spatham Lane, Ditchling, East Sussex BN6 8XL (tel 01273-844919; fax 01273-844914).
Sporting activities including windsurfing, diving and multisports in worldwide destinations all year round. Canary Islands, Spain, the Caribbean, Venezuela, the USA, Turkey and Egypt. Prices £270-£1500 depending on the resort.

Canoeing and Rafting

Worldwide

ADRIFT
Collingbourne House, Spencer Court, 140-142 High Street, London SW18 4JJ (tel 0181-874 4969; fax 0181 875 9236). Internet: http://www.adrift.co.nz
Directors: Cam McLeay.
In business since 1992.
Member of ABTA, CAA, and ATOL holder.
Specialists in whitewater rafting journeys around the globe and throughout the year. Seven, ten, fourteen and 31-day trips, rivers grade two to five. Remote and exotic locations. Maximum 19 team members per departure in three paddle or oar-powered rafts. Experienced kayakers welcome. Camping and cooking around campfires beside the river. No experience required. Exploratory expeditions annually for experienced rafters. Prices from £870 including meals and accommodation.

England

ARCTIC LIGHT ADVENTURE
8 The Speares, Saltash, Cornwall PL12 4UQ (tel 01752-847762). E-mail: arcticLA@aol.com
Director: Mr S R Burge. Secretary: Dr S C Charlton.
In business since 1995.
Recognised by the BCU.
Kayaking tours and day trips. One-week long Isles of Scilly tour in Spring and Autumn based at a campsite on St Mary's, with daily journeys exploring the other islands. Group size limited to eight people. Price: £300 per person including all camping and kayaking equipment; and ferry fare. B&B hotel accommodation can be arranged if requested. Reduced prices with provision of your own equipment.
Kayaking day trips available in South West England (for those with no experience) exploring the estuaries and coastline. £50 per person. All equipment provided.
No age limits.

BOWLES OUTDOOR CENTRE
Eridge Green, Tunbridge Wells TN3 9LW (tel 01892-665665).

Canoeing courses. Basics taught in the Centre swimming pool, then progressing to the River Medway and the Sussex Coast. Advanced courses on British white water. Price per weekend from £74.
Minimum age: nine years.

CALSHOT ACTIVITIES CENTRE
Calshot Spit, Fawley, Southampton S045 1BR (tel 01703-892077).
Recognised by the BCU.
Sea canoeing at the largest sea canoeing centre in Britain offering all types of courses from one-star to coach. Single canoeing days for groups and weekend and expedition courses for both young people and adults. Fleet of over 100 canoes and kayaks. Sheltered water and open water for the more advanced. Adult weekend courses start from £100 (non-residential) £115 fully residential. All specialist equipment and clothing provided.
Minimum age; 13 years.

EUROYOUTH
301 Westborough Road, Westcliff, Southend-on-Sea, Essex SS0 9PT (tel 01702-341434; fax 01702-330104).
Canoeing courses at Southend for individuals and groups. Three weeks June, July and August. Accommodation arranged with families. No experience needed.
Minimum age: 14 years. Unaccompanied teenagers: 16+.

OUTDOOR ADVENTURE
Atlantic Court, Widemouth Bay, Nr Bude, Cornwall EX23 0DF (tel 01288-361312).
Member of: BCU, RYA, BSA, MLTB, BAHA.
The Seafront Centre offers canoeing as part of a week, three-day break or weekend adventure sports holiday for adults. Individuals and groups. All abilities. Equipment, local transport and experienced, qualified instruction included. Other activities include windsurfing, sailing, surfing, ski-surfing, climbing and mountain biking. Price for weekends £127 and weeks from £297. Twin rooms, full board and lively bar. Vegetarians and special diets catered for.
Minimum age: 16.

THE OUTDOOR TRUST
Belford, Northumberland NE70 7QE (tel/fax 01668 213289).
BCU and holiday courses in Inland Kayaking, Open Canoeing and Sea Kayaking for beginners to advanced level. All courses are directed by an examiner with coach, senior instructor and advance proficiency qualifications.

SKERN LODGE OUTDOOR CENTRE
Appledore, Bideford, North Devon EX39 1NG (tel 01237-475992).
River and surf canoeing for beginners and enthusiasts throughout the year. Full board and accommodation provided. Canoeing on the rivers Taw and Torridge, and participants with some experience canoe in the surf off Westward Ho beach. Instruction in capsize drill and rescue techniques as laid down by the BCU. Single canoes with buoyancy and safety toggles, and special surf skis are used.
No experience needed. Participants must be able to swim 50 metres.
Minimum age: nine years (unaccompanied).

YHA ACTIVITY CENTRE
Rowland Cote, Nether Booth, Edale, Derbyshire S30 2ZH (tel 01433-670302).
Placid water canoeing weekends for beginners and improvers, leading to BCU one and two star grades. Learn and develop skills with experienced instructors, plus evening lectures. Price of £83 (weekend) includes full board accommodation.

Scotland

ABERNETHY TRUST
Nethy Bridge, Inverness-shire PH25 3ED (tel 01479-821279).
Introductory canoeing or kayak courses on flat and white water in the Spey Valley area for individuals and groups. One week June-September. Prices from £205-£240, including accommodation, meals and equipment and instruction.
Instruction using modern, plastic slalom kayaks and open canoes by BCU Qualified staff. White water techniques, a river expedition and (weather permitting) kayak surfing on the Moray coast are possible.
'The staff are committed Christians and enjoy sharing their faith with visitors to the Centre'.
Ability to swim 50 metres required.
Minimum age: 16 years.

ARCTIC LIGHT ADVENTURE
8 The Speares, Saltash, Cornwall PL12 4UQ (tel 01752-847762).

Wilderness kayaking 5-day 'tasters' for those with moderate kayaking experience. Operating from Knoydart and Skye in Spring and Autumn. Groups of up to six catered for. Price for five days, £250 per person including all kayaking and camping equipment, food and professional guide. Participants must supply own sleeping bags and waterproofs.
No age restrictions.

GLENCOE OUTDOOR CENTRE
Glencoe, Argyll PA39 4HS (tel 01855-811350).
Qualified instruction for individuals and groups of up to 35. Available from May to October. Price from around £70 per weekend including full board and accommodation, instruction and use of equipment. Canoeing is also available as part of a multi activity course.
No experience needed.
Minimum age: ten years (12 if unaccompanied).

SCOTTISH VOYAGEURS
1 Craigdam Cottages, Tarves, Ellon, Aberdeenshire AB41 7NR (tel 01651-851215).
Proprietor: Mr Dave Horrocks.
In business since 1997.
Holidays for around 100 arranged annually.
Journeys by traditional Canadian fur trade canoe in various locations, including the Caledonian Canal and West Coast of the Scottish Highlands. Holidays operate June to September. Prices from £155 for three days to £310 for six days, inluding fully catered camping in tepees, hotel and guesthouse accommodation. Sleeping bags not included but can be hired. Participation is expected in cooking on camping trips. No experience necessary.
'A unique perspective on the landscape from a beautiful and versatile traditional craft. The camaradarie of a group working as a team'.
Minimum age: eight years (accompanied); 12 years (unaccompanied).

Wales

MONMOUTH CANOE & ACTIVITY CENTRE
Old Dixton Road, Monmouth, Gwent NP5 4DP (tel 01600-713461/716083).
Partners: G C Symonds and S A Symonds.
In business since 1981.
Licensed Centre for under 18's.
Canoeing in the Wye Valley from March to October. Individuals and groups catered for. Instruction can be provided. Overnight stays or up to a week. Accommodation is not included in the price, but bed and breakfast accommodation, camping facilities and youth hostels are available locally.
Minimum age: 11 years.
Unaccompanied young people are accepted if an instructor is booked.
(Also instructor-led caving and rock climbing/abseiling, maximum group size is eight).

OUTER LIMITS
Pwll-y-Garth, Prenmarhno, Gwynedd LL25 0HJ (tel/fax 01690-760248).
One to five-day kayaking courses. Introductory flat water sessions on lakes and slow moving rivers. Moving water skills, white water and surf techniques, and safety proficiency instruction available. No experience necessary. Prices from £20 per day for instruction only, all equipment included. Accommodation available in bunkhouse (£8.50 per night including breakfast), or in local guesthouses.
Minimum age: 14 years (accompanied); 16 years (unaccompanied).
Physically, visually and mentally challenged people welcome.

PLAS MENAI NATIONAL WATERSPORTS CENTRE
Llanfairisgaer, Caernarfon, Gwynedd LL55 IUE (tel 01248-670964).
Beginners, Improvers and Advanced sea and inland canoeing and kayaking courses all year round. Weekend or five-day courses. The Menai strait, Snowdonia and Anglesey surf beaches provide water conditions ranging from still water lakes to white water tidal races. Prices: two-day courses from £104, five-day courses £260 includes all instruction, equipment, shared room and full board.
Minimum age: 14 years. (for youth courses see *Young People's Holidays*).

PRESELI VENTURE
Parcynole Fach, Mathry, Haverfordwest, Pembrokeshire SA62 5HN (tel 01348-837709).
BCU/WCA Approved, Wales Tourist Board Accredited Centre.
Sea kayaking courses and holidays on the unspoilt and spectacular north Pembrokeshire coast. Enjoy sea cliffs, caves, seals and

secluded beaches. Also, 'Coasteering', an unforgettable coastal adventure with scrambling, climbing, swimming and cliff-jumping. Mountaineering also available. Prices £129 for weekend, including accommodation, food and activities.
Minimum age: 14 years (accompanied).

Ireland

ASSOCIATION FOR ADVENTURE SPORTS
Tiglin, The National Adventure Centre, Ashford, Co. Wicklow, Ireland (tel (+353) 404-40169; fax (+353) 404-40169). E-mail: mail@tiglin.le
Whitewater and introductory canoeing courses at the National Adventure Centre near Dublin. The Centre is situated near a lake only eight miles from the sea and within easy reach of several excellent whitewater rivers. Weekends and holiday breaks. Instruction by experienced and qualified staff. Accommodation with full board. Prices from IR£80, all equipment provided.
Canoe touring on the River Barrow in Southern Ireland. Five days July-August. Prices from IR£150.
'The tours are conducted by friendly and very experienced guides. The informality of our small groups generates friendliness and enthusiasm'.
Minimum age: 16 years.

Europe

ADRIFT
Collingbourne House, 140-142 Wandsworth High Street, London SW18 4JJ (tel 0181-874 4969; fax 0181-875 9236).
Whitewater river journeys on the spectacular Grade 5 river Coruh in northeast Turkey. Departures from May to August. River grade three to five, seven, ten and 14-day trips including a trekking option in the Kackar mountains and discovering Istanbul. Experienced kayakers welcome. Prices from £870 including meals and accommodation. Trekking option £155.

EXPLORE WORLDWIDE LTD
1 Frederick Street, Aldershot, Hants GU11 1LQ (tel 01252-344161; fax 01252-343170).
Dordogne river running trip. Eight days camping/rafting/cycling/walking through rural France. Small two-person inflatable boats which you paddle yourself. Explore castles, caves and unspoilt villages. June to September. Around £300, including transfers from London. Also rafting on the Dunajec river in the Slovak Republic from £730.
Minimum age: 17 years.

HEADWATER HOLIDAYS
146 London Road, Northwich, Cheshire CW9 5HH (tel 01606-48699).
Canoeing holidays for independent travellers in France, April to October. Price from £429 which includes ferry crossing hotel accommodation, private bathroom, dinner, bed and breakfast. No experience required.
Physically challenged people catered for.

INTERNATIONAL ADVENTURE
43 East Hatley, Hatley St. George, Sandy, Bedfordshire SG19 3JA (tel 01767-650312; fax 01767-650725).
Partners: A & S Miller.
In business since 1984.
Holidays for 500 arranged annually.
Timber rafting and canoeing safaris in Sweden for ten to 20 days between June and March. Construct your own timber raft from logs and rope and gently cruise the rivers 'living like Tom Sawyer'. Accommodation is either in tents erected on the raft or on the river banks. At the journeys end the rafts are dismantled allowing the logs to float away to the paper mill at Karlstad.
Canoeing safaris in the lakeland region of central Sweden camping at the waters edge. All equipment and food is carried in the canoe. Groups consist of about 18 people. Prices from £400-£450 for rough camping (no showers or toilets). Some canoe trips are fully catered. Sleeping bags are not provided.
Minimum age: 16 years (accompanied).

MOSWIN TOURS
Moswin House, 21 Church Street, Oadby, Leicester LE2 5DB (tel 0116-2719922; fax 0116-2716016).
Canoe holidays in Germany suitable for singles, couples, families and groups. Canoeing packages on the Moselle are for either four days (weekend package) or seven days, and are based on camping overnight in various villages and towns along the river. Seven-day holidays either begin in Trier and

end in Traben-Trarbach, or begin in Traben Trarbach and end in Alken. Canoeing holidays are also offered on the Danube Elbe, Main, Lahn, Neckar and Weser rivers in addition to the Rheinsberger Lakes in north-eastern Germany. Prices start at £255 for four days and participants must be able to swim for fifteen minutes.

Americas

ADRIFT
Collingbourne House, 140-142 Wandsworth High Street, London SW18 4JJ (tel 0181-874 4969; fax 0181-875 9236). E-mail: adrift — raftingemsn.com
Whitewater river journeys in the splendour of the South America rain forests in the Amazon Basin. Departures from December to February. River grade four to five. Experienced kayakers welcome. Prices from £1284 for a 14-day trip including meals and accommodation.

AMERICAN ROUND-UP
Oxenways, Membury, Axminster, Devon EX13 7JR (tel 01404-881777; fax 01404-881778).
Whitewater river rafting, snow mobiling, ranch and riding holidays in the USA and Canada all year round. No experience necessary. Prices range from £900 to £2000 (typical holiday costs £1200) and generally include cabin accommodation, three meals daily and all equipment.
'Riders and non-riders alike have a chance to experience the excitement and wilderness adventure of a whitewater expedition'.
Minimum age for river rafting: eight years. No maximum age.

AMERICAN WILDERNESS EXPERIENCE INC
P O Box 1486, Boulder, Co 80306, USA (+ 1-303-444-2622; fax + 1 303 444 3999).
Sea kayaking and canoe trips in the USA and Canada. The waterways of Vermont (six days); canoeing in Costa Rica (ten days); Alaska Glacier Bay National Park Sea Kayak expeditions and marine mammal discovery. Sample prices for five days $1100; seven days $1500.

ARCTIC LIGHT ADVENTURE
8 The Speares, Saltash, Cornwall PL12 4UQ (tel 01752-847762).
Two-week long kayaking tours of Prince William Sound, Alaska. Tours operate from mid-May to mid-September. Groups of up to 5 people catered for. Tailor-made itineraries depending on experience and preference of the group. All camping and kayaking equipment provided and included in the price, around £1500. Enjoy the stunning scenery and spectacular wildlife including sea otters, eagles, bears, whales and porpoises. Equipment and staff of the highest quality.
'Our trips are about wilderness living, good food and fine company — of an adventure shared with friends'.

CANOE COUNTRY ESCAPES
194, South Franklin Street, Denver, Co 80209, USA (tel + 1 303 722-6482).
President: Eric Durland.
In business since 1980.
National Assoc. of Canoe Liveries and Outfitters.
Holidays for 100 arranged annually.
Guided canoe trips from mid-May to the end of September. Trips last six days and take place in the Minnesota Ontario Boundary Waters canoe area on the Canadian border with Minnesota. Various trip emphases e.g. lodge-to-lodge, seniors, families, etc. Tailor-made trips can be organised for any group. No experience is needed as canoe practice and instruction session is included. Prices $395 (about £243) for a child, $695 (about £430) for an adult. Inexpensive car rentals can be arranged from Duluth (Minnesota) airport.
Minimum age: five years (family trips); ten years (lodge-to-lodge), 12 years (other trips). Unaccompanied minors not accepted.
'We have taken what is normally considered to be a rugged, wilderness experience and softened it with experienced guides and meals and lodging at a beautiful lodge the nights before and after the trip.'

EXPEDITIONS INC
625 N Beaver Street, Flagstaff, Arizona 86001 USA (tel + 1 520-779 3769; fax + 1 520-774 4001). E-mail: expedgc@aol.com
Proprietors: Dick and Susan McCallum.
In operation since 1970.
Grand Canyon raft and kayak supported river trips lasting from five to 14 days from April to October. Camping equipment is provided (tents furnished). All meals are included in the prices of $1000-$2395 (about £620-£1480).

Minimum age: 16 years (unaccompanied); otherwise eight years.

EXPLORE WORLDWIDE LTD
1 Frederick Street, Aldershot, Hants GU11 1LQ (tel 01252-344161; fax 01252-343170).
Rafting on Peru's Urubamba River after trekking on the Inca Trail to Machu Picchu. No experience necessary. Fifteen days from £1160. Canoeing to Angel Falls in Venezuela from £1395, fifteen days.

MAINE WATERS
PO Box 3, Bethel, Maine 04217, USA (tel/fax +1 207 824-3694).
Trade Association Director: Wende Gray.
In operation since 1996.
Holidays for 30,000 arranged annually.
White water rafting, kayaking, canoeing and windjammer cruises around inland and coastal Maine. Trips last three to six days from June-September. Groups of eight to 15 people catered for. Prices from $208-$382 (about £128-£235) for three days including all meals and cabin accommodation. Wet suits can be hired ($15 per day) if necessary. Memorable highlights include moose, bear, osprey and eagle viewing.
Minimum age: 12 years (accompanied).

MAPACHE LODGE WILDERNESS CAMP
Boca Taboga, Sierpe de Osa, Puntarenas, Costa Rica (tel +506-7866565; fax +506-7866358). UK agent: Mike Boston (tel/fax 01631-770214).
Internet: http://www.greenarrow.com/travel/mapache.htm
Kayak trek for 223km (expert kayakers only) around Osa, tavelling the rivers and meeting the big waves of the Pacific Ocean. Eleven-day tour from December-April, $1990. River and sea kayaking for all abilities around the Osa Peninsula, visiting National Parks and the best coral reef in Costa Rica. Six-day tour from December-April.

PEAK INTERNATIONAL
15 Moor Park, Wendover, Aylesbury, Bucks. HP22 6AX (tel/fax 01296-624225).
Canoe expeditions to most parts of North America, in three main areas. All are suitable for novices and experts alike:
The Boundary Waters Wilderness is where you can follow the old voyager canoe routes and see track wolves, black bears, loons, bald eagles and moose. Camp by the waters edge each night, cook your supper on an open fire whilst you gaze north looking for the spectacular display of the northern lights. August and September two week special 'fly in' trip using a float plane to access remoter areas £785 (15 days) inclusive ex Minneapolis.
Guided and self guided tours of the Yukon, Teslin or Big Salmon Rivers from £15 per day. Guided trips from £675 for eight days. July and August.
Every type of waterway explored in a Sunshine Florida trip in February. Explore the clear warm spring waters north of Orlando, the St. John's River teeming with birdlife, the remote Peace River (to boost your alligator count) and the mangroves of the Everglades. Camp on secluded sub tropical Gulf Coast islands. Ideal for novices. £695 + food kitty (15 days) ex Orlando. Price includes canoes, ancillary kit, camping kit, guiding, instruction, camping fees and transport throughout the state.

WORLDWIDE JOURNEYS AND EXPEDITIONS
8 Comeragh Road, London W14 9HP (tel 0171-381 8638; fax 0171-381 0836).
Rafting in Ecuador. Tailor-made tours for small groups and individuals. No previous experience necessary. Can be combined with treks and wildlife viewing. Fully inclusive package.

Africa

ACACIA EXPEDITIONS
27D Stable Way, London W10 6QX (tel 0181-9605747; fax 0181-9601414).
E-mail: acacia@afrika.demon.co.uk
Canoeing safaris on the Zambezi river. Four-day tours offering unrivalled scenery, wildlife and camping on the riverbanks of the lower Zambezi. All equipment and food supplied.

ADRIFT
Collingbourne House, 140-142 Wandsworth High Street, London SW18 4JJ (tel 0181-874-4969; fax 0181 875 9236).
Pioneers of new rafting journeys on the African continent. Explore the real heart of Africa. 14-day trips including safari. Choose from Zambezi in Zimbabwe, Zambia (river grade four/five, August to December), Omo in Ethiopia (river grade two, September to November). The White Nile in Uganda (river grade five all year). Experienced

kayakers welcome on the Zambezi and White Nile. Prices from £970 including meals and accommodation.

AFRICA EXCLUSIVE
66 Palmerston Road, Northampton NN1 5EX (tel 01604-28979).
Canoeing and rafting on the Zambezi river in Zambia all year round. Prices from £2500 include air fares and ground arrangements. Accommodation is in high quality safari lodges, and four or five star hotels on a fully inclusive basis.
Minimum age: 12 years (accompanied).

EXODUS EXPEDITIONS
9 Weir Road, Balham, London SW12 0LT (tel 0181-675 5550 or 0181-673 0859 24 hrs).
Four-day canoeing and camping safaris on the banks of the Zambezi in Zimbabwe including 15-day Rhino safari from £1550. Also canoeing in 'Mokoro', local dug out canoes, in Botswana's the Okavango Delta during a 15-day safari, from £1580.

EXPLORE WORLDWIDE LTD
1 Frederick Street, Aldershot, Hants GU11 1LQ (tel 01252-344161; fax 01252-343170).
Canoeing on the Okavango Delta in Zimbabwe and Botswana or the Zambezi in Zambia; plus optional white water rafting at Victoria Falls. Small exploratory groups. Flight and tours from £1460.

OKAVANGO TOURS AND SAFARIS
Gadd House, Arcadia Avenue, London N3 2JT (tel 0181-343 3283; fax 0181-343 3287).
Canoeing and white water rafting holidays in Zimbabwe and Zambia. The Zambezi river offers you the opportunity to explore its beautiful reed lined channels on the Zimbabwe side with a unique safari by canoe. Zambia provides fully serviced permanent camps along the safari trail whilst Zimbabwe offers participation safaris with tented accommodation being erected each night on a different sand bank. Canoeing experience is not necessary as tuition is provided. Prices start at £450 for three nights/four days excluding long-haul flights.
Also white water rafting at the Victoria falls as one of the most exciting day's adventure activities offered in Africa. Available from Victoria Falls Town in Zimbabwe or Livingstone in Zambia. Prices start at £55 per run including lunch.

Asia

ADRIFT
Collingbourne House, 140-142 Wandsworth High Street, London SW18 4JJ (tel 0181-874-4969; fax 0181 875 9236).
Whitewater river journeys on the best of the Nepalese rivers. 14-day expeditions including safari options on the Sun kosi (river grade three to four, September to October). Experienced kayakers welcome. Price from £1000 including meals and accommodation.

ENCOUNTER OVERLAND
267 Old Brompton Road, London SW5 9JA (tel: 0171-370 6845).
Whitewater river running in Nepal from October to May. Camping and cooking around campfires beside the river. All equipment supplied and carried in the rafts. Experienced helmsmen accompany each trip. No experience required, though must be able to swim. Trips range from three to ten days and depart from Kathmandu.

EXPLORE WORLDWIDE LTD
1 Frederick Street, Aldershot, Hants GU11 1LQ (tel 01252-344161; fax 01252-343170).
Rafting included in trips to Nepal. Combined with jungle treks in small groups. Price including flights from London £1289.

EXODUS EXPEDITIONS
9 Weir Road, Balham, London SW12 0LT (tel 0181-675 5550 or 0181-673 0859 24 hrs).
Whitewater rafting on the Trisulu River in Nepal, plus visits to Chitwan Park and trekking in the Annapurna region. 18 days from £1160. Canoeing along the coast included in a 25-day adventure trip in Indonesia, from £1590.

HIMALAYAN RIVER EXPLORATION (PVT) LTD.
Durbar Marg, PO Box 242, Kathmandu, Nepal (tel (+977) 1 411225;fax (+977) 1 414075). E-mail: tiger@mtn.mos.com.np
Internet: http://www.tigermountain.com
Directors: AVJ Edwards and Steve Webster.
In business since 1964.
Pioneers of white water rafting and kayaking river trip expeditions in Nepal. Choose

from a wide range of trips from two to ten days and from scenic floating to exciting high grade rapids. Operating on all major rivers in Nepal, combined with visits to local villages and chances to observe local widlife. River guides are experienced and are all trained in first aid and survival.
Book direct or through: ExplorAsia Ltd (tel 0171-973 0482); Abercombie & Kent Travel (tel 0171-730 9600) or Worldwide Journeys & Expeditions (tel 0171-381 8638).
'Pioneers of environmentally sensitive adventure holidays in Nepal'.

ULTIMATE DESCENTS
UK Agent: 43 St Quentin Avenue, London W10 6NZ (tel 0171-912 0228; fax 0171-565 8211). E-mail: 101542.573@compuserve.com
Nepal Office: P O Box 6720, Kathmandu (tel/fax +977 1411933). E-mail rivers@ultimate.wlink.com.np
Proprietor: David Allardice.
Operating since 1985.
Holidays for 4,000 arranged annually.
White water rafting expeditions for individuals and private groups. Kayak clinics for beginners and refresher courses, all in Nepal. Trips last from two to 12 days and the main seasons are spring and autumn. However, some short expeditions operate year round. The group size is from six to 20 people. Prices from £500-£1200. A typical trip including international flights costs about £1081. No previous experience is needed as full training is given.

Commonsense age limits: children aged four and five have been on easy river trips and fit 70-year-olds have been on the tough ones.

WORLD PEACE TREKKING (P) LTD
PO Box 550, Thamel, Kathmandu, Nepal (tel 01424-220892).
E-mail: worldpeace@dial.pipex.com
Internet: http://www.pavilion.co.uk/website-designs/world- peace/
Directors: K L Tamang and A Tamang.
In business since 1992.
Holidays for 150 arranged annually.
White water rafting in Nepal and Tibet available all year round. Choose from tours lasting from five to 60 days. Individuals and groups of any size catered for. Prices range from $200-$6000 including camping and all meals. Flights and hotel accommodation in Kathmandu not included in the holiday price. Bookings available on the internet only (see website address for details).
Minimum age: 16 years (unaccompanied).
No maximum age limit.
'We specialise in off-the-beaten-track trekking and rafting. We are not a soft option)'.

WORLDWIDE JOURNEYS AND EXPEDITIONS
8 Comeragh Road, London, W14 9HP (tel 0171-381 8638; fax 0171-381 0836).
Rafting holidays in Nepal. Tailor-made tours for small groups and individuals. No previous experience necessary. Can be combined with treks and wildlife viewing. Fully inclusive packages.

Sailing

Worldwide

ADVENTURE UNDER SAIL
in the UK:'Eye of the Wind', 102 High Street, Crediton, Devon EX17 3LF (tel 01363-777990; fax 01363-773545); In Australia: P O Box 33, Salamander Bay, NSW 2317 (tel +61 49 807647; fax +61 49 846 174).
Ltd company in Australia.
Owner: Capt. Anthony Timbs.
Established approximately 1976.
Sailing adventures for about 300 arranged annually.
Sail training and crewing a tallship *Eye of the Wind* (awarded the Concours d'Elegance in the 1994 Cutty Sark Tall Ships Race. The ship has been in operation for over 80 years, is 132 feet overall and traditionally (brigantine) rigged with a sail capacity of 8,000 sq feet. She undertakes a variety of voyages all year round from short diving and holiday cruises to longer ocean passages and sail training ventures. The itinerary goes all over the world and legs cost from £350 (Penzance to Milford Haven, seven days, Darwin to Bali, twenty days). Prices include all meals and comfortable, modernised accommodation for up to 24 crew in twin-berth cabins.

CHALLENGE ADVENTURE SAILING
The Challenge Business Ltd, Trepen House, Menheniot, Liskeard, Cornwall PL14 3PN (tel 01579-348387; fax 01579-347255). E-mail: 101372.150@compuserve.com
Internet: http://www.challengebus.co.uk

Challenge Adventure Sailing offers the opportunity to sail a high profile ocean racer (those used in the BT Global Challenge Yacht Race) in some remarkable locations. The voyages focus on either the challenge and ultimate personal achievement of the trip undertaken, or the region being sailed. A Challenge yacht is able to provide an adventure experience not normally possible on smaller, cruising yachts. Sailing further and faster makes for an exhilarating experience. Regions visited include southern Chile around Cape Horn and Tierra del Fuego, South Africa's Garden Route coast, the Indian Ocean, the Caribbean, the sub-tropical islands of the Azores, the Fastnet Rock Challenge, beyond the Arctic circle up to Spitsbergen and UK coastal areas. Durations from four days upwards and all voyages are under the expert guidance of a professional skipper and mate.

CREWSEEKERS
Hawthorn House, Hawthorn Lane, Sarisbury Green, Southampton SO31 7BD (tel & fax 01489-578319). E-mail: pstock@crewseekers.co.uk
Internet: http://www.crewseekers.co.uk
Partners: Paul and Tina Stock.
In business since 1990.
International yacht crewing agency bringing owners and crew together for worldwide sailing opportunities including daily sailing, offshore cruising, competitive racing, deliveries and professional sailing positions. All experience levels welcome, including novices. Specialists in introducing amateur crew for daily, weekend and holiday leisure cruising. Regularly updated directory contains information on yachts located worldwide requiring crew. Additional expenses include membership (£40 for 12 months) and food kitty once on board (about £10 per day). Accommodation provided on board. Individual participation expected in day-to-day sailing and domestic duties.
Minimum age: 18 years unaccompanied.

SUNSAIL
The Port House, Port Solent, Portsmouth, Hants PO6 4TH (tel 01705-222222).
Flotilla, bareboat and skippered sailing holidays in the Mediterranean, Caribbean and exotic destinations including Australia, the Seychelles and Thailand. Sunsail also have nine Beach Clubs in the Mediterranean. These shore-based Clubs are for those who want to enjoy dinghy sailing, windsurfing, and day yachting plus the chance to explore ashore. Prices start from £295 for a one-week flotilla and from £395 for a one-week holiday at a Sunsail Club. Both prices are per person and include flights and transfers.

England

ACORN ACTIVITIES
P O Box 120, Hereford HR41 8YB (tel 01432-830083; fax 01432-830110).
Two and five-day courses for beginners and RYA levels. Wayfarers and toppers. Individuals, families, couples and groups. Courses £110-£275. Accommodation from £16 for groups, or £22 per night for farmhouse and £32 per night for hotels. Can be combined with other watersports and activities (see entry in *Multi Activity* section).

ANVIL YACHT CHARTERS
13 Harbour View Road, Parkstone, Poole, Dorset BH14 0PD (tel 01202-741637).
Directors: R J & B Saunders.
In business since 1968.
Holidays for 1200 arranged annually.
One or two week self-sail cruises from Poole for up to 12 people (March to November). Choice of ten or 12 berths; complete self-catering. Oilskins needed but can be hired. Mini cruises last four days. Skippers available.

BLUE PETER SAILING
5 Rowley Close, Botely, Southampton SO30 2FT (tel 01489-781136; fax 01489-780887).
Self charter of various size yachts sleeping four to eight persons. Price range depending on size £250-£800 Friday evening to Sunday evening £450-£2000 per week.

Group sailing with skipper. Group not less than four persons. Accommodation on board. From Friday evening to Sunday evening £180 per person.

CALSHOT ACTIVITIES CENTRE
Calshot Spit, Fawley, Southampton SO45 1BR (tel 01703-892077).
Recognised by the RYA.
Dinghy sailing courses at all levels. Dinghies available include Optimists, Toppers, Picos and Wayfarers. Courses range from single day Optimist courses for the eight to twelve age range through the full range of RYA personal performance awards levels one to five and Instructor and Senior Instructor

courses. Course fees start at £21 for a single day through to £120 for a fully residential adult weekend.

EAST ANGLIAN SEA SCHOOL
Studio 1, Fox's Marina, The Strand, Ipswich, Suffolk IP2 8NN (tel 01473-684884; fax 01473-780877).
Proprietor: P W Smith.
In business since 1973.
Recognised by RYA, member of NFSS.
Holidays for 950 arranged annually.
Offshore and coastal sailing based at Ipswich and sailing to Belgium, Holland and the Channel Islands. Weekends, one week and two-week trips April-October. Weekend prices from about £110. Accommodation aboard modern cruising yachts with access to shore-based marina facilities at most stops.
Also a comprehensive programme of professionally organised RYA courses leading to cruising, shorebased and powerboating certificates. No previous experience needed.
Ages: 17 to 80 years.
No unaccompanied people under 17.

EUROYOUTH
301 Westborough Road, Westcliff, Southend-on-Sea, Essex SS0 9PT (tel 01702-341434; fax 01702-330104).
Sailing courses at Southend for individuals and groups. Accommodation arranged with families. Three weeks June, July and August.
No experience needed.
Minimum age: 14 years.
Unaccompanied teenagers: 16 years + .

FELLOWSHIP AFLOAT
The Sail Lofts, Woodrolfe Road, Tollesbury, Essex CM9 8SE (tel 01621-868113; fax 01621-869771). E-mail: info@fact.keme.co.uk
Charitable Trust.
Director: David Hillyer.
RYA Recognised.
Holidays for 2000 arranged annually.
Dinghy sailing courses in the Blackwater Estuary off the East Coast from April to October. The Trust's base is in a converted Trinity House Light Vessel with accommodation for 36. Individuals and groups accepted. Possibility to mix sailing with other activities including music, extended dinghy expeditions with overnight camping and windsurfing. Prices: £57 (weekend), £199 (week) including full board and accommodation aboard the permanently berthed lightship.
Minimum age: eight years (accompanied), otherwise ten years (unaccompanied).
Physically challenged people catered for.

FOWEY CRUISING SCHOOL
32 Fore Street, Fowey, Cornwall PL23 1AQ (tel 01726-832129; fax 01726-832000).
Proprietor: J G Myatt.
Established 1972.
Members of RYA, NFSS and Cornwall Tourist Board.
Holidays arranged for 200 annually.
Practical and theoretical RYA tuition courses from Competent Crew to Yachtmaster throughout the year. Also family cruising holidays. Prices from £325 including accommodation. No experience necessary. Groups catered for (five maximum per yacht).
Ages: four to 70 (unaccompanied young people from 14 years).
Physically challenged people catered for.

ISLAND CRUISING CLUB
10 Island Street, Salcombe, South Devon TQ8 8DR (tel 01548-843481; fax 01548-843929).
Sailing and cruising holidays from March to October. Weekends, mid-week breaks, five-day, or one- to two-week holidays. Full range of courses on offer. Individuals or groups of up to 60 welcome. Group discounts available. Wide range of dinghies, and keelboats — 420s, Lasers, Wayfarers, Enterprises, Toppers, Solings and Squibs. Club base is a former Mersey ferry which is moored permanently on the Salcombe estuary, a Site of Special Scientific Interest. ICC works together with schools to put together tailor-made three, four and five-day sailing and coastal study packages. Cruises normally start from Salcombe and visit West Country, Channel Islands and French ports. Longer cruises spend time in Brittany. Cruising is in modern five to six berth yachts or in classic sailing schooners or yawls sleeping up to 12. Prices from £250 per week include all on-board meals and accommodation and life jackets.
Minimum age: seven years.
Special weeks for Cadets and Young Members (16-18 years).

JOHN SHARP SAILING (FOWEY)
Brockles Quay, St Veep, Lostwithiel, Cornwall PL22 0NT (tel 01208-872470).
Proprietor: John Sharp.
In business since 1972.

RYA Senior Instructor.
Weekly holiday dinghy sailing training in the Fowey Estuary and along the adjacent coast. Courses operate April-October. Price: £56-£100 per week including instruction, use of boat and personal buoyancy. Accommodation not included, camping, self-catering and hotels nearby. Wet weather gear required.
No experience necessary.
Minimum age: eight years.
Unaccompanied children accepted.
'We like pupils to learn to sail; not to sit in a boat and go for a ride.'

LIBERTY YACHT CHARTERS
Queen Anne's Battery Marina, Plymouth, Devon PL4 OLP (tel 01752-227911; fax 01752-229122).
Director: S Beeby.
In business since 1986.
YCA member.
Liberty Yachts offer courses and yacht charters on boats ranging from 31 to 41 feet long, with six to ten berths available on each yacht. Courses available from beginner to yachtmaster, with no experience being required for five-day Competent Crew course. Prices for courses start from £180, and for yacht charters from £240 for four days on a six-berth yacht. Call for brochure.
Minimum age: 18 if unaccompanied; no restriction if accompanied.

MEDINA VALLEY CENTRE
Dodnor Lane, Newport, Isle of Wight PO30 5TE (tel 01983-522195; fax 01983-825962).
Non-profit making company.
Executive Director: P Savory.
In business since 1963, (formerly The Christian Sailing Centre until 1977).
Holidays and courses for over 2000 arranged annually.
Recognised by RYA and NFSS.
RYA dingy sailing holidays. Full board residential and non-residential. All instructors are RYA qualified. Saftey gear is provided. Full colour brochure and tariff on request.
All ages — all abilities.

NEWTON FERRERS SAILING SCHOOL
Westerly, Yealm Road, Newton Ferrers, Plymouth, Devon PL8 1BJ (tel 01752-872375).
Directors: A P & A E Thomson.
In business since 1958.
Recognised by RYA. Member of NFSPS.
Member of West Country Tourist Board.
Sailing tuition for individuals and groups of up to 12. One or two week courses from April to October. Accommodation and meals available at school headquarters. Prices on application. Oilskins can be hired.
No experience needed.
Minimum age: eight years. Unaccompanied children welcome.

NORFOLK BROADS SCHOOL OF SAILING
The Rhond, Hoveton, Wroxham, Norfolk N12 8UE (tel 01603-783096).
Sole Trader: P C Howe.
In business since 1992.
Holidays for 350 arranged annually.
Sailing holidays on the Norfolk Broads from March-October. Individuals and groups of up to 6 catered for. No experience necessary as tuition is provided by qualified instuctors on the National Keelboat Scheme. Five types of yacht available for weekly hire. Price for five-day sailing course: £400 for two people. Accommodation on yacht, meals not included.
Minimum age: 18 years unaccompanied.

OCEAN YOUTH CLUB
The Bus Station, South Street, Gosport, Hants PO12 1EP (tel 01705-528421; fax 01705-522069).
Internet: http://www.oyc.org.uk/
Registered as an Educational Charity. Number 306078.
Director: David Parkinson.
In business since 1960.
Recognised by the RYA, initiating authority of the Duke of Edinburgh's Award Scheme.
Adventure sailing holidays for young people aged 12 upwards. OYC operates a fleet of modern ocean-going vessels sailing from different ports around the British Isles. Voyages run from March-November. Fees (from £89 for a weekend) include all food, instruction, safety equipment and insurance. Grants are available for those keen to take part but unable to find the money themselves. The Club aims to provide young people no matter what their circumstances with the opportunity to experience the challenge and adventure of life at sea and develop their self-confidence, resourcefulness, co-operation and concern for others.
No previous sailing is experience required.
OYC also offers additional training for those wishing to develop their sailing skills

and access for adults under a Friends' membership scheme.
'Our vessels are large enough to be capable of long passages including ocean crossings and Tall Ships races but also small enough to ensure that everyone on board participates fully in all the activities of running the boat from steering and navigation to cooking and cleaning'.

OUTWARD BOUND TRUST
Watermillock, Cumbria CA11 OJL (tel 0990 134227).
Outward Bound sailing programmes include a Viking Wayfarer, West Coast Passage and a West Coast Explorer. For more information call for a free brochure.

PORTWAY YACHT CHARTERS INTERNATIONAL
Dart Marine Park, Steamer Quay, Totnes, Devon TQ9 5AL (tel 01803-866622; fax 01803-866621).
In business since 1980.
Member of YCA and BMIF.
Skippered and bareboat charters by the day or week from bases in the West Country, the South Coast and the East Coast all year round. Wide range of yacht sizes available. Suitable for cruising the South and East Coasts, Devon and Cornwall, The Scilly Isles, Channel Islands, French and Dutch Coasts. No experience is required for skippered holidays. For bareboat, skippers must be over 21 and suitably qualified and experienced. Charter prices from £350 per week, per boat up to £2500 per week, per boat. No food, fuel or harbour dues are included. Oilskins and sleeping bags can be hired.

SAIL ON OULTON BROAD
Broadland Holiday Village, Marsh Road, Oulton Broad, Lowestoft NR33 9JY (tel 01502-572014).
Principal: Alison Knights.
RYA recognised.
RYA National Dinghy Scheme courses, individual 'one-to-one' tuition or group sessions, on the inland Oulton Broad in Suffolk all year round. Prices: £12 per head for two-hour group session; £195 for individual five-day course. Local accommodation including hotels and chalets available.
Minimum age: seven years unaccompanied.

SOLENT SCHOOL OF YACHTING
The Quay, Warsash, Southampton, Hants. SO3 9FR (tel 01489-583066; fax 01489-572054).
RYA, NFSS.
Practical and theoretical (shorebased) courses in offshore cruising and navigation leading to RYA/DTp qualifications offered all year round. Practical courses last a minimum of five consecutive days. The Solent school complex incorporates estuary waterfrontage, and on-site lecture and assembly rooms, catering and dining facilities, showers and laundry rooms. Individuals, couples, groups of friends and families catered for. Non-certificate activity sailing holidays — weekends, five, seven or 14 days also offered. Prices with meals and on board accommodation supplied on request. Six-day shorebased courses include lunch and RYA notes and lecture pack. Local guest house accommodation can be arranged.
Minimum age: 16 years (unaccompanied).

SUNSAIL UK
The Port House, Port Solent, Portsmouth PO6 4TH (tel 01705-222224).
Learn to sail in the sheltered waters of the Solent and Clyde. Sunsail offer a wide range of RYA sailing courses for adults, children and teenagers on board a modern fleet of dinghies, keelboats and yachts. Sunsail's aim is to make sailing rewarding, accessible and fun for everyone and there are courses for all levels of experience; or none. Prices from £80 for a two-day dinghy course with 'cabin-style' accommodation available on site. For a five-day practical competent crew course, prices start at £180 which includes breakfast, lunch, three evening meals and accommodation.
Special needs groups can be catered for by prior arrangement.

WINDERMERE LAKE HOLIDAYS AFLOAT
Gilly's Landings, Glebe Road, Bowness-on-Windermere, Cumbria LA23 3HE (tel 015394-43415; fax 015394-88721).
Proprietor: Bernard Twitchett.
In business around 60 years.
Holidays for 100's arranged per week .
Sailing and Motor boating holidays on Lake Windermere all year round. Live aboard accommodation. Price £120 plus, excluding meals. Opportunities for other watersports. A qualified leader required on board.

No minimum age if accompanied; unaccompanied young people not accepted.

WINDSPORT INTERNATIONAL
Mylor Yacht Harbour, Nr Falmouth, Cornwall TR11 5UF (tel 01326-377633).
Sailing courses for children, families and adults March to October. Price for a week's course including all equipment is £245.

Scotland

GLENCOE OUTDOOR CENTRE
Glencoe, Argyll PA39 4HS (tel 01855-811350).
Dinghy sailing courses based on Loch Leven (a sheltered sea loch). Individuals and groups of up to 35. RYA qualified instruction. Courses from May to October. Sailing is also available as part of a multi activity course. Price from £70 including full board and accommodation, instruction and use of equipment.
No experience needed.
Minimum age: ten years (12 if unaccompanied).

RAASAY OUTDOOR CENTRE
Raasay House, Isle of Raasay by Kyle, IV40 8PB (tel 01478 660 266).
RYA sailing courses off the Inner Hebridean Isle of Raasay. Prices from £105 to £330 per week. Accommodation in a beautiful Georgian mansion in twin, double, family and alpine-style rooms.

SINBAD CHARTERS
Aidenkyle House, Aidenkyle Road, Kilcreggan by Helensburgh, Dunbartonshire G84 OHP (tel 01436-842247).
Proprietor: P G Waddington.
In business since 1983.
RYA recognised. Scottish Sports Council approved.
Holidays for approx. 150 arranged annually.
Sailing courses (cruising) at all levels aboard the yacht *Zamora*. Also informal sailing and navigation tuition/holiday cruises (skippered) in the Firth of Clyde and associated sea lochs and the Western Isles including Skye and the Outer Hebrides. Duration as client's wishes, but usually one or two weeks. April to October. Itineraries tailor-made to suit clients' wishes and the weather conditions. Berths can be booked by individuals or whole boat charters for up to five people. Prices vary according to season: Single berth £200-£250 per week, wholeboat £800-£1000 per week. Prices do not include food, fuel and berthing charges. Apart from sailing, watching marine mammals such as killer whales, dolphins and innumerable seabirds provides additional pleasure. Beginners welcome.
Some physically and visually challenged clients can be catered for.

SLEAT MARINE SERVICES
Ardvasar, Isle of Skye IV45 8RU (tel 01471-844216/844387).
Proprietor: J Mannall.
In business since 1983
Member of Associated Scottish Yacht Charters, Sail Scotland and British Marine Industries Federation.
Holidays provided for around 500 annually.
Weekly yacht cruising holidays off the West Coast of Scotland from March to October. Groups of up to eight can be catered for. Skippers should be over 24 and be Offshore Standard Yachtmasters. Prices range from £905 to £1530 per boat per week. Food is not included. Sleeping bags may be hired.
No minimum age, but unaccompanied young people are not accepted.

TIGHNABRUAICH SAILING SCHOOL
Tighnabruaich, Argyll PA21 2BD (tel 01700-811396).
Sailing holidays for individuals and groups of up to 40. One or more weeks May to September. All equipment provided. Wide range of accommodation available locally. Courses from £145 per week.
No experience needed.
Minimum age: eight years.

WAVE YACHT CHARTERS
Castlecary Castle, Walton Road, Bonnybridge, Stirlingshire FK4 2HP (tel 01324-841330; fax 01324-841830).
Directors: R L Hunter, R A C Hunter.
In business since 1990.
Member of YCA.
Holidays provided for around 180 annually.
Sailing off the West Coast of Scotland throughout the summer. Charters from one day or a week upwards. Yachts carry a maximum of six passengers, plus skipper and cook. Clients may do as much or as little sailing as they wish. Prices from £65 per person per day including meals, bedding

and oilskins, though you should bring waterproof footwear. Opportunities for walking, climbing, fishing and diving are available. No experience is required.
Minimum age: seven years if accompanied; 16 years if unaccompanied.

YACHT CORRYVRECKAN
Dal an Eas, Kilmore, Oban, Argyll PA34 4XU (tel 01631-770246).
Partners: D Lindsay, M Lindsay.
In business since 1969.
Holidays for 250 arranged annually.
Skippered sailing holidays off the West Coast of Scotland in the custom built (1990) 65 foot yacht *Corryvreckan*. Cruises start and finish in Oban. Mid-April to mid-October. Accommodation is in five two-berth cabins. Clients on skippered holidays are encouraged to join in all aspects of sailing the yacht from washing up to navigating. Prices £425 to £480 per person per week including cordon bleu catering. Only extra costs, drinks and postcards.
Minimum age: 12 years (accompanied) for skippered charter.

Wales

OCEAN YOUTH CLUB
South Street, Gosport, Hampshire PO12 1EP (tel 01705-528421/2).
Adventure sailing from Holyhead and many ports nationwide. Two, seven or more days March-November. Inclusive prices from £89 for a weekend.
No experience needed.
Ages: 12-24 years. Adult voyages also available.

PLAS MENAI NATIONAL WATERSPORTS CENTRE
Caernarfon, Gwynedd LL55 1UE (tel 01248-670964).
RYA courses in dinghy, keelboat and catamaran sailing at all levels. Weekend and five-day courses. Prices from: £132 (two days), £318 (five days) includes all equipment, tuition and full board, shared accommodation.
Minimum age: 14 years (unaccompanied).
For youth courses, see *Young People's Holidays*.

ZINDERNEUF SAILING
PO Box 105,Macclesfield, Cheshire, SK10 2EY (tel 01625-431712; fax 01625-619704).
Director D M Walker.
In business since 1991.
Holidays arranged for around 30-40 annually.
Learn to sail in the unspoilt scenic beauty of Tremadoc and Cardigan Bay areas from April to October. Prices from £85 for a weekend to £275 for five days, includes all meals, engine fuel, cooking gas, harbour dues and tuition. Groups of four maximum.
Ages: 16-70.
Minimum age: seven years (accompanied).

Ireland

GLENANS IRISH SAILING CLUB
5 Lower Mount Street, Dublin 2, Ireland (tel +353 1 6611481/82; fax +353 1 6764249).
Voluntary, non-profit organisation.
In operation since 1969.
Irish Tourist Board, Irish Yachting Association, Irish Association of Sail Training.
Sailing courses for 2,600 arranged annually.
One- and two-week sailing courses offered from April to September at Baltimore and Westport (Co Mayo). Also introductory weekend sailing from mid-June to mid-May and from mid-October to mid-November. Courses in all levels of dinghy, boardsailing, catamaran sailing and cruising. Individuals and groups of up to 25 accepted. Prices from IR£239 (includes membership fee) to IR£285, depending on the season. Prices include dormitory accommodation, instruction, equipment and all food. Members must share the daily cooking and cleaning jobs.
Minimum ages for courses: 14 years (junior); 18 years (adult).
Physically challenged people catered for.
'A Glenans Sailing Course also fosters firm friendships that last long after the sails have been furled... It is also why people keep coming back to Glenans year after year'.

ROSSBRIN YACHT CHARTERS
Rossbrin, Schull, W. Cork, Ireland (tel +353 28 37165).
Proprietor: A Stott.
In business since 1973.
Irish Tourist Board approved.
Skippered yacht charter off south west Ireland all year round. Rustler class (36ft.)

sailing yacht sleeps two couples plus skipper. £690-£1110, per week depending on NUS, for the boat. Food not included but estimated at £30 per head a week. Help with cooking and cleaning expected. Shore accommodation can also be arranged if preferred. Day sailing also available at £95.

SHARE CENTRE
Smith's Strand, Lisnaskea, Co. Fermanagh, Northern Ireland BT92 0EQ (tel 013657-22122/21892; fax 013657-21893).
One week and weekend sailing/cruising holidays on Lough Erne from March to October. Inclusive prices from £35 (weekend) and £130 (one week).
Also learn-to-sail and improvers week/weekend courses available. Viking Adventure week/weekend courses also offered, sailing in a longship along Lough Erne!
Minimum age (unaccompanied): 14 years.

Europe

JUBILEE SAILING TRUST
Jubilee Yard, Hazel Road, Woolston, Southampton SO19 7GB (tel 01703-449138; fax 01703-449145).
National registered charity that offers voyages in the Canary Islands (November-March) and United Kingdom (April-October) aboard tall ship *STS Lord Nelson* specially designed to enable both physically disabled and able-bodied people to share the challenge of tall ship sailing. Prices from £295-£850 depending on duration. No experience necessary. Ages 16-70+.
'For physically challenged and able-bodied people to share the experience of crewing a tall ship at sea'.
Shipbuilding holidays are now available as the JST are building a second ship at Southampton. Mixed ability people work alongside professional shipwrights in all aspects of shipyard life. Price £100 for six days. No experience necessary but would be an advantage.

NAUTILUS YACHTING
4 Church Street, Edenbridge, Kent TN8 5BD (tel 01732-867445; fax 01732-867446.)
Directors: Howard Richardson and Nicola Richardson.
In business since 1986.
ATOL members, 3016.
Sailing holidays provided for 400-600 each year.
Bareboat and skippered yacht charter in Europe and the Caribbean. Destinations include Greece, Turkey, Majorca, Sardinia, Corsica, South of France, Denmark, Malta and the Caribbean. For bareboat charter at least one member of the group should have previous chartering experience or an RYA qualification. For the less experienced there are flotillas in Greece and Turkey, along with sailing tuition in Greece. £250-£600 per head, including flight. Food and fuel is extra. Yachts range in size from 27' suitable for two people to 55' for groups of up to ten. Whole boat charter only (except sailing tuition).

OCEAN YOUTH CLUB
South Street, Gosport, Hampshire PO12 1EP (tel 01705-528421/2).
Sailing in North European waters for individuals and groups of 12, March-November. Vessels based in Holyhead, Liverpool, Belfast, Glasgow and Southern England. Prices from £89 for a weekend, including meals, safety equipment and oilskins.
No experience needed.
Ages: 12-24: Adult voyages also available.

RIVIERA SAILING HOLIDAYS
45 Bath Road, Emsworth, Hants PO10 7ER (tel 01243-374376).
Proprietor: M V Coop.
In business since 1968.
Self-sail yachting holidays on the French Riviera and in Greece. Attended craft also available.

PORTWAY YACHT CHARTERS INTERNATIONAL
Dart Marine Park, Steamer Quay, Totnes, Devon TQ9 5AL (tel 01803-866622; fax 01803-866621).
Self Sail and Skippered sailing holidays from Portway managed bases in the Canary Islands and Turkey. Sailing holidays also arranged in Malta, Greece and Portugal.

SAILING HOLIDAYS LTD
105 Mt Pleasant Road, London NW10 3EH (tel 0181-459 8787; fax 0181-459 8798).
Directors: B E Neilson and H S Neilson.
In business since 1976.
Fully bonded member of AITO, ATOL 2580.
Holidays for 3000 annually.
Flotilla sailing holidays in the Greek Islands from May to October. Choose from a variety of different cruises and a range of yachts. For couples, families and groups up

to about 40. No experience necessary, and strict safety conditions. Prices from £345 to £875 including flights and accommodation on-board, with meals usually taken in local tavernas. Extra items such as windsurfers can be hired.

SAIL TRAINING ASSOCIATION
2a The Hard, Portsmouth, Hampshire PO1 3PT (tel 01705-832055/832056).
Patron: HRH The Duke of Edinburgh.
In operation since 1956.
Member of the Association of Sea Training Organisations, Royal Yachting Association and the Central Council for Physical Recreation.
Voyages provided for 1,800 each year.
The renowned tall ships, *Sir Winston Churchill* and *Malcolm Miller* provide a real taste of adventure for young men and young women aged 16 to 24 years. During the course of a fortnight's voyage, up to 1000 miles are sailed, visiting two or three foreign ports. No previous sailing experience is required. All safety equipment, instruction and food is included. Grants are available.
Also, adult voyages in the Canaries for varying age groups from 16 to 69 years old.
The Association also organises the annual *Cutty Sark* Tall Ships Races where young people from all nations compete.

TOP YACHT CHARTER LTD
Andrew Hill Lane, Hedgerley, Bucks, SL2 3UW (tel 01753-646636; fax 01753-645539).
Directors: D Mitchell, R Mitchell, M Gale.
In business since 1982.
Member of AITO, ABSC, ATOL 1761.
Bareboat charter sailing around Turkey and Greece from May to November. Plan own cruise. Price: £600 per person, travel inclusive, two weeks. Skippers should be competent yachtsmen. Also crewed yachts and motor sailers.
'Exciting sail, beautiful anchorages, warm sea, lots of sun and good breezes.'
Ages: one to 80 years.

Americas

PENELOPE KELLIE WORLDWIDE YACHT CHARTER & TOURS
Steeple Cottage, Easton, Winchester, Hants S021 1EH (tel 01962-779317; fax 01962-779458). E-mail pkellie@yachtors.u-net.com
Member of the Yacht Charter Association, Latin America Travel Association and American Society of Travel Agents.
Yacht charters worlwide in well appointed and prestigious yachts with excellent crews. Charterts can be arranged to suit individual requirements as well as on shore itineraries. Special naturalist and diving cruises worldwide, but especially to the Galapagos Islands of Equador.

Asia

J & C VOYAGEURS
Buckridges, Sutton Courtenay, Abingdon, Oxfordshire OX14 4AW (tel 01235-848747).
Sailing holidays on Eastern Mediterranean (Turkey) charters. Sail on a 60 foot luxury motor yacht. Equipment on board includes windsurfers, Laser sailing dinghy, Avon sports boat, water skis, snorkelling equipment and sunbeds. Destinations can include uninhabited islands, deserted coves, Lycean, Hellenistic and Byzantine remains, ports etc. Visits can be arranged to places of architectural interest such as Ephesus, Myra, Didime, Patara and Termessos. Breakfast and lunch or dinner on board, one meal a day eaten on shore. Operates May to October from £750 for one week to £1,250 for two weeks in October.

McCULLOCH YACHT CHARTER
32 Fairfield Road, London E3 2QB (tel 0181-983 1487).
Proprietors: Dr Marc E Heine.
In business since 1985.
Holidays for approx. 200 annually.
Gulet cruising around Turkey from April to October. Wide range of motored crewed sailing yachts for families, groups or business entertaining. Prices from £200 per day per yacht. Double cabins, cook provided. Food and flights extra.
Accompanied children only; Maximum age: 75 depending on fitness.

Middle East

WEXAS INTERNATIONAL
45-49 Brompton Road, London SW3 1DE (tel 0171-589 3315).
Member ABTA number 91989, IATA number 91212122.

Nile cruising between Luxor and Aswan in Egypt, with a variety of boats from traditional wooden feluccas to luxury cruisers. Duration from seven to 15 days including full sightseeing in Cairo, Luxor and Aswan.

Scuba Diving and Snorkelling

Worldwide

AQUATIC ENCOUNTERS INC
1966 Hardscrabble Place, Boulder, Co 80303 USA (tel +1 303 494 8384; +1 303 494 1202).
President: Marc Bernardi.
In business since 1987.
About 250 holidays arranged annually.
Specialises in adventurous scuba diving tours though snorkellers are also welcome. Sites include Galapagos Islands, Papua New Guinea, Ningaloo Reef (Australia) and Thailand. Dates vary according to the area: e.g. Ningaloo April/May, Galapagos May/June and December/January. Divers must have scuba certification for open water. Prices range from $4000 to $6,000 (about £2,469-£3703) which includes live aboard boats and hotel accommodation at the beginning/end of a trip, tanks and weights. Other personal equipment such as a diving suit can be hired. The range of sea life encountered is staggering from whale sharks to playful sea-lion cubs that nip the divers' fins.

ARC JOURNEYS
102 Stanley Road, Cambridge CB5 8ZB (tel 01223-779200; fax 01223-779090).
Tours to many of the world's best diving sites. Destinations include Sulawesi, Flores, Moluccas, Thailand, Borneo, Austrailia, Vietnam, Madagascar and the Galapagos Islands. Typical prices from £500 per week (flights extra) including good accommodation and breakfast. Individuals and groups catered for. No age limits, but unaccompanied young people are not accepted.

BRITISH SUB-AQUA CLUB
Telford's Quay, Ellesmere Port, South Wirral, L65 4FY (tel 0151-350 6200).
Founded in 1953 the BSAC is the governing body for the sport of scuba diving in Britain and offers instruction through its 1,500 branches and over 250 schools in the UK and overseas.

FRONTIER
77 Leonard Street, London EC2A 4QS (tel 0171-613 2422; fax 0171-613 2992).
E-mail: enquiries@frontier.mailbox.co.uk
Internet: www.mailbox.co.uk/frontier
Frontier conservation expeditions are looking for divers to survey coral reefs, mangrove wetlands and seagrass, which dominate the coastal margins of Tanzania and Mozambique. Survey work is undertaken through general habitat mapping and coral reef survey, complimented by studies of natural resource utilisation by local inhabitants. Each project runs throughout the year for ten week stints and is self-funded, which means each volunteer will need to raise between £2800 and £3000 which covers flights, insurance, food, accommodation, field equipment and a residential briefing weekend. Enthusiasm and tolerance are the most important qualities needed as all the work will be supervised by qualified scientific and logistical staff (most of whom are former volunteers). If you think you can rise to the challenge ask for a free information pack.

REEF & RAINFOREST TOURS LTD
Prospect House, Jubilee Road, Totnes TQ9 5BP (tel 01803-866965; fax 01803-865916).
Diving holidays all year round in Belize's Barrier Reef, Costa Rica's Cocos Island, Indonesia which has the greatest aggregate length of coastline in the world for diving, the Bay and Islands of Honduras and Oman. Open Water Dive Courses are available for beginners in most shore-based locations, but others are only suitable for experienced divers. Prices £1000-£2500, including flights.

REGAL DIVING AND TOURS LTD
22 High Street,, Sutton, Ely, Cambs. CB6 2RB (tel 01353-778096; fax 01353 777897).
E-mail: andy@regal-diving.co.uk
Internet: http://www.regal-diving.co.uk
Director: ART Telford, M Telford.
In business since 1986.
Member BS-AC, PADI.
Diving holidays for over 6000 provided every year.
Individuals and groups catered for. Holidays operate all year round in Egypt, Jordan, Maldives, Caribbean, Galapagos and Solomon Islands. Non-experienced to experienced divers welcome. Prices

£299-£3000 for range of accommodation from self-catering to five star hotel. Equipment provided and can also be hired. Windsurfing and safaris also available.
Minimum age: 12 years (accompanied); 18 years (unaccompanied).
Maximum age: 70 years.

England

DIVING LEISURE UNLIMITED
Rockley Park, Hamworthy, Poole, Dorset BH15 4LZ (tel 01202-680898; fax 01202-680898). E-mail: steve.axtell@btinternet.com
Proprietors: S Axtell.
In operation since 1985.
PADI Five Star Instructor Development Centre & Training Facility.
Scuba diving holidays all year round based at Poole in Dorset. Various courses available including a five-day beginners' course. Price includes all equipment, certification, air etc. Accommodation in luxury caravans or local bed & breakfast. Tuition available up to instructor level. Certification is recognised by the Duke of Edinburgh Award scheme. Qualified divers welcome all year round for pleasure diving, also diving holidays abroad organised for qualified divers.
Minimum age: 12 years.

FALMOUTH UNDERWATER CENTRE
Maenporth Beach, Falmouth, Cornwall TR11 5HN (tel 01326-250852; fax 01326-378776).
Directors: H K Bazeley, S A Bazeley, K West.
In business since 1983.
PADI, BSAC, Falmouth Hotels Association.
Holidays for 500 arranged annually.
Scuba diving courses all year round based at Falmouth in Cornwall. Individuals, and groups of up to 22 catered for. Qualification courses (from two to five days) include BSAC Novice Diver (upgrade to Novice II), BSAC Sports Diver, PADI Open Water Diver, PADI Advanced Open Water Diver. Boat diving trips for qualified divers. Accommodation available locally. Prices from £99-£380 including all equipment. No experience necessary.
Physically, visually and mentally challenged people catered for.
Minimum age: 12 years (accompanied); 15 years (unaccompanied).

FORT BOVISAND UNDERWATER CENTRE
Fort Bovisand, Plymouth PL9 0AB (tel 01752-408021; fax 01752-481952).
Directors: D Welsh & D Carter.
In business since 1970.
Member of West Country Tourist Board, PADI 5-star facility, BSAC, World Underwater Federation, Plymouth Marketing Bureau.
Diving holidays and Sailing courses throughout the year. Based at a nineteenth century coastal fort on Plymouth Sound with own harbour. Courses for all levels plus underwater photography, marine biology and video courses. Prices vary according to accommodation and board, but range from basic bunk-bed in dormitory, to self catering, to en suite rooms with sea views. Price eg: five-day PADI Open Water (novice) £125, or £179 full board.
Minimum age: 15 years.

ISLAND UNDERWATER SAFARIS
'Nowhere', Old Town, St Marys, Isles of Scilly, Cornwall TR21 0NH (tel 01720-422732).
Proprietor: M Groves.
In business since 1984.
Member of BS-AC.
Diving and snorkelling programmes based on the Isles of Scilly. No experience necessary as expert tuition is provided by a qualified and experienced diver. Opportunities to snorkell with seals and marvel at the colourful marine flora and fauna. Operates between Easter and september. No accommodation provided but available locally. Diving Safari prices: £31 for three hours instruction/diving, all gear included. P.A.D.I diving courses available; Open Water £187.50 (four days), Advanced Open Water £150 (two days).

MAENPORTH SCUBA SCHOOL
Aqua House, 23 Tregoniggie Estate, Falmouth, Cornwall TR11 4SN (tel 01326-378878; fax 01326-378776).
Directors: H K Bazeley, S A Bazeley, K West and L West.
In business since 1995.
Member of PADI.
Holidays for 700 arranged annually.
Two to five-day scuba diving courses offered all year round in Falmouth. PADI Open Water Diver (Advanced also), Rescue Diver and Divemaster offered.

Prices from £99-£380 including all equipment. Accommodation available locally at all levels. No experience necessary. Groups of up to 20 catered for.
Minimum age: 12 years (accompanied); 15 years (unaccompanied).

Wales

FIELD STUDIES COUNCIL
Head Office, Montford Bridge, Shrewsbury SY4 1HW (tel 01743-850674; fax 01743-850178).
Specially for experienced divers with an interest in marine biology, Diving the Skomer Marine Reserve and Pembrokeshire Offshore Islands at the FSC's Dale Fort centre in Pembrokeshire in August. Dive sites range from the deep breathtaking drop along Skomer's north coast to the fast moving rapids of Little and Jack Sounds. Price from about £200 for five days inclusive of full board accommodation, tuition, air and the use of boats.
Minimum age: 16 years.

Ireland

D V DIVING
138 Mountstewart Road, Newtownards, Co. Down BT22 2ES (tel 01247-464671).
Proprietor: David Vincent.
In business since 1990.
Member of BS-AC, Association of BS-AC and H & SE Diving Contractor.
Holidays for around 100 annually.
Sub-aqua diving courses in clear water teeming with wildlife, from Easter to October. Also technical diving courses, nitrox, extended range, tri-mix gas blender, nitrox instructor.'Safe, enjoyable tuition by fully qualified instructors'. Prices from £40 to £350. Accommodation in B&Bs from £12 and local hostel from £7.70 to £17.70 full-board. Participants must be able to swim 100m and some courses require a medical certificate. For individuals and groups up to eight.
Minimum age: 14 years (accompanied); 16 years (unaccompanied).
Physically and visually challenged people welcome.

Europe

CALYPSO DIVING CENTRE
Marasli 24, Corfu 41900, Greece (tel +30 661-53101; fax +30 661-34319/53369)
Proprietor: Andreas Dukakis.
In business since 1986.
Member: PADI, SSI, ANIS, CMAS, BS-AC.
Calypso is the only diving school in Greece recognised by the Italian National Federation and has been awared PADI International Resort Centre status (NR 7893). Week-long diving courses for all levels of divers from April to the end of October. Courses start weekly. Also dive packs (six boat dives). Individuals and groups of up to 25. Prices vary according to season from US$290-$390 (about £180-£240) per week and from US$165-US$185 (about £100-£115) for dive packs. Prices include accommodation, breakfast and dinner and airport transfers. Self-catering accommodation can also be provided at the Calypso Diving Centre 16kms from Corfu town.

Calypso Diving centre has permission to dive the entire length of the western coast of Corfu (30 miles) as well as the outlying islands, such as Paxos. The use of the centre's high powered boats enables divers to reach spectacular and little-dived sites. Experienced site guides help divers to get the best out of the diving experiences.

Diving is adapted to the the experience of individual divers. Separate groups are made for beginners, intermediate and advanced divers.

Special dives and courses such as night, wreck and cave can be organised on request. A non-divers boat and beach excursions can also be arranged.

'Opportunities for deep dives, scenic dives for photographers. Some highlights include fascinating caves full of sea life, groupers and undersea arches.'

The latest and finest diving equipment is available for hire.

CORONA HOLIDAYS OF LONDON LTD
73 High Road, South Woodford, London E18 2QP (tel 0181-530 3747; fax 0181-530 3636).
Directors: A Cornish, J Cornish.
In business since 1981.
Holidays arranged for 4000 annually.

Dive the Canaries: Tenerife, Lanzarote, Gran Canaria and Fuerteventura at PADI dive centres all year. Trips run to the deep channel between Tenerife and Gomera, providing opportunity to view schools of pilot whales which can be found cruising year round. Prices from £300-£600, including self-catering accommodation. Diving equipment can be hired locally at the resorts. Individuals and groups up to 12.
Can cater for physically challenged people if already qualified divers.

DIVE CLUB NAUTIQUE
Puerto Deporitvo Marina del Este, 18690 Almunecar, Granada, Spain (tel/fax +34 58-827514).
Directors: Eddie and Walter.
In business since 1987.
Recognised by BSAC, CMAS, FEDAS and PADI.
Diving courses and packages for all levels operating throughout the year in a beautiful, rugged and unspoilt area 80kms east of Malaga. Full packages organised including car hire, accommodation and diving. For individuals and groups of up to 40. Dive Club Nautique has its own, charming, rustic characterful ten-room hotel (Hotel California tel +34 58 881038) with satellite T.V., Video etc. Bathroom or en suite.

THE LONDON UNDERWATER CENTRE
13 Glendower Road, London SW14 8NY (tel 0181-876 0735).
Director: Mr R Vallintine.
In business since 1981.
BS-AC recognised school (No. 14).
Scuba diving holidays in the Mediterranean from one to three weeks. Individuals and groups of up to 20 may be catered for. A BS-AC Novice Diver certificate is usually required and training to Novice is available before leaving. Courses leading to this and more advanced qualifications are run at the centre. Price includes accommodation and full board. Personal diving equipment is not included but may be hired.
Minimum age: 17 years.
Unaccompanied young people sometimes accepted according to circumstances.

OCTOPUS DIVING CENTRE
PO Box 124, Larnaca, Cyprus (tel/fax +357 4 646571).
In business since 1988.
BSAC School No R99 and PADI dive centre.
BSAC and PADI nitrox courses available.
Diving holidays based in Larnaca, Cyprus, 11 months of the year. Individuals and groups of up to 20 catered for. Prices from £13 a dive. Diving from the shore or from the dive centre's own purpose built hard boat *Zenobia II*. Licensed to dive the wreck *Ro Ro Zenobia*. Equipment hire and instruction available. Prices on request.
Minimum age: 12 years.
For more information contact Ian direct.

SUNVIL HOLIDAYS
7 & 8 Upper Square, Old Isleworth, Middlesex TW7 7BJ (tel 0181-847 4748).
Scuba diving holidays in Cyprus throughout the year in conjunction with Cydive, a BSAC/PADI five star school catering for beginners upwards.
Individuals and groups welcome. Price range from £350-£700 per person. Accommodation varies from self-catering apartment to half board hotel. Travel insurance (£21 for two weeks) not included.

Americas

DIVE BVI LTD
PO Box 1040, Virgin Gorda, British Virgin Islands (tel +1 809 495-5513; fax +1 809 495-5347).
Director: Joseph T Giacinto.
In business since 1975.
A PADI 5 Star Dive Center and NAUI Dream Resort.
Scuba diving adventures in the Caribbean for certified divers and beginners. Various courses from Open Water Upgrade to a Rescue Diver Course taught by highly trained Instructors and Divemasters. Prices around $640 for seven nights/five days diving. Range of local resort accommodation in five locations: Virgin Gorda Yacht Harbour; Leverick Bay, Virgin Gorda; Peter Island Hotel, Peter Island and Little Dix Bay Hotel, Virgin Gorda and Marina Cay.
Minimum age: 12 years (accompanied).
Some facilities are suitable for physically challenged people.

HARLEQUIN WORLDWIDE TRAVEL
Harlequin House, 2 North Road, South Ockendon, Essex RM15 6QJ (tel 01708 852780; fax 01708 854952).
Directors: Barry Fehler, Jaslyn Fehler.
In business since 1990.
Holidays for 1000 arranged annually.

Caribbean specialist for diving. Minimum seven nights, all year round. No experience needed as beginners can take a training course. Prices £600 to £2000. Wide choice of destinations and also whale and dolphin watching dive holidays. Any equipment needed can be hired.

THE LONDON UNDERWATER CENTRE
13 Glendower Road, London SW14 8NY (tel 0181-876 0735).
Scuba diving holidays in the Caribbean, from one to three weeks throughout the year. Individuals and groups of up to 20 may be catered for. A BS-AC Novice Diver certificate is usually required. Courses leading to this and more advanced qualifications are run at the centre. Price includes accommodation and full board. Personal diving equipment is not included but may be hired.
Minimum age: 17 years.
Unaccompanied young people sometimes accepted according to circumstances.

Africa

ACACIA EXPEDITIONS
27D Stable Way, London W10 6QX (tel 0181-960 5747).
Diving in Kenya all year. Individuals and groups. Tailor-made i.e. charters possible. No frills diving available.
PADI courses from Beginner to Dive Master.

SEYCHELLES UNDERWATER CENTRE
PO Box 384, Victoria, Mahe, Seychelles (tel +248 247357; fax +248 344223).
E-mail: divesey@seychelles.net
Internet: http://www.seychelles.net/divesey
Directors: G Sanders, D Rowat.
In business since 1985.
A PADI 5-star centre, Seychelles Professional Divers' Association, Seychelles Marine Charter Association, BS-AC.
Holidays provided for over 4,000 each year.
Scuba diving trips and training in the Seychelles all year round, although the best diving times are the spring and autumn. Individuals and groups of up to 16 may be catered for. No experience is required, though for advanced trips you will need a log book, diving licence and medical certificate. Price for two boat dives with tank, air, weights rental, plus bed and breakfast hotel accommodation in twin room is about £115. This includes use of bottles, air and weights but no scuba gear. Bring your own or hire gear from the centre. Multi-lingual, English, French and German speaking staff.
Minimum age: 12 years.

WEXAS INTERNATIONAL
45-49 Brompton Road, London SW3 1DE (tel 0171-589 3315).
Member ABTA number 91989, IATA.
Diving holidays and courses in the Indian ocean off the coasts of Kenya and Zanzibar. Options from seven days to 15 days for all grades from beginners to experts.

Asia

DIVE & SAIL
Nastfield Cottage, The Green, Frampton on Severn, Gloucestershire (tel 01452-740919; fax 01452-740943).
Proprietor: D Wright.
In business since 1986.
Holidays provided for 200-300 each year.
Member of BS-AC, PADI.
Live-aboard diving expeditions for one or two weeks in Turkey, the Maldives and Thailand throughout the year. Individuals and groups of up to 12 may be catered for. You will need an international diving certificate. Fully inclusive prices on enquiry. Yachts are crewed and have professional cooks. Personal diving equipment is not included in the price but may be hired.
Minimum age: 14 years.
Unaccompanied young people accepted.

FANTASEA DIVERS
PO Box 20, Patong Beach, Phuket, Thailand 83150 (tel +66 76 340088; fax +66 76 340309). E-mail: info@fantasea.net
Internet: http://www.fantasea.net
Director: J Deknatel M N Brusselers.
In business since 1979.
Member of DAN, PADI 5-star dive centre.
Holidays provided for 6000+ annually.
Phuket's quality Dive Centre. Daytrips, instruction and Live-Aboard cruises. Two 20 pax dive boats with daily trips to Phuket's dive-sites. Diving courses for all levels by multi-lingual instructors. Six and nine-day Live-Aboard cruises on yacht Colona II. All prices include tanks and weights, other

equipment for hire. Divers must show valid certificate.

UNDERWATER SAFARIS LTD
25c Barnes Place, Colombo 7, Sri Lanka (tel +94 1-694012/699756; fax +94 1-694029).
Managing Director: H Ekanayake.
In business since 1968.
Recognised by the Sri Lanka Tourist Board.
PADI Dive Centre — Resort Centre.
Scuba diving, underwater photography, continuing education programmes, naturalist, multi-level, boat deep, night and wreck diving. Foreign instructors. For individuals and groups. Daily diving excursions at Hikkaduwa (south-west coast) Coral Gardens Hotel from October to April. All equipment available for hire. Approximately US$33 per dive inclusive of boat and equipment. Open Water Diver course US$ 385; advanced course US$285. Prices include lectures, equipment, boat etc.

Australasia

DIVE & SAIL
Nastfield Cottage, The Green, Frampton on Severn, Gloucestershire (tel 01452-740919; fax 01452-740943).
Live-aboard diving expeditions for one or two weeks in Australia around the Great Barrier Reef, throughout the year. Individuals and groups of up to 12 may be catered for. You will need an international diving certificate. Fully inclusive prices on request. Yachts are crewed and have professional cooks. Personal diving equipment is not included in the price but may be hired.
Minimum age: 14 years.
Unaccompanied young people sometimes accepted.

EXMOUTH DIVING CENTRE
P O Box 573, Exmouth 6707, Western Australia (tel +61 8 99 491201; fax +61 8 99 491680).
Directors: M Toole, R Hall, T Medcraft, D Hall.
In business since 1991.
Exmouth Tourist Bureau and PADI member.
Diving for 8000 people arranged annually.
Whale shark diving, diving courses, and diving cruises. Cost of a diving course $299. Whale shark dives take place from mid-March to June and cost $299 for a full day which includes transport from your accommodation to Tantabiddi beach to board the vessel, lunch, tea and refreshments, diving and or snorkelling equipment and a scuba dive on the Ningaloo reef for qualified divers. Divemaster guidance throughout the day and on human/shark encounters. A light aircraft is used to track the sharks and guide the boat to them.
Some accommodation on site; otherwise accommodation to suit all budgets can be arranged.

Middle East

DIVE & SAIL
Nastfield Cottage, The Green, Frampton on Severn, Gloucestershire (tel 01452-740919; fax 01452-740943).
Live-aboard diving expeditions ex Sharm-el-Sheik (Red Sea) southwards for one or two weeks throughout the year. Individuals and groups of up to 12 may be catered for. You will need an international diving certificate. Fully inclusive prices given on enquiry. Yachts are crewed and have professional cooks. Personal diving equipment is not included in the price but may be hired.
Minimum age: 14 years.
Unaccompanied young people accepted.

EMPEROR DIVERS
22 High Street, Sutton, Ely, Cambs CB6 2RB (tel 01353-778096; fax 01353-777897).
E-mail: andy@regal-diving.co.uk
Internet: http://www.regal-diving.co.uk
Director: A Telford.
In business since 1986.
BSAC and PADI.
Holidays for 54,000 arranged annually.
Five-day diving courses based at Hurghada and Sharm el Sheikh. Egypt offered all year round. Individuals and groups. Prices from £299, bed and half board accommodation.

THE LONDON UNDERWATER CENTRE
13 Glendower Road, London SW14 8NY (tel 0181-876 0735).
Scuba diving holidays in the Red Sea, from one to three weeks, during the year. Individuals and groups of up to 20 may be catered for. A BS-AC Novice Diver certificate is usually required. Courses leading to this and more advanced qualifications are run at the centre. Price includes accommodation

and full board. Personal diving equipment is not included but may be hired.
Minimum age: 17 years.
Unaccompanied young people sometimes accepted according to circumstances.

SPEEDWING DIVERS
26 Temple Fortune Parade, London NW11 OQS (tel 0181-905 5252; fax 0181-458 3234).
Deputy Chairman: Simon Lewis.
Managing Director: David Kirsch.
In business since 1992.
ABTA, ATOL licensed.
Scuba diving holidays in the Red Sea for seven or 14 nights from October to May .

SUPERSTAR HOLIDAYS
UK House, 180 Oxford Street, London W1N 0EL (tel 0171-9574300; fax 0171-9574399).
Directors: D Saadon and Y Galon.
In business since 1983.
Member of AITO and ABTA.
Holidays for 6000-7000 annually.
Diving for beginners, advanced and experienced divers in Eilat on the Red Sea of Israel, from September to May. See some of the best flora and fauna on the coral reef in the Gulf of Eilat. Prices from £279-£1182 including accommodation in luxury hotels, Israeli buffet breakfast and six-day diving course.
Physically challenged people welcome.

WEXAS INTERNATIONAL
45-49 Brompton Road, London SW3 1DE (tel 0171-589 3315).
Member ABTA number 91989, IATA.
Diving holidays and courses in the Red Sea based at Hurghada, Sharm el Sheikh and Eilat. Options from seven days to 15 days for all grades from beginners to experts, plus live-aboard boat safaris amongst the uninhabited islands of the Red Sea.

Windsurfing and Surfing

England

CALSHOT ACTIVITIES CENTRE
Calshot Spit, Fawley, Southampton SO45 1BR (tel 01703-892077).
Windsurfing courses on the shores of the Solent. Three fleets of boards and a complete range of rig sizes to cater for all levels from beginner through to Instructors. Initial teaching takes place either on specialist simulators and in a sheltered creek, before moving on to more open water. Video coaching and back-up lectures. Weekend and week courses, fully residential and non-residential for both adults and young people. Prices start from £115, non-residential for a weekend coaching course. All specialist equipment including protective clothing is provided.
Minimum age: ten years.

EUROYOUTH
301 Westborough Road, Westcliff, Southend-on-Sea, Essex SS0 9PT (tel 01702-341434; fax 01702-330104).
Windsurfing courses at International Windsurfing School, Southend. Five hours instruction over two weeks June-September. Paying guest accommodation arranged with private families.
No experience needed.
Minimum age: 14 years.
Unaccompanied teenagers: 16 years + .

FREETIME HOLIDAYS
Runnelstone Cottages, St.Levan, Penzance, Cornwall TR19 6LU (tel & fax 01736-871302).
Proprietor: C South.
In business since 1978.
BSA approved, West Country Tourist Board.
Surfing holidays and courses arranged for 500 annually, plus day courses.
Surfing holidays based at Sennen Cove on the Lands End Peninsula, Cornwall. Easter to October. Clients should be able to swim. BSA Fin Award certificates can be awarded. Other activities also available include, bodyboards, mountain biking, climbing/abseiling and coastal walking. Individuals, families and groups of up to 50. Prices from £80 to £280 include self catering, camping and half board accommodation, all equipment and instruction.
Minimum age: 16 (unaccompanied).

HARBOUR SPORTS
The Harbour, Paignton, Devon TQ4 6DT (tel 01803-550180; fax 01803-558084).
Proprietors: F Sobey, J Smith.
In business since 1978.
Approved by the RYA.
Holidays for 500 arranged annually.
Windsurfing tuition in Paignton Harbour on the South Devon coast throughout the year. Accommodation organised locally. Instructors are fully qualified and issue RYA

Certificates. Half day lesson costs £25 including wet suit and other equipment.
Minimum age: 12 years.

HARLYN SURF SCHOOL

Newbrook, Homer Park Road, Trevone, Padstow, Cornwall PL28 8QU (tel 01841-521395).

In operation since 1995.
Member of BSA, NASC and Padstow Area Tourism Association.
Surfing courses for novices and intermediates located at Boobys, Constantine and Harlyn Bay in North Cornwall. Course lengths vary from half/full day to three, five or seven-day programmes between April and November. Prices from £30 per day to £70 for a three-day course (no meals or accommodation). Five-day Youth Hostel package: £210 including accommoodation, full board, surfing tuition, equipment and transport (seven-day package: £250 all inclusive). Hotel, B&B and camping accommodation available locally. Individuals and groups catered for.
Ages: 7-60 years (16 years unaccompanied). Ability to swim essential.

OUTDOOR ADVENTURE

Atlantic Court, Widemouth Bay, Nr Bude, Cornwall EX2 3ODF (tel 01288-361312).

BSA surfing and RYA windsurfing holiday courses for adults. Weeks, three-day and weekend breaks. Surfing for beginners and improvers. RYA levels 1-5. Inland and sea locations. Experienced, qualified instruction. Individuals and groups. Equipment (including full wetsuit) provided. Price for weekend £127 (surfing); £143 (windsurfing) and week £297 (surfing); £327 (windsurfing). Full board in twin rooms at Seafront Centre. Other activities include canoeing, ski-surfing, sailing, climbing and mountain biking. Vegetarians and special diets catered for.
Minimum age: 16 years.

THE OUTDOOR TRUST

Belford, Northumberland NE70 7QE (tel/fax 01668-213289).

RYA Approved Windsurfing School.
Holiday and instructor courses up to level three and personal sailing assessments up to level four. Also Junior Windsurfing. In addition the Trust is an approved RYA powerboat centre and offers instruction in handling and safety techniques.

SPINERD SAILBOARD SCHOOL

Lake 10, Spine Road, Cerney Wick, Cirencester, Glos. GL7 5QH (tel 01285-861555).

Partners: A D Belcher, P M Belcher.
RYA recognised school.
Windsurfing lessons at the Cotswold Water Park throughout the year. Swimming ability necessary. Price £20 for two hours; from £7 per hour to hire. Groups of up to 20 catered for.
Minimum age: 12 years.
Physically and mentally challenged people catered for where possible.

SURFACE WATERSPORTS

Rutland Water, Whitwell Day Sailing Centre, Empingham, Leicestershire LE15 8BL (tel 01780-460464; fax 01780-460632).

Windsurfing courses on Rutland Water, Europe's largest artificial lake. A variety of one-day courses, plus a two-day beginners course, leading to RYA Level One standard in two four-hour sessions. Price for the two-day course is £80, including all equipment. Hotels and bed and breakfast available locally. Also canoeing and sailing courses.
Unaccompanied young people accepted from nine years.

TORQUAY WINDSURFING SCHOOL

55 Victoria Road, Ellacombe, Torquay, South Devon TQ1 1HX (tel 01803-212411; fax 01803-329850).

Partners: A Shorland.
In operation since 1979.
Windsurfing courses run on Torre Abbey Sands from May to September. Prices of £9 per hour including all equipment. Beginners course £72 for eight hours. Only requirements are good health and ability to swim. Groups catered for.
Minimum age: 12 years.

WINDSURFING WORCESTER

Worcester Road, Holt, Worcester WR6 6NH (tel 01905-620044; fax 01905-620022). Internet: http://www.winsurfing-worcester.co.uk

Proprietor: G Wooldridge.
RYA recognised school.
All year round tuition for windsurfing, dinghy sailing and canoeing. All equipment provided. Taster lessons from £10, Level 1 Course £72. Hire available. Caravanners and campers welcome.

Scotland

RAASAY OUTDOOR CENTRE
Raasay House, Isle of Raasay, by Kyle of Lochalsh, Ross-shire, Scotland IV40 8PB (tel 01478-660266; fax 014-660200).
Windsurfing holidays off the Inner Hebridean Isle of Raasay. Other watersports activities include canoeing and sailing. Groups of up to 50 catered for. No experience needed. Prices from £330 per week for adults and £279 per week for children. Accommodation in twin, double, family and alpine-style rooms in a Georgian mansion. Full board, tuition and all equipment provided.
Unaccompanied young people accepted from nine years.

TIGHNABRUAICH SAILING SCHOOL
Tighnabruaich, Argyll, PA21 2BD (tel 01700-811396).
Windsurfing Holidays for individuals and groups of up to 20. One or more weeks from May to September. All equipment provided. Wide range of accommodation available locally. Courses from £135 per week.
Minimum age: 12 years.

Wales

PLAS MENAI NATIONAL WATERSPORTS CENTRE
Llanfairisgaer, Caernarfon, Gwynedd LL55 IUE (tel 01248-670964).
Beginners, Improvers, funboard, and new wave weekends and weeks windsurfing. Courses are based on the Menai Strait and Anglesey which provide a wide range of wind and sea conditions to suit each course level. Weekend and five-day courses. Prices: two-day £115, five-day £295 includes all instruction, equipment, shared accommodation and full board.
Minimum age: 14.
For youth courses, see *Young People's Holidays.*

Ireland

SHARE CENTRE
Smith's Strand, Lisnaskea, Co Fermanagh BT92 OEQ, Northern Ireland (tel 013657-22122/21892; fax 013657-21893).
RYA Windsurfing: Beginners, Improvers and Instructor Training and assessment courses at a lakeside activity centre.
'The aim is for the integration of able-bodied and disabled people.'
Minimum age (unaccompanied): 14 years.

UNIVERSITY OF LIMERICK ACTIVITY AND SAILING CENTRE
Two Mile Gate, Killaloe, Co. Clare, Ireland (tel +353 61-376622; fax +353 61-376765).
Windsurfing courses on Lough Derg in County Clare. No accommodation on site but can be arranged locally.
Minimum age: nine years (accompanied); 16 years (unaccompanied).
Physically challenged people catered for.

Europe

FREEDOM HOLIDAYS
30 Brackenbury Road, London W6 OBA (tel 0181-741 4686; fax 0181-741 9332).
Proprietor: Paul Noyes-Thomas.
In business since 1969.
Member of ABTA; ATOL No 432.
Windsurfing holidays from May to October in Greece (at Club Vassiliki on Levkas, Kefalos Bay on Kos and Paleochora in western Crete. Also, windsurfing at Tarifa, south west Spain and Bitez in Turkey. Prices range from £105 to £130 per week for equipment and tuition, in addition to package holiday prices of £185-£330 (one week) and £215 to £350 (two weeks) depending on the season and quality of accommodation. Travel Insurance: £21/£25 for one/two weeks.

SUNVIL HOLIDAYS
7 & 8 Upper Square, Old Isleworth, Middlesex TW7 7BJ (tel 0181-847 4748).

Windsurfing holidays in Greece from May to October. Two centres: Parga for beginners and improvers and high-wind Paleochora (on Cretan south coast) for intermediates and experts. Tuition available. Price range from £335-£563. Travel insurance not included at £21 for two weeks cover.

SUNWORLD SAILING HOLIDAYS
120 St George's Road, Brighton, E Sussex BN2 1EA (01273-626284 — reservations; 01273-626283 — brochure line).
Windsurfing, sailing and yachting holidays with instruction at all levels in Greece, Turkey and Spain. Summer or winter. Prices include flights, accommodation, equipment and tuition. No experience needed. Mountain biking also available. Families welcome.
Any age.

TARIFIC HOLIDAYS
P.O. Box 88, Chichester, West Sussex PO20 7DP (tel 01243-511139; fax 01243 513132).
Windsurfing holidays in Spain on the Mediterranean at Tarifa ('statistically the windiest place in Europe'). Tarific holidays is the UK booking agent for the Hurricane hotel and can pre-book windsurfer hire or tuition or you can bring your own equipment. Board hire from £125 per week with plenty of opportunity to change equipment on a daily basis to suit the prevailing weather. Clients should also book their own flights although Tarific have a list of providers of flights to nearby Malaga or Gibraltar from many UK airports. Special events are also organised from time to time.Tuition and windsurf hire can be pre-booked or bring your own equipment.

Tarific are also agents for the Peligoni Sailing and Windsurfing Club in Zakynthos, Greece (see *Watersports, General, Europe* page 173).

Middle East

FREEDOM HOLIDAYS
30 Brackenbury Road, London W6 OBA (tel 0181-741 4686; fax 0181-741 9332).
Windsurfing Holidays based at Hurgada or Safaga, Club Mistral on the Red Sea.

Whitewater rafting *Cinnamon Adventure*

Wildlife

One of the fortunate consequences of the increasingly urban lifestyle of modern man is his new awareness of the threats to the environment. Organisations such as the WWF (World Wildlife Fund for Nature) have encouraged the designation of many areas of the world as particularly worthy of preservation. Flora and fauna are protected not only for their varied beauty and interest but also to maintain the ecological balance.

There are seven National Parks in England — Peak District, Lake District, North York Moors, Yorkshire Dales, Northumberland, Dartmoor and Exmoor; and three in Wales — Brecon Beacons, Pembrokeshire Coast and Snowdonia (see map on page 74). Between them they cover nearly 9% of the land area of England and Wales. There are also several Nature Reserves and extensive Forestry Commission areas; and wildlife lovers will also find a great deal to interest them in their local hedgerows and fields.

Details of Britain's National Parks are available from the Countryside Commission, John Dower House, Crescent Place, Cheltenham, Gloucestershire GL50 3RA (tel 01242-521381). For information on National Trust properties, write to the Trust at 36 Queen Anne's Gate, London SW1H 9AS (tel 0171-222 9251). The Young Ornithologists' Club (part of the Royal Society for the Protection of Birds) organises residential birdwatching courses for those aged nine to 16. Individual membership of the RSPB costs about £22 and the YOC £8, from the Club at The Lodge, Sandy, Bedfordshire SG19 2DL (tel 01767-680551).

The Natural History Book Service (2-3 Wills Road, Totnes, Devon TQ9 5XN; tel 01803 865913; fax 01803 865280), book suppliers to the international community of naturalists, scientists and conservationists has now put their comprehensive catalogue on the internet at the NHBS Web Site:http://www.nhbs.co.uk. Access to the Web Site is free and all of the titles can be ordered through e-mail (nhbs@nhbs.co.uk) and free, printed catalogues are also available on request.

The first section of this chapter deals with general and miscellaneous wildlife holidays which range from identifying fungi in Sussex to tracking gorillas in Rwanda. This is followed by separate sections for birdwatching and botanical holidays and finally one for safaris.

General

Worldwide

ANIMAL WATCH
Granville House, London Road, Sevenoaks, Kent TN13 1DL (tel 01732-741612; fax 01732-740736).
Directors: Mr S V Robbens, Mr V G Durrant and Mrs M Robbens.
In business since 1987.
Member of ABTA and IATA.
Holidays for 100-200 arranged annually.
Wildlife watching holidays to destinations worldwide, for one to three weeks all year round. Opportunities to get close to different species of wildlife: mountain gorillas, whales, seal pups, dolphins and polar bears with an emphasis on conservation. Prices from £1600 to £5000. For individuals and small groups of ten.
Possibilities for physically challenged people on some programmes.

CYGNUS WILDLIFE HOLIDAYS
57 Fore Street, Kingsbridge, Devon TQ7 1PG (tel 01548-856178; fax 01548-857537).
Directors: Mr J F Spry, Mrs C Spry.
In business since 1980.
Member of ATOL.
Holidays for 200 arranged annually.
Escorted birdwatching and natural history holidays, guided by experienced ornithologists to destinations worldwide, all year round. Wide range of tours covering Sri Lanka, Northern India, Texas, Northern Argentina, Australia, Nepal, Ethiopia, Majorca, Poland, and more. For individuals and groups of between six and 18 people. Prices from £625 to £3390 including full-board accommodation in three-star hotels, or the best available in remote locations and guide. No experience necessary.

DISCOVER THE WORLD
29 Nork Way, Banstead, Surrey SM7 1PB (tel 01737 218800; fax 01737 362341).
Directors: Clive Stacey and Mark Leaney.
In business since 1991.
Member of ABTA, AITO and ATOL licensed.
Wildlife and wilderness holidays offered worldwide throughout the year, ranging from unusual weekend breaks to complex expeditions lasting for several weeks. Choose from a weekend dolphin watch in Gibraltar (from £315); bird watching in Iceland (from £893); swimming with dolphins in the Bahamas from £1438; blue whale watching in California (about £1400); and many other exciting holidays worldwide. Prices include economy return flights and accommodation which will vary depending on the trip. All the holidays are informative and fun. Group sizes are kept small to reduce the impact on the environment and guides and escorts are experienced and add further insight and knowledge. Discover the World donates a percentage of its income to conservation work — which means that the consumer has a chance to contribute to the conservation of the wildlife observed.
Minimum age: eight years accompanied, 15 years unaccompanied.

FIELD STUDIES COUNCIL OVERSEAS
Montford Bridge, Shrewsbury SY4 1HW (tel 01743-850164/850522);fax 01743 850599/850178).
Flowers, birds, photography, ecology, archaeology, landscapes, conservation, butterflies and dragonflies, mammals and marine life are some of the topics examined in a broad-ranging programme of environmental study tours of one to four weeks' duration, visiting destinations from the Outer Hebrides to the Falkland Islands and from China to Peru. All courses are fully escorted, often by two expert leaders, and fees are fully inclusive (transport, accommodation, meals, local entry fees and full instruction and guidance).

FOOTPRINT
Lincoln LN6 OXD (tel 01522-690852; fax 01522-501392). E-mail sales@footventure.co.uk
Internet: http://www.footventure.co.uk
Directors: Georg Seywald, Jane Seywald.
In business since 1989.
Footprint provide trekking, birdwatching and wildlife holidays. Most tours have been designed to depart at any time with a minimum of two people. Nepal, India, Malaysia, Indonesia, Thailand, Papua New Guinea, New Zealand, Romania, Kenya, Tanzania, Zimbabwe, Uganda, Ethiopia, Namibia, Botswana, Mozambique, South Africa, Costa Rica, Venezuela and Ecuador A network of long-established ground operators and highly qualified local guides is used. On most tours, clients are met on arrival and transferred to their hotel.

FOREST TRAILS LTD
Oakdene, High Street, Heathfield, East Sussex TN21 0UP (tel 01435-864078; fax 01435-867921).
Directors: A H Brooking and M P Brooking.
In business since 1992.
Wildlife and Eco-Tourism trips to Central America, South America, the Caribbean, Spain and Borneo, throughout the year. See the spectacular range of birds, butterflies, rainforests and orchids of Costa Rica, or visit the exotic Amazonian forest by dugout canoe; the birds and flowers of Catalonia in Northern Spain, the coral reefs of Trinidad and Tobago and the Proboscis Monkeys of Borneo. Prices from £900 to £2000 including full-board accommodation in hotels and lodges, guides and airport transfers. Personalised itineraries or guided groups for between of six to ten people.
Minimum age: 18 years (younger if accompanied).

Physically challenged people welcome where possible.

GULLIVER'S NATURAL HISTORY TOURS
Oak Farm, Stoke Hammond, Milton Keynes MK17 9DB (tel 01525-270100; fax 01525 270777).
Birdwatching, plant hunting and the general enjoyment of nature worldwide. Holidays include tropical adventure in Costa Rica, Cyprus in springtime, Crete flora and fauna, Israel migration, flowers and birds in Uzbekistan and the Pyrenees, summer birdwatching in Hungary, and nature tours to the Seychelles and scenery birds and wildlife in Zimbabwe. Tours of various lengths up to about 15 days depending on destination. Prices from £699 for a week in Cyprus to £2399 for two weeks in Costa Rica.

MURPHY'S WILDLIFE HOLIDAYS
12 Belvoir Close, Belvoir Park, Belfast, Northern Ireland BT8 4PL (tel 01232-693232; fax 01232-644681).
Proprietor: C W Murphy.
In operation since 1990.
Holidays for approximately 250 arranged annually.
Wildlife watching holidays in Britain, Ireland and abroad throughout the year. From weekends to two weeks. Groups of four to 12 led by expert guides. Weekends from £125, weeks from £400 and fortnights from £600. Comfortable accommodation and full board are included in the prices.
Minimum age: 15 (unaccompanied).

NATURAL HABITAT ADVENTURES
2945 Center Green Court, South Boulder, Colorado-80301, USA.
In business since 1985.
Holidays for 800-1,000 arranged annually.
Wildlife adventures/photo safaris organised worldwide including Canada, USA, Mexico, Ecuador, Malaysia and Africa. Trips take place all year round. Individuals and groups of any size catered for. Themes include polar bear watching on the Hudson Bay, whale watching in the lagoons of Mexico's Baja peninsula, seal watching in the Gulf of St Lawrence, swimming with dolphins in the Bahamas and more. Trip lengths vary from six to 14 days. Prices from £900-£3,000 include the best possible accommodation in the area.
Physically challenged people catered for.
UK Agent: The Faraway Traveller, Gallery Travel Ltd, Old Manor House, High Street, Mayfield, East Sussex TN20 6AL (tel 01435-873666).

THE NATURAL WORLD
57 Church Street, Twickenham TW1 3NR (tel 0181-744 0474; fax 0181-744 0574).
A range of adventurous wildlife tours at sea, up rivers and on land lasting from nine to 22 days in Madagascar, Mauritius, the Galapagos, Guyana, Newfoundland, Uganda, Brazil, Borneo, Costa Rica, California (The Bay of Cortez), Zambia, Tanzania, Botswana and Nepal.

WILDLIFE DISCOVERY
Lesbourne House, South Road, Reigate, Surrey RH2 7JS (tel 01737-223903; fax 01737-241102).
Director: Charles Robinson.
General and specialist wildlife and ornithological tours to Africa, North and South America, India, South-East Asia and Australasia all year round. Prices £1600-£2500. Quality accommodation in hotels, lodges and tented camps whichever is the most appropriate to be close to the wildlife.
No age limits.
Physically challenged people catered for at particular destinations — happy to accommodate if/where possible.

WILDLIFE TRAVEL
Green Acre, Wood Lane, Oundle, Peterborough PE8 5TP (tel 01832-274892).
Directors: David Bodger, Richard Hobbs, Michael Singh.
In business since 1988.
Member of Green Flag International and Wildlife Trusts Partnership.
Holidays for 150 arranged annually.
Wildlife holidays with walking and painting in various locations worldwide — the Alps, Mediterranean, Canada, China, Nepal, Sikkim, South Africa and Australia, from February to October. For groups of 12-20 people. Prices from £550-£2,500 including two to four-star hotel accommodation, most meals and expert leaders as guides. Profits donated to conservation projects at home and abroad.
Minimum age: ten years (accompanied).

WILDLIFE WORLDWIDE
170 Selsdon Road, South Croydon, Surrey CR2 6PJ (tel 0181-667 9158; fax 0181-667 1960).
Partners: Chris Breen, David Mills.
In business since 1992.
AITO member.
Journeys for 150 to 200 arranged annually.

Wildlife holidays of varying duration offered all year round worldwide including, Zambia, Botswana, Zimbabwe, Namibia, Tanzania, Kenya, Uganda, Malawi, South Africa, India/Nepal, Bhutan, Indonesia, Australia, New Zealand, Brazil, the Antarctic and European fly-drives. Most journeys last ten to sixteen days except the Subantartic voyages which last eight to 29 days and the Antarctic voyages which last between 14 and 20 days. Prices from £1000 to £10,000 per person with a typical price of about £2,500. Prices are generally fully inclusive.
Minimum age: generally 11 years is the minimum for full appreciation.

England

ACORN ACTIVITIES
P O Box 120, Hereford HR4 8YB (tel 01432-830083; fax 01432-830110).
Wildlife weekends, birdwatching, photography, painting and drawing in Herefordshire, Shropshire and Wales. Sites of Special Scientific Interest. Last vestige of real woodland, wildlife and habitats. Also marine life including seals, porpoises and bottle-nosed dolphins and a day on Skomer Island with spectacular sea bird colonies. Choice of hotels, farmhouses, group accommodation and self-catering. Prices: Accommodation from £22 per night; Activities from £40 per day.

CASTLE HEAD FIELD CENTRE
Grange-over-Sands, Cumbria LA11 6QT (tel 015395-34300).
Natural history and wildlife observation in South Lakeland; courses arranged for viable groups of young people. Heated accommodation and meals in field centre. Facilities include a well-equipped laboratory and a nature reserve. Wide range of habitats to be visited including the inter-tidal areas of Morecambe Bay, limestone fringe and the high fells of Lakeland.
'The only requirement is a genuine interest in the natural world.'
Minimum age: nine years.

THE EARNLEY CONCOURSE
Earnley, Chichester, West Sussex PO20 7JL (tel 01243-670392).
Administered by The Earnley Trust Ltd. In business since 1952 (Earnley Concourse since 1975).
Recognised by ETB.
Holidays for 4000 arranged annually.
Wildlife courses for individuals and groups with tuition and full board accommodation. Instruction given in birdwatching, wildflower studies and photography.
Minimum age: 16 years.

FIELD STUDIES COUNCIL
Head Office, Montford Bridge, Shrewsbury SY4 1HW (tel 01743-850674; fax 01743-850178).
Badgers, bats, butterflies — the FSC has a huge range of wildlife study courses to choose from, running throughout the year at its seven residential field centres in England. The choice includes courses studying a particular topic, like the Small Mammal Weekend at Flatford Mill in Suffolk, or Looking at Ladybirds at Juniper Hall in Surrey; or general natural history courses like Lakeland in Spring or Discovering Shropshire.
No experience needed on many courses. Prices from about £250 for a week, £95 for a weekend including full board accommodation and tuition.
Minimum age: 16 years, except on courses arranged for families.

HF HOLIDAYS LTD
Imperial House, Edgware Road, London NW9 5AL (tel 0181-905 9556).
Wildlife holidays at one of many HF country locations nationwide. Price from £280 for seven nights full board. Five to eight miles walking per day. No experience needed. Call for a Special Interest Holidays brochure.

TRIPS WORLDWIDE
9 Byron Place, Clifton, Bristol BS8 1JT (tel 0117 987 2626; fax 0117 987 2627).
Wildlife, birdwatching, botanical, trekking, safari and rainforest trips worldwide but with emphasis on Central America. Runs a special interest and adventure travel agency. Does tailormade and also takes individuals.

Tailor made tours to Central America and the Alternative Caribbean including, Mexico, Belize, Guatemala, Honduras, Costa Rica, Cuba, Trinidad and Tobago, Dominica and Surinam.

All itineraries for individuals and groups can be based around particular interests:

diving, wildlife, Mayan culture, archaeology, conservation, birds, fishing and trekking.

Tailormade itineraries start at £1200 based on two people sharing for a two-week itinerary including flights and accommodation.

THE WILDAID FOUNDATION TRUST
Staffordshire Wildlife Rescue and Rehabilitation Centre
Spinks Lane, Kingsley, Nr. Cheadle, Staffordshire ST10 2BX (tel 01538-754784).
Curator: Jonathan Hodges.
Registered Charity No 1001595.
Situated in the beautiful Churnet Valley, the sanctuary offers a unique experience, and close encounters with many species of birds and mammals from all over the world, in a natural woodland setting. Educational and guided tours for day visitors at 11am and 2.30pm from April to November. No-one under five years old can be accommodated. Visitor Centre with shop and light refreshments.

Scotland

C-N-DO SCOTLAND
77 John Player Building, Springbank Road, Stirling FK7 7RP (tel/fax 01786-445703).
Established 1984.
Year round Scottish walking holidays for individuals or groups with or without walking experience with much to interest birdwatchers and wildlife enthusiasts. Prices from £75. A variety of accommodation is available. Some equipment can be hired. 'We come across wildlife at ease in its natural environment: a fawn asleep, ptarmigan roosting, ospreys fishing. . .'
Minimum age (unaccompanied): 18 years.
Physically challenged people can often be catered for.

HF HOLIDAYS LTD
Imperial House, Edgware Road, London NW9 5AL (tel 0181-905 9556).
General study of wildlife on Arran in May and September. Also Loch Leven. Price around £290 for seven nights full board. Clients should be confident of being able to walk five to ten miles over rough ground and steep ascents. No experience needed. Call for a Special Interest Holidays brochure.

ISLE OF COLONSAY HOTEL AND CHALETS
Isle of Colonsay, Argyll PA61 7YP (tel 01951-200316).
Partners: Kevin & Christa Byrne.
In business since 1977.
Holidays for 1400 guests annually.
Wildlife holidays on a remote island off the west coast. Hotel or chalet accommodation available throughout the year. The island is home to wild goat, otters, 150 types of British bird and 500 species of flora. Other activities available include sailing, cycling and golf.
Book direct or through ABTA agents.

KINDROGAN FIELD CENTRE
Enochdhu, Blairgowrie, Perthshire PH10 7PG (tel 01250- 881286).
In operation since the 1960s.
Residential courses with full board and lodging. All aspects of natural history including bird watching, mountain flowers and fungi. Also, art and photography and skiing in winter.

WILD EXPLORER HOLIDAYS
Skye Environmental Centre, Broadford, Isle of Skye IV49 9AQ (tel 01471-22 487).
Directors: Paul and Grace Yoxon.
In operation since 1984.
Holidays for 1200 arranged annually to 12 Hebridean Islands. Wildlife, natural history, geology and archaeology holidays, weekends to weeks during most of the year. Prices from £290 including full board, transport and guide.
Wild Explorer Holidays is a registered charity whose profits go directly into wildlife conservation.
Minimum age: ten years.
'Otters and Golden Eagles provide memorable highlights to any visit'.

Wales

FIELD STUDIES COUNCIL
Head Office, Montford Bridge, Shrewsbury SY4 1HW (tel 01743-850674; fax 01743-850178).
Badgers, bats, butterflies, the FSC has a huge range of wildlife study courses to choose from, running throughout the year at it's three residential field centres in Wales.

The choice includes courses studying a particular topic, like the Introduction to Butterflies and Moths course at Rhyd-y-creuau in Snowdonia, or Insects and other Invertebrate Life of Pembrokeshire at Dale Fort; or general natural history courses like Natural History of the Pembrokeshire Coast and Offshore Islands or Bat Ecology. No experience needed on many courses. Price of about £250 includes full board accommodation and tuition.
Minimum age: 16 years, except on courses arranged for families.

FOCUS HOLIDAYS AT 'ARGOED'
'Argoed' Guest House, Crafnant Road, Trefriw, County of Conwy LL27 0TX (tel 01492-640091).
Proprietors: P Booth and K A Booth.
In business since 1987.
Wildlife walks and birdwatching holidays in Snowdonia. Weekends and weeks from March to October. Groups of up to 12 catered for. Prices range from £70 for a weekend to £220 for a week, including accommodation and all meals.
Unaccompanied children not accepted.

Europe

WILD EXPLORER HOLIDAYS
Skye Environmental Centre, Broadford, Isle of Skye IV49 9AQ (tel 01471-822487).
Wolf and bear watching in the wild in the Taiga forest of Russia. Prices include full board, transport and guides. Profits from the holiday go into the Central Forest Biosphere Reserve which is where the trip is based, and so participants have the knowledge that their money goes directly into helping and preserving the bears and wolves they are seeing.

Americas

ECOSUMMER EXPEDITIONS
1516 Duranleau Street, Vancouver V6H 3S4, British Columbia, Canada (tel +1 604 669-7741; fax +1 604 669-3244).
Expedition Director & Founder: Jim Allan.
In business since 1976.
Sea Kayaking expeditions with emphasis on understanding the need for preservation of the world's wildlife areas. May-September British Columbia, N.W.T., Yukon, High Arctic and Greenland; January-April Belize, Bahamas and Mexico; September-November Irian Jaya, Tonga, the South Pacific and Central Asia. For the 18th year — Orca Waters Sea Kayaking Venture — 'mixes the tranquillity of camping with the exhilaration of paddling amidst these powerful but gentle creatures'. Prices around CA$1095 (about £485) for seven days. Accommodation is in tents, most meals are cooked around the campfire by the guides. No experience is necessary as the double kayaks are very seaworthy and easy to handle. Maximum group size of ten with two experienced and knowledgeable guides. Children aged eight plus on some trips.
Maximum age — not as important as physical fitness.

EXODUS EXPEDITIONS
9 Weir Road, Balham, London SW12 0LT (tel 0181-675 5550 or 0181-673 0859 24 hrs).
Exploration of the Galapagos Islands combined with a short jungle safari in Ecuador's Cuyabeno National Park in search of giant turtles, iguana, sea lions and many varieties of birdlife. Tours take place from March to August and in October, from £2150 for 21 or 22 days. Also a special project to observe Polar Bears on their traditional migration route at Cape Churchill in Canada during September and October, from £1460 for ten days. Other wildlife treks and adventure holidays in Peru, Venezuela, Bolivia, Costa Rica, Argentina, Chile, Mexico and Brazil's Pantanal; also Trinidad and Tobago and Beluga whale tours in Canada's Hudson Bay.

EXPLORE WORLDWIDE LTD
1 Frederick Street, Aldershot, Hampshire GU11 1LQ (tel 01252-344161; fax 01252-343170).
Small group exploratory holidays lasting two to four weeks. 22-day tours of the Galapagos and Amazon, using small charter launches to explore the flora and fauna of the islands. Price from £2099. Also visits to Brazil's Mato Grosso and nature reserves in the Pantanal region. 29 days from £2,690.

FIELD STUDIES COUNCIL OVERSEAS
Montford Bridge, Shrewsbury, SY4 1HW (tel 01743-850164).

Natural history tours to Guatemala, the Falkland Islands, the White Mountains and the Canadian Rockies.

GEODYSSEY
29 Harberton Road, London N19 3JS (tel 0171-281 7788; fax 0171-281 7878).
Small group journeys and specialist for Venezuela for birdwatching, photography and history. Tours are designed to see major habitat types and a wide range of species. Transport by 4WD vehicles, mules, light planes and native dugout boats. Prices from £995-1545 including most meals and all accommodation, from hotels, lodges and simple guest houses to hammocks and tents. Insurance and international flights not included in price. No experience necessary.
Minimum age : 14 years (younger people catered for on tailor-made family tours).
Maximum age: 65 years (without a doctor's certificate).

HOSKING TOURS LTD
Pages Green House, Wetheringsett, Stowmarket, Suffolk IP14 5QA (tel 01728-861113).
Wildlife photographic holidays on The Falkland Islands in December/January. See the flora and fauna of the South Atlantic. £3550. Camera equipment and film not included. Clients are asked to attend a pre-tour meeting where they will be advised which equipment would be useful and where to get it from. Groups of up to eight.
Minimum age: 18 years.

NATURETREK
Chautara, Bighton, Nr Alresford, Hampshire SO24 9RB (tel 01962-733051).
Whale watching holidays in Newfoundland in July. Opportunity to watch seabirds, dolphins and porpoises at close range. Also chance to explore the wild landscapes of Newfoundland, including walking amongst the fjords, lakes and waterfalls and the Long Range mountains of the Gros Morne National Park. Price approximately £1500.
Also wildlife holidays to Ecuador and the Galapagos Islands incorporating exploration by private motor yacht of the 'enchanted isles' and visit to Cotopaxi. Optional seven-day safari into the Amazon Jungle. 20 days, £3190; Amazon extension £890. Led by experienced ornithologist/ botanists. Groups of up to 15.

REEF & RAINFOREST TOURS LTD
Prospect House, Jubilee Road, Totnes, Devon TQ9 5BP (01803 866965; fax 01803 865916).
See hundreds of bird species, giant otters, seven species of macaw, and six of monkeys on a 14-day tour of the Manu Biosphere Reserve in Peru. Descent from the Andes through cloud forest to Amazonia and stay in a lodge in the most biologically diverse reserve in the world. Price: from £1598 per person sharing, plus flights from £600.
Also available: wildlife tours of Belize, Costa Rica, Venezuela. Also Papua New Guinea and Madagascar.

WILD QUEST EXPEDITIONS
29 Kings Court, Bishops Stortford, Herts, CM23 2AB (tel 01279-658714).
In business since 1986.
Adventurous expeditions (holidays) to the rainforests of Belize, Central America. No experience necessary — aimed at people looking for an unusual experience. The prices is £1600 for three weeks in Belize which includes all flights, food and accommodation. A large proportion of each trip is spent camping in the jungle. Mosquito nets, hammocks and group camping gear is supplied. Bring your own boots, rucksack, cutlery and a snorkel and mask for the Barrier Reef visits.
'A chance to experience Tropical Rainforest and the Caribbean culture first hand.'

WORLDWIDE JOURNEYS AND EXPEDITIONS
8 Comeragh Road, London W14 9HP (tel 0171-381 8638; fax 0171-381 0836).
Tailor-made tours of the rainforests of Ecuador and the Galapagos Islands for individuals and small groups. Fully inclusive packages.

Africa

ABERCROMBIE & KENT TRAVEL
Sloane Square House, Holbein Place, London SW1W 8NS (tel 0171-730 9600).
Directors: T D Holderness-Roddam, Mrs P H Stobbs, M C Thompson, D Weber, S Feagler, B S Whittaker, R D Winder.
In business since 1962.
Game viewing, trekking, safaris and hot air balloon trips in Kenya. Accommodation in

Kichwa Tembo luxury tented camp in Masai Mara Game Reserve, Ngorongoro Crater Lodge, Tanzania and Windsor Golf and Country Club in Nairobi.
North American headquarters: 1520 Kensington Road, Oak Brook, IL 60521, USA.

EXPLORE WORLDWIDE
1 Frederick Street, Aldershot, Hampshire GU11 1LQ (tel 01252-344161; fax 01252-343170).
Small group exploratory holidays using land rovers and trucks or on foot, exploring game reserves in Kenya, Uganda, Tanzania, Malawi, Zimbabwe, Zambia, South Africa, Botswana and Namibia. Two to four weeks from £1165. Accommodation in hotels and lodges and under canvas.

LET'S GO TRAVEL
P O Box 60342, Nairobi, Kenya (tel +254-2 213033 & 340331; fax +254-2-214713 & 254-2-336890).
Walking, trekking, horseback, camel back safaris in Kenya. Four-day camping safari in Uganda to search for gorillas. 13-day birding safari in Kenya April, May and June (Mt. Kenya, Rift Valley Lakes, Kakemega Forest and the Masai Mara).

Arctic

FIELD STUDIES COUNCIL OVERSEAS
Montford Bridge, Shrewsbury SY4 1HW (tel 0743-850164).
Environmentally aware wildlife study courses and exploration visits to the Canadian Arctic, Spitsbergen and Iceland under the expert guidance of tutors with an in depth knowledge of the countries visited.

Asia

ABERCROMBIE & KENT TRAVEL
Sloane Square House, Holbein Place, London SW1W 8NS (tel 0171-730 9600).
Treks, soft adventure and wildlife holidays in the Himalayas. Accommodation in tented camps (all meals included) and hotels. White water rafting down Nepal's rivers and tiger tracking by elephant in the jungles of Chitwan National Park. Opportunities to see the endangered Indian, one-horn rhinoceros as well as many other species of tropical flora and fauna. Also available: jeep safaris and treks in India; private tours in Bhutan, Tibet, Ladakh and Pakistan and the Silk Road from China.

EXODUS EXPEDITIONS
9 Weir Road, Balham, London SW12 0LT (tel 0181-675 5550 or 0181-673 0859 24 hrs).
Explore nature reserves for Himalayan flora and fauna as part of a wide choice of treks and adventure holidays. Visits to the Wolong Nature Reserve in China to see giant pandas and to Indonesia's Komodo Island to find its large monitor lizards. Elephant safaris in Nepal's Chitwan National Park, seeing rhino and tigers during 17-day tour costing around £1,150.

EXPLORE WORLDWIDE LTD
1 Frederick Street, Aldershot, Hampshire GU11 1LQ (tel 01252-344161; fax 01252-343170).
Small group exploratory holidays in Nepal. Game viewing in Chitwan National Park using elephants or dugout canoes. 17 to 25 days from £1289. Also tiger safaris in India's northern game parks from £1369.

NATURETREK
Chautara, Bighton, Nr Alresford, Hampshire SO24 9RB (tel 01962-733051).
Wildlife and trekking holidays in the jungles of Bhutan, Southern India, Rajasthan, the Himalayas, Malaysia and Ladakh. Two, three and four-week holidays which operate throughout the year. Led by experienced ornithologist and/or botanist.

TIGER TOPS NEPAL
P O Box 242 Kathmandu, Nepal (tel +977 1 411225; fax +977 1 414075/419126). E-mail: tiger@mtn.most.com.np
Tiger Tops Jungle Lodge in the Royal Chitwan Park is built with materials from the surrounding forest. Activities at the lodge include nature walks, wildlife viewing on elephant back, landrover drives, boat trips, jungle treks, birdwatching excursions and photographing from machans (blinds), slide shows and the services of experienced naturalists.

Australasia

NATURETREK
Chautara, Bighton, Nr Alresford, Hampshire SO24 9RB (tel 01962-733051).
Wildlife holidays in Western Australia looking at mammals and wildflowers (22 days, £2490) and the National Parks of New Zealand incorporating North and South Island, Stewart Island and Fiordland, plus two short treks. Groups of up to 15. Led by experienced botanists and/or ornithologists.

Birdwatching

Worldwide

ABERCROMBIE & KENT TRAVEL
Sloane Square House, Holbein Place, London SW1W 8NS (tel 0171-7309600; fax 0171-7309396).
Escorted birdwatching tours to Ethiopia, Kenya, Tanzania, Zambia, Zimbabwe, Botswana, Madagascar, India, South and Central America.

BIRDQUEST LTD
Two Jays, Kemple End, Birdy Brow, Stonyhurst, Lancashire BB6 9QY (tel 01254-826317; fax 01254-826780).
Directors: M Beaman and M Morton.
In business since 1981.
ATOL no. 2937.
Holidays arranged for 600 annually.
Long distance birdwatching holidays all year round on every continent including pioneering journeys to the world's last wild frontiers. Over 50 countries visited and a choice of over 70 tours. Prices for between 8 and 30 days from £1050-£5000 includes suitable accommodation and all meals. Group size is limited: seven to 12 people, plus one-two expert leaders and guides.
Minimum age: 16 years.

FIELD STUDIES COUNCIL OVERSEAS
Field Studies Council, Montford Bridge, Shrewsbury SY4 IHW (tel 01743-850164; fax 01743-850599).
Birdwatching courses organised worldwide, from the Scilly Isles, Islay, Mull and the Outer Hebrides throughout Europe in Andalucia, Mallorca, Camargue, Cevennes, Pyrenees, Picos de Europa, Poland and Morocco, also further afield to Guatemala, Peru, the Galapagos, the Falkland Islands, India and Nepal. Small groups of ten to 15 people; all abilities welcome, especially beginners and anyone wishing to expand identification skills.

GOURMET BIRDS
Birdwatching holidays, Windrush, Coles Lane, Brasted, Westerham, Kent TN16 1NN (tel 01959-563627; fax 01959-562906).
Proprietors: David & Janet Tomlinson.
In business since 1984.
Holidays for 40-70 arranged annually.
Worldwide birdwatching holidays from January to December. For individuals and groups up to 12. Prices from £180 to £3300 including quality accommodation, all food and wine. Some birdwatching experience advised.
Minimum age: 12 years (accompanied).

LIMOSA HOLIDAYS
Suffield House, Northrepps, Norfolk NR27 0LZ (tel 01263-578143; fax 01263-579251).
Partners: Chris & Barbara Kightley, Keith Beswick, Steve Madge.
In business since 1985.
Member of AITO and ATOL/CAA.
Holidays arranged for 300-400 annually.
Wide-ranging programme of escorted birdwatching tours throughout Europe and selected destinations worldwide all year round. All levels of experience catered for from beginner to expert. Individuals or groups up to 14 guided by one/two experienced leader(s). £600-£3500 including full-board accommodation in hotels, motels, lodges or camps, depending on destination. Own optical equipment needed.
Minimum age: 18 years.
Maximum age: 80+.

England

THE EARNLEY CONCOURSE
Earnley, Chichester, West Sussex PO20 7JL (tel 01243 670392).
Birdwatching courses for individuals and groups. Accommodation available. Field trips arranged to explore the birdlife in the variety of habitats in West Sussex, including wetlands and estuaries, woods and downland.
No experience needed.
Minimum age: 16 years.

FIELD STUDIES COUNCIL
Head Office, Montford Bridge, Shrewsbury SY4 1HW (tel 01743-850674; fax 01743-8501780).
Bird study courses throughout the year, with tuition on identification, at five of the FSC's centres in England. The choice includes: Spring Birds and their Songs weekends at Flatford Mill in Suffolk, In Search of the Red Kite at Preston Montford in Shropshire in July and Birds of High Summer at Nettlecombe in Somerset. Prices from about £255 for a week, £100 for a weekend inclusive of accommodation, all meals, tuition and transport. No experience needed on many courses.
Minimum age: 16 years, except on Young Ornithologists' Club courses arranged at Flatford Mill.

HF HOLIDAYS LTD
Imperial House, Edgware Road, London NW9 5AL (tel 0181-905 9556).
Birdwatching weeks based at HF Country Houses located nationwide. Daily expeditions to wide range of bird habitats with slides, recordings and lectures in the evenings. Participants are asked to bring binoculars, strong footwear, waterproofs, notebook and pocket field guide. Prices from £334 for seven nights full board and accommodation. Reduced rate rail travel available. No experience needed. Call for a Special Interest Holidays brochure.

NORTH WEST BIRDS
Barn Close, Beetham, Cumbria LA7 7AL (tel/fax 015935-63191). E-mail: 101456.3506@compuserve.com
Sole Trader: Mike Robinson.
In business since 1996.
Member of Cumbria Tourist Board, Bird Information Service.
Weekend and week long birdwatching breaks in Cumbria all year round. Groups of up to 4 catered for. Prices from £119-£320 including full board, twin rooms, packed lunch and transport. No experienced required. Binoculars and equipment not included in the price but can be provided.
'A new birdwatcher saw 108 birds in one weekend, including eagles and a bittern in the same day.'
Minimum age: 14 years (unaccompanied).

Wales

FIELD STUDIES COUNCIL
Head Office, Montford Bridge, Shrewsbury SY4 1HW (tel 01743-850674; fax 01743-850178).
Bird study courses throughout the year, with tuition on identification, at the FSC's three centres in Wales. The choice includes: Recording Birdsongs at Dale Fort in Pembrokeshire in April and Spring Birds of Snowdonia at Rhyd-y-creuau in May. Prices from about £255 for a week, £100 for a weekend inclusive of accommodation, all meals, tuition and transport.
Minimum age : 16 years (except on Young Ornithologists Club arranged at Dale Fort).

Europe

HONEYGUIDE WILDLIFE HOLIDAYS
36 Thunder Lane, Thorpe St Andrew, Norwich NR7 0PX (tel/fax 01603-300552).
Proprietor: Chris Durdin.
In business since 1991.
Holder of ATOL no. 3253, Member of many conservation organisations.
Holidays arranged for around 80 annually.
Birdwatching and wildlife holidays in Crete, Fuerteventura,Spanish Pyrenees, Menorca, France and Italy, March-June. Good quality accommodation, off the beaten track, normally country houses or small hotels with full board. £720-£1100 for one or two weeks. All holidays include a £25 donation per person to a project run by the local bird protection society in the country visited. 'By staying in the community and meeting local conservationists, the holidays are more than just a birdwatching trip'.

POLNET TRAVEL
10 The Mead, Beckenham, Kent BR3 5PE (tel 0181-6500286; fax 0181-4026678).
Eight-day ornithological tour of the Bialowieza Forest and Biebrza Marshes in Poland. Itinerary includes a Bison reserve visit, boat trip on the Narew River and a guided city tour of Warsaw. Prices include

accommodation in hotels and boarding houses, half board, ground transportation, English speaking guide and city tour (£395 per person for a double room, single supplements available).

SUNBIRD
PO Box 76, Sandy, Bedfordshire SG19 1DF (tel 01767-682969; fax 01767-692481).
E-mail: sunbird@sunbird.demon.co.uk
Directors: David Fisher, Bryan Bland, Steve Rooke and Will Russell (USA).
In business since 1979.
Birdwatching tours throughout the year to Finland, Mallorca, Spain, Morocco, the Canary Islands, Slovakia, Poland, Cyprus, Austria, Norway, Romania, Greece, Czech Republic, Israel and Egypt. Small groups led by full-time professional leaders in self-drive minibuses for maximum flexibility. Suitable for beginners and more experienced birdwatchers. Tour price includes flights from London, all transport, accommodation and meals. 200-page brochure free on request.

Africa

NATURETREK
Chautara, Bighton, Nr Alresford, Hampshire SO24 9RB (tel 01962-733051).
Birdwatching holidays in Africa. 15-day holiday to the High Atlas Mountains of Morocco, incorporating eight-day trek in Mount Toubkal National Park. Price £990. Tours led by experienced botanist and/or ornithologist. Groups of up to 15 catered for. Prices range from £790-£3490. Accommodation is fully serviced camping or luxury hotels and lodges in cities. Sleeping bags and outdoor clothing not included but can be hired. Some meals, airport taxes and drinks not included.
Minimum age; 15 years.
Maximum age: 80 years.

OKAVANGO TOURS AND SAFARIS
Gadd House, Arcadia Avenue, London N3 2JT (tel 0181-343 3283; fax 0181 343 3287).
Directors: Peter Sandenberg and Jane Durham.
In business in Africa since 1985, in London since 1989.
Photographic birdwatching safaris for the casual and serious ornithologist in Botswana, Zambia, Zimbabwe and Namibia. Visit during November to March to catch the migratory birds but the remaining months are rich with birdlife varieties. Individual and small groups are catered for. Prices start from approx. £2100 including long-haul flight from UK.
Minimum age: 12 years (accompanied).

SUNBIRD
PO Box 76, Sandy, Bedfordshire SG19 1DF (tel 01767-682969).
Birdwatching tours throughout the year to Egypt, Morocco, Gambia, Gabon, Ethiopia, Kenya, Cameroon, Zimbabwe, Namibia and South Africa. Small groups led by full-time professional leaders in self-drive minibuses for maximum flexibility. Suitable for beginners and more experienced birdwatchers. Tour price includes flights from London, all transport, accommodation and meals. 200-page brochure free on request.

Americas

SUNBIRD
PO Box 76, Sandy, Bedfordshire SG19 1DF (tel 01767-682969; fax 01767-692481).
Birdwatching tours throughout the year to Point Pelee and Churchill in Canada, Cape May, Texas and Arizona, California, Peru, Trinidad and Tobago, Jamaica, Bolivia, Venezuela, Ecuador, Argentina and Mexico. Small groups led by full-time professional leaders in self-drive minibuses for maximum flexibility. Suitable for beginners and more experienced birdwatchers. Tour price includes flights from London, all transport, accommodation and meals. 200-page brochure free on request.

Arctic

ARCTIC ODYSSEYS
2000 McGilvra Blvd East, Seattle, WA 98112, USA (tel +1 206-3251977; fax +1 206-7268488).
Ornithological odyssey to Siberias Lena River Delta State Nature Reserve. Provides the ultimate in Arctic birdwatching. Price for 13 days, $5980 (about £3700) ex Seattle.

EXPLORE WORLDWIDE LTD
1 Frederick Street, Aldershot, Hants GU11 1LQ (tel 01252-344161: fax 01252-343170).
Birdwatching and nature walks in Iceland. Small group tours led by experts. Travel by four-wheel drive mountain bus. Ten or 14 days from £1160.

Asia

NATURETREK
Chautara, Bighton, Nr Alresford, Hampshire SO24 9RB (tel 01962-733051).
Birdwatching holidays in the Langtang valley of Nepal (24 days, £1890) and Bhutan's Bumthang Valley (three weeks, £2990). Groups of up to 15. Led by experienced ornithologists.

Botanical

Worldwide

DAVID SAYERS TRAVEL
54 High Street, Uppingham, Rutland LE15 9PZ (tel 01572-821330; fax 01572-821072).
Escorted botanical tours in Europe and beyond. Destinations vary each year but some of the previous ones include the Azores, Spain, Cyprus, Dominica, New Zealand and India. Individuals and groups of about 12 people (never larger than 18). Itineraries generally encompass scenic, natural, historical and local ethnic aspects. Trips to individual Azore islands also arranged.

FIELD STUDIES COUNCIL OVERSEAS
Field Studies Council, Montford Bridge, Shrewsbury SY4 1HW (tel 01743-850164/850522; fax 01743-850599).
Botanical study courses and wild flower expeditions from the Arctic to the tropics, catering for all levels of knowledge and experience. Groups of ten to 15 people are led by expert botanists to Colonsay, the Burren, the Alps, Pyrenees, Picos de Europa and Canary Islands and further afield to the Canadian Rockies, Arizona, Seychelles, Thailand and South Australia.

England

THE EARNLEY CONCOURSE
Earnley, Chichester, West Sussex PO20 7JL (tel 01243-670392).
Field trips to the Sussex coast and the woodlands and chalk downlands of the South Downs to examine the wild flowers of the area. Help is given with identification, and there are talks and slides of rare and common wild flowers. Price for weekend about £150 including accommodation, meals, tuition and use of facilities.

FIELD STUDIES COUNCIL
Head Office, Montford Bridge, Shrewsbury SY4 1HW (tel 01743-850674; fax 01743-850178).
Flowers, ferns, fungi- grasses, lichens, mosses. The FSC has a huge range of botanical study courses to choose from, running throughout the year at it's seven residential field centres in England. The choice includes courses studying a particular topic, like the Weekend on Lichens course at Flatford Mill in Suffolk, or Wild Flowers of the Borderland at Preston Montford in Shropshire, or more general courses like Mosses, Liverworts and Lichens at Blencathra in the Lake District. Prices from about £255 for a week, £100 for a weekend inclusive of accommodation, all meals and tuition.
Minimum age: 16 years, except on courses arranged for families.

Wales

FIELD STUDIES COUNCIL
Head Office, Montford Bridge, Shrewsbury SY4 1HW (tel 01743-850674; fax 01743-850178).
Flowers, ferns, fungi-grasses, lichens, mosses. The FSC has a huge range of botanical study courses to choose from, running throughout the year at it's three residential field centres in Wales. The choice ranges from courses for beginners, like the Wildflowers for Beginners course at Rhyd-y-creuau in Snowdonia, or the Introduction to Lichens weekend at Dale Fort in Pembrokeshire in October. Also, courses studying a particular subject in depth like Fungi

of Snowdonia at Rhyd-y-creuau in September, and the Botany of Pembrokeshire course at Dale Fort in late May. Prices from £255 a week, £100 for a weekend, inclusive of accommodation, all meals and tuitions. Minimum age: 16 years, except for courses arranged for families.

Europe

RAMBLERS HOLIDAYS
Box 43, Welwyn Garden City, Herts. AL8 6PQ (tel 01707-331133).
Alpine flowers and photography holidays walking in the Pyrenees, Austrian, French and Swiss Alps, Crete and Southern Greece. One or two weeks April-October. Hotel accommodation, half or full pension. Average of five or six hours of hiking daily to upper slopes, ridges, meadows and valleys. As the snow melts, the meadows are covered with narcissi and other alpine flowers. Boots or shoes with moulded rubber soles needed.

Asia

HIMALAYAN KINGDOMS
20 The Mall, Clifton, Bristol BS8 4DR (tel 0177-923 7163; fax 0117-974 4993).
Trek through the beautiful domain of Sikkim, carpeted with orchids and rhododendrons, in both pre- and post-monsoon seasons. Conversely, try the remote and mountainous 'Hidden Kingdom of Bhutan', a land of supernatural legends, ancient monastic fortresses and sacred rituals. Further details available on request.

NATURETREK
Chautara, Bighton, Nr Alresford, Hampshire SO24 9RB (tel 01962-733051).
Bumthang Valley, including seven-day trek through forests of Central Bhutan (three weeks, £2990) and China's Sichuan Province (21 days from around £3000). Groups of up to 15. Led by experienced botanists.

Safari

Africa

ABERCROMBIE & KENT TRAVEL
Sloane Square House, Holbein Place, London SW1W 8NS (tel 0171-730 9600). Bookings in North America through: 1520 Kensington Road, Oak Brook, Ilinois 60521, USA.
Wildlife safaris in the game reserves of Kenya throughout the year. Accommodation in luxury tents, lodges and hotels with all meals. Add-ons available to the Kenya coast for swimming, underwater diving and marlin or shark fishing. Other safaris in Zambia, Tanzania, Uganda, Ethiopia, Zimbabwe, Malawi, Botswana and Namibia available with visits to a variety of game parks, Mount Kilimanjaro, Mount Kenya etc. Prices from £898 including return flight London-Nairobi. Individual arrangements or small escorted tours.

Also four-day gorilla tracking expeditions in Uganda. Camp accommodation. Stalking the gorillas on foot in the Bwindi National Park.

ACACIA EXPEDITIONS
27D Stable Way, London W10 6QX (tel 0181-960 5747; fax 0181-960 1414).
Specilising in adventure holidays and camping safaris in East and Southern Africa, from 3 days to 3 months. Egypt and Morocco also available, including Nile cruises and mountain treks. All safaris are fully inclusive of game park fees, treks, transport, cooking and camping equipment. Priced from just £25 per day including meals. An excellent way to experience Africa for budget minded the 18-55's.

AFRICA EXCLUSIVE
66 Palmerston Road, Northampton NN1 5EX (tel 01604-28979).
Safaris arranged all year round in Zimbabwe, Botswana and Namibia individuals and groups of up to 24. Price of £2500 includes air fares and all ground arrangements. Acommodation in high quality safari lodges and four or five star hotels on a fully inclusive basis.
'Genuine small group African adventure with a high standard of comfort and very

professional guide. Many locations are remote'.
Minimum age: 12 years (accompanied).

AFRICA TRAVEL CENTRE
Cleveland Travel Ltd, Leigh Street, London WC1H 9QX (tel 0171-387 1211; 0171-383 7512).
In business since 1986.
Wildlife safaris in Africa throughout the year. All major destinations featured: South Africa, Zimbabwe, Namibia, Botswana Kenya and Tanzania.

All grades and types of trip: overland tours, camping trips, luxurious lodges and tented camps. Also specialist flight only department.

Prices from £295 for a two-week gorilla safari.

Unaccompanied children not accepted.

ART OF TRAVEL LTD
21 The Bakehouse, Bakery Place, 119 Altenburg Gardens, London SW11 1JQ (tel 0171-738 2038; fax 0171-738-1893). E-mail: artravel@dircon.co.uk
Tailor-made safaris in East, central and southern Africa, all year round. Trips include opportunities for ballooning, canoeing, rafting, riding, walking, diving, camel riding and other activities. Prices vary between £2500 and £3500, depending upon tour budget and requirements.
Unaccompanied young people may be accepted from 16 years.

CAMPFIRE CLASSIC ADVENTURES
Lowlands, Homanton, Shrewton, Salisbury SP3 4ER (tel/fax 01980-620839).
Wildlife tracking, river, elephant back, train and photography safaris in Botswana, Zimbabwe and South Africa. Individuals and groups catered for. Typical price: £2,000 (all inclusive). Accommodation in camps and lodges. Detailed information pack available on request.
Minimum age: 12 years (unaccompanied).

DRAGOMAN ADVENTURES
28 Camp Green, Debenham, Suffolk IP14 6LA (tel 01728-861133; fax 01728-861127).
Three to ten-week safaris in southern, central and East Africa. Variety of trips including visits to the Gorillas in Uganda, Serengeti and Ngorongoro Crater in Tanzania, South Luangwa National Park in Zambia, Matobo and Lake Kariba in Zimbabwe, Chobe National Park, the Okavango Delta in Botswana, Kruger National Park in South Africa, Etosha National Park and Cape Cross Seal Colony in Namibia. Accommodation mainly camping. Transport by expedition vehicle. Groups prepare three meals a day on equipment provided. Prices from £180 a week including fuel, tolls, vechicle, crew, plus kitty for food, campsites, etc.
Minimum age: 18 years.

ELITE VACATIONS
Elite House, 98-100 Bessborough Road, Harrow, Middlesex HA1 3DT (tel 0181-864 9818; fax 0181-426 9178).
Safaris in Kenya, Tanzania, Namibia, Zimbabwe and South Africa. As well as fixed itinerary safaris, Elite can also tailor make 'adventure' safaris including camel-trekking, ox-wagon safaris, fishing safaris, climbing Mts. Kilimanjaro and Kenya. Safaris last eight, nine or 16 days. Prices from £898 (seven nights Kenya) to £1897 Kenya/Tanzania spectacular (13 nights).Different types of accommodation can also be arranged. Together with Kingfisher Elite offer traditional tented safaris mainly based in the secluded areas of the the Tsavo East National Park in Kenya. One safari includes 11 nights at the Kingfisher Lodge and three nights on an exclusive, private safari on a full board basis £1557-£1785.

ENCOUNTER OVERLAND
267 Old Brompton Road, London SW5 9JA (tel 0171-370 6845).
Safaris in East and Southern Africa from two to nine weeks. Game parks in Uganda, Tanzania, Ethiopia, Zambia, Zimbabwe, Botswana, Namibia and South Africa, with options to climb Kilimanjaro or see the mountain Gorillas. Travel in four-wheel drive safari trucks. All camping equipment supplied (except sleeping bag) and all meals are included in the price.
Exciting new 28-day trip called the Roots of Southern Africa, from Capetown to Harare visiting South Africa, Lesotho, Swaziland, Mozambique and Zimbabwe. Cost £1063.

EXODUS EXPEDITIONS
9 Weir Road, Balham, London SW12 0LT (tel 0181-675 5550 or 0181-673 0859 24 hrs).
Wildlife safaris to see Rhino on the Zambezi in Zimbabwe, mountain gorillas in their natural habitat in Zaire and chimpanzees in Tanzania. Also game viewing safaris by foot or vehicle in Kenya, Zambia, Uganda, Botswana, Namibia, Swaziland and Zambia. Prices range from £570 to £2600, six to 24 days with departures all year round.

EXPLORE WORLDWIDE LTD
1 Frederick Street, Aldershot, Hants GU11 1LQ (tel 01252 344161; fax 01252-343170).
Wide range of small group safaris, including Kenya, Zambia, Uganda, Zimbabwe, Zambia, South Africa, Madagascar, Tanzania, Namibia, Malawi and Botswana. Take in some of Africa's best game reserves. Highlights include climbing Mount Kilimanjaro, Tanzania's Selous Reserve and big game spotting. Camping, hotels and mountain huts. Prices, including flight from London, from £928.

FOOTPRINT ADVENTURES
5 Malham Drive, Lakelands, Lincoln LN6 OXD, Lincs. (01522-690852; fax 01522-501392). E-mail: sales@footventure.co.uk
Internet: http://www.footventure.co.uk
Footprint provides a wide range of wildlife, birdwatching and walking safaris to east and southern Africa. These can be hotel-based, or in lodges or camping. The majority of the tours are based on scheduled departures, all year round, visiting the major game parks in Kenya, Tanzania and Uganda including climbing Mt Kenya, Kiliminjaro and Ruwenzori trekking. The southern Africa safaris cover national parks in South Africa, Zimbabwe, Botswana, Namibia and Mozambique.

GRENADIER SAFARIS
11-12 West Stockwell Street,Colchester C01 1HN.
Managing Director: J Ewart.
In business since 1986.
ATOL no 2955.
Safaris of any duration in Zimbabwe, Zaire, Uganda, Kenya, South Africa, Malawi, Namibia, Botswana, Zambia and Tanzania, all year round. Camping or canoe safaris, as well as more luxurious tours. Prices range between £1900 and £3000. All prices include full board.
Minimum age: 12 years, if accompanied.

GUERBA EXPEDITIONS LTD
Wessex House, 40 Station Road, Westbury, Wiltshire BA13 3JN (tel 01373-826611).
'Africa in Close-up' safaris throughout Africa including West Africa, Kenya, Tanzania, Zimbabwe, Botswana, Namibia, South Africa. Departures all year round are fully escorted, mostly in Guerba's own vehicles. All camping equipment supplied but own sleeping bag needed.

HARTLEY'S SAFARIS, UNITED KINGDOM
3 Bailgate, Lincoln, LN1 3AE (tel 01522-511577; fax 01522-538580). E-mail: hartleys@easynet.co.uk
Operating since 1988.
Member of SATOA, ATTA, SATSA, ATOL 3958.
Tailor made Safaris incorporating various forms of travel including (horse, elephant, walking, rafting, canoeing and ballooning) in the southern part of the African contiment in Botswana, Zimbabwe, Zambia, Malawi, Namibia and South Africa) and the Indian Ocean Islands (Mauritius, Benguerra Island and the Comores). Price range of £2500-£3,500 per person for two weeks all inclusive. Tours operate all year round. Accommodation varies and may include safari tents, lake houseboats, safari lodges and country house hotels and island lodges.

HOOPOE ADVENTURE TOURS
Suite F1, Kebbell House, Carpenders Down, Watford WD1 5BE (tel 0181-4288221; fax 0181-4211396). E-mail: hoopoeuk@aol.com
Directors: P Lindstrom, S Laiser, O Davidson, S Khetia.
In business since 1991.
Member of ATTA.
Tailor-made safaris to Tanzania and Kenya operating all year. Holidays include trekking, hiking, mountain climbing, wildlife viewing and scuba diving options. Thirteen-day safari begins and ends in Arusha National Park, with stops at Kiruruma, the Ngorongoro Crater, Lake Natron, Lake Manyara and Tarangire National Park. Seven-day safari includes highlights of the Serengeti and Ngorongoro. Both safaris combine canvas and lodge accommodation. Limited of eight people per group. Prices from $1500 including luxury meals (drinks extra).
Unaccompanied young people not accepted.

HOSKING TOURS LTD
Pages Green House, Wetheringsett, Stowmarket, Suffolk IP14 5QA (tel 01728-861113; fax 01728-860222).
Wildlife photographic holidays on a Kenyan safari from October. Highlights include: the open Savannah, woodlands and rivers of the Masai Mara Game Reserve, occupied by herds of wildebeest, and the Lakes of the Rift Valley to which wildlife is drawn. Price £2790. Camera equipment and film not

included. Clients are asked to attend a pre-tour meeting where they will be advised which equipment would be useful and where to get it from. Groups of up to 12.
Minimum age: 18 years.
'Close encounters with nature and being able to record this on film.'

J & C VOYAGEURS
Buckridges, Sutton Courtenay, Abingdon, Oxfordshire OX14 4AW (tel 01235-848747).
Directors: Jennie Humphreys; Caroline Newell. In business since 1989. Member of Worldwide Fund for Nature.
Safaris include: wildlife safari in Botswana's Okavango Delta and the Kalahari Desert, February to December for 11 to 12 days from £2400. Also safaris in Kenya, Tanzania, Uganda, Malawi, Zambia, South Africa and Zimbabwe by four-wheel drive, boat or walking. Climbing and whitewater river rafting opportunities. Groups of four to eight people. General prices approximately £2500 which include tents and all meals. Led by experienced guides.
Minimum age: 12 years.
'Special holidays in countries of intrinsic interest preferably in remote places off the usual tourist routes.'
For young peoples' safari see *Young People's Holidays* section.

LET'S GO TRAVEL
P O Box 60342, Nairobi, Kenya (tel +254-2 213033 & 340331; fax +254-2-214713 & 254-2-336890).
Established 1979.
Member: IATA, Kenya Assoc. of Tour Operators.
Camel back safaris, horse riding safaris, walking safaris, camping and gorilla tracking in Kenya, Tanzania and Uganda throughout the year. Accommodation can be camping or lodge or a mixture. Safaris can be from one and a half days (e.g. flying safari from Nairobi to Masai Mara) to sixteen days (Samburu, Lake Naivasha and 11 nights under canvas in the Masai Mara with horse riding and game viewing from vehicles). Prices from $280-$4070. Book by faxing or e-mailing direct.

NATURETREK
Chautara, Bighton, Nr Alresford, Hampshire SO24 9RB (tel 01962-733051).
Walking wildlife safari in Malawi exploring Liwonde and Lengwe National Parks, the underwater world of Lake Malawi and walking for 11 days on Zomba and Mulanje Mountains and the Nyika National Park. Operates August or November. Price £2490 for three weeks. 19-day mammal and bird-watching safari in Uganda including an expedition into the Bwindi Impenetrable Forest to search for the mountain gorilla. Price from around £2800. 19-day wildlife safari in search of the birds and mammals of Namibia's unique desert habitats including Etosha Pan, the Namib Desert, the Waterberg mountains, Damaraland and the Skeleton Coast. Price £2590. Tours led by experienced botanist/ornithologist. Groups of up to 15 catered for. Prices range from £790-£3490. Accommodation is fully-serviced camping or luxury hotels and lodges in cities. Sleeping bags and outdoor clothing not included but can be hired. Some meals, airport taxes and drinks not included.
Minimum age; 15 years.
Maximum age: 80 years.

OKAVANGO TOURS AND SAFARIS
Gadd House, Arcadia Avenue, London N3 2PT (tel 0181-343 3283; fax 0181-343 3287).
The company specialises in tailor-made safari holidays for individuals and small groups in Botswana, Zambia, Zimbabwe and Namibia. A fortnight's holiday from the UK starts at approx. £2000 per person sharing which includes full board, game excursions, park fees, transfers and sheduled and light aircraft flights where applicable. A wide range of accommodation is available from thatched bungalows with en suite facilities, to luxury safari tents with private bathrooms to romantic reed bungalows overlooking the Zambezi river, 'There is something to suit everyone. . .' Activities include walking and vehicle safaris, canoeing safaris, white water rafting trips, horse safaris and hot-air ballooning trips over the Namib Desert of Namibia.

REX SAFARIS managed by Marketing and Reservations International (MRI)
9 Galena Road, London W6 OLT (tel 0181-741 5333; fax 0181 741 9030). E-mail: mrirex@compuserve.com
Directors: J S Penman, M V Patel.
In business since 1983.
Members of Kenya and Tanzanian Associations of Tour Operators, Zambian Hotel & Catering Assocation.
Holidays for approx 1000 arranged annually.
Specialists in tailor made and set departure safaris in Kenya, Tanzania and Zambia.Safaris operate all year except in Zambia

which is seasonal from June to October. Two to 14 nights' duration. Prices from £150 for a two-night camping safari excluding flight. Price ranges to £1000 for ground arrangements only. Usually includes accommodation from tented camps to luxury lodges and full board. On a camping safari, tents and sleeping bags can be hired. Additional expenses are National Park entrance fees for mountain climbs and Zambian walking safaris which are payable locally. Individual participation in the day-to-day running is expected for the basic camping safaris only.
Book direct in UK or at African agents: in Kenya — Rhino Safaris, Nyere Avenue, Mombasa (tel +254 11 311755); in Tanzania — Kudu Safaris, POB 1404, Arusha (tel +255 57 8193/6065); Zambia — Wilderness Trails, Lusaka (+2601 220112/3/4).
Minimum recommended age: not under six years because of long road journeys; for Zambia 12 years.

SAFARI CONSULTANTS LTD
Orchard House, Upper Road, Little Cornard, Suffolk CO10 ONZ (tel 01787-228494).
ATOL No. 3783 and AITO 1091.
Director: W B Adams, J A Campbell.
In business since 1983.
Holidays provided for 300 annually.
African safaris for approximately two weeks throughout the year. Groups of six to eight people can be catered for. Prices from £1500 to £5000, including full board and tented/lodge accommodation. All equipment is included, except for sleeping bags on some of the cheaper safaris.
No minimum age, but unaccompanied young people are not accepted.
Physically challenged people catered for.

SAFARI DRIVE LTD
Wessex House, 127 High Street, Hungerford, Berkshire RG17 0DL
Directors: C Norwood and M Turner.
In business since 1993.
Self Drive safari holidays in Zimbabwe, Botswana, Namibia, Zambia and Tanzania. The ultimate safari for those that crave remoteness and adventure. Drive in fully equipped Land Rovers across the endless game filled plains of Africa. This can be tailored as an independent safari to suit your personal requirements. Alternatively you can be part of a small escorted trip accompanied by a cook and professional guide, exploring some of Africa's least accessible areas. Prices from £1900 for two weeks, all inclusive.

SARTRAVEL
Regency House, 1-4 Warwick Street, London W1R 5WA (tel 0171-2871133; fax 0171-2871134).
Directors: K Holmes, K Makhetha.
In business since 1953.
Member of ATOL, SATOA, ATTA.
Holidays for around 2,500 arranged annually.
Tailor-made walking, vehicle and horse riding safaris in Southern Africa all year round. Itineraries include canoeing and white water rafting options. Choose from over 20 lodges in a variety of game reserve locations close to the famous National Parks. All prices are tailor-made. Individuals and corporate groups catered for. Arrangements can be made for physically and mentally challenged people.

SOUTHERN AFRICA TRAVEL
1 Pioneer Business Park, Amy Johnson Way, York YO3 4TN (tel 01904-692469; fax 01904-691340). London: 7 Buckingham Gate, London SW1E 6JX (tel 0171-630 0100; fax 0171-630 9900).
ABTA, ATOL 3067.
Safaris in Zimbabwe, Botswana, South Africa, Kenya and Tanzania. Examples include The Bushman Trail Safari in Namibia (12 days), including a visit to a true wilderness area where a minimum of two 4x4 vehicles are required to travel in convoy and spending four days with the Bushmen who will endeavour to pass on some of their local knowledge and skills including tracking, gathering of foodstuffs and their cultural customs and beliefs. There is a wide choice of safaris from traditional to Connoisseur. The latter with exclusive accommodation often with a choice of watersports and leisure activities depending on location.

TAMBOPATA JUNGLE LODGE
PO Box 454, Avenida Pardo 705, Cusco, Peru (tel (+51) 84-225701; fax (+51) 84-228911).
Manager: Tom Hendrickson.
In business since 1991.
A rustic, but very comfortable lodge located amidst the magnificent rainforest within the Tambopata Candamo reserve of Southern Peru. Access is via Puerto Maldonado a

20-minute flight from Cusco and a 3½ hour river trip by motor canoe. Programmes are all inclusive and vary from three to five days, or longer. Running water, good food, nature guides and structured daily programmes are available. There is a high and low forest, visits to lakes, a clear forest stream and lots to see for those interested in botany, birdwatching or nature in general. Prices are around US$50 per day.

TANA TRAVEL
2 Ely Street, Stratford-Upon-Avon, Warwickshire CV37 6LW (tel 01789-414200; fax 01789-414420).
Managing Director: N W Basnett. Chairman: S R Newman.
In business since 1984.
Holders of ABTA, IATA and ATOL licences.
Holidays for 1600 each year.
Tailor-made holidays, to suit individual clients' budgets, in eastern and southern Africa, the Indian Ocean, India, Australia and New Zealand.

Arranges horseback safaris in South Africa, Botswana, Malawi or Kenya. Also climbs of Kiliminjaro or Mt Kenya.

Other activities include deep sea fishing in Mauritius, canoeing and bird watching safaris in Zimbabwe or South Africa and wine tours of South Africa, Australia or New Zealand.

Any special interest can be catered for, ranging from bungy jumping to hunting.

TIM BEST TRAVEL
68 Old Brompton Road, London SW7 3LQ (tel 0171-591 0300; fax 0171-591 0301).
Directors: Tim & Sophie Best.
In business since 1994.
African adventure safaris in East and Southern Africa (Kenya, Tanzania, Zimbabwe, Botswana, Zambia, Namibia and South Africa) all year round. Activities include white water rafting, walking, climbing, diving, canoeing, whale watching, golf or simply relaxing on a beach. Prices from £1600 to £3000 including flights, all accommodation in tented camps or lodges, guides, meals and airport transfers. Individual, tailor-made itineraries.

THOMSON
Greater London House, Hampstead Road, London NW1 7SD (tel 0171-387 9321).
Managing Director: Charles Newbold.
ABTA, IATA, ATOL licensed.
Range of safari holidays covering most of the Kenyan game reserves. One, two, three and four-night safaris beginning and ending in Mobasa and visiting Tsavo East and West and Shimba Hills and including from ten to 13 nights at a Mombasa beach hotel (total holiday duration of 14 nights. Seven-night safaris starting in Nairobi and visiting Treetops, Samburu Game Reserve, the Great Rift Valley, Lake Nakuru, Lake Naivasha and the Masai Mara, combined with seven or 14 nights at a Mombasa beach hotel. Five-night safari to Tanzania visiting Ngorongoro, Serengeti and Tarangire combined with nine nights at a Mombassa beach hotel. Prices from £929 (three nights' safari and eleven nights beach hotel, departing in May 1998).

TONGABEZI
Private Bag 31, Livingstone, Zambia (tel +260 3 324450; fax +260 3 323224).
E-mail: tonga@zamnet.zm
Zambia and Zambezi river specialists. The Tongabezi main camp is on the rivers edge, Sindabezi Island, exclusive Livingstone Island (on the vey edge of Victoria Falls), plus new Sausage Tree Camp and Potato Bush Camp (in the lower Zambezi National Park). Upper and lower Zambezi canoe safaris. Kafue National Park and Lower Zambezi walking safaris. Tongabezi air safaris in six-seater Cherokee air-craft.

TRACKS
Evegate Park Barn, Smeeth, Ashford, Kent TN25 6SX (tel 01303-814949).
Adventure safaris in East Africa and in particular Tanzania. Trips from one to 36 weeks duration, all year round. There are fixed dates for departures but tailor-made, group tours can be arranged at any time. Visit remote and fascinating areas off the beaten track in four-wheel drive trucks. Connecting flights and details of other areas covered including Mt Kilimanjaro climb and Mombasa beach holiday from the above address. Fifteen days from £660. Prices do not include flights, sleeping bags or personal equipment.
All ages.

WEXAS INTERNATIONAL
45-49 Brompton Road, Knightsbridge, London SW3 1DE (tel 0171-589 3315).
Wildlife safaris in Kenya, Tanzania, Botswana, Malawi, South Africa and Namibia.

Camping and accommodation in hotels and lodges. Safaris three days to four weeks.

WILD AFRICA SAFARIS
20, Pimlico Road, London SW1W 8LJ (tel 0171-259 9909; fax 0171-259 9949); Zimbabwe (Harare) Office (tel +263 4-738329/0; fax +263 4-737956); Canada Office (tel +1 604-6821610; fax +1 604-6821615).
Director: Bryan Smith.
In business since 1989.
Member of SATOUR, ATOL, AETA & ATTA.
Holidays arranged for 2500+ annually.
Safari holidays to Zimbabwe, Botswana, South Africa, Zambia, Malawi, Namibia, Swaziland, Kenya, Tanzania, Mauritius, Seychelles and Zanzibar. Holidays are tailor-made to suit any client, budget, schedule and style. Other activities can be arranged. Prices from £600 to £6000. Flights, accommodation and transportation can be included according to requirements. Accommodation varies from hotels and lodges to tented camps.
Minimum unaccompanied age varies from 12 to 18 years.

WORLDWIDE JOURNEYS AND EXPEDITIONS
8 Comeragh Road, London W14 9HP (tel 0171-381 8638; fax 0171- 381 0836).
Safaris throughout Africa, including Kenya, Tanzania, Zambia, the Seychelles, Mauritius, Malawi, Botswana and Zimbabwe. Tours last between 13 and 23 days and prices range from around £1800 to around £3000

Asia

CHANDERTAL TOURS
20 The Fridays, East Dean, Nr Eastbourne, Sussex BN20 ODH (tel & fax 01323-422213).
Jeep safaris, treks, mountain biking, riding, white-water rafting, paragliding and wildlife holidays in India, Nepal, Burma and Thailand including the Himalayas and wildlife parks. Specialists for Himachal Pradesh, Zanskar and Ladakh in North India and Rajasthan and Gujurat in southern India. Available April-November for two to eight

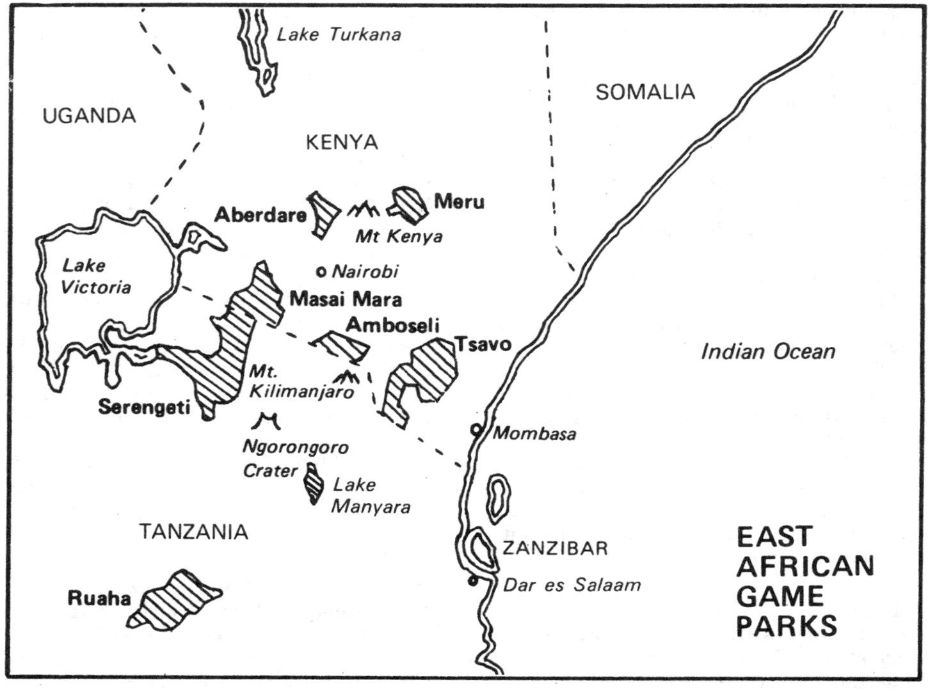

weeks. No experience required. Free expedition planning service. Free information service. Specialist wild flower, mahseer fishing and mountaineering tours. Price £950-£1750 includes return flight to London, accommodation (tents on treks, otherwise five star hotels), meals, tours, guides and all equipment. Sleeping bags can be hired. Travel in small groups or individuals, maximum twelve persons.
Minimum age if unaccompanied: 16 years.
Chandertal Tours also owns a company in India - Himalayan Folkways in the Banon Resort of Manali, (see separate entry).

EXPLORE WORLDWIDE LTD
1 Frederick Street, Aldershot, Hants GU11 1LQ (tel 01252-344161; fax 01252-343170).
Safari lasting 22 days in Rajasthan State, India, including a three-day camel safari through the Great Thar Desert to Jaisalmer. Travel in small groups, maximum 18 persons. Tented accommodation during safari, hotels and resthouses elsewhere. All equipment (except sleeping bag) provided. Price including flight from London from £1299 October to March. Also safaris by elephant in Nepal, staying at a jungle lodge in Chitwan National Park, travelling by dugout canoe. 17 days from £1289. A wildlife and tiger safari which takes in four of India's best game parks, £1369 for 22 days.
Minimum age: 17 years.

TIGER TOPS
Durbar Marg, PO Box 242, Kathmandu, Nepal (tel +977 1 411225; fax +977 1 414075/419126).E-mail: tiger@mtn.mos.com.np
Internet: http://www.tigermountain.com
Director: AVJ Edwards and Chuck McDougal.
In business since 1964.
Pioneers of environmentally sensitive adventure holidays in Nepal, Tiger Tops use an ecotourism level to base their expeditions on. Experience elephant safaris, jungle walks & drives, canoe rides and jungle treks based around a jungle lodge and tented camps in Royal Chitwan, and Karnali in the Royal Bardia National Park. All activities are accompanied by experienced and professional nature guides and naturalists. See the elusive Royal Bengal tiger, Greater One-Horned rhinoceros, Gharial crocodile and over 450 species of birds and wildlife. Safaris on elephant back to see these and many more.
Bookings through Abercombie & Kent Travel (tel 0171-730 9600) or Worldwide Journeys & Expeditions (tel 0171-381 8638).

WORLDWIDE JOURNEYS AND EXPEDITIONS
8 Comeragh Road, London, W14 9HP (tel 0171-381 8638; fax 0171-381 0836).
Wildlife safari tours in Assam, taking in the Bharatpur Bird Sanctuary, Fatehpur Sikri, the Kanha Tiger Reserve and the Kaziranga National Park. Also tours to Nepal and Sri Lanka. Tours last 19 days and cost around £2,000.

Australasia

AAT KINGS TOURS (UK) LTD
Bishop's Palace House, Bishops Hall, Kingston-upon-Thames, Surrey KT1 1QN (tel 0181-974 9922; fax 0181 974 8877).
ABTA: VO584.
Chairman: Mayer Ronald Page
Director: Dallas Newton.
In business since 1927.
Four-wheel drive adventures, camping safaris, farmstays — tours throughout Australia. Opportunities to visit remote outback areas, National Parks, World Heritage sites, the Great Barrier Reef; experience Aboriginal culture, see unique wildlife, go bushwalking, swimming etc.
A wide range of fully inclusive tours including travel by luxury coach and accommodation in first class hotels or camping adventures accompanied by a safari leader and cook/hostess. Our tours give you the opportunity to explore remote and unique areas of Australia, with the benefit of travelling with local experts.

Index of Companies and Organisations

Advertisers are shown in **bold**

The first entry for each organisation (indicated by the first page reference) includes more details than subsequent entries.

AAK Europe — 105
AAT Kings Tours — 219
Abercrombie & Kent Travel — 80, 206, 207, 208, 212
Abernethy Outdoor Centre — 19
Abernethy Trust — 17, 43, 99, 104, 172, 175
Above the Clouds — 70
Acacia Expeditions — 179, 194, 212
Acorn Activities — 10, 49, 58, 71, 95, 121, 139, 140, 142, 144, 171, 182, 203
Action Holidays — 38
Action Vacances (UCPA) — 45
Active Edge — 51
Adrenalin Pump — 32
Adrift — 174, 177, 178, 179, 180
Adventure and Computer Holidays — 38
Adventure Balloons — 49
Adventure Cycling Association — 66
Adventureline — 71, 86
Adventure South America — 113
Adventure Sports — 171
Adventure Travel Centre — 83, 86, 113
Adventure under Sail — 181
Adventure World Interlaken — 24, 96
Africa Exclusive — 86, 180, 212
Africa Explored — 113
Africa Travel Centre — 213
Airborne Hang Gliding & Paragliding Centre — 51
Airwaves — 154, 156
Albion Rides — 121
Allnatt Centres — 10
Alp Active — 24, 62
Alpine Adventures/Mountain Reality — 101, 105
Alpine Guides — 103
Alpine Helicopters — 84
Alps Mountain Bike Tours — 63
Alston Training Centre — 10, 59
Alternative Travel Group — 80, 146
Alto Aragón — 80
AmeriCan Adventures Inc — 29, 113
American Round-Up — 128, 178
American Wilderness — 46, 84, 128, 135, 178
Amizade — 148
Andean Trails — 84
Andes — 84, 107
Anglia Cycling Holidays — 59
Anglia Summer Schools — 38
Anglian Activity Breaks — 10
Anglo Dutch Sports — 63
Animal Watch — 200
Anvil Yacht Charters — 182
Aqua Sports Company — 38
Aquatic Encounters — 190
Arblaster & Clark Wine Tours — 158
Arc Journeys — 70, 149, 159, 190
Arctic Experience — 33, 87, 113, 149, 152
Arctic Light Journeys — 174, 175, 178
Arctic Odysseys — 109, 150, 210
Arcturus Expeditions — 109, 150, 152
Ardmore Adventure — 39
Armathwaite Hall Hotel — 121, 143
Arran Outdoor Centre — 17
Art of Travel — 213
Asian Journeys — 159
Asian Pacific Adventures — 159
Atelier de la Rose — 133, 135
Association for Adventure Sports — 22, 99, 100, 101, 141, 177
Association Nationale de Tourisme Equestre Hippotour — 127
Austral Tours — 84, 128
Australian Pacific Tours — 113
Austravels Great Escape — 159
Avalon Trekking — 75
Avon Ski Centre/Mendip Riding Centre — 10
Avril Dankworth National Children's Music Camps — 39
Ayrshire Equitation Centre — 125

Barend Properties Ltd — 125
Barry Skinner (Traeth) — 95
Bath Balloons — 49
Battisborough House — 39
Bedfordshire School of Flying — 55
Belle France — 63, 80
Bents Bicycle & Walking Tours — 63, 80
Bicycle Beano — 61
Bicycle Breaks — 59
Biggin Hill School of Flying — 55
Bike & Sun Tours — 155
Bike Tours — 58
Bird Quest — 208
Blackbushe School of Flying — 55
Black Dragon Outdoor — 19, 77, 100
Black Mountain Activities — 19
Blakes Holidays Ltd — 153
Blenheim Lodge — 10
Blue Green Adventures — 128
Blue Peter Sailing Ltd — 182
Blue Ridge Travel — 45, 46
Blue Skies Parachute Training — 53
Bobsport — 132, 143
Boojum Expeditions — 130
Border Parachute Centre — 53
Borlum Farm Country Holidays — 125
Boswednack Manor — 144
Bowland Bowtops — 151
Bowles Outdoor Centre — 11, 97, 104, 174
Bradwell Field Studies & Sailing Centre — 171
Brathay Exploration Group — 39
Breakaway Survival School — 143
Breton Bikes — 63
Bristol & Gloucestershire Gliding Club — 50
British Parachute School — 53
British Sub-Aqua Club — 190
British Universities Accommodation Consortium Ltd — 144
Bufo Ventures Ltd — 88, 102
Bukima Africa — 114
Burrendale Hotel & Country Club — 22
Butterfields — 19

Cabair Flight Training — 55
Caledonian Discovery — 75
Cairnwell Hang Gliding Centre — 52
Cairnwell Mountain Sports — 17, 52, 104
Caledonian Discovery — 17
Calshot Activities Centre — 39, 59, 98, 104, 175, 182, 196
Calvert Trust Kielder — 11
Calypso Diving Centre — 192
Caminhos do Alentejo (CDA Portugal) — 127
Camp Alaska — 29
Campfire Classic Adventures — 129, 152, 213
Canoe Country Escapes — 178
Cantref Riding Centre — 125
Carlingford Adventure Centre — 22, 45
Castle Head Field Centre — 39, 203
Cathy Matos Mexican Tours — 149
Cedarberg Travel — 159
Chalet Snowboard — 107, 110
Challenge Activ — 24, 105
Challenge Adventure Sailing — 181
Chandertal Tours — 88, 218
Chichester Interest Holidays — 145
Cinnamon Adventures — 11, 20
Classic Nepal — 88, 99, 102
Clive Powell Mountain Bikes — 61
Club Med — 7
Clwych Farm — 20
Clyne Farm — 20, 43
CMC Pensarn Harbour — 19, 44
C-N-DO Scotland — 75, 94, 204
Cold Keld Guided Walking Holidays — 71
Collineige — 81, 96
Compagnie des Guides de Chamonix — 96
Compass Christian Centre Ltd — 17, 104
Compass Holidays — 59, 71
Compass West ISR — 11, 24
Conservation Volunteers Northern Ireland — 137
Contessa Riding Centre — 121
Contiki — 110
Coral Cay Conservation — 156
Corona Holidays of London — 192
Corpo Vivo, Actividades Recreativas — 64
Council for British Archaeology — 133
Countrywide Holidays — 71, 145
Craigower Lodge Outdoor Centre — 17, 43, 76
Crewseekers — 182
The Cruise People — 150
Crusader Travel — 127
Crystal Holidays — 24, 105
Cuban Cigar Tours — 159
Cuillin Guides — 95
Cultural Pursuits — 160
Cwm Pennant Centre — 20
Cycleactive — 66
Cyclists' Touring Club — 59, 64, 66
Cygnus Wildlife Holidays — 201

David Sayers Travel — 211
Deborah Baynes Pottery Studio — 134
Denham School of Flying — 56
Derbyshire & Lancashire Gliding Club — 50
Dick Phillips — 87
Dinefwr Treks — 77
Discover — 45, 114
Discover the Pyrenees — 81
Discover the World — 201
Discovery Initiatives — 157
Dive BVI — 193
Dive Club Nautique — 193
Dive & Sail — 194, 195
Diving Leisure Unlimited — 191
Dorset Adventure Holidays — 11, 40
Dovey Valley — 139, 143
Dragoman Ltd — 29, 32, 33, 114, 213
Drystone Walking — 71
Dubbelju — 155
D V Diving — 143, 192

The Earnley Concourse — 203, 208, 211
Earthwatch — 157
East Anglian School of Sailing — 183
Eastbourne Marine — 12
Eclipse Outdoor Discovery — 105
Ecosummer Expeditions — 88, 152, 205
Eldertreks — 160
Elite Vacations — 213
Emperor Divers — 195
Encounter Overland — 88, 114, 180, 213
Endon Riding School — 122
English Wanderer — 71
Equitour — 121
Equus Horse Safaris — 129
Erna Low Consultants — 24
Errislannan Manor — 126
European Bike Express — 64
Euroyouth — 40, 122, 175, 183, 196
Exmoor Riding Centre — 122
Exmouth Diving Centre — 195
Exodus Expeditions — 24, 29, 32, 34, 81, 84, 86, 89, 101, 102, 114, 151, 160, 180, 205, 207, 213
Expeditions Inc — 178
Explore Worldwide — 25, 29, 33, 64, 81, 84, 86, 89, 114, 149, 151, 177, 179, 180, 205, 207, 211, 214, 219

Falmouth Underwater Centre — 191
Fantasea Divers — 194
Fellowship Afloat Charitable Trust — 183
Field Studies Council — 40, 44, 72, 78, 94, 96, 131, 132, 133, 134, 135, 136, 137, 140, 141, 142, 145, 192, 203, 204, 209, 211
Field Studies Council Overseas — 132, 141, 142, 151, 157, 201, 205, 207, 208, 211
Finnish Tourist Board — 81, 132
Finlandia — 25, 152, 153
First Challenge — 46
Five Valley Treks — 89
Fly High — 54
Focus Holidays at 'Argoed' — 78, 133, 205
Footloose — 81
Footprint Adventures — 201, 214
The Forest Experience — 140
Forest Trails — 201
Fort Bovisand Underwater Centre — 191
Fowey Cruising School — 183
Freedom Holidays — 64, 127, 198, 199
Freetime Activities — 135
Freetime Holidays — 196
Freewheeling — 64
French Country Cruises — 154
Frontier — 157, 190
Frontier Ski — 107

Galapagos Adventure Tours — 160
Galloway Sailing Centre — 172
Gambia Experience — 147
Gane & Marshall International — 7, 23
Geodyssey — 29, 206
Gina & Val's Hols — 72
Glenan's Irish Sailing Club — 187
Glencoe Outdoor Centre — 18, 76, 95, 99, 104, 176, 186
Glenmore Lodge National Outdoor Training Centre — 18, 43

Global Gypsies — 115
Goodwood Travel — 161
Gourmet Birds — 127, 208
Graham Baxter Sporting Hols — 64
Great Glen School of Adventure — 18
Greco-File — 146
Greenholme Holidays and Tours — 72, 76
Greenscape (UK) — 72
Grenadier Safaris — 214
Guerba Expeditions — 85, 89, 115, 214
Guildford Boathouse — 153
Gullivers Natural History Holidays — 202

Harbour Sports — 196
Hargrave Cattle & Guest Ranch — 135
Harlequin Worldwide Travel — 193
Harlyn Surf School — 197
Hartley's Safaris — 214
Hayfield Riding Centre — 125
Headcorn Parachute Club — 54
Head for the Hills — 77
Headwater Holidays — 25, 64, 81, 105, 177
Heart of Wales Riding Holidays — 44
HC Travel — 154
HF Holidays — 59, 72, 76, 98, 122, 140, 142, 172, 203, 204, 209
High Adventure — 12, 51
Highland Activity Holidays — 76
Highlander Mountaineering — 99
High Places — 67, 85, 87, 89, 91, 161
High Trek Snowdonia — 78
Hillscape — 78
Himalayan Kingdoms — 34, 89, 98, 101, 102, 212
Himalayan River Exploration — 180
Himalayan Roadrunners — 155
Hinterland Travel — 115
Holmhead — 59
Holts Battlefield Tours — 149
Honeyguide Wildlife Holidays — 209
Hoopoe Adventures — 214
Horetown House Riding Centre — 126
Horse Racing Abroad — 161
Hoseasons — 154
Hosking Tours — 156, 206, 214
Huntly Nordic Ski Centre — 61, 95
Huski — 105
Hyde House — 40

Imaginative Traveller — 34, 35, 60, 65
Incredible Adventures — 30, 85
India Link — 161
Inntravel — 65, 82, 128
Insight Travel — 148
Instep Linear Walking — 73
International Adventure — 177
International Centre, Gibbon Studies — 147
Intourist Travel — 161
Ipswich Parachute Centre — 54
Irish Cycling Safaris — 62
ISCA Children's Holidays — 40
Ishestar (Icelandic Riding) — 128
Island Cruising Club — 40, 143, 183
Island Underwater Safaris — 191
Isle of Colonsay Hotel and Chalets — 204

Jasmine Tours — 89
J & C Voyageurs — 130, 189, 215
Jersey Cycle Tours — 65
Jim Russell Racing — 140
John Bull School of Adventure — 12, 43, 144
John Sharp Sailing — 183
Jon Hurley's Wine Weekends — 144
Journey Latin America — 116
Jubilee Sailing Trust — 188

K E Adventure Travel — 96, 97
Kentwell Hall — 138
Kevin Walker Mountain Activities — 79, 96, 100
Kids Klub Activity Centre — 41
Killary Tours — 62, 79
Kindrogan Field Centre — 204
Kingair Flight Centre — 56
Knowle Riding Centre — 122
Kootenay Helicopter Skiing — 107
Kumuka Expeditions — 8, 86, 116

Lakeland Canoe Centre — 23
Last Frontiers — 30
Laurentian Ski School — 108
Lena & Friends — 25
Leicester Study Groups (see LSG)
Lejair — 56
Let's Go Travel — 33, 87, 97, 130, 151, 207, 215
Liberty Yacht Charters — 184
Limosa Holidays — 208
Little Killary Adventure Centre — 23
Llangollen YHA Centre — 21
Loch Insh Watersports & Skiing Centre — 173
Loch Ness Riding Centre — 125
Loch Rannoch Hotel — 18
London School of Flying — 56
London Underwater Centre — 193, 194, 195
Lower Aston House Pottery & Painting Summer School — 134
Lower Shaw Farm — 145
LSG Theme Holidays — 25, 141, 146
Lydford House Riding Stables — 122
Lyncombe Lodge Riding Hols — 12, 122

Maenporth Scuba School — 191
Magic Carpet Travel — 91, 103, 116, 161
Magic of Bolivia — 116
Maine Waters — 179
Malaysia Experience — 34
Mapache Lodge Wilderness — 30, 179
Marco Polo Experience — 161
Mark Warner — 173
Marlborough College Summer School — 41, 145
Marle Hall — 44
Marmot Trails — 82
Martin Moran Mountaineering — 100, 101, 103
Maya Mountain Lodge — 158
McCulloch Yacht Charter — 189
Medina Valley Centre — 12, 184
Mendip Outdoor Pursuits — 12, 136, 172
Meriski — 106
Midas Battlefield Tours — 149
Midland Gliding Club — 50
Mill on the Brue — 13
Millfield Village of Education — 13, 41
Monmouth Canoe Hire — 176
Montana Raft Company — 30
Moswin Tours — 26, 65, 82, 152, 154, 177
Motor Racing International — 162
Mountain Craft — 76, 100
Mountain Experience — 106
Mountain Goat Holidays — 73
Mountain Travel Nepal — 90
Mountain Treks & Training — 158
Mountain Ventures — 21
Mountain Walking in Lakeland — 41
Mount Severn Centre — 44
Multitours (Russia) — 162
Murphy's Wildlife Holidays — 202
Mysteries of India — 34

Naburn Grange Riding Centre — 123
The National Trust Working Holidays — 136
Natural Habitat Adventures — 202
Natural Heights — 26
The Natural World — 202
Naturetrek — 87, 90, 206, 207, 208, 210, 211, 212, 215
Nautilus Yachting — 188
Neuchâtel Tourism — 26, 106
Newton Ferrers Sailing School — 184
HJHC Dutch Youth Hostel Assoc — 26
Norfolk Broads School of Sailing — 184
Northern Microlight School — 56
North Humberside Riding Centre — 123
Northumbria Horse Holidays — 123
North-West Birds — 209
North-West Frontiers — 76
North York Moors Centre — 13

Ocean Contact — 162
Ocean Youth Club — 184, 187, 188
Octopus Diving Centre — 193
Offshore Sports — 60
Okavango Tours & Safaris — 130, 180, 210, 215
One World Workforce Hands-on Conservation — 138
Origins — 8
Ossian Guides — 95
Outback UK — 162
Outdoor Adventure — 13, 60, 145, 175, 197
Outdoor Trust — 13, 41, 98, 139, 175, 197
Outer Limits — 21, 100, 176
Outward Bound Trust — 14, 41, 73, 76, 79, 99, 138, 139, 185
Overland Latin America — 116

J Padwick — 162
Pan-Andean Tours — 162
Panorama Tunisia — 147, 163
Paramania — 52
Parc le Breos Riding Holiday Centre — 126
Parallel Pursuits — 26
Passage to South America — 163
Pathways — 73, 82
Peak District Hang Gliding Centre — 51
Peak International — 35, 65, 66, 67, 82, 85, 87, 90, 103, 109, 129, 130, 139, 153, 179
Peak National Park Centre — 14
Peak School of Hang Gliding — 51
Pedals & Boots — 60, 73
Peligoni Club — 173
Penelope Kellie Worldwide Yacht Charter & Tours — 189
Penshurst Off Road Club — 41, 138
Perthshire Activity Line — 18
PGL Adventure — 42, 45
Phil Parish Photography — 142
Phoenix Overland — 117
Photo Travellers — 142
Pilgrim Adventure — 77, 79
Piste Artiste — 108
Plas Caerdeon Outdoor Centre — 21
Plas Menai Watersports — 44, 143, 176, 187, 198
Pleasure in Leisure — 14, 42
Plus Travel — 65, 82
Polar Travel Company — 151
Polnet Travel — 27, 209
Port Edgar Sailing School — 173
Portway Yacht Charters — 185, 188
Preseli Venture — 61, 176
The Project Partnership — 31
Project Trust — 37
Puffin Cycle Tours & Walking Holidays — 79

Quark Expeditions — 163
Quasar Nautica Galapagos Expeditions — 163
Quest Australia — 163

Raasay Outdoor Centre — 18, 186, 198
Ramblers Holidays — 73, 90, 106, 212
Ranch America — 31
Raven Tours — 31
Redesdale Riding Centre — 123
Red Kite Activities — 62
Reef & Rainforest Tours — 31, 190, 206
Regal Diving — 190
Regent Holidays — 156, 164
Rex Safaris — 215
Rhiwiau Riding Centre — 79, 126
Ride World Wide — 121
Riviera Sailing Holidays — 154, 188
Roama Travel — 90, 103
Robin Hood Riding Holidays — 123
Rock Lea Activity Activity Centre — 14, 60, 73, 99, 136, 139
Rossbrin Yacht Charters — 187
Rough Tracks — 27, 65
Roxton Bailey Robinson — 131
Ru'a Reidh Lighthouse Outdoor Centre — 77
The Russia Experience — 164
Russell Hafter Holidays — 82

Safari Consultants Ltd — 216
Safari Drive Ltd — 117, 216
Sail on Oulton Broad — 185
Sail Training Association — 189
Sailing Holidays Ltd — 188
SAR Travel — 216
Scottish Border Trails — 61
Scottish Conservation Projects Trust — 137
Scottish Cycling Holidays — 61
Scottish Gliding — 50
Scottish Voyageurs — 176
Scottish Youth Hostels Association — 61, 125
Scot-Trek — 77
Scripture Union Holidays — 42
Sealyham Activity Centre Ltd — 21
Seychelles Underwater Centre — 194
Share Centre — 23, 188, 198
Sherpa Co-operative Trekking (P) Ltd — 91
Shoreline Leisure Services — 14
Silk Steps — 164
Sinbad Charters — 186
SITA World Travel (India) Ltd — 91
Skaigh Stables — 123
Skern Lodge Outdoor Centre — 15, 175
Ski Club Holidays — 106, 108
Ski Gourmet — 106
Ski Independence — 108
Skiworld — 107, 108
Skydive Tandem — 55
Skydive Unlimited — 53
Skydragons Paragliding — 49, 54
Skye Mountain Guides — 100
Sky Systems — 52
Slatterys Travel — 62, 152
Sleat Marine — 186
Smugglers' Notch Resort — 109
Snowdonia Guided Walks — 79
Snowdonia Mountain Centre — 21
The Soaring Centre — 50
Sociétée Spéléologique de Wallonie — 136

Solent School of Yachting — 185
Sourdough Outfitters Inc — 31
South American Experience — 164
Southern Africa Travel — 216
Sovereign Scanscape — 83
Speedwing Divers — 196
SPICE — 15
Spinerd Sailboard School — 197
Sportif International — 8, 174
STA Travel — 117
St George's House — 15
Step by Step — 73
Steppes East — 91, 117, 130
Stiftelsen Stjärnsund — 146
Stirling Parachute Centre — 54
Stracomer Riding Centre — 127
Suffolk Cycle Breaks — 60
Summer Academy — 146
Summitreks — 15
Sun Blessed Holidays — 35
Sunbird — 210
Sunsail Clubs — 42, 138, 182, 185
Sunseed Desert Technology — 138
Suntrek — 117
Sunvil — 149, 193, 198
Sunworld Sailing Holidays — 173, 199
Suomen Latu Ry — 83, 107
Superchoice — 42
Superstar Holidays — 164, 196
Surface Watersports — 197
Susi Madron's Cycling for Softies — 65
Sussex Hang Gliding — 52
Sutherland Lodge Activity Centre — 43
Swallow Tandems — 62
Symbiosis Expedition Planning — 164

Tall Stories — 27
Tambopata Jungle Lodge — 216
Tana Travel — 217
Tangent Expeditions International — 102, 109
Tarific Holidays — 199
Tenerife Tracks & Trails — 83
Thistle Camps — 137
Thomson — 217
Tiger Tops — 34, 207, 219
Tighnabruaich Sailing School — 186, 198
Tikota Tours — 67
Tim Best Travel — 217
TM International School of Horsemanship — 124
Tongabezi Safaris — 217
Tony Doyle Pursuits — 66
Top Deck Travel — 117
Top Yacht Charter — 189
Torquay Boardsailing Centre & School — 197
Totnes School of Guitarmaking — 134
Tracks — 117, 217
Trailfinders — 118
Trans Indus — 35
Travelbag Adventures — 8
Travelbound — 27
Travel Choice — 28
The Travellers' Club — 165
Treble Cone Ski Area — 110
Trek America — 118
Trek & Dive — 8
Trekforce Expeditions — 158
Trekking Hellas — 28, 83
Trigpoint 49 — 15
Trips Worldwide — 32, 146, 203
Trireme Trust — 133
Truck Africa — 118
Tucan South America — 32, 85, 118
Tusk Tours — 33
Twr-y-Felin — 22, 44
Ty Coch Farm — 126

UCPA (see Action Vacances) — 46, 107
Uist Outdoor Centre — 19
Ultimate Descents — 181
Underwater Safaris Ltd — 195
United Touring Company — 119
University of Limerick Activity Centre — 23, 198
USA Tailor-made Holidays — 135, 155

Valkenberg & Mergelland — 28
VFB Holidays — 28
Vigvatten Natur Klubb — 28, 46
Virgin Balloon Flights — 49

Wave Yacht Charters — 186
Waymark Holidays — 83, 107
Weekend Escape — 139
Wellfield Trekking — 124
Wellington Riding — 124
Welsh Hang Gliding Centre — 52
Welsh Wayfaring Holidays — 79
Wenford Bridge Pottery — 134
Western Encounters — 129
West of Ireland Activity Centre — 45
West Wales Windsurf & Sail — 173
WEXAS International — 91, 119, 151, 189, 194, 196, 217
Whale Watch Azores — 158
Wheal Buller Riding School — 124
Wheely Wonderful Cycling — 60
Wheely Wonderful Walking — 75
White Hall Centre for Open Country Pursuits — 16
The Whodunnit Company — 140
Wight Water Adventure Sports — 16, 172
Wild Africa Safaris — 218
Wild Explorer Holidays — 204, 205
Wild Geese School of Adventure Training — 55
Wild Quest Expeditions — 143, 206
Wildaid Foundation Trust — 204
Wildlife Discovery — 202
Wildlife Tours — 33
Wildlife Travel — 202
Wildlife Worldwide — 202
Wilton House Hotel — 22
Wiltshire Hang Gliding — 52
Wind, Sand & Stars — 165
Windermere Lake Holidays Afloat — 185
Windsport International — 172, 186
Windsurfing Worcester — 197
Winetrails — 75, 83, 141, 144
Wintergreen Dogsledding Lodge — 153
Wolds Silver — 134
World Challenge Expeditions — 38, 85, 91, 97, 101, 102, 104, 165
World Peace Trekking — 103, 181
Worldwide Fishing Safaris — 132
Worldwide Journeys & Expeditions — 86, 87, 97, 179, 181, 206, 218, 219
WWOOF — 131

Yacht Corryvreckan — 187
YHA Activity Centre — 16, 43, 99, 136, 141, 175
YHA Northern Region — 75
YMCA National Centre, Fairthorne Manor — 16
YMCA National Centre, Lakeside — 16
Young Archaeologists' Club — 43
Youth Travel Bureau — 165

Zara Training Centre — 124
Zinderneuf Sailing — 187